Larousse Treasury of Country Cooking

Around the World

LAROUSSE
TREASURY of

COUNTRY
Cooking
Around the World

HAMLYN
LONDON · NEW YORK · SYDNEY · TORONTO

Most of the recipes in *Larousse Treasury of Country Cooking Around the World*
have been adapted from
  Les cuisines régionales by Marie Maronne and Rose Montigny
and *Cuisine à travers le monde* by Rose Montigny

Translated by the Translation Company of America

First published in 1975 by
Crown Publishers, Inc., New York
Published simultaneously in Canada by
General Publishing Company Limited

An original work created and produced by
Vineyard Books, Inc.
159 East 64th Street, New York, New York 10021

This edition published in 1977 by
The Hamlyn Publishing Group Limited
London · New York · Sydney · Toronto
Astronaut House, Feltham, Middlesex, England

ISBN 0 600 35506 3

Phototypeset by Tradespools Limited, Frome, Somerset

Printed in Spain by Mateu Cromo, Madrid

Contents

*The discovery of a new dish does more for the
happiness of mankind than the discovery of a star.*

—JEAN-ANTHELME BRILLAT-SAVARIN,
The Philosopher in the Kitchen

Preface

Gathered together in this book are hundreds of regional recipes, evolved over the centuries in country kitchens of many lands by ingenious, painstaking and imaginative cooks.

Provincial cookery, using fresh, low-cost, locally available ingredients, is the cornerstone of any great cuisine. It is on these simple and sensible recipes that the elaborate, heavily sauced dishes one orders at astronomical prices in gourmet restaurants have been built. But in today's fast-paced world most people no longer care to indulge in pretentious five-course dinners. For reasons of health, vitality, weight and even boredom, the trend in contemporary life style is towards simplicity. Informal entertaining and a worldwide move back to the basics are reasons for a renewed interest in simple foods, simply prepared.

This widely varied collection of recipes has been assembled with four specific goals in mind. First, the element of cost. Second, the availability of the ingredients. Third, the preferences and biases of Anglo-American cooks and consumers. Finally, ease of preparation.

The editors are quick to admit that 'cost' is an elusive term, dependent on season and geography. Some ingredients—leeks and cauliflower, for example—may be low-priced in London and relatively expensive in New York. There are even wide variations in the price of a given item between New Orleans and Denver, Oxford and Glasgow, Melbourne and Perth. In most cases, however, this book lives up to its purpose and shows the average cook how to make a little go a long way (stews and casseroles); how to make inexpensive cuts really tasty (marinades and slow cooking); how to use every part of the animal (fat for cooking and bones for stock); how to devise dozens of variations for daily staples (meat in France, pasta in Italy). Where cost *is* ignored is in the few instances where a specific ingredient, while abundant in its native land, may be expensive or rarely found on our own shores. A few such recipes *were* kept for the festive occasions when one might want to splurge in order to reproduce a recipe that would not be authentic without the use of, let's say, truffles or pâté de foie gras.

Wherever possible the editors offer acceptable substitutes for items that are unavailable or prohibitively expensive outside the country of origin. By way of example, white mushrooms are suggested in lieu of cèpes and chanterelles, Dublin Bay prawns for langoustines, olive oil for goose fat.

Another significant change resulted from the fact that the original Larousse recipes were generalised and often non-specific—a clear tribute to the expertise and inventiveness of French cooks. Since English-speaking readers prefer step-by-step instructions in preparing dishes, the editors meticulously adhered to the content and intent of the Larousse recipes while adapting them for non-French kitchens. With each recipe the home chef is told how much time is needed to prepare a given dish and how much time it will take to cook. A 'Fundamentals' chapter at the end of the volume explains cookery terms, and recipes are given for such basics as hollandaise and béchamel sauces, which are used again and again with various recipes in the book.

Since France has been recognised for centuries as the home of superlative provincial cooking, more than half the recipes in this book originated in Gallic kitchens. All the historic provinces are represented—Normandy and Brittany, Alsace and Lorraine, Provence and the Île de France, along with dozens of others.

Almost an equal number of culinary gems included are indigenous to over fifty other nations. There are Spring Rolls plus a score of others from China. Baked Clams Oregano and Brisket of Beef with Fruit partially represent Italy and Israel. Baked Lamb with Cracked Wheat comes from Lebanon and Tongue with Almond Sauce from Argentina.

The *Larousse Treasury of Country Cooking Around the World* makes no pretence of being an encyclopedic work. It is highly selective, hugely diversified. Many if not all the foreign recipes will appeal immediately to the English or American palate. An effort has been made to make this collection truly international in scope and at the same time appeal to the armchair traveller. Ideas abound from all corners of the earth for every occasion—twosomes and family meals; buffets and dinner parties; teas, cold suppers and snacks.

More than anything else, this is a Discovery Cookbook. It contains the unexpected and the unique. It is down to earth and easy to follow. It should be a boon to the family budget and a delight to all those whose taste buds are receptive to new dishes in their day-to-day menus.

Appetisers and Hors D'Oeuvre

AVOCADO DIP

Mexico

Preparation time: 10 minutes

Ingredients

2 avocados, peeled and
stoned

Juice of 1 lemon

1 onion, finely chopped

1 to 2 cloves garlic,
crushed

1 green chilli pepper,
finely chopped

Salt

1 tomato, peeled, seeded
and chopped

Mayonnaise for coating

1. In a non-metallic bowl lightly mash the avocados to chunky consistency.

2. Add the lemon juice, chopped onion, crushed garlic and chilli pepper. Mix thoroughly, then season to taste with salt.

3. Stir in the chopped tomato, then transfer to a serving bowl.

4. Using a broad spatula, spread a very thin layer of mayonnaise over the dip, cover the bowl with foil and refrigerate until needed.

Serves 4 to 6

CAULIFLOWER AND TURNIP DIP

Preparation time: 20 minutes

Cooking time: 5 minutes
Refrigeration time: 1 hour

USSR

Ingredients

*1 head cauliflower,
   broken into florets*

*6 young turnips, scraped
   and cut into sticks*

Russian Mayonnaise:

3 egg yolks, hard-boiled

1 teaspoon dry mustard

*¾ pint/4½ dl. soured
   cream*

4 tablespoons olive oil

1½ tablespoons vinegar

*2 tablespoons chopped
   capers*

*1 tablespoon chopped
   fresh parsley*

Salt

Freshly ground pepper

1. Parboil the cauliflower and turnips in separate saucepans of boiling salted water until barely tender. (This will take about 5 minutes.) Refresh under cold running water, drain and reserve.

2. Push the egg yolks through a sieve into a mixing bowl. Add the dry mustard and beat in the soured cream. Drop by drop, gradually beat in the oil and then stir in the vinegar.

3. Add the chopped capers and parsley. Season to taste with salt and pepper. Scrape into a serving bowl.

4. Place the serving bowl in the centre of a platter and surround with the cooled cauliflower and turnips. Chill for at least an hour before serving.

Serves 6 to 8

CHICK-PEA APPETISER

Israel

Preparation time: 15 minutes

Ingredients

A 20-oz./567-g. can
  chick-peas
4 oz./100 g. tahini
  (sesame seed paste)
Salt

1 clove garlic, crushed
Juice of 1 lemon
Cayenne pepper
Chopped fresh parsley
  for garnish

1. Drain the chick-peas and reserve the liquid. Purée the chick-peas using a sieve or blender, adding as much of the liquid as needed to make a smooth paste.

2. In a bowl, combine the chick-pea purée and the *tahini*. Blend thoroughly, then season to taste with salt, crushed garlic, lemon juice and cayenne pepper.

3. Transfer mixture to a serving dish and garnish with chopped parsley. Serve at room temperature as a dip or a spread with savoury biscuits, Arab bread (page 374) or bite-sized raw vegetables.

Serves 8 to 10

AUBERGINE DIP

Preparation time: 15 minutes   **Cooking time:** 40 minutes   *Lebanon*

Ingredients

1 large aubergine

2 oz./50 g. tahini
(sesame seed paste)

1 clove garlic, crushed

1½ tablespoons lemon juice

1½ tablespoons olive oil

Salt

Chopped fresh parsley
for garnish

1. Set oven at 400°F., 200°C., Gas Mark 6.

2. Bake the aubergine until tender, about 40 minutes.

3. Allow the baked aubergine to cool enough to be handled, then peel. Discard skin.

4. Place the aubergine pulp in a mixing bowl and mash with a fork.

5. Add the *tahini*, garlic, lemon juice and olive oil to the mashed pulp. Mix thoroughly, then season to taste with salt.

6. Cover bowl and store in the refrigerator until needed.

7. Before serving, stir dip thoroughly, then transfer to a serving bowl and garnish with chopped fresh parsley. Serve at room temperature.

Serves 2 to 4

Serve as a salad or as a spread with Arab bread (page 374) and bite-sized raw vegetables.

NIÇOISE 'CAVIAR'

France

Preparation time: 10 minutes

Ingredients

6 anchovy fillets

12 oz./350 g. olives, stoned

3 oz./75 g. tuna fish packed in olive oil

2 tablespoons olive oil

Freshly ground pepper

2 to 4 garlic cloves, crushed

1. Rinse the anchovy fillets under running cold water. Pat dry.

2. Put the olives, anchovy fillets and tuna fish through a sieve or blender. Beat in the olive oil. Season to taste with freshly ground pepper and garlic.

3. Serve in a small earthenware dish with fresh French bread or toast.

Serves 4 to 6

VARIATION: *Blend hard-boiled egg yolks in during Step 2. Stuff the mixture into the egg whites.*

ARTICHOKES WITH GREEN VINAIGRETTE

France

Preparation time: 20 minutes   **Cooking time:** 40 minutes

Ingredients

4 artichokes

1 lemon, cut in half

4 peppercorns

Green Vinaigrette Sauce:

4 tablespoons red wine
    vinegar

3 cloves garlic, crushed

1 tablespoon dry mustard

1 teaspoon salt

1 teaspoon freshly
    ground pepper

⅓ pint/2 dl. olive oil

6 tablespoons finely
    chopped fresh herbs
    (parsley, tarragon, basil)

1. In a large pot bring 3 pints/1½ litres of salted water to a rapid boil.

2. Cut off the stems of the artichokes, remove the tough bottom leaves and rub the base of each artichoke with lemon. Put the artichokes into the water with the lemon and peppercorns and bring back to the boil. Partially cover and boil gently until a centre artichoke leaf pulls out easily, about 40 minutes.

3. When the artichokes are done, remove them from pot and place upside down to drain.

4. Make the vinaigrette sauce, combining the vinegar, garlic, mustard, salt and pepper and blending well, then adding the oil and the chopped herbs.

5. Serve the artichokes at room temperature with the green vinaigrette sauce on the side.

Serves 4

GRATED CARROT HORS D'OEUVRE

France

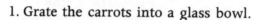

Preparation time: 15 minutes   **Marination time:** 2 hours

Ingredients

*8 oz./225 g. carrots,
    peeled*
2 shallots, finely chopped
4 tablespoons olive oil
Juice of ½ lemon

*Lettuce leaves for
    garnish*
*Chopped parsley for
    garnish*

1. Grate the carrots into a glass bowl.

2. Combine the carrots with the shallots, olive oil and lemon juice. Marinate for 2 hours.

3. To serve, arrange on a bed of lettuce and sprinkle with chopped parsley.

Serves 4

CELERY-ROOT RÉMOULADE

Preparation time: 30 minutes   **Refrigeration time:** overnight

France

Ingredients

1 celeriac (root or knob
celery), peeled, washed
and cut in julienne
strips
1 teaspoon salt
1 tablespoon vinegar

Mustard Mayonnaise:
6 tablespoons mayonnaise
1½ tablespoons dry
mustard
1½ tablespoons lemon juice

1. Place the celeriac strips in a glass bowl. To prevent discolouring, cover with cold water and add the salt and vinegar. Allow to stand for 15 minutes, then drain.

2. Blanch the celeriac strips in boiling water for 30 seconds. Drain, refresh under cold running water, then pat dry.

3. Prepare the mustard mayonnaise by combining the three ingredients.

4. Place the celeriac strips in a glass bowl and toss gently with the mustard mayonnaise. Cover and refrigerate overnight.

Serves 4

AUBERGINE FAREED

Lebanon

Preparation time: 10 minutes
Aubergine stands—30 minutes

Cooking time: 6 minutes
Prepared dish chills—
3 hours

Ingredients

2 small aubergines, peeled
and cubed

Salt

5 tablespoons olive oil

1 clove garlic, crushed

¼ medium onion, minced

Juice of 1 lemon

1½ tablespoons chopped
fresh parsley

⅓ pint/2 dl. yoghurt

Chopped fresh mint for
garnish

Thinly sliced black
bread

1. Put the aubergine cubes in a non-metallic colander. Salt cubes lightly, then cover colander with a cloth and rest over a plate (or in the sink) for 30 minutes.

2. Drain aubergine thoroughly and dry on absorbent paper.

3. Heat half the oil in a frying pan. Add the aubergine and sauté over moderate heat until tender, about 6 minutes. Remove from heat.

4. In a mixing bowl, combine the sautéed aubergine, garlic, onion, lemon juice and remaining olive oil. Toss until well mixed.

5. Stir in the parsley and yoghurt. Adjust seasonings.

6. Transfer the aubergine to a serving bowl, cover and refrigerate for at least 3 hours.

7. Serve at room temperature, garnished with chopped fresh mint and accompanied by thinly sliced black bread.

Serves 4 to 6

FENNEL ANTIPASTO

Preparation time: 10 minutes   **Marination time:** 2 hours   *Italy*

Ingredients

1 fennel bulb, trimmed
and thinly sliced

6 tablespoons olive oil

Juice of ½ lemon

Salt

Freshly ground pepper

1. Place the fennel in a glass bowl. Coat the fennel with the olive oil and the lemon juice. Add salt and pepper to taste.

2. Cover and let stand at room temperature for at least 2 hours. Stir occasionally.

3. Serve as part of an antipasto or as part of a green salad, using the marinade as the base for the salad dressing.

Serves 2 to 4

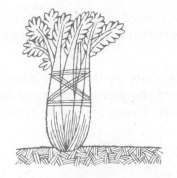

very nice!

CRACKED WHEAT SALAD (Tabbouleh)

Syria

Preparation time: 10 minutes
Cracked wheat soaks—15 minutes

Ingredients

5 oz./150 g. cracked wheat

6 spring onions, chopped

6 tablespoons finely chopped fresh parsley

4 tablespoons finely chopped fresh mint or 2 tablespoons crushed dried mint

3 large tomatoes, peeled and finely chopped

3 tablespoons olive oil

3 tablespoons lemon juice

Salt

Freshly ground pepper

Lettuce for garnish

Sliced cucumbers for garnish

Black olives for garnish

1. Soak the cracked wheat in a bowl of water for 15 minutes. Drain and squeeze dry.

2. Transfer the cracked wheat to a mixing bowl. Add the remaining ingredients, except for the garnishes, and mix well.

3. Line a serving platter with lettuce leaves. Heap the salad in the centre of the platter and garnish with cucumber slices and black olives.

Serves 6

but Munzar's recipe is even better!

KIDNEY BEAN SALAD

Preparation time: 10 minutes   **Marination time:** 12 hours   *Cuba*

Ingredients

1 lb./450 g. canned red
  kidney beans, drained

1 onion, finely chopped

1 clove garlic, crushed

1 tablespoon olive oil

1 tablespoon red wine
  vinegar

¼ teaspoon dry mustard

¼ teaspoon salt

⅛ teaspoon curry powder

1. Combine all the above ingredients in a glass bowl. Mix well.

2. Cover bowl tightly with plastic wrap. Allow mixture to marinate at room temperature for at least 12 hours.

Serves 4

MARINATED LEEKS WITH RICE

France

Preparation time: 10 minutes

Cooking time: 20 minutes
Refrigeration time: 1 hour

Ingredients

3 to 4 leeks
6 tablespoons water
1½ tablespoons olive oil
1 tablespoon rice

¼ tablespoon salt
Juice of ½ lemon
Lemon wedges for garnish

1. Cut off the roots and the upper thirds of the green part of the leeks. Pull off tough outer leaves. Wash thoroughly to remove all traces of sand.

2. Cut the leeks into 1-inch/2½-cm. pieces. Rinse again.

3. Place the leeks in a saucepan. Add the water, oil, rice and salt. Bring to the boil, then cover and simmer over low heat for 20 minutes.

4. With a slotted spoon, transfer leeks and rice to a serving dish. Sprinkle with lemon juice and refrigerate for at least 1 hour. When ready to serve, garnish with lemon wedges.

Serves 2 to 4

MUSHROOMS ÎLE DE FRANCE

Preparation time: 30 minutes   **Cooking time:** 20 minutes   *France*

Ingredients

1 lb./450 g. firm white
  mushrooms, finely
  chopped
1 onion, finely chopped
⅓ pint/2 dl. water
Bouquet garni (thyme,
  basil, oregano)

1½ tablespoons lemon juice
2 tablespoons salt
Freshly ground pepper
4 eggs
6 tablespoons cream

1. Set oven at 400°F., 200°C., Gas Mark 6.

2. In a saucepan, combine the mushrooms, onion, water, bouquet garni, 1 tablespoon lemon juice, salt and pepper. Cook rapidly until the water has evaporated, about 10 minutes. Remove bouquet garni.

3. In a bowl, beat the eggs and the cream.

4. Remove the mushroom mixture from the heat and add the remaining lemon juice. Taste and correct seasoning.

5. Add the mushroom mixture to the cream and egg mixture.

6. Ladle the mixture into individual ovenproof ramekins. Place in a shallow pan of hot water and bake until set, about 20 minutes.

7. Serve warm as a first course or chilled as a spread with hot buttered toast.

Serves 4

CREAMED MUSHROOMS WITH CHEESE

France

Preparation time: 20 minutes   **Cooking time:** 10 minutes

Ingredients

3½ oz./90 g. butter
1 lb./450 g. small white
   mushrooms, cleaned
   and sliced
¼ teaspoon grated
   nutmeg
Salt
Freshly ground pepper

3 tablespoons double
   cream
8 1-inch/2½-cm. slices
   French bread
2 oz./50 g. Gruyère or
   other Swiss cheese,
   grated

1. Preheat oven to 400°F., 200°C., Gas Mark 6.

2. Melt the butter in a large frying pan and cook mushrooms rapidly over a high heat until they begin to give off steam.

3. Lower heat and add nutmeg, salt and pepper to taste and stir in cream.

4. Arrange the slices of bread on a baking sheet. Make a slight hollow in the middle of each slice.

5. Spoon the creamed mushrooms over the slices and sprinkle with the grated cheese.

6. Bake until golden, about 10 minutes, and serve.

Serves 4 to 8

GRILLED STUFFED MUSHROOM CAPS

Italy

Preparation time: 20 minutes   **Cooking time:** 25 minutes

Ingredients

12 large white mushrooms
1 clove garlic, crushed
3 shallots, finely chopped
1½ oz./40 g. butter
3 tablespoons olive oil
1 oz./25 g. breadcrumbs
2 oz./50 g. Parmesan
  cheese, grated

1 teaspoon basil
2 tablespoons chopped
  parsley
Salt
Freshly ground pepper

1. Wipe the mushrooms with a damp cloth. Remove the stems and chop them finely and squeeze dry in absorbent paper.

2. Preheat oven to 350°F., 180°C., Gas Mark 4.

3. In a small saucepan, sauté the garlic and shallots in 1 oz./25 g. of the butter and 1 tablespoon of the olive oil. Add the chopped mushroom stems and stir over moderate heat until mushroom liquid has evaporated, about 5 minutes. Remove from heat.

4. Mix the remaining ingredients into the mushroom stem mixture. Taste and correct seasoning.

5. Stuff the mushroom caps with the mixture. Top each cap with a dot of the remaining butter.

6. Arrange the caps in a shallow well-oiled ovenproof dish and bake about 25 minutes. Serve hot.

Serves 2 to 4

GREEN PEPPERS GABOR

Hungary

Preparation time: 20 minutes

Ingredients

8 oz./225 g. cottage cheese

8 anchovy fillets, finely
  chopped

2 tablespoons capers

4 medium onions, finely
  chopped

Salt

Freshly ground pepper

6 small green peppers,
  halved and seeded

3 eggs, hard-boiled and
  quartered

6 slices black bread,
  buttered and quartered

1. In a large bowl, combine the cottage cheese, anchovies, capers and onions. Season to taste with salt and pepper.

2. Fill the peppers with the cottage cheese mixture.

3. Arrange the stuffed peppers and hard-boiled eggs on a platter. Garnish with the slices of buttered black bread.

Serves 6

ANTIPASTO OF STUFFED PEPPERS

Italy

Preparation time: 20 minutes   **Cooking time:** 30 minutes

Ingredients

*2 to 4 cloves garlic,
   crushed*

*3 firm ripe tomatoes,
   peeled, seeded and
   chopped*

*12 anchovy fillets,
   coarsely chopped*

2 tablespoons olive oil

*6 sweet peppers, seeded
   and quartered*

2 oz./50 g. butter

1. Set oven at 350°F., 180°C., Gas Mark 4.

2. In a bowl, mix the garlic, tomatoes and anchovy fillets with the olive oil.

3. Stuff each pepper section with some of the mixture and dot with the butter.

4. Arrange the peppers on an oiled baking sheet. Bake for 30 minutes. Remove baking sheet from oven and allow peppers to cool to room temperature.

5. Serve accompanied by olive oil and vinegar.

Serves 4 to 6

A combination of red and green peppers makes an attractive presentation.

CRISPY VEGETABLES

India

Preparation time: 1 hour

Cooking time: 3 minutes per batch

Ingredients

4 oz./100 g. wholewheat flour
½ teaspoon salt
6 tablespoons vegetable oil
6 tablespoons water
3 potatoes, peeled
½ teaspoon each ground cumin and coriander
2 onions, chopped
1 clove garlic, crushed
¼ teaspoon ground turmeric

½ teaspoon garam masala
2 teaspoons lemon juice
Vegetable oil for frying
1 green pepper, chopped
1 cauliflower, broken into florets
1 bowl chopped spinach
2 tomatoes, chopped
4 carrots, peeled and chopped

1. In a large mixing bowl, combine the flour, ¼ teaspoon salt and 3 tablespoons of oil. Add the water, a little at a time, to form a stiff dough. Knead until smooth, about 10 minutes. Roll into a ball, brush with oil and reserve.

2. Boil the potatoes in salted water until tender, about 25 minutes. Mash lightly. Heat 3 tablespoons of oil. Add the cumin, coriander, half the chopped onions, the garlic and turmeric. Cook until the onions are tender, about 5 minutes. Add the potatoes, ¼ teaspoon salt, the garam masala and lemon juice. Cook for 5 minutes. Remove from heat.

3. Roll out the dough to ¼-inch/5-mm. thickness. Cut the dough into 2-inch/5-cm. rounds. Place a spoonful of the potato mixture in the centre of each round. Fold into crescents and pinch to seal.

4. Pour the vegetable oil to a depth of 3 inches/7½ cm. in a deep-frier. Heat to sizzling, then reduce heat to moderate. Fry a few crescents at a time until golden brown, about 3 minutes. Drain. Place the crescents in a serving dish, accompanied by bowls of the chopped vegetables.

Makes about 36 turnovers

CHEESE TRUFFLES

Preparation time: 20 minutes

Ingredients

4 oz./100 g. unsalted
  butter, at room
  temperature
1½ oz./40 g. Gouda or
  Cheddar cheese, grated

Salt

Freshly ground pepper
Paprika
4 slices stale pumpernickel
  bread (without crusts),
  very finely crumbled

The Netherlands

1. In a mixing bowl, cream the butter well with a wooden spoon.

2. Gradually blend in the grated cheese, then season with salt, freshly ground pepper and paprika. Reserve.

3. Using a spoonful of the cheese mixture at a time, shape the mixture into small balls. Reserve.

4. Spread the breadcrumbs out on greaseproof paper. Season with freshly ground pepper.

5. Roll the cheese truffles in the seasoned breadcrumbs until well coated, then transfer the truffles to a serving plate. Chill until needed.

Makes about 36 truffles

BURGUNDY CHEESE RING

France

Preparation time: 20 minutes

Cooking time: 35 minutes

Ingredients

12 fl. oz./3½ dl. water
4½ oz./125 g. butter
2 teaspoons salt
6 oz./175 g. sifted flour
6 eggs, beaten

8 oz./225 g. Gruyère or
other Swiss cheese,
grated
1 egg, beaten, for glazing

1. Set oven at 400°F., 200°C., Gas Mark 6.

2. Bring the water, butter and salt to the boil in a saucepan. When the butter has melted, remove the pan from heat and vigorously beat in all the flour at once. Continue beating until flour is totally incorporated.

3. Return saucepan to moderate heat. Beat constantly with a wooden spoon until the dough forms a ball and comes away from the sides of the pan (about 2 to 4 minutes).

4. Remove saucepan from the heat. Beat in the eggs a little at a time, making sure each addition is well incorporated before adding the next. Gradually beat in the grated cheese.

5. With moist hands, form the dough into a sausage shape and twist the roll into a ring.

6. Place on a greased baking sheet, make a few slits on the surface of the dough with a knife and, to glaze, brush with the beaten egg.

7. Bake 30 to 35 minutes, until the cheese pastry is golden brown on the outside and has puffed up. (Do not open the oven door during baking.) Slice and serve immediately as an appetiser.

Serves 4 to 6

MELTED CHEESE APPETISERS LORRAINE

France

Preparation time: 35 minutes   **Grilling time:** 5 minutes

Ingredients

8 slices white bread
Butter
12 fl. oz./3½ dl. beer
8 oz./225 g. Gruyère
  or other Swiss cheese,
  grated

Dash cayenne pepper
1½ oz./40 g. butter
4 slices ham

1. Preheat grill.

2. Lightly toast the bread and butter it.

3. In a saucepan reduce the beer by half over moderate heat. Add the grated cheese, stirring until the mixture has the consistency of paste. Season with cayenne pepper.

4. In a frying pan melt the butter and fry the slices of ham over moderately high heat. Place the ham slices on toast, cover with the cheese mixture and top with the remaining toast, butter side up.

5. Put the sandwiches under the grill until the toast is golden.

6. Serve very hot, accompanied by cold beer at lunch, or cut into quarters as an appetiser.

Makes 4 sandwiches

LITTLE UKRAINIAN PIES

USSR

Preparation time: 30 minutes
Sour cream pastry chills—1 hour

Cooking time:
15–20 minutes

Ingredients

Sour Cream Pastry:
14 oz./400 g. plain flour
1 teaspoon baking powder
½ teaspoon salt
4 oz./100 g. butter, chilled
2 eggs, lightly beaten
¼ pint/1½ dl. soured cream

Mushroom Filling:
6 spring onions, chopped
12 oz./350 g. mushrooms, chopped

2 oz./50 g. butter
1 tablespoon flour
2 tablespoons soured cream
3 tablespoons fresh dill
Pinch allspice
Salt
Freshly ground pepper
2 hard-boiled eggs, chopped

———

Beaten egg for glazing

1. Prepare the pastry: Sift the flour, baking powder and salt into a large bowl. Cut the butter into the flour until it is the consistency of breadcrumbs. In another bowl, combine the eggs and the soured cream until smooth, then blend in the flour mixture. Knead the dough on a floured board until smooth. Cover and chill for 1 hour.

2. Sauté the spring onions and mushrooms in the butter until golden. Remove and reserve. Sprinkle in the flour and stir over moderate heat for 1 minute. Blend in the soured cream and remove from heat. Return the spring onions and mushrooms to the pan. Mix thoroughly, then add the dill, allspice, salt, pepper and chopped eggs.

3. Preheat the oven to 400°F., 200°C., Gas Mark 6. Roll out the dough to ¼-inch/5-mm. thickness. Cut into 3½-inch/8½-cm. rounds. Place a tablespoon of filling in the centre of each round. Fold into crescents and pinch the edges. Place on a buttered baking sheet. Brush with the egg and bake until golden, about 15 to 20 minutes.

Makes 36 pies

VEAL AND CHIVE TURNOVERS

Preparation time: 20 minutes   **Cooking time:** 20 minutes
Refrigeration: pastry—1½ hours
                    filling—1 hour

France

Ingredients

Flaky Pastry:
8 oz./225 g. plain flour
½ teaspoon salt
6 oz./175 g. butter
7 tablespoons iced water

Filling:
10 oz./275 g. minced veal
  (shoulder or rump)

2 teaspoons salt
Freshly ground pepper
⅛ teaspoon nutmeg
2 eggs, whole
1 egg, separated
¼ pint/1½ dl. double cream
1½ tablespoons chopped
  chives

1. Prepare flaky pastry (page 474) and chill for about 1½ hours.

2. Place the minced veal in a bowl. Add the seasonings and beat in the whole eggs. Beat the extra egg white until stiff and fold into the veal. Refrigerate mixture for 1 hour.

3. Set oven at 425°F., 220°C., Gas Mark 7.

4. Beat the cream until stiff and fold into veal. Add the chives.

5. Roll out a third of the pastry to ¼-inch/5-mm. thickness and cut into 3-inch/7½-cm. circles. Roll out the remaining pastry and cut into 4-inch/10-cm. circles.

6. Put a tablespoon of the filling onto each small circle. Moisten the edges of the circles with water, cover with the larger circles and seal. Slit tops of turnovers, then transfer to a buttered baking sheet. Beat the remaining egg yolk with a little water and brush onto the pastry. Bake for 20 minutes. Serve hot.

Makes about 20 individual turnovers

SPRING ROLLS

China

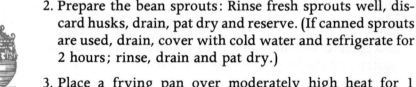

Preparation time: 1¼ hours
Canned sprouts chill—2 hours

Cooking time:
Filling—12 minutes
Spring rolls—4 minutes
per batch

Ingredients
Filling:

8 oz./225 g. lean boneless
  pork, cut into julienne
  strips

1 teaspoon cornflour

1 lb./450 g. fresh mung
  bean sprouts or 1 large
  can bean sprouts

4 tablespoons vegetable
  oil

3 to 4 thick slices fresh
  root ginger, peeled

8 oz./225 g. small prawns,
  shelled, de-veined and
  halved

1½ teaspoons salt

1 tablespoon Chinese rice
  wine or dry sherry

10 small white
  mushrooms, sliced

2 leeks (white parts only),
  chopped

1 tablespoon soy sauce
——

3 packets of spring roll
  wrappers

1 egg, lightly beaten

1½ pints/9 dl. vegetable oil
  for deep-frying

1. Toss the pork with the cornflour in a bowl. Cover and reserve.

2. Prepare the bean sprouts: Rinse fresh sprouts well, discard husks, drain, pat dry and reserve. (If canned sprouts are used, drain, cover with cold water and refrigerate for 2 hours; rinse, drain and pat dry.)

3. Place a frying pan over moderately high heat for 1 minute. Add 1 tablespoon of the oil. Wait ½ minute, then add the ginger. Fry for 1 minute, stirring.

4. Raise heat and add the prawns. Briskly stir in ¼ teaspoon of the salt and the rice wine (or sherry). Stirring constantly, cook until the prawns are pink, about 1 minute. Remove prawns with a slotted spoon and reserve on a heated platter.

5. Add another tablespoon of the oil to the pan. Heat a few seconds, then briskly stir in the pork strips. Fry for 2

minutes, then lower heat, add mushrooms and fry for another 1½ minutes, stirring. Remove with a slotted spoon and add to the prawns.

China

6. Add the remaining oil to the pan. Raise heat and add the leeks and the sprouts. Fry for 1 minute.

7. Return the prawn mixture to the pan. Stir briefly over high heat, then add the soy sauce and the remaining salt. Remove pan from heat.

8. Using a slotted spoon, transfer filling to absorbent paper. Drain well. Place in a bowl, cover and cool to room temperature. (Filling may be prepared in advance and stored in the refrigerator.)

9. To fill spring rolls: Place 3 to 4 tablespoons of filling in the centre of a wrapper; mould filling into a sausage shape; roll into a compact cylinder, tucking in the ends and sealing edges with beaten egg. Repeat until all the filling is used.

10. In a heavy saucepan, heat the 1½ pints/9 dl. oil to 375°F., 190°C.

11. Gently lower 4 to 6 spring rolls at a time into the oil and fry until crisp and golden, about 4 minutes. Remove with a slotted spoon, drain on absorbent paper and keep warm in a slow oven. Repeat until all the spring rolls have been fried.

Makes about 24

Spring rolls may be assembled in advance and frozen. Defrost to room temperature and deep-fry as directed.

ANCHOVY CANAPÉS

France

Preparation time: 15 minutes

Ingredients

2 2-oz./57-g. cans
anchovy fillets, drained
and chopped

2 to 3 cloves garlic, crushed

1 tablespoon olive oil

1 tablespoon vinegar

6 shallots, finely chopped

3 tablespoons chopped
fresh parsley

4 tomatoes, peeled, seeded
and chopped

Freshly ground pepper

Thinly sliced French
bread, rubbed with
garlic and fried on one
side in olive oil

1. Set oven at 400°F., 200°C., Gas Mark 6.

2. In a mortar combine the anchovies and garlic. Grind mixture to a paste, then transfer to a mixing bowl.

3. Gradually beat the olive oil into the anchovy-garlic mixture. Continue beating until oil is thoroughly incorporated, then beat in the vinegar.

4. Add the shallots, parsley and tomatoes. Blend thoroughly, then season to taste with freshly ground pepper. Reserve.

5. Arrange the thinly sliced bread (fried side down) on a baking sheet. Make a slight depression in the unfried side of each slice of bread and spread the anchovy mixture on top.

6. Before serving, place baking sheet in oven until canapés are heated through, about 3 minutes, then arrange the hot anchovy canapés on a platter and serve hot.

Serves 4

SMOKED FISH ROE DIP

Preparation time: 20 minutes

Greece

Ingredients

*3 slices white bread,
   crusts trimmed*

*Milk or water for
   soaking bread*

*A 3-oz./85-g. jar tarama
   or smoked cod roe*

1 to 2 cloves garlic, crushed

¼ medium onion, grated

5 tablespoons olive oil

*2 to 3 tablespoons lemon
   juice*

Toasted white bread

Black olives

1. Soak the bread in a little milk or water. Squeeze out excess liquid.

2. Crush the roe in a mortar and add the bread a little at a time. Then crush in the garlic and grated onion. Blend thoroughly.

3. Beating vigorously, as for a mayonnaise, gradually add the olive oil and the lemon juice, a tablespoon at a time. Taste as you go along until the flavour seems right.

4. Serve on toast accompanied by black olives.

Serves 4

CHRISTMAS PICKLED HERRING

Denmark

Preparation time: 20 minutes
Herring soaks—overnight

Marination time: 4 days

Ingredients

16 herring fillets
4 onions, thinly sliced
1¼ oz./35 g. pickling spice
   mixture

Marinade:

1½ pints/9 dl. white
   vinegar
1½ pints/9 dl. water
2 oz./50 g. brown sugar

1. Soak the herring fillets overnight in cold water.

2. Drain the fillets and, if necessary, remove the black membranes. Cut fillets into bite-sized pieces.

3. Place a layer of herring in a large earthenware dish. Cover with a layer of sliced onions and a generous sprinkling of pickling spices. Continue layering and seasoning until dish is three-quarters full.

4. In a non-metallic bowl, combine the marinade ingredients. Mix thoroughly, then add to the dish.

5. Cover dish tightly and marinate herring in a cool place or refrigerator for 3 days. Gently stir herring with a wooden spoon, then re-cover dish and marinate for at least 1 more day.

Serves 12 to 16

Although pickled herring is delicious all year round, traditionally it is a Christmas season favourite. Since the herring 'gathers virtue' with prolonged marination, a large batch is often prepared at the end of November so that it will be at its best for the holidays.

MARINATED HERRING WITH 3 DRESSINGS

Finland

Preparation time: 30 minutes
Raw herring marinates—3 hours

Ingredients

2 oz./50 g. salt

$\frac{3}{4}$ pint/4$\frac{1}{2}$ dl. water

$\frac{1}{3}$ pint/2 dl. vinegar

5 lb./2$\frac{1}{4}$ kg. herring fillets

$\frac{1}{3}$ pint/2 dl. white wine

1 oz./25 g. sugar

2 onions, thinly sliced

2 lemons, thinly sliced

2 teaspoons peppercorns

$\frac{1}{2}$ teaspoon crushed dried chilli peppers

2 bay leaves, crushed

Cream Cheese Dressing:

3 oz./75 g. cream cheese

6 tablespoons single cream

1 tablespoon lemon juice

1$\frac{1}{2}$ tablespoons chopped chives

Mustard Mayonnaise:

1$\frac{1}{2}$ tablespoons mustard

$\frac{1}{3}$ pint/2 dl. mayonnaise

1$\frac{1}{2}$ tablespoons herring marinade

Dill Dressing:

$\frac{1}{3}$ pint/2 dl. soured cream

1 small onion, minced

3 tablespoons vinegar

6 tablespoons chopped dill

1. Combine the salt, water and vinegar. Add the fillets and marinate for 3 hours. Drain the fillets and reserve.

2. Pour the marinade into a small saucepan. Add the wine and sugar. Boil rapidly for 2 minutes, remove from heat and cool.

3. Roll up the herring fillets. Layer the fillets in 3 glass pickling jars, covering each layer of herring with a layer of onions, lemon and flavourings. Pour in the marinade. Cover and refrigerate for 24 hours.

4. Prepare the three dressings in separate bowls, blending the ingredients listed above for each. To serve, drain the fillets and cut into bite-sized pieces. Add a third of the fillets to each dressing and mix gently.

Serves 12

MARINATED FISH

Mexico

Preparation time: 15 minutes   **Refrigeration time:** 3 hours

Ingredients

8 oz./225 g. halibut fillets or other firm white fish, diced

8 oz./225 g. scallops, diced

Juice of 2 limes or lemons

1 ripe avocado

8 oz./225 g. tomatoes, peeled, seeded and chopped

½ green pepper, seeded and diced

3 tablespoons olive oil

3 tablespoons chopped parsley

2 to 4 spring onions, white part only, diced

Pinch cayenne

Salt

Freshly ground pepper

1. Put the fish and scallops in a glass bowl, toss with lime (or lemon) juice, cover and refrigerate for 2 hours, stirring occasionally.

2. Peel and dice the avocado.

3. Add the avocado and the remaining ingredients to the fish. Toss and correct seasoning. Refrigerate for at least 1 hour.

4. Serve on a bed of lettuce or in individual chilled glass bowls.

Serves 4

SALMON WITH DILL SAUCE

Preparation time: 1 hour

Ingredients

2½ lb./1¼ kg. salmon, cleaned

2 tablespoons coarse salt

1½ tablespoons sugar

1 tablespoon pepper

1 tablespoon vegetable oil

1 tablespoon cognac or other brandy

1 large bunch fresh dill

Marination time: 2 days

Dill Sauce:

2 tablespoons Dijon or dark mustard

1 tablespoon sugar

1½ tablespoons white vinegar

6 tablespoons vegetable oil

6 tablespoons chopped fresh dill

Salt and pepper

Sweden

1. Cut the salmon in half lengthwise. Bone. Pat dry and reserve.

2. In a small bowl, combine the salt, sugar and pepper.

3. Rub both sides of the salmon with oil and brandy, then season with half the sugar, salt and pepper mixture.

4. Spread a third of the dill in a shallow baking dish. Place one piece of fish (skin side down) on top. Sprinkle on half the remaining dill. Cover with the second piece of fish (skin side up), then sprinkle on the remaining dill.

5. Cover with a double thickness of aluminium foil, place a plate on top and weight. Refrigerate for 2 days, turning and basting the fish every 12 hours.

6. Prepare sauce: Combine mustard, sugar and vinegar in small bowl. Using a wire whisk, beat in the oil, as for a mayonnaise (page 476), then add the dill, salt and pepper.

7. Slice the cured salmon in long, thin strips and serve with the dill sauce, lemon wedges and black bread or toast.

Serves 6 to 8

PRAWNS MARINATED WITH DILL

Sweden

Preparation time: 25 minutes

Marination time: 3 hours

Ingredients

Court Bouillon:

1 onion, chopped

1 stick celery, chopped

1½ pints/9 dl. water

2 bay leaves

6 peppercorns

½ tablespoon salt

30 prawns

⅓ pint/2 dl. tarragon vinegar

4 bay leaves, crushed

6 peppercorns

3 tablespoons chopped fresh dill

1. In a large saucepan, combine the court bouillon ingredients listed above. Boil rapidly for 15 minutes.

2. Add the prawns to the court bouillon. Return to the boil, then lower heat and simmer until shells of prawns turn pink, about 3 to 5 minutes.

3. Remove prawns with a slotted spoon, shell and de-vein, then chop coarsely.

4. In a non-metallic bowl, combine the chopped prawns, vinegar, bay leaves, peppercorns and dill. Mix gently, then cover and let stand at least 3 hours.

5. Before serving, drain well, then transfer to a serving bowl and surround with thinly sliced black bread.

Serves 4

POTTED SHRIMPS

Preparation time: 20 minutes   **Cooking time:** 5 minutes
Prepared dish chills—30 minutes

Great Britain

Ingredients

1 lb./450 g. tiny shrimps
*Bouquet garni (bay leaf,
   parsley, 5 peppercorns,
   thyme)*
*8 oz./225 g. butter, at
   room temperature*
1 tablespoon lemon juice

½ teaspoon ground mace
Pinch cayenne pepper
Salt
*Freshly ground black
   pepper*
Fresh toast triangles

1. Drop the shrimps and the bouquet garni into a pot of lightly salted boiling water. Reduce heat to moderate and cook shrimps until firm and pink, about 5 minutes. Remove from heat, drain and allow to cool to room temperature.

2. Shell and de-vein the shrimps. Finely chop half the shrimps and reserve.

3. Place the remaining shrimps in a blender or mortar. Add half the butter and the lemon juice. Purée mixture to a paste.

4. Mix the reserved chopped shrimps into the paste. Add the mace and cayenne pepper, then season to taste with salt and black pepper.

5. Press the shrimp mixture into a 1¼-pint/¾-litre mould.

6. Melt the remaining butter in a small saucepan and pour it into the mould. Refrigerate mould until the butter is firm, about 30 minutes.

7. Present the potted shrimps in the mould or unmould and serve as a spread on hot buttered toast triangles.

Serves 6

STUFFED MUSSELS

France

Preparation time: 20 minutes   **Cooking time:** 5 minutes

Ingredients

3 pints/1½ litres mussels

3 tablespoons water or dry white wine

6 oz./175 g. lightly salted butter, at room temperature

2 cloves garlic, crushed

4 teaspoons finely chopped fresh parsley

1. Wash the mussels thoroughly, using a stiff brush to scrub the shells. Discard any that are open. Rinse with cold running water until there is no trace of sand.

2. Put them in a large covered pan with the water (or white wine). Cover and steam over high heat until shells open (about 5 minutes).

3. Set oven at 475°F., 240°C., Gas Mark 9.

4. Transfer mussels to a baking sheet and discard one shell from each mussel. Do not use mussels that have not opened.

5. Cream the butter in a bowl with the crushed garlic and parsley. Stuff each mussel with ½ teaspoon of the mixture.

6. Bake until butter mixture bubbles, a few minutes. Serve piping hot.

Serves 4

SALT COD WITH GARLIC MAYONNAISE AND GARNISHES

France

Preparation time: 20 minutes   **Cooking time:** 30 minutes
Salt cod soaks—10 hours

Ingredients

1½ lb./700 g. salt cod
8 new potatoes
8 small carrots, diced
4 white turnips, diced
4 small Jerusalem
    artichokes
24 canned snails

Garlic Mayonnaise:

8 cloves garlic, peeled
3 egg yolks
Pinch salt
¾ pint/4½ dl. olive oil
Juice of ½ lemon
Freshly ground pepper

1. Soak the cod in cold water for 10 hours to remove the salt. Change the water 3 or 4 times.

2. Cook vegetables in separate pots of boiling salted water until tender. Drain and reserve.

3. Meanwhile, prepare the garlic mayonnaise: a) Crush the garlic; b) add the yolks and salt and beat thoroughly; c) add the oil drop by drop, beating constantly, as for a mayonnaise (page 476); d) when thickened, add the lemon juice and pepper.

4. Rinse the cod a final time, place in a saucepan and cover with cold water. Bring to the boil, then reduce heat and poach fish until it flakes when tested with a fork, about 10 minutes. Drain and cut into serving pieces.

5. Arrange the cod, vegetables and snails on separate serving platters. Serve the mayonnaise in a bowl as an accompaniment.

Serves 4

Garlic mayonnaise, the 'butter of Provence', is also served as a sauce for hearts of palm, eggs, tomatoes, green peppers and meat.

BEAN AND TUNA FISH ANTIPASTO

Italy

Preparation time: 15 minutes
Beans soak—overnight

Cooking time: 2½ hours

Ingredients

14 oz./400 g. dried haricot beans
1 Spanish onion, sliced thinly
¼ pint/1½ dl. olive oil
1½ tablespoons wine vinegar

Freshly ground pepper
Salt
2 7-oz./198-g. cans tuna fish packed in olive oil, broken into chunks
Chopped parsley for garnish

1. Put the beans in a bowl and add enough cold water to reach 3 inches/7½ cm. above level of the beans. Let beans soak at room temperature overnight. Drain.

2. Put the beans in a saucepan and add enough cold water to cover. Bring rapidly to the boil. Lower heat, cover and simmer until tender, about 2½ hours. Remove from heat and drain.

3. In a bowl, combine the beans with the onion, olive oil, vinegar, freshly ground pepper and a little salt. Cover and let the mixture cool to room temperature.

4. Add the tuna fish and toss briefly. Sprinkle with the parsley before serving.

Serves 4 to 6

SMOKED FISH MOUSSE

Preparation time: 25 minutes

Cooking time: 10 minutes
Refrigeration time: 1 hour

Great Britain

Ingredients

12 oz./350 g. filleted
   haddock or other fish

Bouquet garni (bay leaf,
   parsley, peppercorns)

3 oz./75 g. smoked trout

2 oz./50 g. butter,
   creamed

3 tablespoons dry white
   wine

1 tablespoon unflavoured
   gelatine

3 tablespoons water, boiling

½ pint/3 dl. mayonnaise

¼ medium onion, grated

6 tablespoons double
   cream

Salt

Freshly ground pepper

Horseradish Cream:

⅓ pint/2 dl. double cream

1 tablespoon grated fresh
   horseradish

Salt

1. Place the fillets and bouquet garni in a saucepan. Cover with water. Bring to the boil, then lower heat, cover and simmer until fish flakes when tested with a fork, about 10 minutes. Remove pan from heat and cool fish in its liquid.

2. Drain the fillets and transfer to a large mortar or bowl. Add the smoked trout. Mash the fish to a paste with a pestle or wooden spoon. Add the paste to the butter. Mix thoroughly.

3. Pour the wine into another bowl. Sprinkle in the gelatine, then pour in boiling water. Cool slightly. Blend in mayonnaise and onion. Add to the fish mixture. Mix well.

4. In a small bowl, beat the cream until stiff. Fold the cream into the fish mixture and season to taste. Pour into an oiled mould. Refrigerate until set, about 1 hour.

5. Whip the cream until stiff. Fold in the horseradish and adjust seasoning. Unmould the mousse and serve with the bowl of horseradish cream.

Serves 6

CHICKEN TERIYAKI

Japan

Preparation time: 15 minutes
Chicken marinates—4–6 hours
Ingredients

Cooking time:
6–8 minutes

Teriyaki Marinade:
5 tablespoons soy sauce
*5 tablespoons sake or
pale dry sherry*
*2 teaspoons peeled and
crushed fresh root ginger*

*8 oz./225 g. chicken livers,
halved*
*1 lb./450 g. chicken
breasts, skinned, boned
and cut in cubes*
Fresh watercress

1. In a cup, combine the marinade ingredients listed above. Reserve.

2. Place the chicken livers and chicken breast cubes in a non-metallic bowl. Pour in the marinade. Stir gently until meat is thoroughly coated, then cover and let stand at room temperature for 4 to 6 hours.

3. Thread the marinated chicken and chicken liver pieces onto small bamboo skewers. (Alternate chicken pieces with chicken liver pieces when threading.) Reserve marinade.

4. Brush the *teriyaki* with the marinade and then grill over charcoal (or under the grill) for 3 minutes.

5. Turn skewers and brush *teriyaki* with the marinade, then continue grilling until chicken is tender, about 4 minutes.

6. When the *teriyaki* is done, arrange on a heated platter, garnish with fresh watercress and serve immediately.

Serves 2 to 4

VARIATION: *Prepare a beef teriyaki. Substitute 1 lb./450 g. sirloin steak cut in 1-inch/2½-cm. cubes for the chicken and chicken livers. Proceed as above and serve hot, garnished with raw mushroom slices.*

FIVE SPICED COLD BEEF

Preparation time: 10 minutes

Cooking time: 1 hour
Cooling time: 1 hour

China

Ingredients

A 1-lb./450-g. piece
  topside of beef

3 tablespoons soy sauce

1 tablespoon Chinese rice
  wine or dry sherry

1 teaspoon sugar

3 $\frac{1}{2}$-inch/1-cm. cubes fresh
  root ginger, peeled

1 whole star anise or 8
  pieces anise

1$\frac{1}{3}$ pints/8 dl. cold water

4 hard-boiled eggs, thinly
  sliced

8 oz./225 g. ham or
  prosciutto, thinly sliced

1. In a heavy pan, combine the beef, soy sauce, rice wine
   (or sherry), sugar, ginger, anise and cold water.

2. Bring to the boil, then lower heat. Simmer for 1 hour,
   turning meat frequently. Remove from heat.

3. Remove meat from pot and cut into very thin slices.

4. Return sliced meat to pot. Allow liquid to cool to room
   temperature, then remove meat slices and reserve.

5. To serve, arrange the slices of beef in the centre of a
   serving platter and surround with the eggs and ham.

Serves 4 to 6

ROAST SPARE RIBS

China

Preparation time: 5 minutes
Ribs marinate—2 hours

Cooking time: 40 minutes

Ingredients

A 2-lb./1-kg. strip spare ribs, trimmed but uncut

Marinade:

3 tablespoons soy sauce

1 teaspoon sugar

2 tablespoons Chinese rice wine or dry sherry

1 tablespoon anise powder or hoisin sauce

2 teaspoons honey

1. Combine marinade ingredients in a small bowl.

2. Place ribs in a shallow dish. Pour on marinade, spoon over ribs several times to coat evenly, then let stand at room temperature for at least 2 hours. Baste occasionally.

3. Preheat oven to 475°F., 240°C., Gas Mark 9.

4. Transfer ribs to a rack placed in a roasting tin and roast for 20 minutes, basting occasionally with the marinade.

5. Lower heat to 375°F., 190°C., Gas Mark 5.

6. Turn ribs over and baste well. Continue roasting until crisp, about 20 minutes. Remove pan from oven.

7. Carve strip into individual ribs with a knife or cleaver.

8. Serve hot or cold.

Serves 4 to 6

CALVES' BRAINS VINAIGRETTE

Preparation time: 20 minutes **Cooking time:** 25 minutes
Calves' brains soak—2 hours **Prepared dish chills**—2 hours

France

Ingredients

1 to 2 pair calves' brains
6 fl. oz./1¾ dl. white
vinegar
1 leek, chopped
1 onion, chopped
2 carrots, peeled and
chopped
2 teaspoons lemon juice
Bouquet garni (bay leaf,
thyme, parsley)
5 peppercorns
1 teaspoon salt

Vinaigrette:

6 tablespoons olive oil
2 tablespoons red wine
vinegar
1 teaspoon dry mustard
Salt
Freshly ground pepper
1½ tablespoons chopped
fresh parsley
1½ tablespoons chopped
chives

1. Rinse the brains under cold running water and place in a large non-metallic bowl. Cover with cold water and add a third of the white vinegar. Soak brains for 40 minutes, then drain. Repeat soaking process 2 more times and drain.

2. Place the brains in a large saucepan. Cover with cold water and add the leek, onion, carrots, lemon juice, bouquet garni and seasonings. Cover and simmer for 25 minutes. Using a slotted spoon, plunge the brains into a bowl of iced water. Drain, pat dry and reserve.

3. Prepare the vinaigrette sauce (page 482). Pour the vinaigrette sauce over the brains and refrigerate for 2 hours.

4. To serve: Cut the brains into even slices and arrange on a bed of lettuce. Spoon remaining vinaigrette over the slices.

Serves 2 to 4

JELLIED CALVES' FEET

USSR

Preparation time: 30 minutes

Cooking time: 4 hours

Refrigeration time: 2 hours

Ingredients

4 calves' feet, split
1 veal knuckle
1 stick celery
2 carrots
2 onions
2 garlic cloves, crushed
Bouquet garni (bay leaf, peppercorns, parsley)

2 teaspoons salt
3 to 4 tablespoons vinegar
5 hard-boiled eggs, sliced
Lettuce
Parsley sprigs and lemon wedges for garnish

1. Drop the calves' feet into a large pot of boiling water. Blanch for 2 minutes, drain and rinse.

2. In a large saucepan cover the calves' feet, veal knuckle, celery, carrots, onions, garlic and bouquet garni generously with salt water. Bring to the boil and skim until liquid clears. Lower heat, cover and simmer until the meat is tender, about 3 hours.

3. Skim the fat, then remove the calves' feet and veal knuckle. Cut the meat from the bones and reserve. Return the bones to the pan. Return stock to a rapid boil, then lower heat, cover and simmer for 1 more hour.

4. Skim the fat again. Discard the bouquet garni and bones. Strain the stock into a large bowl. Pour 3 tablespoons of vinegar into the stock. Adjust seasonings and add more vinegar, if necessary. Let stand 15 minutes.

5. Arrange the eggs and the meat in an oiled mould. Pour in the stock. Cover and refrigerate until set, about 2 hours. To serve, unmould onto a bed of lettuce and garnish with parsley sprigs and lemon wedges.

Serves 8

COUNTRY PÂTÉ

Preparation time: 30 minutes   **Cooking time:** 1½ hours   *France*

Ingredients

8 oz./225 g. pork loin

8 oz./225 g. boneless veal

12 oz./350 g. fresh pork fat

8 oz./225 g. ham

8 oz./225 g. pig's liver or
chicken livers

2 cloves garlic, crushed

2 eggs

3 tablespoons dry white
wine

1½ tablespoons cognac

2 teaspoons salt

1 teaspoon pepper

¼ teaspoon allspice

Pinch thyme

Pinch ground bay leaf

1. Set oven at 350°F., 180°C., Gas Mark 4.

2. Mince together the pork loin, the veal and a third of the pork fat. Finely dice the ham and half the remaining pork fat. In a blender, purée the pig's (or chicken) liver, garlic, eggs, wine, cognac and seasonings.

3. In a large bowl, combine the purée, the minced ingredients and the diced ingredients. Mix thoroughly.

4. Slice the remaining pork fat. Line a 2½-pint/1¼-litre terrine or baking dish, reserving a few slices to cover the pâté. Fill the terrine with the pâté. Arrange the pork fat on top, then cover tightly with a double thickness of aluminium foil.

5. Set the terrine in a pan of water and bake in oven until pâté comes away from the sides of the terrine, about 1½ hours.

6. Remove terrine from the oven and cover with a board or lid that fits inside the terrine. Weight the board and cool to room temperature. (The excess fat will overflow as the pâté cools and firms.) Remove weights and chill. Serve the pâté in the terrine, or warm terrine slightly, unmould and transfer to a platter. Slice thinly and serve.

Serves 10 to 12

CHICKEN LIVER PÂTÉ

Canada

Preparation time: 20 minutes
Pâté chills—2 hours

Cooking time: 15 minutes

Ingredients

1 onion, finely chopped

1 clove garlic, crushed

1 oz./25 g. chicken fat
or bacon dripping

1 lb./450 g. chicken livers,
trimmed

4 oz./100 g. butter

¼ teaspoon salt

Freshly ground pepper

⅛ teaspoon nutmeg

½ teaspoon basil

¼ teaspoon marjoram

¼ teaspoon thyme

2 tablespoons cognac

2 tablespoons double
cream

1 egg, hard-boiled

Chopped chives

1. Sauté the onion and garlic until translucent in the chicken fat. Add the chicken livers, cover and cook over low heat for 10 minutes. Cool slightly, then purée using a sieve or blender.

2. Melt the butter in the same saucepan. Add the seasonings, cognac and cream. When heated through, add to the chicken purée and blend until the consistency of whipped cream.

3. Pour the purée into a lightly oiled mould and chill, covered, for 2 hours or more. To serve, unmould the pâté onto a serving plate. Garnish with the sieved yolk of the egg and the chives. Surround the base of the pâté with finely minced egg white.

Serves 4

Soups

CHERRY SOUP

France

Preparation time: 20 minutes   **Cooking time:** 25 minutes

Ingredients

1½ lb./700 g. sour cherries
1½ oz./40 g. butter
4 teaspoons flour
2 pints/generous litre
  boiling water
1 oz./25 g. sugar

4 tablespoons kirsch
1 piece lemon peel
⅓ pint/2 dl. cold water
6 slices French bread,
  fried in butter

1. Wash the cherries and remove stones. Reserve the stones.

2. Melt the butter in a large saucepan. Stir in the flour and continue stirring for 1 minute. Do not let the flour brown.

3. Stirring constantly, slowly pour in the boiling water. Add the cherries, sugar, kirsch and lemon peel. Bring to the boil, then lower heat, cover and simmer for 20 minutes. Discard peel.

4. Combine the reserved cherry stones and the cold water in a small saucepan. Cook over moderate heat for 15 minutes.

5. Line a heated soup tureen with the fried bread. Strain the cherry stone liquid into the tureen, then pour in the cherry soup. Serve immediately.

Serves 4

COCONUT SOUP

Preparation time: 25 minutes   **Cooking time:** 10 minutes   *Tahiti*
Coconut bakes—25 minutes

Ingredients

2 coconuts

Pinch nutmeg

1½ pints/9 dl. chicken
  stock

Cayenne pepper

1. Puncture the 'eyes' of the coconuts and drain, reserving the milk.

2. Split the coconuts. Remove the flesh, paring the brown skin. Finely dice enough flesh to make 4 oz./100 g. Grate the remaining flesh.

3. Toast the diced coconut in a cool oven (300°F., 150°C., Gas Mark 2) until light brown, about 25 minutes.

4. In a heavy saucepan, combine the reserved coconut milk, grated flesh, nutmeg and chicken stock. Season to taste with cayenne pepper. Simmer over low heat for 10 minutes.

5. Strain soup, then return to saucepan and reheat gently.

6. Serve accompanied by the toasted diced coconut.

Serves 4

COLD CUCUMBER-YOGHURT SOUP

Turkey

Preparation time: 15 minutes
Cucumbers stand—20 minutes

Refrigeration time: 1 hour

Ingredients

4 cucumbers, peeled,
  seeded and chopped

Salt

4 cloves garlic, peeled

3 tablespoons olive oil

2 pints/generous litre yoghurt

$\frac{1}{3}$ pint/2 dl. cream

1$\frac{1}{2}$ tablespoons chopped
  fresh parsley

White pepper

Chopped fresh mint for
  garnish

1. Put the chopped cucumbers in a glass bowl. Salt lightly and toss. Cover bowl and let stand at room temperature for 20 minutes. Drain cucumbers, pat dry and reserve.

2. Crush the garlic into a large glass bowl. Add 1 teaspoon salt, then gradually beat in the olive oil.

3. Add the reserved cucumbers, yoghurt, cream and parsley. Mix thoroughly, then cover and refrigerate for at least 1 hour.

4. Before serving, season to taste with salt and white pepper and garnish with chopped fresh mint.

Serves 6

GAZPACHO ANDALUZ

Preparation time: 15 minutes   **Refrigeration time:** 2 hours

Spain

Ingredients

2 slices dry white bread,
   crumbled

3 tablespoons olive oil

1½ tablespoons wine
   vinegar

1¼ pints/7 dl. chicken stock

2 cloves garlic

2 lb./1 kg. large ripe
   tomatoes, peeled,
   seeded and chopped

4 large spring onions,
   chopped

1 cucumber, chopped

1 green pepper, chopped

¼ teaspoon cumin

Pinch cayenne

Salt

Freshly ground pepper

Chopped fresh parsley
   (or other chopped fresh
   herbs: basil, dill,
   tarragon, chervil) for
   garnish

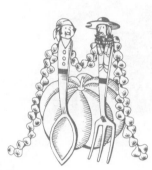

1. In a non-metallic bowl, combine the crumbled bread with the olive oil, vinegar and chicken stock. With a press, crush the garlic into the mixture.

2. Add the tomatoes, spring onions, cucumber, green pepper, cumin and cayenne. Blend well.

3. Add salt and pepper to taste (remember that when chilled, the soup will taste less salty). Refrigerate for a minimum of 2 hours. Serve in chilled soup cups with a sprinkling of chopped parsley or other fresh herbs.

Serves 4

There are as many variations of gazpacho as there are cities in Spain. Some cooks make gazpacho in a blender and offer bowls of croûtons, chopped cucumber, green pepper, celery, onions or chives to sprinkle over the soup.

BORSCHT

Poland

Preparation time: 30 minutes

Cooking time: 2½ hours

Ingredients

2 oz./50 g. butter

2 lb./1 kg. raw beetroots, scraped and grated

2 celery sticks, diced

3 leeks, chopped

½ cabbage, shredded

2 carrots, shredded

2 onions, chopped

1 clove garlic, chopped

1 lb./450 g. brisket of beef, cut in ½-inch/1-cm. cubes

3¼ pints/1¾ litres water

1 tablespoon salt

Bouquet garni (bay leaf, peppercorns, parsley, 2 cloves)

2 egg yolks

⅓ pint/2 dl. soured cream

Chopped fresh dill for garnish

Soured cream for garnish

1. Melt the butter in a large saucepan and sauté the beetroots, celery, leeks, cabbage, carrots, onions and garlic until the green vegetables are slightly limp.

2. Add the beef, water, salt and bouquet garni. Bring to the boil and skim the surface. Cover and simmer over low heat for 2½ hours, skimming occasionally. Discard bouquet garni.

3. Just before serving, beat the egg yolks in a bowl with the ⅓ pint/2 dl. soured cream. Add some soup, a spoonful at a time, to the egg mixture, then gently stir the mixture into the remaining soup, taking care not to let it boil.

4. Serve in warmed soup bowls topped with a sprinkling of dill and a spoonful of soured cream.

Serves 6

VARIATION: *For a clear chilled borscht, proceed through Step 2. Strain the soup, pour into individual cups and refrigerate. Serve garnished with cucumber slices, fresh dill and soured cream.*

SHREDDED CABBAGE SOUP

Preparation time: 20 minutes   **Cooking time:** 25 minutes   *Portugal*

Ingredients

½ medium cabbage
1½ tablespoons olive oil
1 onion, thinly sliced
1¼ pints/7 dl. chicken stock

3 medium potatoes,
  peeled and sliced
Salt
Freshly ground pepper

1. Shred the cabbage as finely as possible. (The strands should be almost threadlike.) Reserve.

2. In a large saucepan, heat the oil and gently sauté the sliced onion until translucent, about 5 minutes.

3. Add the stock, potatoes, salt and pepper. Bring to the boil, then lower heat and simmer until potatoes are tender, about 15 minutes. Remove from heat.

4. Using a sieve or blender, purée the soup to the consistency of cream.

5. Return soup to saucepan, add the reserved cabbage and boil, uncovered, for 3 minutes. Remove from heat.

6. Taste and correct seasoning, if necessary. Serve piping hot.

Serves 4

GARLIC BROTH PROVENÇAL

France

Preparation time: 5 minutes   **Cooking time:** 8 minutes

Ingredients

2½ pints/1¼ litres water
1½ teaspoons salt
6 cloves garlic, crushed
1 sprig sage or 1 teaspoon
    dried sage
½ bay leaf

1 small sprig thyme or 1
    teaspoon dried thyme
1 egg
Salt
Freshly ground pepper
4 to 6 slices French bread,
    fried in olive oil

1. Bring the salted water to the boil in a large saucepan.
   Add the crushed garlic and herbs. Boil for an additional
   8 minutes, then remove from heat.

2. Beat the egg in a large bowl.

3. Beating well, gradually strain the broth into the bowl.
   Add salt and pepper to taste.

4. Serve in soup bowls garnished with the fried French
   bread.

Serves 4 to 6

BEER SOUP

Preparation time: 5 minutes   **Cooking time:** 25 minutes

Germany

Ingredients

2 oz./50 g. butter
1½ tablespoons flour
1½ pints/9 dl. beer
Pinch salt
Pinch nutmeg
Pinch ginger

Pinch cinnamon
4 egg yolks
1 tablespoon sugar
⅓ pint/2 dl. dry white wine
Grated peel of 1 lemon

1. Melt the butter in a large saucepan. Stirring constantly to avoid lumps, gradually blend in the flour and cook over moderately low heat until the flour is golden.

2. Still stirring, slowly pour in the beer. Add the salt, nutmeg, ginger and cinnamon. Simmer gently for 20 minutes.

3. While the beer is simmering, beat the egg yolks well in a bowl. Add the sugar, then beat in the white wine and the grated lemon peel.

4. Drop by drop, beat 3 tablespoons of the hot beer into the egg mixture.

5. Gently stir the egg and beer mixture into the remaining hot beer. Heat through, making sure the soup remains below the simmering point. Taste and correct seasoning, if necessary.

Serves 4

EGG AND LEMON SOUP

Greece

Preparation time: 15 minutes   **Cooking time:** 25 minutes

Ingredients

*3¼ pints/1¾ litres strong
  chicken stock*

4 tablespoons rice

3 to 4 eggs

Juice of 2 lemons

*Chopped fresh parsley
  or chives for garnish*

1. In a saucepan, bring the stock to the boil. Add the rice, cover and cook over low heat until the rice is tender, about 20 minutes.

2. Beat the eggs in a bowl until light and frothy. Add the lemon juice. Beating constantly, gradually add ⅓ pint/ 2 dl. of the hot stock to the egg and lemon mixture in the bowl. When thoughly mixed, beat in another ⅓ pint/ 2 dl. of the stock.

3. Return the saucepan with stock to low heat. Slowly ladle in the egg and lemon mixture, stirring constantly to prevent curdling. Heat through, but do not allow the soup to simmer.

4. Serve immediately, garnished with parsley or chives.

Serves 6 to 8

BLACK BREAD SOUP

Preparation time: 5 minutes   **Cooking time:** 10 minutes   *Norway*

Ingredients

*1½ pints/9 dl. chicken
    stock*
*1 teaspoon grated lemon
    peel*
Pinch nutmeg
Pinch cinnamon

2 oz./50 g. brown sugar
¾ pint/4½ dl. brown ale
4 slices black bread
*⅓ pint/2 dl. soured cream
    for garnish*

1. In a large saucepan, combine the stock, lemon peel, nutmeg, cinnamon, brown sugar and ale. Bring to the boil, then lower heat and simmer for 10 minutes.

2. Line a warmed soup tureen with the slices of black bread. Pour in the soup.

3. Serve the soured cream separately.

Serves 4

HOT AND SOUR SOUP

China

Preparation time: 45 minutes   **Cooking time:** 20 minutes

Ingredients

5 dried Chinese mushrooms
1 tablespoon dried shrimps
4 oz./100 g. lean pork
4 oz./100 g. chicken breast
2 oz./50 g. bamboo shoots
2 bean curd cakes
2½ pints/1¼ litres chicken stock
A 1-inch/2½-cm. cube root ginger, crushed
1 spring onion, finely chopped

½ teaspoon salt
1½ tablespoons vinegar
Freshly ground pepper
2 teaspoons soy sauce
2 tablespoons cornflour mixed with 3 tablespoons cold water
1 egg, beaten
Finely chopped spring onions
Sesame seed oil

1. Soak the mushrooms and shrimps in separate bowls of warm water for 30 minutes. Drain the mushrooms and slice into julienne strips. Reserve ⅓ pint/2 dl. of the liquid. Drain and rinse the shrimps. Slice the next 4 ingredients into julienne strips.

2. In a large saucepan, combine the chicken stock and the mushroom liquid. Bring to the boil, then add the mushrooms, shrimps, pork, chicken, bamboo shoots and ginger. Return to the boil, then lower heat, cover and simmer for 10 minutes.

3. Add the bean curd and spring onion. Re-cover and simmer for 3 more minutes. Season the soup with the salt, vinegar, pepper and soy sauce, then gently stir in the cornflour paste. Continue stirring until soup thickens, about 2 minutes. Slowly dribble in the egg, remove from heat and garnish with spring onions and sprinkle with a few drops of sesame seed oil.

Serves 4 to 6

WONTON SOUP

Preparation time: 35 minutes   **Cooking time:** 10 minutes
Standing time: 45 minutes

Ingredients

Wonton Wrappers:
6 oz./175 g. flour
¾ teaspoon salt
1 egg, lightly beaten
2 to 3 tablespoons water

Filling:
1 lb./450 g. pork, minced
6 spring onions, finely chopped
1 green pepper, finely chopped

4 thick slices root ginger,
  peeled and finely chopped
½ teaspoon salt
1 tablespoon soy sauce
4 oz./100 g. prawns, diced
—
1 egg, lightly beaten
3¼ pints/1¾ litres stock
1 tablespoon oil
½ teaspoon soy sauce
Spring onions

1. Sift the flour and salt into a large bowl. Incorporate the egg and just enough water to form a stiff dough. Knead until smooth, cover with a damp cloth and refrigerate for 45 minutes. Knead gently, then roll out to an ⅛-inch/3-mm. thickness. Cut into 3-inch/7½-cm. squares.

2. Combine the filling ingredients and let stand at room temperature for 30 minutes.

3. To assemble the wonton, place 1 tablespoon of filling in the centre of each wrapper, then fold one corner over the filling, tucking the tip under the filling to secure. Fold the 2 small sections of the wrapper towards the centre, pressing down the edges to seal, then brush the remaining section with the egg and roll up the wonton.

4. Drop the wontons into a pot of rapidly boiling water and simmer until tender, about 10 minutes. Drain.

5. Bring the stock to the boil. Add the oil and soy sauce, then pour over the wontons. Garnish with chopped spring onions and serve immediately.

Serves 6 to 8

VEGETABLE SOUP

Finland

Preparation time: 20 minutes   **Cooking time:** 30 minutes

Ingredients

1 small cauliflower,
   divided into florets

1 lb./450 g. fresh green
   peas, shelled

8 oz./225 g. fresh French
   beans, snapped in half

6 small carrots, sliced

2 new potatoes, sliced

4 radishes, halved

3¼ pints/1¾ litres water

2 teaspoons salt

4 oz./100 g. fresh spinach,
   shredded

1 oz./25 g. butter

1½ tablespoons flour

⅓ pint/2 dl. milk

1 egg yolk

3 tablespoons cream

8 oz./225 g. prawns
   de-veined (optional)

Salt and pepper

Chopped fresh parsley

1. In a large saucepan, combine the cauliflower, peas, French beans, carrots, potatoes, radishes, water and salt. Bring to the boil and cook until vegetables are barely tender, about 10 minutes. Add the spinach and cook for 5 more minutes. Strain liquid into a bowl. Reserve vegetables in another bowl.

2. Melt the butter in the saucepan. Stirring constantly over moderate heat, blend in the flour and cook for 1 minute. Pour in the liquid. Stir vigorously until well blended, then cook over moderate heat for 10 minutes. Stir in the milk.

3. Beat the egg yolk and cream together. Stirring vigorously, gradually add ⅓ pint/2 dl. of the hot soup. When well mixed, stir back into the remainder of the soup.

4. Add the reserved vegetables (and prawns) to the soup. Heat just to simmering point, then remove from heat. Season with salt and white pepper. Pour soup into a heated tureen, garnish with parsley and serve.

Serves 8

CHICKEN VEGETABLE SOUP

Preparation time: 15 minutes   **Cooking time:** 25 minutes   *Japan*

Ingredients

1 tablespoon groundnut oil

1 large carrot, peeled and diced

1 medium potato, peeled and diced

2 oz./50 g. radish, diced

8 oz./225 g. canned bamboo shoots, diced

1 whole chicken breast, boned, skinned and diced

2½ pints/1¼ litres chicken stock

1½ tablespoons soy sauce

1 tablespoon sake or dry sherry

1 teaspoon fresh peeled and finely chopped root ginger

1 tablespoon cornflour, dissolved in 2 tablespoons water

3 spring onions, chopped

1. Heat the oil in a large saucepan. Add the carrot, potato, radish and bamboo shoots. Stir briskly over moderately high heat for 2 minutes.

2. Add the diced chicken and continue stirring over high heat until the chicken pieces turn colour, about 2 or 3 minutes.

3. Add the chicken stock, soy sauce, *sake* (or sherry) and ginger. Bring to the boil, then lower heat and simmer gently until the vegetables are barely tender, about 15 minutes.

4. Stir 3 tablespoons of the hot stock into the cornflour, then stir it into the soup. Simmer for another 5 minutes.

5. Pour soup into a heated tureen, add the chopped spring onions and serve.

Serves 6

CHICKEN SOUP WITH CLAMS AND SPINACH

Korea

Preparation time: 15 minutes **Cooking time:** 15 minutes

Ingredients

16 clams or mussels

1 tablespoon groundnut oil

1½ teaspoons finely chopped fresh root ginger

1 clove garlic, crushed

3 spring onions, chopped

1 chicken breast, skinned, boned and shredded

1½ pints/9 dl. chicken stock

12 oz./350 g. fresh spinach, washed and chopped

1 teaspoon sunflower seed oil

1. Using a stiff brush, scrub the clam (or mussel) shells and rinse thoroughly in cold water until no sand remains. Discard any with open shells.

2. Heat the oil in a large saucepan. Add the ginger, garlic, spring onions and chicken. Fry over high heat for 30 seconds, stirring constantly.

3. Add the chicken stock and bring to the boil. Lower heat and simmer for 5 minutes.

4. Add the clams. Return to a simmer, cover and cook clams until shells open, about 8 minutes. Discard any clams with unopened shells.

5. Add the spinach to the soup, stir briefly, then remove saucepan from heat.

6. Stir in the sunflower seed oil and serve immediately.

Serves 4

CHEESE AND VEGETABLE SOUP

Preparation time: 20 minutes
Beans soak—overnight

Cooking time: $3\frac{1}{4}$ hours

*The
Netherlands*

Ingredients

7 oz./200 g. dried haricot
  beans
$3\frac{1}{2}$ oz./90 g. butter
4 leeks, thinly sliced
4 sticks celery, thinly
  sliced
2 onions, thinly sliced
8 oz./225 g. cabbage,
  shredded
$2\frac{1}{2}$ pints/$1\frac{1}{4}$ litres chicken
  stock

1 tablespoon chopped fresh
  parsley
1 tablespoon cream
6 oz./175 g. Edam cheese,
  grated
Salt
Freshly ground pepper

1. Soak the beans overnight in cold water.

2. Drain the beans, transfer to a saucepan and cover with
   cold water. Bring to the boil, then lower heat, cover and
   simmer until tender, about $2\frac{1}{2}$ hours. Drain.

3. Mash the beans or purée them in a blender. Reserve.

4. Melt the butter in a large saucepan. Add the leeks, celery,
   onions and cabbage. Sauté until the vegetables are tender
   but not browned.

5. Add the bean purée and the chicken stock. Simmer for
   25 minutes.

6. Add the parsley, cream and grated cheese. Season to
   taste with salt and pepper. Heat through and serve.

Serves 4 to 6

TOMATO AND CHEESE SOUP

France

Preparation time: 15 minutes

Cooking time: 1 hour

Ingredients

1 tablespoon olive oil or
   goose fat

2 large onions, sliced

1 clove garlic, finely
   chopped

1 lb./450 g. tomatoes,
   peeled, seeded and
   chopped

2½ pints/1¼ litres water

Salt

Freshly ground pepper

12 slices French bread,
   fried in olive oil or goose
   fat

3 oz./75 g. Gruyère or other
   Swiss cheese, grated

1. Heat the oil in an enamelled cast-iron casserole and gently
   cook the onions for 10 minutes over moderate heat. Do
   not let them brown.

2. Add the garlic, tomatoes and water. Season with salt and
   pepper. Bring to the boil, then lower heat and simmer for
   45 minutes. Taste and correct seasoning, if necessary.

3. Preheat grill.

4. Put half the fried bread slices at the bottom of an ovenproof tureen and sprinkle with half the grated cheese.
   Strain the stock into the tureen. Top with the remaining
   fried bread slices and cheese.

5. Place under the grill for about 5 minutes to brown the
   cheese. Serve immediately.

Serves 6

ONION SOUP LYONNAISE

Preparation time: 10 minutes   **Cooking time:** 50 minutes

France

Ingredients

1 oz./25 g. butter
1½ tablespoons oil
5 large onions, sliced
3¼ pints/1¾ litres beef stock
Freshly ground pepper

12 slices French bread, toasted
6 oz./175 g. Gruyère or other Swiss cheese, grated

1. Heat the butter and the oil in an enamelled cast-iron casserole. Add the onions and cook over low heat until translucent, about 10 minutes. Do not allow onions to brown.

2. Add the stock and season to taste with pepper. Bring quickly to the boil. Boil rapidly for 5 minutes, then lower heat and simmer for 25 minutes. Taste and correct seasoning if necessary.

3. Preheat grill.

4. Place half the toasted bread slices in an ovenproof tureen. Cover with half the grated cheese and then pour in the soup. Add the remaining slices of bread and top with the rest of the cheese.

5. Put the tureen under the grill until the top is browned, about 3 to 5 minutes.

Serves 6

PYRENEES HAM AND ONION SOUP

Spain

Preparation time: 10 minutes   **Cooking time:** 40 minutes

Ingredients

5 tablespoons olive oil
5 onions, thinly sliced
4 oz./100 g. ham, cut
  into julienne strips
1 bay leaf
1 teaspoon thyme

Freshly ground pepper
2½ pints/1¼ litres stock
4 egg yolks
4 to 8 slices French bread
  fried in oil and rubbed
  with garlic

1. In a large saucepan, heat the olive oil. Add the onions and sauté over low heat until limp, about 10 minutes.

2. Add the ham, bay leaf and thyme. Season with pepper. Pour in the stock and bring to the boil, then lower heat and simmer for 25 minutes.

3. Beat the egg yolks well in a bowl. Beat in ⅓ pint/2 dl. of the hot stock, a little at a time, then gently stir mixture into the remainder of the soup. Quickly heat through, but do not allow soup to come to the boil.

4. Place the fried bread slices in a warmed soup tureen. Pour in the hot soup and serve immediately.

Serves 4 to 6

CREAM OF ONION SOUP
ÎLE DE FRANCE

France

Preparation time: 10 minutes **Cooking time:** 35 minutes

Ingredients

1 oz./25 g. butter
*8 oz./225 g. onions, thinly
  sliced*
1½ tablespoons flour
2½ pints/1¼ litres hot milk
Salt

Freshly ground pepper
4 egg yolks
*12 fl. oz./3½ dl. single
  cream*
*4 to 6 slices French bread,
  fried in butter (optional)*

1. Melt the butter in a large saucepan and sauté the onions
   until they become translucent. Do not let them brown.

2. Stir in the flour and mix thoroughly. Add the hot milk,
   salt and pepper. Cook for 30 minutes, stirring frequently
   to prevent lumps. Remove sauce from heat.

3. In a bowl, beat the egg yolks and cream. Beating constantly, very slowly drip ⅓ pint/2 dl. soup into the egg
   mixture. Beat this mixture into the saucepan, then heat
   to thicken slightly. Do not boil.

4. Pour soup into a warmed tureen and garnish with the
   fried bread, if desired.

Serves 4 to 6

PEANUT SOUP

Ghana

Preparation time: 20 minutes

Cooking time: 1 hour

Ingredients

1 lb./450 g. shelled roasted
  peanuts
1 oz./25 g. butter
1 onion, finely chopped
2 sticks celery, finely
  chopped
2½ pints/1¼ litres beef
  stock
1 tablespoon cornflour

⅓ pint/2 dl. milk
⅓ pint/2 dl. cream
Salt
Cayenne pepper
Chopped parsley for
  garnish
Chopped peanuts for
  garnish

1. In a blender or grinder, grind the peanuts to a fine consistency.

2. Heat the butter in a large, heavy saucepan and gently sauté the onion and celery until translucent. Do not brown.

3. Add the ground peanuts and all but 3 tablespoons of the stock. Bring to the boil, then lower heat and simmer for 30 minutes. Remove from heat.

4. Mix the cornflour with the remaining stock and stir into the soup.

5. Return soup to low heat. Add the milk and cream. Season to taste with salt and cayenne pepper (the soup should be spicy). Cover and simmer very gently for 30 minutes.

6. Serve garnished with chopped parsley and peanuts.

Serves 6

In South Africa this soup is laced with liberal amounts of cayenne. It is even better made in advance and reheated a day later.

HARICOT BEAN SOUP

Preparation time: 20 minutes **Cooking time:** 3 hours *USA*
Beans soak—overnight

Ingredients

12 oz./350 g. dried haricot
 beans

1 ham bone, cracked

4¾ pints/2¾ litres cold
 water or beef stock

Bouquet garni (bay leaf,
 parsley, 3 cloves)

1 tablespoon salt

¼ teaspoon pepper

1 oz./25 g. butter

2 onions, chopped

2 sticks celery, chopped

2 carrots, chopped

6 tablespoons dry sherry

1 lemon, thinly sliced

1. Soak beans overnight in cold water.

2. Discard any beans floating on top of the water. Drain the remaining beans and transfer to a large saucepan. Add the ham bone and the cold water (or beef stock). Bring rapidly to the boil. Skim the surface, then add the bouquet garni, salt and pepper. Lower heat, cover tightly and simmer until beans are tender, about 2½ hours.

3. While the beans are cooking, heat the butter in a frying pan and sauté the vegetables until the onions are translucent but not brown. Remove from heat and reserve.

4. When the beans are tender, add the sautéed vegetables to the saucepan. Return to the boil, then lower heat, re-cover and simmer for another ½ hour. Remove from heat. Skim the soup, then discard the ham bone and bouquet garni.

5. Purée the soup in a blender or through a sieve. Taste and adjust seasoning.

6. Return soup to the saucepan and heat through. Stir in the sherry. Pour into a warmed tureen, top with the lemon slices and serve immediately.

Serves 8 to 10

SPLIT PEA SOUP

Canada

Preparation time: 15 minutes
Split peas soak—overnight

Cooking time: 3 hours

Ingredients

1 lb./450 g. dried split
 peas

4¾ pints/2¾ litres cold
 water

8 oz./225 g. streaky
 bacon, chopped

2 medium onions, chopped

3 carrots, chopped

¼ teaspoon powdered
 savory

Bouquet garni (bay leaf,
 2 sprigs parsley, 3
 cloves)

Freshly ground pepper

Salt

French bread, diced
 and fried in butter for
 croûtons

1. Soak the split peas overnight in cold water.

2. Drain the peas and transfer to a large saucepan. Pour in
   the cold water and bring rapidly to the boil.

3. Skim the surface, then add bacon, onions, carrots, savory
   and bouquet garni. Season with pepper and a little salt.

4. Return to the boil, then lower heat, cover and simmer for
   3 hours.

5. Remove bouquet garni and correct seasoning. Pour into
   a heated soup tureen and serve garnished with the
   croûtons.

Serves 8 to 10

SOUP WITH LIVER MEATBALLS

Preparation time: 20 minutes **Cooking time:** 15 minutes

Austria

Ingredients

*2 slices stale bread, soaked
  in milk*
*8 oz./225 g. pig's liver,
  minced*
2 oz./50 g. butter
1 medium onion, chopped
1 clove garlic, crushed
2 eggs, well beaten

Pinch powdered marjoram
Salt
Freshly ground pepper
*2½ pints/1¼ litres beef
  stock*
*Chopped fresh parsley
  for garnish*

1. Squeeze the milk from the bread, then crumble in a large bowl. Add the minced liver and mix well. Reserve.

2. Heat ½ oz./15 g. of the butter in a frying pan. Add the onion and garlic. Sauté over low heat until the onion is limp, about 5 minutes. Transfer to the liver and bread mixture.

3. Bind the mixture with the beaten eggs, then season with the marjoram, salt and pepper. Mix thoroughly, then shape into small meatballs.

4. In a large frying pan, heat the remaining butter and sauté the meatballs until nicely browned. Remove from heat.

5. In a large saucepan, bring the beef stock to the boil. Add the meatballs. Lower heat and simmer for 5 minutes.

6. Pour into a heated soup tureen, garnish with chopped parsley and serve.

Serves 4 to 6

TYROLEAN BEEF SOUP

Austria

Preparation time: 20 minutes   **Cooking time:** 1½ hours

Ingredients

5 onions, finely chopped
3 oz./75 g. lard or oil
2 cloves garlic
1 teaspoon cumin seeds
1 teaspoon marjoram
1 teaspoon paprika
3¼ pints/1¾ litres beef stock

1 lb./450 g. good quality braising steak, diced
Salt
Freshly ground pepper
2 tablespoons flour
1 lb./450 g. potatoes, peeled and diced

1. In a large heavy saucepan, sauté the onions in the lard (or oil) until translucent but not brown.

2. While the onions are cooking, crush the garlic, cumin seeds and marjoram together in a mortar. Reserve.

3. Sprinkle the onions with paprika and stir in all but ⅓ pint/2 dl. of the stock. Bring to the boil and add the diced beef. Return to the boil, then lower heat and simmer gently for 20 minutes.

4. Add the crushed garlic, cumin seeds and marjoram to the soup. Season with salt and pepper, then cover and simmer over low heat for 45 minutes or until the meat is tender.

5. Gradually stir the remaining cold stock into the flour. Stirring constantly to avoid lumps, slowly pour the mixture into the hot soup.

6. Add the potatoes to the soup and continue simmering until the potatoes are done, about 15 minutes.

7. Pour into a heated soup tureen and serve.

Serves 6

VEGETABLE SOUP PROVENÇAL

Preparation time: 25 minutes
White beans soak—overnight

Cooking time: 1½ hours

France

Ingredients

*1 lb./450 g. dried haricot
  beans*

3¼ pints/1¾ litres water

2 teaspoons salt

*4 oz./100 g. green beans,
  sliced*

*3 large potatoes, peeled
  and diced*

2 courgettes, sliced

3 carrots, sliced

*4 oz./100 g. canned
  kidney beans, drained*

2 oz./50 g. vermicelli

½ teaspoon pepper

Pistou:

4 cloves garlic, crushed

*3 tablespoons chopped
  fresh basil or 1½
  tablespoons dried basil*

*4 large tomatoes, peeled,
  seeded and chopped*

3 tablespoons olive oil

*4 oz./100 g. grated
  Gruyère cheese for
  garnish*

1. Soak the haricot beans overnight. Drain and reserve.

2. Bring the water to the boil in a large saucepan. Add the
   salt, fresh vegetables and haricot beans. Lower heat and
   simmer gently for 1¼ hours. Add the kidney beans,
   vermicelli and pepper. Cook an additional 15 minutes.

3. Make the pistou: Place the garlic, basil and tomatoes in a
   mortar and crush to a paste. Add the olive oil, drop by
   drop, as for a mayonnaise.

4. Stirring well, add the pistou to the soup. Bring back to
   the boil and immediately remove from heat. Adjust
   seasoning. Serve with a dish of grated cheese.

Serves 6

BASQUE BEAN AND CABBAGE SOUP

Spain

Preparation time: 20 minutes
Beans soak—overnight

Cooking time: 3 hours

Ingredients

*10 oz./275 g. dried haricot
    beans*
2 medium onions, sliced
3 cloves garlic, crushed
*2 oz./50 g. lard or olive
    oil*
1 white cabbage, shredded

Salt
Freshly ground pepper
4¾ pints/2¾ litres water
*1 teaspoon red wine
    vinegar per person
    (optional)*

1. Soak beans overnight. Drain and reserve.

2. In a large saucepan, brown the onions and garlic in the lard (or olive oil).

3. Add the cabbage, beans, salt, pepper and water.

4. Bring soup to the boil. Lower heat, cover and simmer for 3 hours. Taste and adjust seasoning if necessary.

Serves 8 to 10

The Basques traditionally add a touch of vinegar to their soup plates.

SCOTCH BROTH

Preparation time: 30 minutes

Cooking time: 2½ hours

Scotland

Ingredients

8 oz./225 g. breast of
lamb, cut into pieces

8 oz./225 g. neck of lamb,
chopped

3¼ pints/1¾ litres water

3½ oz./90 g. pearl barley

2 oz./50 g. butter

3 carrots, peeled and
diced

2 turnips, peeled and
diced

2 onions, chopped

2 leeks, chopped

2 sticks celery, chopped

Bouquet garni (thyme,
bay leaf, parsley)

Salt

Freshly ground pepper

Chopped fresh parsley

1. In a large saucepan, combine the meats and 2½ pints/1¼
   litres of the water. Bring to the boil and skim off any
   foam that appears. Lower heat, cover and simmer for 20
   minutes.

2. In a small saucepan, bring the remaining water to the
   boil. Stir in the barley and cook, uncovered, over high
   heat for 10 minutes. Drain barley and reserve.

3. Melt the butter in a frying pan. Add the carrots, turnips,
   onions, leeks and celery. Sauté until the onions are golden.

4. Add the vegetables, reserved barley and bouquet garni
   to the soup. Simmer for 2 hours, skimming off foam
   occasionally.

5. Discard the bouquet garni. Remove the bones from the
   soup. Cut any meat remaining on the bones into small
   pieces and return it to the broth. Discard the bones.
   Skim off any fat on the surface of the soup, then season
   to taste with salt and pepper. Garnish with chopped fresh
   parsley and serve immediately.

Serves 6

LAMB AND VEGETABLE SOUP WITH VERMICELLI

North Africa

Preparation time: 20 minutes

Cooking time: 2¾ hours

Ingredients

1½ lb./700 g. lean lamb
2 lamb bones, cracked
3¼ pints/1¾ litres cold
 water
Salt
Freshly ground pepper
Pinch cayenne pepper
4 oz./100 g. dried apricots
3 tablespoons oil
4 onions, coarsely chopped

3 green peppers, seeded
 and coarsely chopped
1 to 1½ tablespoons chopped
 fresh mint leaves
4 tomatoes, peeled, seeded
 and chopped
4 oz./100 g. large
 vermicelli
1 tablespoon lemon juice
Chopped fresh parsley
 and mint for garnish

1. Put the meat and bones in a large heavy pan and cover with the cold water. Add salt, pepper and cayenne. Bring to the boil and skim the surface. Add the apricots, then lower heat, cover and simmer for 1½ hours.

2. Heat the oil in a frying pan. Add the onions, peppers and mint leaves and cook until the onions are limp.

3. Add the onions, peppers, mint leaves and tomatoes to the soup. Continue simmering for 1 hour.

4. Remove the meat and bones from the soup. Discard bones and cut the meat into bite-size chunks. Return meat to soup.

5. Adjust seasoning, then bring to the boil. Add the vermicelli and cook for 5 minutes, or to desired tenderness.

6. Pour into a heated soup tureen, stir in the lemon juice and garnish with chopped parsley and mint.

Serves 6

MINESTRONE

Preparation time: 20 minutes
Beans soak—overnight

Cooking time: 3 hours

Italy

Ingredients

8 oz./225 g. dried haricot
   beans

6 tablespoons olive oil

4 onions, chopped

2 leeks, chopped

1 clove garlic, crushed

2 sticks celery, diced

8 oz./225 g. fresh green
   beans, sliced

2 courgettes, diced

8 oz./225 g. potatoes,
   peeled and diced

2 ripe tomatoes, diced

3½ pints/2 litres beef
   stock

4 oz./100 g. macaroni

½ tablespoon chopped fresh
   sage

½ tablespoon chopped fresh
   basil

½ tablespoon chopped fresh
   parsley

Salt

Freshly ground pepper

Freshly grated Parmesan
   cheese

1. Soak haricot beans overnight in cold water.

2. Drain them and transfer to a saucepan. Cover with cold water. Bring to the boil, then lower heat, cover and simmer until nearly tender, about 2 hours. Drain and reserve.

3. Heat the olive oil in a large saucepan and stir in the onions, leeks, garlic and celery. Sauté until the onions are translucent but not browned.

4. Add the reserved haricot beans, the remaining vegetables and the stock. Cover and simmer for 40 minutes.

5. Uncover and turn up heat. When the soup comes to the boil, add the macaroni, chopped herbs, salt and pepper. Cook uncovered for 20 minutes. Pour into a tureen and serve with freshly grated Parmesan.

Serves 6 to 8

MAIN-COURSE CABBAGE AND BEAN SOUP BÉARNAIS

France

Preparation time: 15 minutes
Beans soak—overnight

Cooking time: 2½ hours

Ingredients

9 oz./250 g. dried haricot
beans

1 lb./450 g. potatoes,
peeled and quartered

A 1½-lb./700-g. bacon
joint

4 cloves garlic, crushed

Bouquet garni (bay leaf,
parsley, thyme, 8
peppercorns)

4¾ pints/2¾ litres water

2½ lb./1¼ kg. green
cabbage, coarsely
chopped

2 carrots, peeled and
quartered

1 leg preserved goose
(optional, page 477)

Freshly ground pepper

Salt

1. Soak beans overnight. Drain and reserve.

2. Put the potatoes, bacon joint, garlic, bouquet garni and
   water in a large enamelled cast-iron casserole. Bring to
   the boil. Lower heat, cover and simmer for 1 hour.

3. Add the beans, cabbage and carrots (and goose). Cover
   partially and simmer for 1½ hours.

4. Salt and pepper to taste.

5. Before serving, remove the meats, cut into serving
   pieces and return to the casserole.

Serves 8 to 10

GRISONS-STYLE BEEF AND BEAN SOUP

Switzerland

Preparation time: 20 minutes
Beans soak—overnight

Cooking time: 3 hours

Ingredients

8 oz./225 g. dried haricot
   beans

Meat bones

8 oz./225 g. salted beef
   e.g., silverside, diced

8 oz./225 g. braising steak,
   cut into strips

3¼ pints/1¼ litres cold
   water

10 oz./275 g. pearl barley

3 medium potatoes,
   peeled and quartered

1 lb./450 g. cabbage,
   coarsely chopped

2 sticks celery, chopped

Salt

Freshly ground pepper

6 fl. oz./1¾ dl. cream

1 tablespoon cornflour

Chopped fresh parsley for
   garnish

1. Soak the beans overnight. Drain and reserve.

2. Combine the beans, meat bones, meats and water in a large saucepan. Bring to the boil, then lower heat and simmer, uncovered, for 2 hours.

3. Add the barley, potatoes, cabbage and celery. Season with salt and pepper. Cover and simmer over low heat for 1 hour. Remove meat bones.

4. Five minutes before serving, blend the cream and cornflour together in a bowl. Stirring constantly, add the mixture to the soup and cook very gently for a few minutes. Do not let the soup boil.

5. Sprinkle with parsley and serve.

Serves 4

ALBIGEOIS MAIN-COURSE SOUP

France

Preparation time: 30 minutes
Beans soak—overnight

Cooking time: 3½ hours

Ingredients

1 lb./450 g. dried haricot
  beans

6½ pints/3½ litres water

1 veal knuckle

1 meat bone

2 lb./1 kg. beef shin

A 1-lb./450-g. bacon joint

6 carrots, peeled and
  quartered

6 leeks, white parts only

4 cloves garlic, crushed

Bouquet garni (bay
  leaves, parsley, thyme,
  peppercorns)

1 onion stuck with 4 or
  5 cloves

1 tablespoon salt

2 teaspoons freshly ground
  pepper

1 cabbage, cut into
  quarters

2 lb./1 kg. garlic sausage
  or Italian cotechino

¼ preserved goose (optional,
  page 477)

1. Soak beans overnight. Drain and reserve.

2. Put the water in a very large saucepan. Add the veal
   knuckle, meat bone, beef shin, bacon, carrots, leeks,
   garlic, bouquet garni, onion, salt and pepper. Bring to the
   boil and skim off the foam. Cover and simmer for 2½ hours.

3. Blanch the cabbage and the beans for 2 minutes in a
   separate large pot of rapidly boiling water. Drain and
   refresh.

4. Add the cabbage, beans, sausage (and goose) to the soup.
   Simmer, uncovered, for another hour. Taste and correct
   seasoning. Discard bouquet garni.

5. Using a slotted spoon, arrange the meats, vegetables and
   beans on a heated platter. Pour the broth into a warmed
   tureen and serve at the same time.

Serves 8 to 10

MAIN-COURSE BOILED BACON SOUP

France

Preparation time: 30 minutes
Bacon soaks—4 hours

Cooking time: 2 hours

Ingredients

A 3-lb./1⅓-kg. bacon joint
4 pints/2¼ litres water
8 leeks, trimmed
8 carrots, peeled and quartered
1 onion stuck with 4 cloves
4 shallots, chopped
Bouquet garni (parsley, bay leaf, garlic clove)

1 celeriac (celery root), quartered
Freshly ground pepper
1 small cabbage, quartered
8 oz./225 g. runner beans, sliced
1 lb./450 g. peas, shelled
8 slices French bread, toasted

1. Soak the bacon in cold water for 4 hours, changing the water twice.

2. Put the bacon in a large saucepan with the water, leeks, carrots, onion, shallots, bouquet garni and celeriac. Season with pepper. Bring to the boil and skim the foam off. Reduce heat, cover and simmer for 1½ hours.

3. Blanch the cabbage and runner beans separately in salted boiling water for 5 minutes. Drain and refresh. Add the cabbage to the soup and cook for an additional 20 minutes.

4. Add the beans and peas to the soup and cook until they are tender, about 15 minutes. Discard the bouquet garni.

5. Transfer the bacon and vegetables to a platter. Arrange the bread in a warmed tureen and add the broth. Serve the soup immediately and follow with the meat and vegetables as a main course.

Serves 8

MAIN-COURSE PORK AND VEGETABLE SOUP

France

Preparation time: 30 minutes   **Cooking time:** 3 hours

Ingredients

An 8-oz./225-g. bacon joint
1 lb./450 g. belly of pork
3¼ pints/1¾ litres water
3 carrots, peeled and
   quartered
5 small white turnips,
   peeled and quartered

1 small cabbage,
   quartered
Freshly ground pepper
4 potatoes, peeled and
   quartered
4 fresh sausages
8 thin slices French bread,
   toasted

1. Cut the bacon into chunks and blanch in boiling water for 10 minutes to remove the salt. Drain.

2. Put the bacon and the belly of pork into a large saucepan. Pour in the water. Bring to the boil and skim.

3. Add the carrots, turnips and cabbage. Season with pepper. Simmer for 2½ hours.

4. Add the potatoes and pricked sausages. Simmer for an additional 30 minutes.

5. Remove the vegetables and meat and arrange them on a heated platter. Keep warm.

6. Pour stock into a tureen lined with the bread slices. Serve immediately. The meat and vegetables are served separately.

Serves 4

CALF KIDNEY SOUP

Preparation time: 20 minutes   **Cooking time:** 20 minutes

The Netherlands

Ingredients

2 calves' kidneys
1½ pints/9 dl. chicken stock
2 oz./50 g. butter
1 onion, finely chopped
1 oz./25 g. flour
⅓ pint/2 dl. double cream

1 lb./450 g. mushrooms, chopped
2 tablespoons Madeira
Juice of ½ lemon
1½ tablespoons chopped fresh parsley

1. Prepare the kidneys: Remove the outer membrane and split in half lengthwise. Discard the core of fat and the white veins, then dice the kidneys.

2. In a large saucepan, combine the chicken stock and the kidneys. Bring to the boil, then lower heat, cover and simmer until tender, about 15 minutes.

3. While the kidneys cook, melt the butter in another saucepan and sauté the onion until tender, about 5 minutes.

4. Off the heat, stir the flour into the onion mixture. Return to low heat and stir for 5 minutes. Do not let the flour brown. Add the hot stock, a little at a time, to the flour, stirring constantly to avoid lumps. Cook until thickened.

5. Add the kidneys, cream and chopped mushrooms and heat through but do not boil. Simmer for 5 minutes. Just before serving, stir in the Madeira, lemon juice and the chopped parsley.

Serves 4

VOLGA-STYLE FISH CONSOMMÉ

USSR

Preparation time: 20 minutes

Cooking time: 2 hours

Ingredients

2 lb./1 kg. white-fleshed
   fish (cod, whiting or
   haddock), cleaned

1 small eel, cleaned

3¼ pints/1¾ litres water

2 onions, chopped

3 sticks celery, chopped

1 carrot, peeled and
   chopped

3 tablespoons chopped
   fresh parsley

1 bay leaf

1 teaspoon salt

6 peppercorns

Pinch nutmeg

6 tablespoons dry white
   wine

Chopped fresh dill for
   garnish

1. In a large saucepan, combine the fish, water, vegetables, herbs, salt, peppercorns and nutmeg.

2. Bring to the boil, then lower heat, cover and simmer for 2 hours.

3. Using a fine sieve lined with muslin, strain soup into another large saucepan.

4. Bring strained soup to a simmer. Stir in the wine and heat through.

5. Pour into a warmed tureen, garnish with freshly chopped dill and serve immediately.

Serves 6

FLEMISH FISH SOUP

Preparation time: 20 minutes   **Cooking time:** 25 minutes

Belgium

Ingredients

4 oz./100 g. butter

2 leeks, chopped

2 onions, chopped

2 carrots, sliced

2 lb./1 kg. assorted fish,
    cut into chunks

¾ pint/4½ dl. dry white
    wine

¾ pint/4½ dl. fish stock or
    water

Salt

Freshly ground pepper

Bouquet garni (bay leaf,
    thyme, sage)

Chopped parsley for
    garnish

1. Melt 3 oz./75 g. of the butter in a large saucepan. Add the leeks, onions and carrots; sauté until the onions are translucent but not browned.

2. Add the remaining butter and the fish. Pour in the wine and fish stock (or water). Salt and pepper lightly and add the bouquet garni.

3. Bring soup to the boil, then cover, lower heat and simmer for about 20 minutes, or until all the fish chunks flake easily when tested with a fork.

4. Discard the bouquet garni, correct seasoning and serve piping hot, sprinkled with parsley.

Serves 4

BASQUE FISH AND ONION SOUP

Spain

Preparation time: 10 minutes   **Cooking time:** 1¼ hours

Ingredients

4 medium onions, sliced
6 tablespoons olive oil
2½ pints/1¼ litres water
Bouquet garni (thyme,
    parsley, bay leaf,
    oregano)
1 teaspoon salt

Freshly ground pepper
4 thick pieces hake, cod
    or haddock, boned
4 slices French bread
2 cloves garlic, peeled and
    cut in half

1. In a large heavy pan, sauté the onions in half the olive oil until lightly browned.

2. Add the water, bouquet garni, salt and pepper. Bring to the boil, then cover and cook over moderate heat for 15 minutes.

3. Add the fish, re-cover and simmer over low heat for 1 hour.

4. While the fish is cooking, fry the bread in the remaining olive oil and rub each slice with half a clove of garlic.

5. To serve, carefully remove the fish from the pot with a slotted spoon and arrange in a warmed deep dish. Top each piece of fish with a slice of fried bread. Taste soup and adjust seasoning, if necessary, then pour over the fish. Serve immediately.

Serves 4

BAHIA FISH SOUP

Preparation time: 10 minutes   **Cooking time:** 30 minutes   *Brazil*

Ingredients

1½ tablespoons olive oil

3 cloves garlic, crushed

6 onions, chopped

3 tomatoes, peeled, seeded and chopped

3 green peppers, seeded and chopped

1 lb./450 g. fish fillets, cut into chunks

12 oz./350 g. prawns, shelled, de-veined and halved

2 pints/generous litre chicken stock

Salt

½ teaspoon cayenne pepper

1 teaspoon marjoram

1. In a large saucepan, heat the olive oil with the garlic and sauté the onions until translucent, about 5 minutes.

2. Stir in the tomatoes and green peppers. Cook for 1 minute over moderately high heat, then add the fish and the prawns.

3. Pour in the chicken stock; season with salt, cayenne pepper and marjoram.

4. Bring soup to the boil, then lower heat, cover and simmer until the fish chunks flake easily when tested with a fork, about 20 minutes. Correct seasoning and serve piping hot.

Serves 4

NEW ENGLAND CLAM CHOWDER

USA

Preparation time: 30 minutes   **Cooking time:** 45 minutes

Ingredients

48 clams or mussels

¾ pint/4½ dl. water

3 rashers bacon, chopped

1 medium onion, chopped

3 medium potatoes,
  peeled

Salt

Freshly ground pepper

¾ pint/4½ dl. milk

⅓ pint/2 dl. cream

1½ oz./40 g. butter

1. Wash the clams (or mussels) thoroughly. Place them in a deep pot and add the water. Cover tightly and bring to the boil. Lower heat and simmer until the shells open, about 10 minutes. Discard any that do not open.

2. Drain the clams, reserving the broth. Remove the clams from their shells and chop them finely.

3. Sauté the bacon pieces until crisp and drain. Add the onion to the fat and cook until transparent. Add the clam broth and potatoes. Season with salt and pepper. Cover and simmer until the potatoes are tender, about 30 minutes. Remove from heat.

4. Stir in the milk, cream and butter. Return to heat. When the broth simmers, add the clams and bacon and simmer for about 3 minutes. (Do not let soup boil.) Correct seasoning. Pour into warm soup plates and serve immediately.

Serves 4 to 6

PURÉE OF SHELLFISH SOUP

Preparation time: 20 minutes   **Cooking time:** 1 hour

France

Ingredients

$\frac{1}{3}$ pint/2 dl. dry white wine

8 crayfish, de-veined, or
   8 Dublin Bay prawns
   (scampi)

2 tablespoons olive oil

1 leek, sliced

2 onions, sliced

1 carrot, sliced

1 tablespoon flour

$3\frac{1}{4}$ pints/1$\frac{3}{4}$ litres boiling
   water

Bouquet garni (parsley,
   thyme, rosemary,
   lemon peel)

1 tablespoon salt

Freshly ground pepper

1 egg yolk, beaten

Chopped parsley

1. Bring the wine to the boil in a saucepan. Add the shell-fish, cover and simmer for 10 minutes. Drain, reserving the wine.

2. Heat the oil in a large saucepan. Add the leek, onions and carrot. Cook over moderate heat for 5 minutes.

3. Sprinkle the flour over the vegetables. Stir for 1 minute, then slowly pour in the wine and the water. Add the bouquet garni, salt and pepper. Bring soup to a slow boil and reduce to 2 pints/generous litre. (This will take about 30 minutes.)

4. While the soup is reducing, mince the shellfish in a mincer or blender. Reserve.

5. Strain the soup back into the saucepan. Add the shell-fish. Bring to the boil, lower heat, cover and simmer for 15 minutes.

6. Just before serving, combine 6 tablespoons of soup with the egg yolk, then gently stir the mixture back into the soup. Heat through, but do not bring to the boil. Pour the soup into a warmed tureen and sprinkle with parsley.

Serves 4

FISHERMAN'S BOUILLABAISSE

France

Preparation time: 20 minutes   **Cooking time:** 10–12 minutes
Fish marinates—1 hour

Ingredients

3 lb./1⅓ kg. assorted white
  fish (halibut, cod,
  whiting, haddock)

4 cloves garlic, crushed

4 tomatoes, peeled
  seeded and chopped

2 onions, sliced

1 tablespoon salt

Freshly ground pepper

Bouquet garni (fennel,
  bay leaf, savory,
  parsley)

6 tablespoons olive oil

12 slices French bread

3¼ pints/1¾ litres boiling
  water

½ teaspoon saffron

Chopped fresh parsley

1. Wash the fish and cut into 2-inch/5-cm. chunks.

2. Put the fish in a large pan. Add the garlic, tomatoes, onions, salt, pepper, bouquet garni and olive oil. Marinate at room temperature for 1 hour, stirring occasionally.

3. While the fish is marinating, dry (but do not brown) the slices of French bread in a cool oven (300°F., 150°C., Gas Mark 2).

4. Remove the fish chunks and reserve. Add the boiling water and the saffron to the pan and cook over high heat for 6 minutes. Return the fish to the pot and boil rapidly until the fish flakes easily, about 5 minutes.

5. Remove the fish and arrange on a platter. Sprinkle with the chopped parsley. Place the toasted bread slices in a warm tureen, pour in the stock and serve with the fish.

Serves 6

Fish and Shellfish

FISH SOUP AND STEW PROVENÇAL

France

Preparation time: 20 minutes

Cooking time: 20 minutes

Ingredients

2 lb./1 kg. white fish (cod, halibut, flounder), cut in chunks

5 potatoes, peeled and thickly sliced

1 onion, sliced

2 tomatoes, peeled, seeded and chopped

2 cloves garlic, crushed

Bouquet garni (parsley, fennel, celery, orange peel, bay leaf)

6 tablespoons olive oil

1 tablespoon salt

Freshly ground pepper

3¼ pints/1¾ litres boiling water

Rouille:

1 slice white bread

1 hot red chilli pepper

1 clove garlic

6 tablespoons olive oil

Salt

Chopped fresh parsley

8 to 12 thinly sliced pieces of French bread, toasted

1. In an enamelled cast-iron casserole, combine the fish, potatoes, onion, tomatoes, garlic, bouquet garni, oil, salt and pepper. Pour in the boiling water and cook uncovered over moderately high heat for 20 minutes.

2. While the fish is cooking, prepare the *rouille*: Briefly soak the bread in water and squeeze dry. In a mortar, pound the bread, chilli pepper and garlic into a smooth paste. Add the oil by drops, beating as for mayonnaise. Add 1½ tablespoons of the fish stock and season with salt and pepper. Reserve.

3. Transfer the fish and potatoes to a warmed platter. Sprinkle with parsley and keep warm. Line a soup tureen with the toasted bread and strain in the stock. Serve the fish and potatoes separately, with the *rouille* on the side.

Serves 6

NEAPOLITAN FISHERMAN'S STEW

Italy

Preparation time: 10 minutes **Cooking time:** 35–45 minutes
Fish pieces marinate—2–3 hours

Ingredients

½ red pepper, diced
2 onions, finely chopped
1 to 2 cloves garlic, crushed
1 teaspoon marjoram
Salt
Freshly ground pepper
3 tablespoons olive oil
1¼ pints/7 dl. red wine
1½ tablespoons lemon juice

*3 lb./1⅓ kg. assorted fish,
cut into serving pieces*
*24 uncooked prawns,
cleaned, shelled and
de-veined*
24 clams or mussels
1½ oz./40 g. butter
1½ tablespoons flour
Chopped fresh parsley

1. Combine the first nine ingredients and marinate the fish in this mixture for 2 to 3 hours at room temperature.

2. Transfer the fish and the marinade to a cast-iron saucepan. Bring to the boil, then lower heat and simmer fish for 10 minutes. When nearly tender, add the prawns. Simmer until the fish flakes easily and the prawns are pink.

3. Remove the fish and prawns, then reduce the liquid by a third.

4. Steam the clams (or mussels) until the shells open, about 10 minutes. Drain and discard any that do not open. Keep warm.

5. Melt the butter, then sprinkle in the flour and cook for 1 minute, stirring constantly. Blend in the reduced liquid and continue stirring until sauce is smooth. Correct seasoning.

6. Arrange the fish and shellfish in a heated serving dish, cover with the sauce and garnish with the parsley.

Serves 8

SOLE AND MUSSEL STEW

France   **Preparation time:** 20 minutes   **Cooking time:** 20 minutes

Ingredients

$3\frac{1}{2}$ oz./90 g. butter
2 lb./1 kg. sole fillets
1 onion, chopped
4 oz./100 g. mushrooms
Freshly ground pepper
12 fl. oz./$3\frac{1}{2}$ dl. dry cider
  or dry white wine
$1\frac{1}{2}$ tablespoons brandy

24 mussels, scrubbed
3 tablespoons white wine
2 tablespoons flour
6 tablespoons single cream
Salt
6 slices French bread, fried
  in butter

1. Heat 2 oz./50 g. of the butter in a large frying pan and lightly brown the fish. Remove and reserve.

2. Sauté the onion and mushrooms in the frying pan for 5 minutes. Return the fillets to the pan. Season with pepper, then pour in the cider and brandy. Cover and simmer until the fish flakes easily, about 10 minutes. Remove the shells, saving 6 whole mussels for final warm.

3. Boil the mussels in the wine over high heat until the shells open, about 5 minutes. Discard any mussels that have not opened. Drain mussels and reserve liquid. Remove the shells, saving 6 whole mussels for final decoration. Arrange the shelled mussels with the sole.

4. Combine the fish and mussel liquids and reduce over high heat to 6 tablespoons.

5. Make a roux (page 478) with the remaining butter and the flour. Slowly add the cream. Stir the roux into the liquid and adjust seasoning. Pour the sauce over the fish, then garnish with the fried bread and the reserved whole mussels.

Serves 6

ANGOUMOIS FISH STEW

Preparation time: 15 minutes   **Cooking time:** 35 minutes

France

Ingredients

3½ oz./90 g. butter
4 medium onions, sliced
Bouquet garni (bay leaf,
   3 cloves, parsley, dill)
1 clove garlic, crushed
1 teaspoon salt
Freshly ground pepper

1½ pints/9 dl. dry white
   wine, or half wine, half
   water
2½ lb./1¼ kg. white
   fish fillets (sole, whiting,
   flounder), cut in chunks

1. Melt the butter in a large heavy pan and sauté the onions for 5 minutes.

2. Add the bouquet garni, garlic, salt and pepper. Cover with the white wine and simmer for 15 minutes.

3. Add the fish to the pot, cover and simmer until the fish is tender, about 15 minutes.

4. Using a slotted spoon, transfer the fish to a heated dish and keep warm.

5. Reduce stock by half and pour over fish.

Serves 4 to 6

VARIATION: *Add small whole potatoes to the mixture at Step 2.*

SEA BASS WITH GINGER

China

Preparation time: 10 minutes

Cooking time: 25 minutes

Ingredients

1½ lb./700 g. sea bass

5 1-inch/2½-cm. slices fresh
root ginger

3 spring onions, finely
chopped

Salt

3 tablespoons groundnut
oil or flavourless
vegetable oil

2 spring onions, shredded

2 slices fresh root ginger,
peeled and slivered

2 tablespoons soy sauce

1. Rinse the fish in cold water, then wrap in a thin layer of muslin.

2. Pour enough cold water into an enamelled cast-iron casserole to completely cover the fish when it is cooking. Add the ginger, spring onions and salt, then bring rapidly to the boil.

3. Add the wrapped fish to the casserole and return to the boil.

4. As soon as the water reaches a full boil, cover casserole and remove from heat. Allow fish to cook (off heat) until the flesh flakes when tested with a fork, about 25 minutes. (Do not uncover casserole during this time.) While the fish cooks, heat the oil in a small heavy saucepan. Keep hot.

5. Remove the cooked bass from the casserole and drain, then gently unwrap and transfer to a heated platter.

6. Salt fish lightly, then top with the shredded spring onions. Keep hot.

7. Bring the hot oil almost to the smoking point, then add the slivered ginger. Remove from heat immediately and pour over the fish.

8. Sprinkle fish with the soy sauce and serve immediately.

Serves 3

BAKED SEA BREAM PROVENÇAL

Preparation time: 20 minutes   **Cooking time:** 40 minutes   *France*

Ingredients

A 5-lb/2¼-kg. sea bream
    or sea bass

5 to 6 sprigs fennel or 1
    tablespoon fennel seed

4 tablespoons olive oil

6 tomatoes, peeled and
    quartered

3 onions, thinly sliced

1½ tablespoons chopped
    fresh parsley

1 tablespoon chopped fresh
    thyme, or 1 teaspoon
    dried thyme

Salt

Freshly ground pepper

1 lemon, thinly sliced

2 tablespoons vinaigrette
    dressing (page 482)

Lemon wedges and parsley
    sprigs for garnish

1. Set oven at 400°F., 200°C., Gas Mark 6.

2. Wash and dry fish.

3. Insert fennel into fish cavity.

4. Pour the oil into a baking dish. Add the fish and coat with oil on both sides. Surround fish with the tomatoes, onions, parsley and thyme. Season with salt and pepper. Place lemon slices on top of fish.

5. Bake fish for 30 minutes, then add the vinaigrette dressing. Baste fish and vegetables thoroughly.

6. Continue baking until fish flakes easily when tested with a fork, about 10 minutes.

7. To serve, transfer fish to a heated platter. Arrange tomatoes and onions on the side and sprinkle the pan juices over the fish. Garnish with lemon wedges and sprigs of parsley.

Serves 8

GRILLED FISH WITH WHITE WINE SAUCE

France

Preparation time: 15 minutes
Fish marinates—2 hours

Cooking time: 12 minutes

Ingredients

3 lb./1⅓ kg. bream, pike, or cod, cleaned and split

2 tablespoons olive oil

Salt

Freshly ground pepper

1½ tablespoons mixed herbs (chervil, dill, thyme, basil)

1 oz./25 g. butter

Sauce:

3 shallots, finely chopped

6 tablespoons dry white wine

1 teaspoon mustard

5 oz./150 g. butter

2 hard-boiled egg yolks, sieved

Juice of 1 lemon

1½ tablespoons parsley

1. Put the fish on a plate, skin side down. Sprinkle with the oil, salt and pepper. Rub the mixed herbs into the flesh and marinate for 2 hours.

2. Preheat grill.

3. Pat the fish dry and place on the grill pan. Dot with the 1 oz./25 g. butter. Grill the fish until it flakes easily, about 12 minutes. Baste frequently.

4. While the fish is grilling, make the sauce: a) In a small saucepan, combine the shallots and wine; b) reduce over moderately high heat until almost all the liquid has evaporated; c) remove from heat and beat in the mustard; d) place the pan over hot water; e) beating constantly, add the butter, a little at a time, then the egg yolks, salt and pepper. Keep warm.

5. Transfer the fish to a heated serving dish. Beat the lemon juice and parsley into the sauce and pour over the fish.

Serves 6

very nice with cod. Added mushrooms

TURBOT IN WHITE WINE

Preparation time: 10 minutes   **Cooking time:** 30 minutes   *France*

Ingredients

1½ lb./700 g. turbot, cod
   or haddock, cut in
   ¾-inch/2-cm. slices
Flour for dusting fish
5 tablespoons olive oil
1 lb./450 g. tomatoes,
   peeled, seeded and
   chopped
2 shallots, sliced

Salt
Freshly ground pepper
Bouquet garni (bay leaf, *tarragon*
   parsley, thyme,
   peppercorns)
6 tablespoons dry white
   wine

1. Rinse the fish under cold running water. Pat dry and dust lightly with flour.

2. Heat the oil in a frying pan. Add the fish and brown on both sides over moderately high heat. Remove fish with a slotted spoon and reserve.

3. Add the tomatoes and shallots to the pan. Sauté for 5 minutes.

4. Season with salt and pepper and add the bouquet garni. Pour in the white wine and bring to the boil.

5. Return the slices of fish to the pan, reduce heat and cover. Simmer gently until fish flakes when tested with a fork, about 20 minutes.

Serves 4

COLD MARINATED CARP

France

Preparation time: 20 minutes   **Cooking time:** 20 minutes
Fish marinates—12 hours   **Prepared dish chills**—24 hours

Ingredients

2 lb./1 kg. carp, pike,
  cod or hake, boned and
  cut into serving pieces

Marinade:

6 tablespoons dry white
  wine

Salt

Freshly ground pepper

2 onions, chopped

1 clove garlic, crushed

Bouquet garni (dill,
  chervil, peppercorns,
  thyme)

——

3 shallots, chopped

2 tablespoons olive oil

1 tablespoon flour

⅓ pint/2 dl. water

1 tablespoon chopped
  fresh parsley

1. Place fish in a glass bowl with the marinade of white
   wine, salt, pepper, chopped onion, garlic and bouquet
   garni. Cover and marinate in the refrigerator for 12
   hours.

2. Remove fish from bowl and reserve. Strain marinade and
   reserve.

3. In a saucepan, cook the shallots with the oil until translucent, about 5 minutes.

4. Stir in the flour and cook for 1 minute. Slowly pour in
   the water and strained marinade. Bring to the boil.

5. Add the fish, then cover and simmer gently until the fish
   pieces flake easily when tested with a fork, about 15
   minutes.

6. Remove fish and arrange on a serving platter.

7. Reduce the sauce by half over high heat. Strain, add the
   chopped parsley and pour over the fish. Cover and keep
   in the refrigerator until the following day.

Serves 4 to 5

CARP WITH RED WINE SAUCE

Preparation time: 15 minutes   **Cooking time:** 40–45 minutes

France

Ingredients

2 lb./1 kg. carp, perch, pike, cod or hake, cleaned and boned

¾ pint/4½ dl. red wine

12 small white onions

1 clove garlic, crushed

½ teaspoon salt

Freshly ground pepper

Bouquet garni (bay leaf, chervil, dill, basil, peppercorns)

1 oz./25 g. butter, at room temperature

1 oz./25 g. flour

Chopped fresh parsley for garnish

1. Cut the boned fish into 2-inch/5-cm.-thick serving pieces. Reserve.

2. Pour the wine into an enamelled cast-iron casserole. Add the onions, garlic, salt, pepper and bouquet garni. Boil for 10 minutes.

3. Add the fish to the casserole. Lower heat, cover and simmer gently, until fish flakes easily with a fork, about 15 to 20 minutes.

4. Prepare a *beurre manié* by blending together the butter and flour. Reserve.

5. Using a slotted spoon, remove the fish and onions. Arrange on a heated platter and keep warm.

6. Strain the casserole liquid through a fine sieve into a small saucepan. Reduce over moderate heat for 10 minutes. Remove from heat and beat in the *beurre manié*. Return to the boil for 1 minute, stirring constantly.

7. Pour the sauce over the fish, sprinkle with chopped parsley and serve.

Serves 4 to 5

CARP STUFFED WITH FOIE GRAS

France

Preparation time: 25 minutes   **Cooking time:** 30 minutes

Ingredients

A 2-lb./1-kg. carp or
   perch

Stuffing:

3 oz./75 g. breadcrumbs

6 tablespoons milk

1 oz./25 g. butter

Carp's or perch's roe,
   chopped

2 oz./50 g. foie gras

Salt

Freshly ground pepper

—

1 pint/6 dl. cream

1. Clean and bone the fish. Reserve.

2. Set oven at 350°F., 180°C., Gas Mark 4.

3. Briefly soak the breadcrumbs in the milk. Squeeze out the excess milk and reserve breadcrumbs.

4. Heat the butter in a frying pan and sauté the chopped roe for 5 minutes. Remove from heat. Add the breadcrumbs, *foie gras*, salt and pepper. Mix thoroughly.

5. Fill the carp (or pike) with the stuffing, then sew up. Place in a buttered baking dish. Salt the fish and cover with the cream.

6. Basting frequently, bake fish until it flakes easily when tested with a fork, about 30 minutes.

Serves 3 to 4

SUMMER FISH SALAD

Preparation time: 35 minutes
Prepared dish chills—1 hour

Cooking time: 15 minutes

West Indies

Ingredients

Court Bouillon:

2 pints/generous litre water

6 tablespoons dry white wine

Bouquet garni (bay leaf, thyme, parsley, peppercorns)

2 carrots, chopped

2 sticks celery, chopped

Salt

—

1 lb./450 g. cod, boned

Vinaigrette Sauce:

⅓ pint/2 dl. olive oil

1 clove garlic, crushed

6 tablespoons lemon or lime juice

Salt

Freshly ground pepper

—

2 onions, grated

3 tomatoes, peeled and diced

3 tablespoons chopped fresh parsley

Watercress for garnish

1. Using the ingredients listed above, prepare a court bouillon (page 473) in a large saucepan. Simmer for 20 minutes.

2. Add the fish, cover and simmer until fish flakes easily when tested with a fork, about 15 minutes. Remove from heat and allow fish to cool in stock.

3. Drain fish, then flake in a large bowl. Reserve.

4. Using the ingredients listed above, prepare a vinaigrette sauce (page 482).

5. Add the onions, tomatoes and chopped parsley to the fish. Mix, then toss with the vinaigrette. Correct seasoning.

6. Cover bowl and refrigerate for 1 hour. Garnish with watercress when served.

Serves 2

COD BAKED IN SOURED CREAM

Norway

Preparation time: 15 minutes   **Cooking time:** 20 minutes

Ingredients

2 oz./50 g. butter
3 shallots, finely chopped
12 oz./350 g. mushrooms, sliced
1 tablespoon chopped fresh dill
1 tablespoon chopped fresh parsley
Salt
Freshly ground pepper
2 lb./1 kg. fresh cod or any white-fleshed fish, cut in serving pieces

Flour seasoned with salt, pepper and paprika
1½ oz./40 g. Parmesan cheese, grated
2 teaspoons paprika
⅓ pint/2 dl. soured cream
Dry breadcrumbs

1. Set oven at 375°F., 190°C., Gas Mark 5.

2. Heat 1½ oz./40 g. of the butter in a frying pan. Add the shallots and sauté over moderate heat until translucent.

3. Add the mushrooms to the frying pan. Stirring gently over moderate heat, sauté mushrooms until barely golden. Remove frying pan from heat and stir in the dill and parsley. Season to taste with salt and pepper. Reserve.

4. Rinse the fish pieces under cold water, then pat dry and dust with the seasoned flour.

5. Arrange half the mushrooms in a buttered dish. Cover with the fish, then top with the remaining mushrooms.

6. Sprinkle on the grated cheese and paprika, spoon in the soured cream and top with a thin layer of breadcrumbs.

7. Dot dish with the remaining butter and bake until the fish flakes easily when tested with a fork, about 20 minutes. Serve from the baking dish.

Serves 4

CREAMED SALT COD

Preparation time: 25 minutes
Cod soaks—10 hours

Cooking time: 10 minutes

France

Ingredients

1½ lb./700 g. salt cod
  fillets
14 fl. oz./4 dl. olive oil,
  warmed
1 clove garlic, crushed
⅓ pint/2 dl. single cream,
  warmed

Salt
Freshly ground white
  pepper
4 to 6 slices French bread,
  cut in triangles and fried
  in olive oil

1. Soak the cod fillets in cold water for 10 hours, changing the water 3 or 4 times.

2. Rinse the fillets under cold water and place in a large saucepan.

3. Cover with cold water. Bring to the boil, then lower heat and poach fish gently for 8 minutes. (Do not let water boil while fish poaches.)

4. Drain the fillets and separate into flakes.

5. Pour 4 tablespoons of the warmed olive oil into a saucepan. Place over low heat. Using a wooden spoon, mash the cod flakes and the garlic into the oil.

6. Make a thick paste of the mixture and continue to mash, adding the remaining oil and the cream a tablespoon at a time. Mash until all the liquid has been thoroughly absorbed. Do not allow mixture to boil.

7. Add salt and pepper to taste, garnish with the fried bread triangles and serve immediately.

Serves 4

If salt cod is unavailable, use fresh cod fillets and omit Step 1.

BAKED SALT COD IN TOMATO SAUCE

Portugal

Preparation time: 15 minutes   **Cooking time:** 35 minutes
Salt cod soaks—10 hours

Ingredients

1½ lb./700 g. salt cod fillets

3 tablespoons olive oil

1 lb./450 g. tomatoes, peeled, seeded and chopped

2 shallots, finely chopped

1 clove garlic, crushed

4 onions, thinly sliced

Freshly ground pepper

3 pimentos, cut into strips

3 tablespoons dry bread-crumbs

1 oz./25 g. butter

1. Soak cod fillets for 10 hours in cold water to desalt. Change the water 3 or 4 times.

2. Heat the oil in a frying pan. Add the tomatoes, shallots, garlic and onions. Cover and simmer over very low heat until the mixture is creamy. (Stir occasionally during cooking to prevent sticking.) Season with pepper, then remove from heat. Reserve.

3. Rinse the cod fillets under cold water. Place in a saucepan and cover with cold water. Bring to the boil, then lower heat and simmer for 8 minutes. Remove fillets and drain.

4. Set oven at 400°F., 200°C., Gas Mark 6.

5. Pour the tomato and onion mixture into a buttered baking dish, add the fish and garnish with the pimento.

6. Sprinkle on the breadcrumbs, dot with the butter and brown in oven for 10 to 15 minutes.

Serves 4

If salt cod is unavailable, use fresh cod fillets and omit Step 1.

EEL IN WHITE WINE SAUCE

Preparation time: 1 hour

Cooking time: 30 minutes

France

Ingredients

Court Bouillon:

1¼ pints/7 dl. dry white wine

1¼ pints/7 dl. water

2 cloves garlic, crushed

2 shallots, chopped

1 carrot, sliced

1 onion, sliced

Bouquet garni (rosemary, thyme, chervil, bay leaf)

Salt

10 peppercorns

1½ lb./700 g. eel, skinned and cut into serving pieces

Flour for dusting eel

3½ oz./90 g. butter

6 tablespoons cognac, warmed

8 Dublin Bay prawns (scampi), de-veined

1½ tablespoons cream

1 egg yolk, beaten

1. Prepare the court bouillon (page 473). Simmer for 30 minutes.

2. Lightly dust the eel with flour, then sauté in 1½ oz./40 g. butter. Add the warmed cognac and flambé.

3. Add the eel to the court bouillon, cover and simmer over low heat for 25 minutes. Add the shellfish and cook until pink. Remove the eel and shellfish to a heated serving dish.

4. Reduce the court bouillon to ¾ pint/4½ dl. and strain. Over low heat, beat in the remaining butter, a little at a time, then stir in the cream.

5. Beat 3 tablespoons of the sauce into the egg. Stirring constantly, pour the mixture back into the sauce. Heat through, then pour over the eel and shellfish and serve.

Serves 4

FROGS' LEGS WITH GARLIC HERB BUTTER

France

Preparation time: 15 minutes **Cooking time** 8–10 minutes

Ingredients

6 pairs frogs' legs
1½ pints/9 dl. water
3 tablespoons white wine vinegar
Milk for coating frogs' legs
Flour for coating frogs' legs
1 oz./25 g. butter

Garlic Herb Butter:

2 oz./50 g. butter
2 cloves garlic, crushed

1 tablespoon finely chopped fresh basil
1 tablespoon chopped fresh oregano
1 tablespoon chopped fresh tarragon
1 tablespoon chopped fresh thyme

—

Chopped fresh parsley for garnish
Lemon slices for garnish

1. Place frogs' legs in a shallow, non-metallic dish. Pour in the water and white vinegar. Soak frogs' legs for 10 minutes, then remove and pat dry.

2. Dip frogs' legs in milk, then in flour.

3. Heat the 1 oz./25 g. butter in a frying pan. Add the frogs' legs and sauté on both sides until tender, about 4 minutes per side. Transfer to a heated platter and keep warm.

4. While the frogs' legs are cooking, melt the 2 oz./50 g. butter in a small heavy saucepan; blend in the garlic and herbs. Stir over low heat for 3 minutes.

5. Pour garlic herb butter over frogs' legs, sprinkle with fresh chopped parsley and garnish with lemon slices.

Serves 2

OSLO FISH PUDDING

Preparation time: 45 minutes

Cooking time: 1 hour

Norway

Ingredients

1 lb./450 g. haddock or
   cod fillets, chopped

3 oz./75 g. butter

3 eggs, separated

1½ tablespoons flour

6 tablespoons milk

Peel of 1 lemon, grated

1 tablespoon fresh dill

Pinch nutmeg

Salt

Freshly ground pepper

⅓ pint/2 dl. double cream,
   whipped

Dill Sauce:

1 oz./25 g. butter

1½ tablespoons flour

⅓ pint/2 dl. fish stock,
   heated

⅓ pint/2 dl. double cream

6 oz./175 g. cooked prawns,
   chopped

Salt

Freshly ground pepper

1½ tablespoons fresh dill

———

Fresh dill for garnish

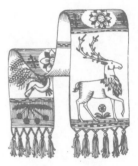

1. Grind the fish to a fine paste. Gradually incorporate the butter. One by one, add the egg yolks. Beat until fluffy. Sprinkle in the flour, then beat in the milk. Stir in the lemon peel, dill, nutmeg, salt and pepper.

2. Set oven at 325°F., 160°C., Gas Mark 3. Beat the egg whites until stiff. Fold the egg whites into the fish mixture, then fold in the cream. Pour into a buttered 3½-pint/2-litre mould. Cover with buttered paper and place in a shallow pan of hot water. Bake until set, about 1 hour. Run a knife around the edge, then quickly invert over a platter.

3. About 10 minutes before serving, prepare the sauce: Melt the butter, sprinkle in the flour and stir over low heat for 1 minute. Beat in the fish stock, then gradually add the cream. Simmer for 3 minutes, then add the prawns. Season, then stir in the dill. Pour the sauce over the pudding and garnish with fresh dill.

Serves 4 to 6

KEDGEREE

Great Britain

Preparation time: 15 minutes   **Cooking time:** 10 minutes

Ingredients

10 oz./275 g. smoked
  haddock fillet, cooked
3 oz./75 g. butter
1 large onion, finely
  chopped
1 lb./450 g. cooked rice,
  heated

2 hard-boiled eggs
Salt
Freshly ground pepper
Cayenne pepper
Parsley sprigs for
  garnish

1. In a large bowl, flake the fish with a fork. Reserve.

2. Melt half the butter in a large frying pan. Add the onion and sauté over moderately low heat until limp, about 5 minutes. Keep hot.

3. Add the flaked fish and mix thoroughly, then add the hot rice and toss well. Keep hot.

4. Coarsely chop the hard-boiled egg whites, then add to the fish and rice. Keep hot.

5. Sieve the hard-boiled egg yolks into the kedgeree, then season highly with salt, pepper and cayenne. Mix well.

6. Dot the kedgeree with the remaining butter, then transfer to a heated platter, garnish with parsley sprigs and serve piping hot.

Serves 4

VARIATION: *Kedgeree may be prepared with any leftover cooked fish.*

CREAMED SMOKED HADDOCK

Preparation time: 10 minutes

Great Britain

Ingredients

8 oz./225 g. smoked
   haddock fillet
¼ pint/1½ dl. cream
Juice of ½ lemon
Salt
Freshly ground pepper

Pinch cayenne pepper
Lemon wedges for
   garnish
Chopped parsley for
   garnish

1. Remove any skin and bones from the haddock and flake
   the fish. Put half the fish in a blender with half the cream
   and purée to a creamy texture.

2. Pour the purée into a bowl and blend the remaining fish
   and cream. Mix the creamed fish together in a bowl.
   Add the lemon juice and season to taste. Place in a
   serving dish and garnish with lemon wedges and parsley.
   Serve with hot buttered toast or crispbread.

Serves 2

FRIED HERRING WITH MUSTARD SAUCE

Scotland

Preparation time: 10 minutes   **Cooking time:** 8–10 minutes

Ingredients

Mustard Sauce:
½ oz./15 g. butter
1 tablespoon flour
⅓ pint/2 dl. milk
2 teaspoons mustard

—

4 fresh herrings, cleaned
  and filleted
1 egg, beaten
6 oz./175 g. coarse oatmeal
2 oz./50 g. butter

1. To prepare the mustard sauce, melt the butter in a small saucepan. Blend in the flour and gradually add the milk. Stir until thickened, then blend in the mustard. Keep warm.

2. Dip the herrings into the egg and coat with the oatmeal.

3. Melt the butter in a frying pan and fry the herrings until tender, about 8 to 10 minutes. Serve with the mustard sauce.

Serves 2

BAKED STUFFED MACKEREL

Preparation time: 15 minutes   **Cooking time:** 20–30 minutes   *France*

Ingredients

4 medium-sized whole
   mackerel, boned

2 oz./50 g. butter, at
   room temperature

3 shallots, finely chopped

3 tablespoons finely
   chopped fresh parsley

1 oz./25 g. spring onions,
   finely chopped

Salt

Freshly ground pepper

Juice of 1 lemon

1. Set oven at 350°F., 180°C., Gas Mark 4.

2. Wash fish and pat dry.

3. Cream the butter in a bowl. Blend in the shallots, parsley, spring onions, salt and pepper. Stuff the fish with this mixture.

4. Wrap each fish in well-buttered aluminium foil, securing the ends to prevent juices from leaking. Place on a baking sheet.

5. Bake for 20 to 30 minutes, depending on size of fish.

6. Before serving, remove foil and sprinkle fish with lemon juice.

Serves 4

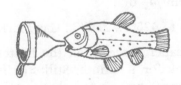

MACKEREL IN CAPER SAUCE

France

Preparation time: 35 minutes
Fish marinates—1 hour

Cooking time: 35 minutes

Ingredients

Marinade:

2 tablespoons olive oil

1 onion, sliced

Salt

Freshly ground pepper

—

4 mackerel (with heads
   and tails reserved),
   filleted

Court Bouillon:

3¼ pints/1¾ litres water

⅓ pint/2 dl. cider vinegar

1 carrot, chopped

1 onion, chopped

Fish heads and tails

1 tablespoon coarse salt

10 peppercorns, crushed

Bouquet garni (bay leaf,
   parsley, thyme)

Caper Sauce:

1½ oz./40 g. butter

2 tablespoons flour

2 tablespoons capers

1 tablespoon finely
   chopped spring onions

Juice of ½ lemon

1. Combine marinade ingredients. Coat the mackerel fillets
   well and let stand 1 hour.

2. Prepare the court bouillon (page 473). Simmer for 30
   minutes. Poach the fillets in the court bouillon for 15
   minutes. Remove and arrange in a flameproof baking
   dish. Strain the court bouillon, bring to the boil and
   reduce to ¾ pint/4½ dl.

3. Preheat oven to 425°F., 220°C., Gas Mark 7.

4. Prepare the caper sauce: Melt the butter, blend in the
   flour and cook for 1 minute. Still stirring, pour in the
   court bouillon. Simmer until thickened, then add the
   capers, spring onions and lemon juice. Cover the fish
   with the sauce. Bake until the fish flakes easily, about 7
   minutes. Serve immediately.

Serves 4

FILLETS OF PERCH IN CHABLIS

Preparation time: 10 minutes **Cooking time:** 20–25 minutes   *France*

Ingredients

2 lb./1 kg. perch fillets

4 shallots, finely chopped

2½ oz./65 g. butter

Salt

Freshly ground pepper

⅓ pint/2 dl. Chablis, hot

1 oz./25 g. fresh bread-
   crumbs

3 oz./75 g. Gruyère or other
   Swiss cheese, grated

1. Set oven at 400°F., 200°C., Gas Mark 6.

2. Place the fillets in a buttered shallow baking dish. Add the shallots and dot with the butter. Season with salt and pepper.

3. Cover fish with the hot wine and bake until fish is almost done, about 15 minutes.

4. Remove dish from oven and sprinkle with the bread-crumbs and grated cheese.

5. Brown under the grill for 5 to 10 minutes and serve immediately.

Serves 4

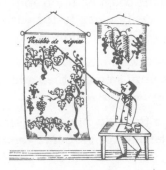

COLD POACHED PIKE WITH BLUE CHEESE SAUCE

France

Preparation time: 20 minutes **Cooking time:** 30 minutes
Court bouillon simmers—30 minutes

Ingredients

Court Bouillon:

3¼ pints/1¾ litres water

¾ pint/4½ dl. dry white wine

Bouquet garni (parsley, bay leaf, thyme, peppercorns)

2 carrots, chopped

2 onions, chopped

Salt

Freshly ground pepper

—

3 lb./1⅓ kg. pike, cleaned

Blue Cheese Sauce:

1 tablespoon grated blue cheese (preferably bleu de Bresse)

1 teaspoon Dijon mustard

5 tomatoes, peeled, seeded and chopped

3 tablespoons chopped fresh parsley

—

Parsley sprigs for garnish

1. Using the ingredients listed above, prepare a court bouillon (page 473). Simmer for 30 minutes.

2. Add the fish to the court bouillon and poach gently until the flesh flakes easily when tested with a fork, about 30 minutes. Remove fish and allow it to cool.

3. Prepare the sauce: Combine the blue cheese and mustard in a bowl. Mix until smooth, then add the tomatoes and chopped parsley. Blend well.

4. To serve: place the cold pike on a serving platter and garnish with parsley sprigs. Serve the sauce separately.

Serves 6

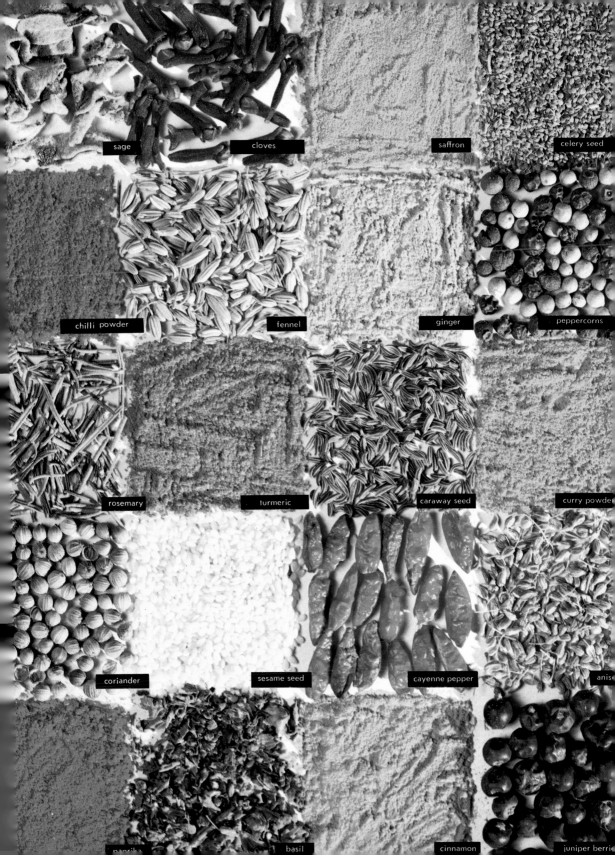

sage

cloves

saffron

celery seed

chilli powder

fennel

ginger

peppercorns

rosemary

turmeric

caraway seed

curry powder

coriander

sesame seed

cayenne pepper

anise

paprika

basil

cinnamon

juniper berries

PIKE POACHED IN CREAM AND ROSÉ WINE

France

Preparation time: 15 minutes   **Cooking time:** 25 minutes

Ingredients

 3 oz./75 g. butter

 3 lb./1⅓ kg. pike, cut into
  serving pieces

 1½ tablespoons eau de vie
  de mirabelle or kirsch,
  warmed

 1¼ pints/7 dl. rosé wine

 2 shallots, finely chopped

 Salt

 Freshly ground pepper

 Bouquet garni (parsley,
  chervil, thyme,
  peppercorns)

 2 tablespoons flour

 ⅓ pint/2 dl. double cream

 8 slices French bread,
  fried in butter

1. Heat half of the butter in an enamelled casserole. Add the pieces of fish and brown lightly. Pour in the warmed *eau de vie* (or kirsch) and flambé.

2. Add the wine, shallots, salt, pepper and bouquet garni. Simmer for 5 minutes. Remove fish and keep warm. Strain the liquid.

3. In a small saucepan prepare a roux (page 478) with the remaining butter and the flour. Stirring constantly, slowly add the liquid to the roux and cook over low heat until the sauce is well blended.

4. Return the fish to the casserole. Cover with the sauce and cook over low heat for 15 minutes. Stir in the cream and heat slightly. Do not boil. Transfer to a deep dish, surround with the fried bread and serve.

Serves 4 to 6

POACHED PIKE WITH MUSTARD HOLLANDAISE

France

Preparation time: 45 minutes   **Cooking time:** 35 minutes

Ingredients

Court Bouillon:

3¼ pints/1¾ litres water

¾ pint/4½ dl. dry white
  wine

6 tablespoons vinegar

1 carrot, sliced

2 onions, sliced

Bouquet garni (chervil,
  dill, fennel, bay leaf,
  basil)

3 to 4 cloves

3 tablespoons coarse salt

10 peppercorns

4 lb./1¾ kg. pike

Mustard Hollandaise:

3 egg yolks

1 teaspoon made mustard

1 tablespoon vinegar

Salt

Freshly ground pepper

6 oz./175 g. butter, at
  room temperature

Chopped fresh parsley for
  garnish

1. Using the ingredients listed above, prepare a court bouillon (page 473) in a fish kettle. Simmer 30 minutes.

2. Add the fish to the court bouillon. Cover and poach gently until the fish flakes easily when tested with a fork, about 35 minutes.

3. While the fish is cooking, prepare the sauce: Beat the egg yolks well with the mustard, then proceed as usual for hollandaise (page 475).

4. Gently transfer the fish from poaching liquid to a heated platter. Garnish with chopped parsley. Serve the mustard hollandaise in a sauce boat.

Serves 6

POACHED FISH WITH MUSHROOMS AND ONIONS

France

Preparation time: 20 minutes   **Cooking time:** 25 minutes

Ingredients

4 carrots, finely sliced

1 onion, chopped

1½ tablespoons chopped parsley

1 tablespoon chopped tarragon

3 shallots, chopped

Salt

Freshly ground pepper

6 oz./175 g. butter

3 lb./1⅓ kg. pike, cleaned, boned and split

¾ pint/4½ dl. champagne or dry white Burgundy

12 tiny white onions

8 tiny mushrooms

1½ tablespoons flour

6 fl. oz./1¾ dl. milk

Salt

White pepper

2 egg yolks

Parsley sprigs and lemon wedges for garnish

1. In an enamelled casserole sauté the carrots, onion, parsley, tarragon, shallots, salt and pepper in 1 oz./25 g. butter. Place the pike on the vegetables and add the wine. Cover and poach until fish flakes when tested, about 20 minutes. Transfer to a hot platter. Strain liquid and reduce to 6 tablespoons.

2. Heat another 1 oz./25 g. butter in a frying pan and sauté the onions until tender. Add the mushrooms and sauté.

3. Prepare a béchamel sauce (page 471): Melt 1 oz./25 g. of the remaining butter, sprinkle in the flour, then stir in the milk, salt and pepper. Beat in the reduced liquid.

4. Beat the egg yolks in a bowl. Gradually stir in 6 tablespoons of the sauce, then slowly beat the egg yolk mixture back into the remaining sauce. Beat in the remaining butter. Add the mushrooms and onions. Do not boil. Cover the fish with the sauce and garnish with parsley and lemon wedges.

Serves 6

STUFFED PIKE WITH HOLLANDAISE SAUCE

France

Preparation time: 20 minutes   **Cooking time:** 35–40 minutes

Ingredients

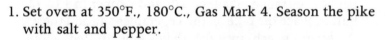

3 lb./1⅓ kg. pike, split and boned

Salt

Freshly ground pepper

Stuffing:

2 oz./50 g. fresh bread-crumbs, moistened

2 eggs, beaten

3 oz./75 g. sorrel or spinach, finely chopped

7 to 8 sprigs parsley or chervil, chopped

2 to 3 sprigs tarragon, chopped

2 shallots, finely chopped

—

1 pint/6 dl. dry white wine

Bouquet garni (rosemary, thyme, peppercorns, bay leaf)

Hollandaise Sauce:

3 egg yolks

1 tablespoon water

Juice of ½ lemon

White pepper

4 oz./100 g. butter

1. Set oven at 350°F., 180°C., Gas Mark 4. Season the pike with salt and pepper.

2. Combine all the ingredients for the stuffing. Mix well, then season with salt and pepper. Stuff the pike and sew up the belly. Place in a buttered baking dish. Pour in ¾ pint/4½ dl. of the wine, add the bouquet garni and bake until fish flakes easily, about 35 minutes.

3. While the fish is cooking, prepare the hollandaise sauce (page 475). Keep warm in a double saucepan.

4. When the pike is done, discard the bouquet garni and transfer fish to a heated serving dish. Keep warm.

5. Add the remaining wine to the baking dish. Place over high heat and reduce liquid by half. Pour the wine sauce over the fish and serve immediately, accompanied by the hollandaise.

Serves 4 to 6

FRIED FISH WITH WHITE WINE AND MUSHROOMS

France

Preparation time: 25 minutes   **Cooking time:** 20 minutes

Ingredients

2 lb./1 kg. pike, cleaned
2 tablespoons milk
Flour for dusting pike
Salt
Freshly ground pepper
3 oz./75 g. butter

¾ pint/4½ dl. dry white wine
12 oz./350 g. mushrooms, quartered
1½ tablespoons chopped fresh parsley

1. Set oven at 400°F., 200°C., Gas Mark 6.

2. Dip pike in the milk and then dust with flour. Season with salt and pepper.

3. Heat the butter in a large frying pan. Add fish and brown on both sides over moderately high heat. Remove pike and place in a lightly buttered baking dish.

4. Pour the wine into the frying pan and scrape up the browned pieces remaining in the pan. Boil for 5 minutes to reduce the liquid a bit.

5. Place the mushrooms around the fish. Season with salt and pepper, then sprinkle with the parsley and pour in the wine mixture.

6. Bake until the fish flakes easily when tested with a fork, about 20 minutes.

Serves 4

FRIED FISH IN SAVOURY SAUCE

Peru

Preparation time: 15 minutes
Fish fillets stand—30 minutes

Cooking time: 15 minutes

Ingredients

2 lb./1 kg. fillet of
  haddock, bass or cod

Salt

4 tablespoons olive oil

1 clove garlic, crushed

2 large onions, sliced

1 egg, lightly beaten

Dry breadcrumbs or
  cornmeal

Vinegar Sauce:

1 bay leaf

8 peppercorns

¼ teaspoon allspice

6 tablespoons cold water

6 tablespoons red wine
  vinegar

———

1 green pepper, cut into
  rings

Chopped coriander

1. Rub fillets with salt and let stand for 30 minutes.

2. In a large frying pan, heat the olive oil and sauté the garlic and half the sliced onions until translucent. Remove with a slotted spoon and reserve.

3. Pat fish dry. Dip in the egg, then in the breadcrumbs. Fry fish over moderately high heat until evenly browned and the flesh flakes easily when tested with a fork.

4. While the fish is cooking, prepare vinegar sauce: In a small saucepan, combine the bay leaf, peppercorns, allspice and water. Bring rapidly to the boil, then lower heat and simmer for 5 minutes. Add the vinegar, sautéed onions and garlic. Simmer for 5 more minutes.

5. Transfer fish to a hot platter and cover with hot vinegar sauce. Top the fish with remaining uncooked onion slices and the green pepper rings. Garnish with coriander.

Serves 4

HALIBUT COZUMEL

Preparation time: 20 minutes   **Cooking time:** 25 minutes   *Mexico*

Ingredients

2 lb./1 kg. halibut

Hot Sauce:

3 tablespoons olive oil

1 medium onion, chopped

1 tablespoon ground
    coriander

$\frac{1}{4}$ teaspoon cayenne pepper

1 pepper (green or red),
    seeded and chopped

2 tomatoes, peeled,
    seeded and quartered

$\frac{1}{3}$ pint/2 dl. lime juice

Salt

Freshly ground pepper

1. Preheat oven to 375°F., 190°C., Gas Mark 5.

2. Rinse fish well under cold water. Pat dry and reserve.

3. In a saucepan, heat the oil and sauté the onion over
   moderate heat until translucent. Stir in the coriander
   and cayenne pepper and blend well. Add the chopped
   pepper and cook for 5 minutes.

4. Add the tomatoes and lime juice. Season to taste with
   salt and pepper. Remove from heat.

5. Arrange the fish in a buttered shallow ovenproof dish.
   Cover with the sauce. Bake, uncovered, until the fish
   flakes easily when tested with a fork, about 25 minutes.

Serves 4

BAKED RIVER FISH

France

Preparation time: 15 minutes   **Cooking time:** 25 minutes

Ingredients

4 char* or 4 small river
    trout, cleaned

1 egg, beaten

Flour for dusting fish

2 oz./50 g. butter

12 oz./350 g. mushrooms,
    sliced

1½ tablespoons cream

¾ pint/4½ dl. dry white
    wine

Salt

Freshly ground pepper

Juice of 1 lemon

2 tablespoons chopped
    fresh parsley

1. Set oven at 325°F., 160°C., Gas Mark 3.

2. Rinse the fish under cold running water and pat dry.

3. Dip in the beaten egg and then in flour.

4. Melt the butter in a long baking dish and add the fish.
   Turn them once to allow undersides to get coated with
   butter. Arrange the mushroom slices around the fish.

5. Mix the cream with the wine and pour around the fish.
   Sprinkle with salt and pepper.

6. Bake until the fish flakes easily when tested with a fork,
   about 25 minutes.

7. Serve in the baking dish, sprinkled with the lemon juice
   and garnished with the chopped parsley.

Serves 4

*Char is a delicate freshwater fish resembling trout, native to
Switzerland and Savoy.*

COLD SALMON IN ASPIC

Preparation time: 4 hours

Cooking time: 30 minutes

Canada

Ingredients

Court Bouillon:
3½ pints/2 litres water
1½ pints/9 dl. dry white wine
2 carrots, chopped
2 sticks celery, chopped
2 onions, sliced
4 sprigs parsley
1 bay leaf
3 cloves

1 tablespoon salt
1 teaspoon thyme
———
4 lb./1¾ kg. salmon
2 oz./50 g. gelatine
2 egg whites, beaten
2 egg shells, crushed
6 tablespoons mayonnaise
*Cucumber and lemon
    slices for garnish*

1. Prepare the court bouillon (page 473). Simmer for 1 hour. Wrap the fish in muslin and poach gently in the court bouillon until the fish flakes easily. Refrigerate the fish. Strain the liquid and reduce to 2½ pints/1¼ litres.

2. Sprinkle the gelatine into 6 tablespoons cold water, then pour in the reduced stock and stir until dissolved. Return the liquid to a saucepan and add the egg whites and egg shells. Bring to the boil, stirring constantly, and cook until foamy. Let cool, then strain through a sieve lined with a damp cloth. Combine ⅓ pint/2 dl. of the aspic with the mayonnaise and refrigerate until thickened. Reserve remaining aspic at room temperature.

3. Coat the salmon with the thickened aspic-mayonnaise mixture, then chill until set. Chill reserved aspic to the point of setting. Apply a thin layer of clear aspic over the fish, then chill until set. Reserve remaining aspic.

4. Repeat layering aspic until the coating is of the desired thickness. Refrigerate until needed and chill the remaining aspic until set. Before serving, finely chop aspic and arrange around fish. Garnish with cucumber and lemon.

Serves 8 to 12

GRILLED SALMON STEAKS WITH MUSHROOMS

France

Preparation time: 10 minutes **Cooking time:** 10–16 minutes

Ingredients

4 salmon steaks

1 egg

3 tablespoons olive oil

Salt

Freshly ground pepper

Fresh breadcrumbs for
   coating fish

3 oz./75 g. butter

1 clove garlic, crushed

12 oz./350 g. mushrooms,
   quartered

2 tablespoons cream

Juice of ½ lemon

Parsley for garnish

Lemon wedges for garnish

1. Rinse the salmon steaks under cold water. Pat dry. In a bowl, beat the egg with 1 tablespoon of the olive oil, salt and pepper.

2. Dip the salmon steaks in the egg mixture and then in the breadcrumbs.

3. In a frying pan, heat the remaining olive oil and half the butter. Over fairly high heat, brown the salmon steaks on both sides. This should take 5 to 8 minutes per side.

4. While the steaks are cooking, heat the remaining butter with the garlic in another frying pan. Add the mushrooms and sauté over moderate heat.

5. Add the cream to the mushrooms and heat slightly.

6. Arrange the fish on a heated platter and sprinkle with the lemon juice. Surround with the mushrooms and a garnish of parsley and lemon wedges.

Serves 4

SEA TROUT STUFFED WITH SORREL

France

Preparation time: 25 minutes   **Cooking time:** 35–45 minutes

Ingredients

Stuffing:

1 oz./25 g. butter

2 shallots, finely chopped

1½ oz./40 g. sorrel or spinach, chopped

Sea trout's roe, chopped

2 oz./50 g. fresh breadcrumbs

1½ tablespoons white wine

1½ tablespoons chopped fresh parsley

1½ tablespoons chopped fresh chervil

Salt

Freshly ground pepper

Freshly grated nutmeg

2 eggs, lightly beaten

—

A 2½- to 3-lb./1¼- to 1⅓-kg. sea trout (with roe), boned

4 leeks (white part only)

1 lb./450 g. sorrel or spinach

¾ pint/4½ dl. white wine

1½ oz./40 g. butter

1. Make the stuffing: a) Melt the butter in a frying pan and cook the shallots over low heat until translucent; b) add the sorrel and cook briefly to wilt; c) add the chopped roe and sauté briefly; d) remove pan from heat and add the breadcrumbs, white wine, parsley and chervil; e) season to taste with salt, pepper and nutmeg; f) bind with the beaten eggs.

2. Preheat oven to 325°F., 160°C., Gas Mark 3. Pat fish dry and lightly salt the inside surfaces. Stuff the fish. Sew up and reserve.

3. Blanch the leeks in a pot of rapidly boiling water. Rinse, then drain. Arrange the leeks and sorrel in an ovenproof dish. Place the fish on the vegetables and cover with the wine. Dot with the butter and bake until fish flakes easily when tested with a fork, about 35 to 45 minutes. Baste frequently.

Serves 4 to 6

COD PALERMO

Italy

Preparation time: 5 minutes

Cooking time: 7 minutes

Ingredients

4 cod steaks
Salt
Freshly ground pepper
Pinch paprika
2 oz./50 g. butter, softened

Fresh parsley for
garnish
Lemon wedges for
garnish

1. Preheat the grill.

2. Pat the cod pieces dry. Season to taste with salt, pepper and paprika. Dot with half the butter.

3. Place the fish on a buttered grill pan and grill for 3 minutes on the top side. Turn the steaks, dot with the remaining butter and grill until light brown, about 4 minutes. Arrange the fish on a heated serving platter, pour over any pan juices and garnish with the parsley and lemon wedges.

Serves 4

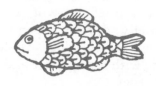

ALPINE BROOK TROUT

Preparation time: 5 minutes
Fish stands—15 minutes

Cooking time: 10–14 minutes

France

Ingredients

4 trout, cleaned
Salt
Freshly ground pepper
Juice of 2 lemons
Flour for dusting fish
1 egg, well beaten
3 tablespoons olive oil
2 tablespoons chicken
   stock, heated

½ oz./15 g. butter, at
   room temperature
1½ tablespoons chopped
   fresh parsley
Parsley sprigs for garnish
Lemon wedges for
   garnish

1. Rinse the trout under cold running water and pat dry. Season with salt, pepper and the juice of 1 lemon. Let stand for 15 minutes.

2. Dust fish with flour and dip in the beaten egg.

3. Heat the oil until sizzling in a frying pan. Add the trout, lower heat and fry until lightly brown, about 5 to 7 minutes on each side. (Fish should flake when tested with a fork.)

4. Arrange fish on a hot platter. Sprinkle on the chicken stock and the juice of the second lemon, then dot with butter and sprinkle on the parsley. Garnish with parsley sprigs and lemon wedges.

Serves 4

STUFFED TROUT

France

Preparation time: 20 minutes   **Cooking time:** 15 minutes

Ingredients

*2 to 3 slices stale bread,
  cut into cubes*

Milk for soaking bread

*3 oz./75 g. foie gras or
  liver pâté*

1 shallot, finely chopped

1 egg, well beaten

Salt

Freshly ground pepper

1 clove garlic, crushed

*1 teaspoon chopped fresh
  parsley*

*1 oz./25 g. butter, at room
  temperature*

*4 trout, cleaned and
  gutted*

2 tablespoons olive oil

1. Briefly soak the stale bread cubes in a little milk. Squeeze out and transfer to a mixing bowl.

2. Add the *foie gras* (or pâté) and shallot. Blend well, then bind with the beaten egg. Season with salt and pepper.

3. Cream the garlic and parsley into the butter. Form into small balls and refrigerate until needed.

4. Stuff each trout with the *foie gras* mixture. Sew up or secure with toothpicks or skewers.

5. Heat the olive oil in a frying pan. Fry the trout over moderately high heat until flesh flakes easily when tested with a fork, about 15 minutes (7½ minutes on each side). Spoon the oil over the fish while they cook.

6. Serve trout piping hot, topping each trout with a piece of the parsley-garlic-butter mixture.

Serves 4

TROUT IN WHITE WINE, DAUPHINÉ

France

Preparation time: 15 minutes   **Cooking time:** 15 minutes

Ingredients

4 trout, cleaned

⅓ pint/2 dl. milk

Flour for dusting fish

3 oz./75 g. butter

2 oz./50 g. mushrooms, diced

Peel of 1 truffle (optional)

⅓ pint/2 dl. dry white wine

1 shallot, finely chopped

Salt

Freshly ground pepper

⅓ pint/2 dl. cream

Juice of ½ lemon

1. Set oven at 425°F., 220°C., Gas Mark 7.

2. Rinse the trout under cold running water and pat dry. Dip in the milk and then dust with flour.

3. Melt 2 oz./50 g. of the butter in a frying pan. Cook the trout over moderately high heat until golden, about 5 minutes on each side.

4. In another frying pan, sauté the mushrooms (and truffle peel) in the remaining butter.

5. When the fish are done, transfer them to a baking dish.

6. Mix the wine into the pan juices, add the shallot, and salt and pepper to taste. Reduce over high heat for 1 or 2 minutes.

7. Add the mushrooms, truffle peel, cream and lemon juice. Pour the mixture over the trout and bake for 5 minutes.

Serves 4

STUFFED FISH EN PAPILLOTE

France

Preparation time: 20 minutes

Cooking time: 20 minutes

Ingredients

2 tench or trout, cleaned

Stuffing:

2 oz./50 g. fresh bread-
    crumbs

1½ tablespoons milk

8 oz./225 g. mushrooms,
    chopped

4 shallots, finely chopped

3 tablespoons chopped
    fresh parsley

Salt

Freshly ground pepper

1 egg, beaten

—

3 oz./75 g. butter

⅓ pint/2 dl. white wine

Lemon wedges for
    garnish

1. Rinse the fish under cold water. Pat dry and reserve.

2. Set oven at 400°F., 200°C., Gas Mark 6.

3. Make the stuffing: a) Combine the breadcrumbs and milk in a mixing bowl; b) add the mushrooms, shallots and parsley; c) season with salt and pepper; d) bind with the beaten egg.

4. Heat half of the butter in a frying pan and briefly sauté the stuffing. Remove pan from heat.

5. Stuff the fish, then rub the skins with the remaining butter. Wrap each fish *en papillote* (in greaseproof paper or parchment).

6. Place the fish in a baking dish. Pour in the wine and bake until fish are cooked through, about 20 minutes.

7. Remove the paper from the cooked fish, then transfer fish to a warmed platter. Spoon the cooking juices over the fish, garnish with lemon wedges and serve immediately.

Serves 2

FRIED FISH IN THE POITOU STYLE

France

Preparation time: 5 minutes   **Cooking time:** 12–15 minutes

Ingredients

2 tench or trout, cleaned
1½ tablespoons olive oil
3 oz./75 g. butter
2 shallots, finely chopped
Salt
Freshly ground pepper

1½ tablespoons white wine
  vinegar
1 clove garlic, crushed
3 tablespoons chopped
  fresh parsley

1. Rinse the fish under cold water. Pat dry.

2. In a frying pan heat the oil and 1 oz./25 g. of the butter. Add the fish and sauté over moderately high heat until nicely browned, about 5 to 7 minutes on each side. Remove to a serving platter. Keep warm.

3. Add the rest of the butter to the frying pan. Stir in the shallots and sauté over moderate heat until lightly browned. Season with salt and pepper.

4. Add the vinegar, garlic and parsley to the frying pan and bring to the boil.

5. Pour over the fish and serve.

Serves 2

FISH FRY NIÇOISE

France

Preparation time: 10 minutes   **Cooking time** 10–15 minutes

Ingredients

12 oz./350 g. tiny fish
(smelts or whitebait)
6 tablespoons white wine
vinegar
Flour for coating fish
4 tablespoons olive oil

3 medium onions, chopped
Salt
Freshly ground pepper
Lemon wedges for
garnish

1. Spread the fish out on a dish and sprinkle with the vinegar.

2. Dry the fish and roll in flour.

3. Heat the olive oil in a large frying pan and add the chopped onions. Brown the onions and then add the fish. Cook over moderately high heat until fish are golden.

4. Season with salt and pepper. Garnish with lemon wedges and serve piping hot.

Serves 2

FISH CURRY WITH RICE

Preparation time: 50 minutes   **Cooking time:** 20 minutes

Rice soaks—1 hour

India

Ingredients

8 oz./225 g. rice

Curry Mixture:

1 tablespoon coriander

2 teaspoons cumin

½ teaspoon ground ginger

1 teaspoon turmeric

½ teaspoon fenugreek

½ teaspoon chilli powder

—

2 tablespoons groundnut oil

4 whole dried chilli peppers

¾ pint/4½ dl. water

1½ lb./700 g. filleted white-fleshed fish, cut into serving pieces

Salt

2 large onions, sliced

1½ tablespoons lemon juice

1. Soak rice in a bowl of cold water for 1 hour.

2. In a small bowl, combine the curry ingredients. Mix thoroughly, then blend in enough water to make a thick paste. Heat half the oil in a flameproof casserole and briskly stir the paste and the chilli peppers over moderate heat until spices darken, about 3 minutes.

3. Blend in the water, then add the fish and season with salt. Bring to the boil, then simmer until fish flakes easily when tested with a fork, about 20 minutes. Carefully remove the fish and keep warm.

4. Heat the remaining oil and sauté the onions for about 5 minutes. Add to the fish liquid and bring to the boil. Stir in the drained rice and the lemon juice. Lower heat, cover and simmer until rice is fluffy, about 15 minutes.

5. When rice is tender, return fish pieces to the casserole. Heat through and serve.

Serves 4

TUNA FISH CROQUETTES

Japan

Preparation time: 10 minutes   **Cooking time:** 8 minutes

Ingredients

2 7-oz./198-g. cans tuna

1 lb./450 g. potatoes,
   boiled and mashed

4 spring onions, chopped

2 eggs, beaten

Salt

Freshly ground pepper

Breadcrumbs for coating
   croquettes

6 tablespoons vegetable
   oil

1. Drain the tuna fish. Transfer to a bowl and flake.

2. Add the mashed potatoes and spring onions. Mix well. Bind with the beaten eggs, then season with salt and pepper.

3. Shape mixture into 8 croquettes. Roll in breadcrumbs.

4. Heat the oil in a frying pan and fry the croquettes until golden brown. Serve immediately.

Serves 4

PASTA WITH RED CLAM SAUCE

Preparation time: 15 minutes   **Cooking time:** 20 minutes

Fresh clams steam—10 minutes

Italy

Ingredients

24 clams or mussels

4 shallots, finely chopped

1 onion, finely chopped

3 cloves garlic, crushed

3 tablespoons oil

8 tomatoes, chopped

1½ tablespoons tomato
   purée

6 tablespoons white wine

½ teaspoon dried oregano

½ teaspoon dried basil

Salt

Freshly ground pepper

1 tablespoon olive oil

8 oz./225 g. thin spaghetti

1 oz./25 g. butter

3 tablespoons chopped
   fresh parsley

1. Prepare the clams (or mussels). Scrub the shells with a
   stiff brush. Rinse until no sand remains. Discard any
   open clams. Steam remaining clams in a little water until
   shells open, about 10 minutes. Drain, discarding any
   unopened clams and reserving ⅓ pint/2 dl. of the liquid.
   Shell, trim and mince the remaining clams. Reserve.

2. Sauté the shallots, onion and garlic in the oil for 5
   minutes. Add the tomatoes, tomato purée, white wine,
   reserved clam juice, oregano and basil. Mix well. Season
   with salt and pepper. Bring to the boil, then lower heat
   and simmer for 20 minutes.

3. Add the olive oil to a large pan of rapidly boiling salted
   water, then cook the spaghetti over moderate heat until
   barely tender (*al dente*), about 10 minutes. Drain and
   return to the pan. Toss with the butter then transfer to
   a platter.

4. Add the clams to the sauce. Heat through, then stir in
   the parsley. Pour sauce over the spaghetti and serve.

Serves 4

SHELLFISH BRILLAT-SAVARIN

France

Preparation time: 30 minutes   **Cooking time:** 30 minutes

Ingredients

3 oz./75 g. butter
1 carrot, thinly sliced
1 onion, sliced
3 shallots, finely chopped
36 crayfish or Dublin
  Bay prawns, cleaned,
  shelled and de-veined
2 tablespoons cognac,
  warmed
3 tomatoes, chopped

Bouquet garni (rosemary,
  thyme, bay leaf,
  peppercorns)
¾ pint/4½ dl. dry white
  wine
Salt
Freshly ground pepper
Cayenne pepper
1 tablespoon flour
6 tablespoons cream

1. In a large frying pan, melt 2 oz./50 g. butter and cook the carrot, onion and shallots for 10 minutes. Add the shellfish and sauté until pink, about 10 minutes.

2. Pour in the warmed cognac and flambé.

3. Add the tomatoes, bouquet garni and white wine. Bring to the boil. Cover, lower heat and simmer for 10 minutes. Stir occasionally and season to taste. Remove the shellfish and arrange on a serving dish. Keep warm.

4. Prepare a *beurre manié* by blending the remaining butter and flour.

5. Strain the cooking liquid and reduce by half over high heat. Lower heat and thicken sauce by beating in the *beurre manié* and the cream. Pour over shellfish and serve immediately.

Serves 6

SHELLFISH IN WHITE WINE SAUCE

Preparation time: 40 minutes   **Cooking time:** 20 minutes

France

Ingredients

2 carrots, finely sliced

2 onions, finely chopped

1 clove garlic, crushed

2 shallots, finely chopped

2 sticks celery, finely sliced

4 oz./100 g. butter

Salt

Freshly ground pepper

24 crayfish or Dublin Bay prawns, cleaned, shelled and de-veined

2 tablespoons cognac, warmed

12 fl. oz./3½ dl. dry white wine

Bouquet garni (parsley, bay leaf, peppercorns)

1 tablespoon chopped fresh tarragon

2 egg yolks

1 tablespoon double cream

1. Sauté the carrots, onions, garlic, shallots and celery in a pan with a quarter of the butter. Season with salt and pepper.

2. Heat the remaining butter in a deep frying pan. Stir in the shellfish and cook until they turn colour, about 10 minutes. Pour the warmed cognac over the shellfish and flambé.

3. Add the wine, sautéed vegetables and bouquet garni. Bring to the boil. Cover and simmer for 5 minutes, stirring occasionally. Remove the bouquet garni and sprinkle shellfish with the chopped tarragon. Transfer shellfish to a warmed shallow dish. Strain the broth and reduce slightly.

4. In a bowl, beat the egg yolks well with the cream. Slowly add 6 tablespoons of the hot broth. Slowly stir the mixture back into the broth. Heat gently until slightly thickened. Do not boil. Pour the sauce over the shellfish and serve.

Serves 4

CRAYFISH TAILS IN CREAM SAUCE

France

Preparation time: 45 minutes   **Cooking time:** 25 minutes

Ingredients

Court Bouillon:
1¼ pints/7 dl. water
12 fl. oz./3½ dl. dry white
  wine
1 onion, finely chopped
Bouquet garni (bay leaf,
  peppercorns, thyme,
  dill)
  —
24 crayfish tails or
  Dublin Bay prawns,
  cleaned, shelled and
  de-veined

Béchamel Sauce:
2 oz./50 g. butter
1 oz./25 g. flour
12 fl. oz./3½ dl. hot milk
  —
3 egg yolks, well beaten
¾ pint/4½ dl. cream
Salt
Freshly ground pepper
4 oz./100 g. Swiss cheese,
  grated

1. Using the ingredients listed above, prepare a court bouillon (page 473). Simmer for 20 minutes.

2. Poach crayfish (or prawns) in the court bouillon for 5 minutes. Remove shellfish with a slotted spoon and keep warm.

3. Using the ingredients listed above, prepare a béchamel sauce (page 471).

4. Set oven at 400°F., 200°C., Gas Mark 6.

5. Remove béchamel from heat and gradually incorporate the egg yolks and cream. Season with salt and pepper. (If sauce is too thick, thin it with a little of the bouillon.)

6. Transfer shellfish to a buttered baking dish, cover with the sauce, then sprinkle evenly with the cheese.

7. Bake until golden, about 25 minutes. Serve in baking dish.

Serves 4

GRILLED BRITTANY LOBSTER

Preparation time: 20 minutes   **Cooking time:** 20 minutes

France

Ingredients

A 2-lb./1-kg. live lobster

Salt

Cayenne pepper

4 oz./100 g. butter, melted

1½ tablespoons Calvados, warmed

⅓ pint/2 dl. crème fraîche or double cream

1 tablespoon chopped fresh chervil, or ½ teaspoon dried chervil

1. Rinse the lobster. Cut its spinal cord by inserting a knife at the juncture where the tail and body meet. Turn lobster on its back and split in half lengthwise. Remove and discard the dark vein, the sac behind the eyes, and gills (dead men's fingers). Separate the tail from the chest. Cut off the claws and crack them.

2. Preheat grill.

3. Place the lobster, flesh side up, in grill pan. Sprinkle with salt and cayenne pepper.

4. Brush lobster with half the melted butter and grill for 12 to 15 minutes. Baste at 3-minute intervals to keep the flesh tender.

5. Transfer lobster to an ovenproof serving dish. Baste with the remaining melted butter and pan juices.

6. Set oven at 425°F., 220°C., Gas Mark 7.

7. Sprinkle lobster with the warmed Calvados and flambé.

8. Pour the *crème fraîche* (page 473) or double cream over lobster and sprinkle with the chervil. Put the dish in the oven for a few minutes to brown. Serve at once.

Serves 2

NORMANDY-STYLE LOBSTER

France

Preparation time: 30 minutes   **Cooking time:** 30 minutes

Ingredients

*A 2-lb./1-kg. lobster,
cleaned (page 476)*

Salt

Freshly ground pepper

3 tablespoons olive oil

*3 tomatoes, peeled,
seeded and chopped*

*1½ tablespoons Calvados,
warmed*

*⅓ pint/2 dl. dry cider
or dry white wine*

½ teaspoon saffron

1 shallot, finely chopped

½ clove garlic, crushed

1 oz./25 g. butter

1 egg yolk

*Chopped fresh parsley
for garnish*

1. Season the lobster pieces with salt and pepper. Heat the oil in a large frying pan and sauté the lobster over high heat for several minutes, turning the shells constantly until bright red. Add the tomatoes and bring to the boil. Lower heat, add the warmed Calvados and flambé. Add the cider (or wine) and saffron. Cover pan and simmer for 20 minutes.

2. Sauté the shallot and garlic in butter until translucent. Add the lobster coral and green liver. Cover and simmer for 3 minutes. Keep saucepan over very low heat.

3. Remove the lobster from the frying pan and keep hot. Reduce the lobster liquid slightly over high heat, then add it to the coral and green liver. Beat the egg yolk well in a bowl. Slowly beat in a few tablespoons of the sauce, then gently stir the mixture into the remainder of the sauce. Heat very gently. Do not boil.

4. Arrange the lobster on a heated serving platter and pour the sauce over it. Garnish with parsley.

Serves 2

MUSSELS ANGOUMOIS IN CREAM SAUCE

France

Preparation time: 50 minutes **Cooking time:** 20 minutes

Ingredients

*5 pints/3 litres mussels,
  scrubbed*
*⅓ pint/2 dl. white wine or
  water*
*Bouquet garni (bay leaf,
  parsley, thyme)*
1 clove garlic
1½ oz./40 g. butter

3 shallots, finely chopped
Freshly ground pepper
1½ tablespoons flour
1 egg yolk
6 tablespoons cream
Juice of ½ lemon

1. In a large pan, combine the mussels with the white wine, bouquet garni and garlic. Cover and steam until shells open, about 10 minutes. Drain, reserving the liquor.

2. Discard the bouquet garni, garlic and any unopened mussels. Remove half the shell from each opened mussel. Arrange on a heated serving platter and keep warm.

3. In a saucepan, heat the butter and sauté the shallots. Season with pepper. Stirring constantly, blend in the flour. Slowly pour in the mussel liquor. Cook for 10 minutes, then remove from heat.

4. Beat the egg yolk and cream in a bowl. Slowly pour a little of the hot sauce into egg mixture, stirring constantly to prevent curdling. Stir this mixture into the sauce. Add the lemon juice and heat through. Do not boil.

5. Pour sauce over mussels and serve at once.

Serves 4

BORDEAUX SCALLOPS

France

Preparation time: 15 minutes   **Cooking time:** 25 minutes

Ingredients

*1 lb./450 g. scallops,
  sliced*

2½ oz./65 g. butter

1 onion, sliced

1 shallot, finely chopped

*2 tablespoons cognac,
  warmed*

*1 tomato, peeled, seeded
  and chopped*

1½ cloves garlic, crushed

Salt

Freshly ground pepper

*6 tablespoons white wine
  (preferably Bordeaux)*

1. Rinse the scallops under cold running water. Pat dry.

2. Heat the butter in a frying pan. Add the onion and shallot and cook over moderate heat until translucent.

3. Add the scallops, raise heat and brown lightly. Pour on the cognac and flambé.

4. Add the tomato and garlic. Season with salt and pepper. Pour in the white wine and simmer for 5 to 6 minutes. Stir gently.

5. Using a slotted spoon, transfer the cooked scallops to 4 warmed scallop shells or individual shallow baking dishes. Keep warm.

6. Reduce the sauce over moderately high heat. Strain through a fine sieve and pour over the scallops. Serve at once.

Serves 4

SAVOURY SAUTÉED SCALLOPS

Preparation time: 10 minutes   **Cooking time:** 17 minutes   *France*

Ingredients

1½ lb./700 g. scallops,
  sliced

4 oz./100 g. butter

2 shallots, finely chopped

1 tablespoon chopped
  fresh chervil, or 1
  teaspoon dried chervil

1 clove garlic, crushed

Pinch freshly grated
  nutmeg

Dash cayenne pepper

Salt

3 oz./75 g. fresh bread-
  crumbs

1½ oz./40 g. dry bread-
  crumbs

1. Rinse the scallops under cold running water. Pat dry.

2. Melt 2½ oz./65 g. of the butter in a saucepan. Add the shallots and chervil and sauté gently for 2 minutes.

3. Add the scallops, garlic, nutmeg, cayenne and salt. Cook for 6 minutes, stirring occasionally.

4. Add the fresh breadcrumbs and continue cooking for 6 more minutes. Remove from heat.

5. Spoon the scallop mixture into 6 scallop shells or individual baking dishes. Sprinkle with the dry breadcrumbs and dot with the remaining butter.

6. Place under the grill until nicely browned, about 3 minutes. Serve piping hot.

Serves 6

PRAWNS BAKED IN PORT, EGGS AND CREAM

Portugal

Preparation time: 20 minutes   **Cooking time:** 35 minutes

Ingredients

2 oz./50 g. butter

8 spring onions, chopped

1 lb./450 g. uncooked, cleaned, shelled and de-veined prawns

3 tablespoons dry port

4 egg yolks

⅓ pint/2 dl. double cream

8 tablespoons coarsely chopped fresh parsley

Salt

Freshly ground pepper

1. Preheat oven to 325°F., 160°C., Gas Mark 3.

2. Melt the butter in a large frying pan. Add the spring onions and sauté over moderate heat until limp.

3. Add the prawns and cook gently until pink, about 5 minutes.

4. Add the port and simmer for 5 minutes.

5. Transfer the prawn mixture to an ovenproof dish. Reserve.

6. In a bowl, beat together the egg yolks and cream. Add the parsley and season with salt and pepper.

7. Pour the custard mixture into the ovenproof dish. Mix thoroughly. Bake until set, about 35 minutes.

Serves 4

BEAN CURD AND PRAWNS

Preparation time: 10 minutes

Cooking time: 7 minutes

Japan

Ingredients

2 teaspoons cornflour

1½ tablespoons vegetable oil

1 thin slice fresh root ginger, peeled and finely chopped

1 lb./450 g. uncooked, cleaned, shelled and de-veined prawns

1¼ pints/7 dl. chicken stock

4 spring onions, cut into 1-inch/2½-cm. pieces

3 tablespoons sake or dry sherry

4 3-inch/7½-cm. squares fresh bean curd (tofu), diced

1. In a cup, dissolve the cornflour in a little water. Reserve.

2. Heat the oil in a frying pan. Add the ginger and prawns. Fry, stirring, over high heat until prawns turn pink, about 3 minutes.

3. Add the stock, spring onions and *sake* (or sherry). Bring to the boil, then reduce heat to low and briskly stir in cornflour mixture.

4. Continue stirring until liquid clears. Add the bean curd and heat through. Serve immediately.

Serves 2 to 4

PRAWN AND OKRA GUMBO

Martinique

Preparation time: 5 minutes **Cooking time:** 20–25 minutes

Ingredients

3 tablespoons vegetable oil

1 onion, chopped

1 lb./450 g. fresh okra, trimmed and sliced

1 lb./450 g. tomatoes, peeled and chopped

1 large banana, peeled and sliced

1 lb./450 g. uncooked, cleaned, shelled, de-veined and coarsely chopped prawns

1½ teaspoons lemon juice

Salt

Cayenne pepper

6 tablespoons boiling water

Boiled rice

1. Heat the oil in a large saucepan. Add the onion and sauté over low heat until translucent, about 5 minutes.

2. Stirring constantly, add the okra and cook over low heat for 2 minutes.

3. Add the tomatoes, then the banana slices and mix thoroughly. Simmer over moderately low heat for 5 minutes.

4. Add the chopped prawns and lemon juice, then season to taste with salt and cayenne pepper.

5. Pour in the boiling water, cover and simmer until prawns are pink and firm, about 10 minutes.

6. Adjust seasonings, transfer to a bed of boiled rice and serve immediately.

Serves 4

FRIED PRAWNS

Preparation time: 15 minutes   **Cooking time:** 7 minutes

China

Ingredients

4 tablespoons peanut oil

1½ teaspoons salt

2 green peppers, seeded and chopped

1 lb./450 g. canned bamboo shoots, diced

3 cloves garlic, crushed

1 thick slice fresh root ginger, chopped

1 lb./450 g. uncooked, shelled, de-veined and diced prawns

1½ tablespoons Chinese rice wine or dry sherry

½ teaspoon sugar

1 tablespoon cornflour

1½ tablespoons chicken stock or water

1. Place a frying pan over high heat for ½ minute. Add 1 tablespoon of the oil and ½ teaspoon of the salt. Wait ½ minute, then add the peppers and fry, stirring, for 1 minute. Remove with a slotted spoon and reserve.

2. Add another ½ tablespoon oil and ½ teaspoon salt to the pan. Wait ½ minute, then add the bamboo shoots and fry for 1 minute, stirring all the time. Remove and reserve.

3. Add the remaining oil and salt to the pan. Wait 10 seconds, then add the garlic and ginger. Still stirring, fry for 1 minute, then raise heat, add the prawns and cook over high heat until pink, about 1½ minutes. Remove pan from heat. Add the rice wine (or sherry) and sugar. Stir briefly to blend, then allow mixture to rest for 1 or 2 minutes.

4. In a cup dissolve the cornflour in the stock (or water). Add reserved peppers and bamboo shoots to the pan, then briskly stir in the cornflour mixture.

5. Return pan to high heat and toss ingredients until the prawns are thoroughly glazed, about 1 minute. Serve immediately.

Serves 3 to 4

PRAWN CROQUETTES

The Netherlands

Preparation time: 30 minutes
Standing time: 1 hour

Cooking time: 8 minutes

Ingredients

3 oz./75 g. butter
3 oz./75 g. flour
⅓ pint/2 dl. milk, heated
⅓ pint/2 dl. double cream, heated
1 lb./450 g. cooked prawns, minced
Salt
Freshly ground pepper

Freshly grated nutmeg
Flour
2 eggs, beaten
Dry breadcrumbs for coating croquettes
Vegetable oil for deep-frying

1. Melt the butter in a saucepan. Sprinkle in the flour, stirring constantly over low heat for 2 minutes. Gradually blend in the milk and the cream. Stir over low heat until sauce thickens, about 10 minutes. Remove pan from heat.

2. Add the prawns and mix thoroughly, then season to taste with salt, pepper and nutmeg. Spread the prawn mixture out on a large platter. Let stand until completely cool, about 30 minutes.

3. Shape the cooled prawn mixture into sausagelike rolls about 2 inches/5 cm. long. On a lightly floured board roll each croquette to lightly coat. Dip in the beaten egg, then roll in the dry breadcrumbs until well coated. Cover and let stand for 30 minutes.

4. Pour enough vegetable oil into a large saucepan to reach a depth of 4 inches/10 cm. Heat oil almost to the smoking point (385°–390°F., 196°–198°C.). Arrange the croquettes in a frying basket. Plunge basket into the hot oil and fry croquettes until crisp and golden, about 8 minutes.

5. Transfer the croquettes to absorbent paper or to a wire rack and drain. Serve piping hot.

Serves 4

POULTRY AND GAME

ROAST CHICKEN IN MADEIRA SAUCE

France

Preparation time: 25 minutes **Cooking time:** 1¾ hours
Truffles and pork fat marinate—4 hours

Ingredients

3 tablespoons cognac

3 tablespoons Madeira

2 oz./50 g. truffles or
mushrooms, cut into
fine strips

8 oz./225 g. fresh pork
fat or bacon, diced

A 4-lb./1¾-kg. chicken

3 oz./75 g. butter, at
room temperature

Salt

Freshly ground pepper

⅓ pint/2 dl. chicken stock

1. In a non-metallic bowl, combine the cognac and Madeira.
   Add the truffle (or mushroom) strips and the diced pork
   fat (or bacon). Marinate for 4 hours, then drain. Reserve
   marinade.

2. Preheat oven to 375°F., 190°C., Gas Mark 5.

3. Insert the truffle strips along the chicken breast between
   the flesh and the skin. Put half the butter and half the
   marinated pork fat inside the chicken. Truss the chicken
   and coat the skin thoroughly with the remaining butter.
   Sprinkle with salt and pepper.

4. Put the rest of the pork fat and the marinade in a flameproof casserole. Add the chicken and roast until tender,
   about 1¾ hours, basting frequently. Transfer chicken to
   a board and carve.

5. Place the casserole over high heat and reduce the juices
   a little. Pour the sauce over and serve immediately.

Serves 4 to 6

ROAST CHICKEN WITH HONEY AND ORANGE SAUCE

Israel

Preparation time: 20 minutes   **Cooking time:** 2 hours

Ingredients

1½ tablespoons chicken
  fat

3 tablespoons honey

1 teaspoon salt

1 teaspoon paprika

A 5-lb./2¼-kg. roasting
  chicken

⅓ pint/2 dl. orange juice,
  heated

¾ pint/4½ dl. orange juice

1½ tablespoons grated
  orange rind

2 spring onions, chopped

¼ green pepper, chopped

½ teaspoon ginger

½ teaspoon prepared
  horseradish

Salt

Orange slices for garnish

1 tablespoon cornflour

1. Preheat oven to 375°F., 190°C., Gas Mark 5.

2. In a saucepan, melt the chicken fat. Remove from heat and blend in the honey, salt and paprika.

3. Place the chicken in a roasting tin. Coat inside and out with the honey mixture, then pour the heated orange juice over the bird. Place the tin in the oven and roast chicken until tender, about 2 hours. (Baste frequently during roasting.)

4. About 20 minutes before chicken is done, combine the ¾ pint/4½ dl. orange juice, rind, spring onions, green pepper, ginger, horseradish and salt. Bring slowly to the boil and simmer for 15 minutes. Keep hot.

5. Transfer the roasted chicken to a platter and garnish with orange slices. Pour the tin juices into the sauce.

6. Dissolve the cornflour in a little cold water, then briskly stir into sauce. Stir over low heat until thickened. Pour into a warmed sauce boat and serve.

Serves 6

CHICKEN WITH CHESTNUT STUFFING

France

Preparation time: 45 minutes   **Cooking time:** 1¼ hours

Ingredients

Stuffing:
24 chestnuts
⅓ pint/2 dl. chicken stock
1 stick celery, chopped
1½ oz./40 g. butter
2 onions, chopped
4 oz./100 g. sausage meat

3 tablespoons chopped
  fresh parsley
Salt
Freshly ground pepper
—
A 3-lb./1⅓-kg. chicken
½ oz./15 g. butter

1. Score the chestnuts and cook in rapidly boiling water for 3 minutes. Drain, peel and skin.

2. In a saucepan, combine the chestnuts with the chicken stock, celery and ½ oz./15 g. of the butter. Cook over low heat for 20 minutes. Drain and chop the chestnuts.

3. Set oven at 425°F., 220°C., Gas Mark 7.

4. In a bowl, mix the chestnuts and celery with the onions, sausage meat and parsley. Season to taste, then brown lightly in the remaining 1 oz./25 g. of the butter.

5. Stuff the chicken with this mixture and truss. Place in a roasting tin and coat with ½ oz./15 g. butter.

6. Roast the chicken for 15 minutes, then reduce heat to 350°F., 180°C., Gas Mark 4 and continue roasting until done, about another hour. Baste chicken frequently as it roasts.

Serves 4

CHICKEN IN SOURED CREAM SAUCE

Sweden

Preparation time: 30 minutes   **Cooking time:** 1¾ hours

Ingredients

A 4-lb./1¾-kg. roasting
   chicken, cleaned

Salt

1 teaspoon dried thyme

1½ oz./40 g. butter

1½ tablespoons vegetable
   oil

3 onions, chopped

1 bay leaf

6 juniper berries or 2
   tablespoons gin

1 teaspoon ginger

Freshly ground pepper

3 rashers lean bacon

¾ pint/4½ dl. soured
   cream

Parsley for garnish

1. Preheat oven to 350°F., 180°C., Gas Mark 4. Dry the chicken well. Season with salt and the thyme. Truss bird and coat with ½ oz./15 g. butter.

2. Heat the remaining butter and the oil in an enamelled cast-iron casserole. Brown the chicken and then reserve.

3. Add the onions, bay leaf, juniper berries (or gin), ginger and pepper to the casserole. Cook briskly for 5 minutes.

4. Cover the breast and legs with the bacon rashers and return the chicken to the casserole. Cover and bake for 1 hour.

5. Add the soured cream. Continue cooking until bird is tender, about 45 minutes. Take casserole from oven and remove chicken. Place casserole over moderate heat and stir to blend sauce. Taste and correct seasoning, if necessary. Keep warm.

6. Carve the chicken. Strain the sauce and pour over chicken. Garnish with parsley.

Serves 4 to 6

CHICKEN IN CHAMPAGNE SAUCE

France

Preparation time: 1 hour

Cooking time: 1¼ hours

Ingredients

Stuffing:

8 oz./225 g. sausage meat	A 3-lb./1⅓-kg. chicken
¾ oz./20 g. butter	1 thin strip pork fat
1 small onion, chopped	4 oz./100 g. bacon, diced
1 shallot, chopped	1 carrot, sliced
½ clove garlic, crushed	1 turnip, sliced
6 tablespoons dry white wine	½ calf's foot
1 chicken liver, chopped	1 stick celery, sliced
3 tablespoons fresh parsley	Salt
Salt	Freshly ground pepper
Freshly ground pepper	¾ pint/4½ dl. champagne
Pinch nutmeg	or dry white wine

1. Brown the sausage meat in a frying pan; remove and reserve. Add the butter to the pan and sauté the onion, shallot and garlic. Pour in the wine and reduce liquid by half. Add liver, parsley, sausage meat, and seasonings.

2. Stuff the chicken with this mixture. Truss and tie the strip of pork fat over the breast. Preheat oven to 375°F., 190°C., Gas Mark 5.

3. In a large flameproof casserole brown the bacon with the carrot and turnip. Add the chicken and brown.

4. Blanch the calf's foot for 5 minutes, then rinse. Add the calf's foot, celery, salt and pepper to the casserole. Pour in the champagne and bring rapidly to the boil. Remove casserole from heat, cover and place in oven. Bake until chicken is tender, about 1¼ hours. To serve, transfer the chicken to a warm platter. Strain sauce, skim and pour into a warm gravy boat.

Serves 3 to 4

BRAISED CHICKEN WITH RED WINE AND ARMAGNAC

France

Preparation time: 40 minutes **Cooking time:** 1½ hours

Ingredients

4 oz./100 g. bacon, diced
1 tablespoon olive oil
A 3-lb./1⅓-kg. chicken
2 tablespoons Armagnac brandy, warmed
1 onion, chopped
1 tablespoon flour
1½ tablespoons tomato purée

1¼ pints/7 dl. red Bordeaux wine
4 shallots, chopped
Bouquet garni (bay leaf, parsley, thyme)
Salt
Freshly ground pepper
1 oz./25 g. butter
8 oz./225 g. mushrooms

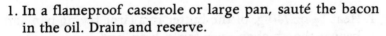

1. In a flameproof casserole or large pan, sauté the bacon in the oil. Drain and reserve.

2. Sauté the chicken until nicely browned, about 10 minutes. Pour in the brandy and flambé. Remove and reserve.

3. Sauté the onion until translucent, about 5 minutes. Stir in the flour and cook for 1 minute, then blend in the tomato purée, wine, shallots and bouquet garni. Season with salt and pepper. Bring rapidly to the boil, then lower heat and add the chicken and bacon. Cover and simmer gently for 45 minutes. Turn the chicken, re-cover and simmer for another 35 minutes.

4. Heat the butter in a frying pan. Sauté the mushrooms until golden, then add to the casserole. Continue cooking until chicken is tender, about 10 minutes.

5. Remove chicken and carve. Remove bouquet garni and reduce the sauce to the desired consistency. Return chicken with juices to the casserole. Heat through.

Serves 3 to 4

CHICKEN LYONNAISE WITH MUSHROOMS

France

Preparation time: 30 minutes   **Cooking time:** 30 minutes

Ingredients

2½ oz./65 g. butter

A 3-lb./1⅓-kg. chicken,
   cut into serving pieces

1 lb./450 g. mushrooms,
   sliced

2 large tomatoes, peeled,
   seeded and chopped

2 tablespoons cognac,
   warmed

6 tablespoons white wine

2 tablespoons rich
   chicken stock

1 clove garlic, crushed

Salt

Freshly ground pepper

Dash cayenne pepper

Chopped fresh parsley
   for garnish

1. Heat 1½ oz./40 g. of the butter in a large frying pan and brown the chicken over fairly high heat.

2. Add the remaining butter, sliced mushrooms and chopped tomatoes to the pan. Sprinkle on the cognac and flambé, then sauté for 5 minutes.

3. Add the wine, chicken stock and crushed garlic. Season lightly with salt, pepper and cayenne pepper.

4. Cover the pan and cook over low heat until chicken is tender, about 30 minutes.

5. Using a slotted spoon, transfer the chicken and mushrooms to a heated serving dish and keep warm.

6. Reduce sauce to desired consistency over high heat. Taste and adjust seasoning, if necessary. Pour over the chicken and garnish with parsley.

Serves 4

POACHED CHICKEN IN 'HALF-MOURNING'

France

Preparation time: 1½ hours
Chicken refrigerated—overnight

Cooking time: 1¾ hours

Ingredients

2 black truffles or large
    mushrooms, sliced

A 4-lb./1¾-kg. chicken
    (with giblets)

Juice of 1 lemon

Stock:

4 pints/2¼ litres water

3 carrots, chopped

3 turnips, chopped

1 celery heart, chopped

4 leeks, chopped

1 onion stuck with 3 or
    4 cloves

Bouquet garni (thyme,
    bay leaf, parsley,
    peppercorns)

4 oz./100 g. bacon, diced

2 veal bones

Chicken's giblets

Salt

Freshly ground pepper

Freshly grated nutmeg

—

Assorted cooked vegetables
    for garnish

1. Insert the truffle (or mushroom) slices between the skin and the flesh of the chicken—use 3 slices in each side of the breast and 2 in each of the thighs. Secure with string. Truss the bird and sprinkle with lemon juice. Cover with foil and refrigerate overnight.

2. In a large saucepan combine all the above-listed stock ingredients. Cover and simmer for 1 hour. Add the chicken. Return to the boil and skim, then reduce heat, cover and poach chicken gently until tender, about 1¾ hours. Strain the liquid in which the chicken has poached and reserve for future use.

3. Transfer the chicken to a warmed platter and garnish with separately cooked assorted vegetables, such as baby carrots, small white onions, tiny green peas, mushrooms and asparagus.

Serves 4 to 6

POACHED STUFFED CHICKEN

France

Preparation time: 30 minutes   **Cooking time:** 1½–2 hours
Court bouillon simmers—30 minutes

Ingredients

*A 4-lb./1¾-kg. boiling
  chicken (with liver
  and giblets)*

Court Bouillon:

4 pints/2¼ litres water

Chicken's giblets

2 leeks

2 carrots

2 turnips

1 stick celery

*Bouquet garni (parsley,
  rosemary, bay leaf,
  sage)*

Salt

Freshly ground pepper

Stuffing:

Chicken's liver, chopped

1 oz./25 g. butter

1 egg, beaten

5 oz./150 g. foie gras

Salt

Freshly ground pepper

*Pinch of freshly grated
  nutmeg*

1. Using the ingredients listed above, prepare the court bouillon (page 473) and simmer for 30 minutes.

2. Lightly sauté the chopped chicken liver in the butter. Remove from heat.

3. Combine the sautéed mixture with the egg, *foie gras*, salt, pepper and nutmeg.

4. Stuff the chicken with this mixture, truss and secure the vent.

5. Add the chicken to the court bouillon and return to the boil. Lower heat, cover and simmer gently until the chicken is tender, about 1½ to 2 hours. Serve with rice.

Serves 4 to 6

A rich broth is left after the chicken is cooked. Rice served with the chicken may be cooked in it, or it can provide the basis for many other soups and sauces.

CHICKEN-IN-THE-POT

Preparation time: 40 minutes
Stock simmers—2 hours

Cooking time: 1¾ hours

France

Ingredients

Stock:

A 2-lb./1-kg. piece beef
  shin

1 beef marrow bone

Chicken's giblets

1 lb./450 g. carrots, sliced

1 lb./450 g. turnips, sliced

4 leeks, sliced

1 celery stick, quartered

1 large onion

Bouquet garni (rosemary,
  parsley, thyme, bay
  leaf)

5 pints/3 litres water

Stuffing:

Chicken's liver

1 oz./25 g. butter

4 oz./100 g. dry bread-
  crumbs

1½ tablespoons milk

8 oz./225 g. ham, diced

2 cloves garlic, crushed

1 shallot, chopped

3 tablespoons chopped
  fresh parsley

Salt

Freshly ground pepper

¼ teaspoon nutmeg

1 egg, beaten

———

A 4-lb./1¾-kg. boiling
  chicken

6 cabbage leaves

4 to 6 potatoes, peeled

1. Combine all the ingredients listed for stock, bring to the boil and skim, then cover and simmer for 2 hours.

2. Lightly sauté the liver in the butter. Chop, then mix with the other stuffing ingredients. Stuff the bird, reserving 6 tablespoons stuffing. Add the chicken to the stock, cover and simmer for about 1½ hours.

3. Blanch the cabbage leaves in boiling water. Place a spoonful of the stuffing on each leaf. Roll into sausage shapes and tie. Add the cabbage and the potatoes to the pan. Simmer until the potatoes are tender, about 20 minutes. Transfer the chicken to a platter and surround with the vegetables. Serve the broth separately.

Serves 4 to 6

SESAME SEED CHICKEN

China

Preparation time: 25 minutes
Chicken steeps—20–30 minutes

Cooking time: 1 hour

Ingredients

A 3-lb./1⅓-kg chicken
Salt

8 spring onions

6 whole peppercorns
(optional)

3 1-inch/2½-cm. lengths
fresh root ginger,
peeled

1½ tablespoons sesame
seed oil

1 tablespoon soy sauce

1 tablespoon sesame
seeds, toasted

1. Wash the chicken under cold running water. Pat dry.

2. Rub the cavity with salt, then insert 2 spring onions (the peppercorns) and the ginger.

3. Place the chicken, breast up, in a heavy pot. Add cold water to half cover the chicken. Season with 1 teaspoon salt.

4. Bring rapidly to the boil, then reduce heat, cover and simmer until chicken is tender, about 1 hour.

5. Remove pot from heat and allow chicken to steep in water for 20 to 30 minutes.

6. Transfer chicken to a cutting board. Remove skin. Cut meat into thin slices, then shred. Cool to room temperature.

7. While the chicken is cooling, mince the remaining spring onions.

8. Transfer the shredded chicken to a bowl. Toss with the sesame oil, the soy sauce and the minced spring onions.

9. To serve, arrange on a platter and garnish with the toasted sesame seeds.

Serves 4

BRAISED CHICKEN WITH PEANUTS

Senegal

Preparation time: 20 minutes   **Cooking time:** 45 minutes

Ingredients

6 tablespoons groundnut
   oil

A 3-lb./1⅓-kg. chicken,
   cut in serving pieces

2 onions, chopped

¾ pint/4½ dl. chicken
   stock, heated

6 tablespoons peanut
   butter

4 oz./100 g. tomato paste

Salt

Freshly ground pepper

Cayenne pepper

Chopped hard-boiled
   eggs for garnish

Chopped roasted peanuts
   for garnish

1. Heat the oil in a large enamelled cast-iron casserole. Add
   the chicken pieces and sauté over moderately high heat
   until nicely browned on all sides, about 10 minutes.

2. Add the chopped onion and stir over moderate heat until
   onion is golden, about 5 minutes. Keep hot.

3. In a bowl, combine the chicken stock, peanut butter and
   tomato paste. Blend until smooth, then pour over the
   chicken.

4. Season casserole with salt, pepper and cayenne, then
   cover and simmer over low heat until chicken is tender,
   about 30 minutes.

5. To serve, arrange on a bed of rice and garnish with
   chopped hard-boiled eggs and chopped roasted peanuts.

Serves 4

CHICKEN BRAISED IN RED WINE

France

Preparation time: 25 minutes   **Cooking time:** 30–40 minutes

Ingredients

3½ oz./90 g. butter

1 large onion, chopped

A 3-lb./1⅓-kg. chicken, cut into serving pieces

4 carrots, sliced

8 oz./225 g. salsify or aubergine, peeled and sliced

1½ tablespoons flour

⅓ pint/2 dl. water

12 fl. oz./3½ dl. red wine

Salt

Freshly ground pepper

Bouquet garni (parsley, bay leaf, thyme)

1. Heat half of the butter in a frying pan and brown the chopped onion and chicken pieces over moderately high heat.

2. Transfer the chicken and chopped onion to an enamelled cast-iron casserole. Reserve.

3. Sauté the vegetables for 8 to 10 minutes in the pan used to brown the chicken. Transfer to the casserole.

4. Melt the remaining butter in the frying pan. Stirring constantly, blend in the flour and cook for 1 minute. Still stirring, gradually add the water and bring the sauce to the boil.

5. Remove sauce from heat and add the wine, salt, pepper and bouquet garni. Blend well, then pour into casserole. Cover casserole and simmer over very low heat until chicken is tender, about 30 to 40 minutes.

Serves 4

CHICKEN WITH RED WINE AUVERGNAISE

France

Preparation time: 30 minutes
Chicken marinates—12 hours

Cooking time: 30 minutes

Ingredients

Marinade:

½ teaspoon thyme
1 bay leaf
3 or 4 sprigs parsley
12 peppercorns
1¾ pints/1 litre red wine

A 5-lb./2¼-kg. chicken, cut
into serving pieces
3½ oz./90 g. butter

4 oz./100 g. bacon, diced
10 small white onions
8 oz./225 g. mushrooms,
sliced
2 tablespoons Armagnac
brandy, warmed
2 tablespoons flour
1 clove garlic, crushed
Salt
Freshly ground pepper

1. Combine the marinade ingredients and marinate chicken for 12 hours. Remove chicken and reserve marinade.

2. Heat 2½ oz./65 g. of the butter in an enamelled cast-iron casserole. Sauté the diced bacon, onions and mushrooms briefly over moderate heat. Add the chicken and brown. Pour in the brandy and flambé.

3. Add 1 tablespoon of the flour, stir constantly for 5 minutes, then strain in the marinade. Secure the strained herbs into a bouquet and add with the garlic to the casserole. Cover and simmer until the chicken is tender, about 30 minutes.

4. Before serving, transfer chicken, bacon, onions and mushrooms to a warm platter. Over high heat, reduce sauce in casserole.

5. Prepare a *beurre manié* (page 471) with the remaining butter and flour and beat into the reduced sauce, simmer for 5 minutes, then pour over chicken.

Serves 6

CHICKEN WITH TOMATOES AND GREEN PEPPERS

France

Preparation time: 25 minutes   **Cooking time:** 30 minutes

Ingredients

A 3-lb./1⅓-kg. chicken,
  cut into serving pieces

Flour for dusting chicken

2 tablespoons olive oil

1 clove garlic

4 oz./100 g. mushrooms,
  sliced

4 tomatoes, peeled, seeded
  and chopped

2 green peppers, seeded
  and sliced

4 oz./100 g. ham, diced

6 tablespoons dry white
  wine

Salt

Freshly ground pepper

Chopped fresh parsley
  for garnish

1. Lightly dust the chicken pieces with flour.

2. Put the oil in an enamelled cast-iron casserole rubbed with the garlic. Add the chicken pieces and brown evenly over moderately high heat.

3. Add the mushrooms and sauté briefly. Stir in the tomatoes, peppers and ham.

4. Pour in the wine and season with salt and pepper. Cover and simmer until chicken is tender, about 30 minutes.

5. Transfer the pieces of chicken to a warmed serving platter. Reduce the sauce over high heat if necessary, then pour over the chicken. Garnish with chopped parsley. Serve with rice.

Serves 4

CHICKEN CASSEROLE WITH SAFFRON RICE

Mexico

Preparation time: 30–40 minutes   **Cooking time:** 50 minutes

Ingredients

2 3-lb./1⅓-kg. chickens,
    cut into serving pieces

6 tablespoons olive oil

3 cloves garlic, crushed

1 large onion, finely
    chopped

1 green pepper, seeded
    and chopped

11 oz./300 g. rice

1 teaspoon oregano

8 oz./225 g. ham, diced

1 tablespoon salt

Freshly ground pepper

1 to 2 teaspoons saffron

8 tomatoes, peeled and
    quartered

¾ pint/4½ dl. water

10 oz./275 g. green peas,
    shelled

2½ oz./65 g. stuffed green
    olives

2 oz./50 g. capers

Fresh parsley, chopped

Pimento for garnish

1. Set oven at 350°F., 180°C., Gas Mark 4. Rinse the chicken pieces and pat dry. Heat the oil in a large flameproof casserole and brown a few chicken pieces at a time. Reserve.

2. Sauté the garlic, onion and green pepper until soft, about 5 minutes. Add the rice and stir to coat. Cook over moderate heat until golden, about 3 minutes.

3. Return the chicken pieces to the casserole. Stir in the oregano, ham, salt, pepper, saffron, tomatoes and water. Bring to the boil on top of the stove. Cover and place in the oven for 30 minutes.

4. Reduce the heat to 250°F., 120°C., Gas Mark ½. Add the peas, olives and capers. Continue baking, uncovered, until chicken is tender, about 20 minutes. Garnish with the parsley and pimento.

Serves 8

ANJOU-STYLE CHICKEN FRICASSÉE

France

Preparation time: 25 minutes   **Cooking time:** 30 minutes

Ingredients

2½ oz./65 g. butter

A 3-lb./1⅓-kg. chicken, cut
   into serving pieces

10 small white onions

8 oz./225 g. mushrooms,
   cut in half

⅓ pint/2 dl. white wine

Salt

Freshly ground pepper

6 tablespoons double
   cream

1. Melt the butter in a large pan and brown the chicken pieces evenly over moderately high heat.

2. Reduce heat and add the onions. Continue cooking for 5 minutes, then stir in the mushrooms.

3. Pour in the wine and season with salt and pepper.

4. Cover pan and simmer over low heat for 30 minutes.

5. Just before serving, stir in the cream and heat through. Do not boil.

Serves 4

EGER CHICKEN PAPRIKA

Preparation time: 30 minutes   **Cooking time:** 30 minutes

Hungary

Ingredients

6 chicken pieces
Flour for dredging chicken
Salt
Freshly ground pepper
3 oz./75 g. butter
1½ tablespoons vegetable
  oil
2 onions, chopped

1 clove garlic, crushed
1½ tablespoons paprika
⅓ pint/2 dl. chicken stock
1 tablespoon double cream
⅓ pint/2 dl. soured cream
Chopped fresh parsley
  for garnish
Paprika for garnish

1. Dry the chicken pieces well, then dredge in flour seasoned with salt and pepper.

2. Heat the butter and oil in a large frying pan or enamelled cast-iron casserole. Add the chicken pieces and sauté until golden. Remove chicken and reserve.

3. Add the onions and garlic and sauté lightly, then stir in the paprika and half the stock. Blend thoroughly. Return the chicken to the pan, cover and simmer for 20 minutes.

4. Add the remaining stock and the cream. Continue simmering, uncovered, until chicken is tender, about 10 minutes.

5. Remove chicken from pan and keep warm. Stir in the soured cream and simmer gently for 5 minutes. Taste sauce and correct seasoning.

6. To serve, arrange chicken on a heated platter, cover with the sauce, garnish with parsley and a sprinkling of paprika.

Serves 6

very nice !

CHICKEN CREOLE

Haiti

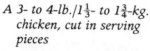

Preparation time: 35 minutes   **Cooking time:** 30 minutes

Ingredients

A 3- to 4-lb./1⅓- to 1¾-kg. chicken, cut in serving pieces

2 tablespoons vegetable oil

2 medium onions, chopped

2 green peppers, seeded and chopped

2 sticks celery, chopped

2 cloves garlic, crushed

1½ tablespoons chopped fresh parsley

2 whole cloves

¼ teaspoon dried basil

3 whole dried red chilli peppers (optional)

¼ teaspoon chilli powder

¼ teaspoon cayenne pepper

¼ teaspoon dried thyme

2 bay leaves, crushed

1 tablespoon salt

Freshly ground pepper

1¼ pints/7 dl. water

1 large can Italian plum tomatoes

8 oz./225 g. raw long-grain rice

1. Wash the chicken pieces and pat dry.

2. Heat the oil in a large enamelled cast-iron casserole. Add the chicken and sauté until nicely browned, about 15 minutes. Remove chicken pieces and reserve.

3. Add the onions, green peppers, celery and garlic to the casserole and sauté over moderate heat until onions are translucent, about 5 minutes. Add the remaining seasonings, water and plum tomatoes (with juice). Mix well.

4. Return the reserved chicken to the casserole. Bring to the boil, then lower heat, cover and simmer gently for 15 minutes.

5. Stir in the rice, then re-cover the casserole and simmer until rice is tender, about 15 minutes. Uncover the casserole, raise heat to moderate and boil briefly until liquid is slightly reduced. Serve immediately from the casserole.

Serves 4 to 6

CHICKEN WITH HOT SAUCE

Preparation time: 30 minutes   **Cooking time:** 40 minutes   *Ethiopia*

Ingredients

A 3-lb./1⅓-kg. chicken, cut into serving pieces

1¼ pints/7 dl. boiling water

Juice of 1 lemon

1 teaspoon salt

2 oz./50 g. butter

6 onions, chopped

1½ tablespoons chilli powder

1½ tablespoons tomato paste

3 tablespoons red wine

½ teaspoon ground ginger

Freshly ground pepper

4 hard-boiled eggs, shelled

1. Place the chicken in a large pot and cover with the boiling water. Add the lemon juice and salt and simmer for 10 minutes. Remove the chicken and reserve the broth.

2. Melt the butter in a large flameproof casserole and sauté the onions for 10 minutes. Add ⅓ pint/2 dl. of hot chicken broth, the chilli powder and tomato paste to the onions. Simmer for 5 minutes, then add the red wine, ginger, pepper and another ⅓ pint/2 dl. of the broth.

3. Place the chicken in the sauce and simmer until tender, about 40 minutes.

4. Prick the hard-boiled eggs with a fork and add to the sauce about 3 minutes before serving.

Serves 4

CHICKEN CURRY

India

Preparation time: 20 minutes **Cooking time:** 20 minutes

Ingredients

Curry Powder:

3 tablespoons cumin

1 tablespoon coriander

1 teaspoon turmeric

1 teaspoon chilli powder

½ teaspoon ginger

½ teaspoon fenugreek

½ teaspoon garam masala
(optional)

—

4 large onions, finely
chopped

4 dried chilli peppers

3 tablespoons groundnut oil

3 tablespoons water

Salt

4 chicken breasts, diced

4 cardamom pods (seeds
only), ground

4 oz./100 g. coconut,
toasted

1 oz./25 g. walnuts,
chopped

12 fl. oz./3½ dl. yoghurt

2 tablespoons lemon juice

Walnut halves

1. Combine all the curry powder ingredients.

2. Sauté the onions and the chillies in the oil for 10 minutes.
   Blend the curry mixture into the onions. Stir over
   moderate heat until the spices darken, about 3 minutes.
   Add 2 tablespoons of the water to prevent scorching.

3. Season with salt, then add the chicken and the cardamom. Stir briskly for 4 minutes, then blend in the remaining water. Add three-quarters of the coconut and
   the walnuts. Mix thoroughly. Reduce heat to low and
   blend in half the yoghurt. Stirring frequently, simmer
   chicken very gently until tender, about 5 minutes. (If
   the heat is too high, the yoghurt will curdle.)

4. Blend in the remaining yoghurt and the lemon juice.
   Heat through. Discard the chillies. Transfer to a heated
   platter and garnish with the remaining coconut and
   halved walnuts. Serve hot with chutney and rice.

Serves 4 to 6

YOGHURT MARINATED CHICKEN

India

Preparation time: 20 minutes
Chicken marinates—24 hours

Cooking time: 40 minutes

Ingredients

A 3-lb./1⅓-kg. roasting chicken

Marinade:

⅓ pint/2 dl. natural yoghurt

3 cloves garlic, crushed

1 teaspoon ginger

1 medium onion, finely chopped

3 tablespoons lemon or lime juice

1 tablespoon coriander

1 teaspoon turmeric

1 teaspoon cumin

1 teaspoon garam masala (optional)

Salt

Freshly ground pepper

3 tablespoons vegetable oil

—

1 onion, thinly sliced

1 lemon or lime, quartered

1. Quarter and skin the chicken. Reserve.

2. In a large bowl, combine the yoghurt, garlic, ginger, onion, lemon (or lime) juice, coriander, turmeric, cumin, *garam masala*, salt, pepper and oil.

3. Cut several deep slits (nearly to the bone) in each piece of chicken, then thoroughly rub with marinade. Place chicken in marinade and refrigerate for at least 24 hours, turning occasionally.

4. Preheat oven to 375°F., 190°C., Gas Mark 5.

5. Transfer chicken pieces to a greased rack in a roasting tin. Baste chicken pieces with the marinade and roast until tender, about 40 minutes. (Baste occasionally during roasting.)

6. To serve, arrange chicken pieces on a heated platter and garnish with onion rings and lemon or lime wedges.

Serves 4

CHICKEN KIEV

Preparation time: 20 minutes   **Cooking time:** 20 minutes

Ingredients

8 oz./225 g. unsalted
   butter, at room
   temperature

2 tablespoons chopped
   parsley

2 cloves garlic, crushed

½ teaspoon tarragon

6 chicken breasts

Salt and pepper

Flour for dredging

1 egg, lightly beaten

4 oz./100 g. dry bread-
   crumbs

Mushroom Cream Sauce:

1½ lb./700 g. fresh
   mushrooms, chopped

6 oz./175 g. butter

1½ oz./40 g. flour

1¼ pints/7 dl. chicken
   stock

Salt and pepper

Pinch cayenne pepper

6 fl. oz./1¾ dl. sherry

⅓ pint/2 dl. single cream

—

Butter or fat for frying

1. Blend the butter, parsley, garlic and tarragon. Shape into 6 small rolls (about 2 inches/5 cm. long and ½ inch/1 cm. thick). Place a roll of butter on each flattened breast of chicken. Sprinkle with salt and pepper. Roll up each chicken breast around the butter, folding in the ends. Skewer with toothpicks. Dredge in flour, dip in egg and thoroughly coat with breadcrumbs. Refrigerate while preparing the sauce.

2. Sauté the mushrooms in butter. Blend in the flour. Mix well. Add the stock and seasonings. Stir constantly for 5 minutes, then add the sherry and simmer for another 5 minutes. Remove from heat, blend in the cream and keep warm.

3. In a large pan, melt enough butter or fat to cover the chicken. Heat to 375°F., 190°C. (or until a 1-inch/2½-cm. cube of bread browns in 1 minute). Fry each roll until golden, about 6 minutes. Drain and place on a heated platter. Serve sauce separately.

Serves 6

CHICKEN WITH BAMBOO SHOOTS AND MUSHROOMS

China

Preparation time: 30 minutes **Cooking time:** 8 minutes

Ingredients

6 dried Chinese
 mushrooms

2 chicken breasts

1 tablespoon cornflour

1½ tablespoons hoisin
 sauce (optional)

1 tablespoon water

2 tablespoons groundnut
 oil

2 oz./50 g. canned bamboo
 shoots, sliced

2 cloves garlic, crushed

1½ tablespoons Chinese
 rice wine or dry sherry

1 to 3 tablespoons soy
 sauce

Salt

1. Soak the mushrooms in a bowl of lukewarm water for 30 minutes. Drain. Discard stems. Dry caps, dice and reserve.

2. Slice chicken into julienne strips, then dice. In a bowl, toss diced chicken with 1 tablespoon cornflour. Reserve.

3. In a cup, combine the hoisin sauce and the water. Reserve.

4. Place a frying pan over high heat for ½ minute. Lower heat and swirl in 1 tablespoon of the oil. Wait ½ minute, then add the bamboo shoots and the mushrooms. Fry, stirring, for 2 minutes. Remove vegetables with a slotted spoon.

5. Add the remaining oil to the pan. Wait ½ minute, then add the garlic and chicken. Still stirring, fry briskly until the chicken changes colour, about 1½ minutes.

6. Over low heat, stir in the rice wine (or sherry), then the hoisin sauce mixture and the soy sauce. Season to taste with salt. Add the mushrooms and bamboo shoots to the pan. Mix briefly and serve immediately.

Serves 2

PINEAPPLE CHICKEN

China

Preparation time: 10 minutes

Cooking time: 6 minutes

Ingredients

2 chicken breasts, diced

1½ tablespoons cornflour

1 medium (14- to 16-oz./ 400- to 450-g.) can pineapple tidbits in juice

1½ tablespoons groundnut oil or flavourless vegetable oil

2 slices fresh root ginger, peeled and finely chopped

½ green pepper, seeded and diced

1 medium onion, finely chopped

1½ tablespoons Chinese rice wine or dry sherry

Salt

1. In a bowl, toss the diced chicken with 1 tablespoon cornflour. Reserve.

2. Drain pineapple tidbits and reserve. Pour juice into a measuring cup. For each ⅓ pint/2 dl. add 1 heaped teaspoon cornflour. Blend well and reserve.

3. Place a frying pan over high heat for ½ minute. Add the oil and swirl pan for ½ minute. Add the ginger and green pepper. Fry, stirring, for 1 minute, then add the chicken pieces and the onion. Fry until chicken changes colour, about 1½ to 2 minutes. Remove pan from heat.

4. Add the wine and salt. Mix, then add the pineapple tidbits.

5. Stir cornflour-pineapple juice to remix, then add to pan.

6. Return pan to high heat. Stir lightly until ingredients are thoroughly coated, then boil until sauce clears. Serve immediately.

Serves 2

CHICKEN WITH ASPARAGUS

Preparation time: 5 minutes   **Cooking time:** 5 minutes   *China*

Ingredients

2 to 3 tablespoons
   vegetable oil

1 thick slice ginger,
   diced

1 clove garlic, crushed

8 oz./225 g. asparagus,
   cut into 1-inch/2½-cm.
   pieces

3 chicken breasts, slivered

3 tablespoons chicken
   stock

1 tablespoon Chinese rice
   wine or dry sherry

1½ tablespoons water

2 teaspoons cornflour

1. Heat 1 tablespoon of the oil in a frying pan. Stirring continuously, fry the ginger and garlic for ½ minute, then add the asparagus and cook for 1 minute. Remove with a slotted spoon.

2. Add 1 or 2 tablespoons of the remaining oil to the pan. Still stirring, fry the chicken for 1 minute, then add the stock, wine and water. Simmer briefly, then sprinkle in the cornflour. Mix well and heat through.

3. Return the asparagus mixture to the pan and toss lightly to coat with the sauce. Serve immediately.

Serves 2 to 3

CHICKEN WINGS WITH GINGER

China   **Preparation time:** 5 minutes   **Cooking time:** 20 minutes

Ingredients

1 tablespoon groundnut oil or flavourless vegetable oil

1 thick slice fresh root ginger, peeled and rinsed

8 chicken wings

1 clove garlic, crushed

1 tablespoon soy sauce

¼ teaspoon salt

2 teaspoons sugar

1 tablespoon Chinese rice wine or pale dry sherry

6 tablespoons water

Cabbage or bok choy (Chinese cabbage) for garnish

1. Place a frying pan over high heat for ½ minute.

2. Swirl in the oil. Heat for ½ minute, then add the ginger and fry, stirring continuously. Add the chicken wings and garlic and fry for 2 minutes.

3. Add the soy sauce. Mix briefly. Then add the salt, sugar and rice wine (or sherry).

4. Pour in the water and bring to the boil, then lower heat and simmer gently for 20 minutes.

5. Serve on a bed of cabbage.

Serves 2

UKRAINIAN CHICKEN PIE

Preparation time: 2¼ hours   **Cooking time:** 45 minutes   *USSR*

Ingredients

2 onions, halved
1 stick celery, halved
1 clove garlic, crushed
2 teaspoons salt
2 pints/generous litre water
A 4-lb./1¾-kg. chicken
Sour Cream Pastry:
14 oz./400 g. flour
1 teaspoon baking powder
½ teaspoon salt
4 oz./100 g. butter, chilled
2 eggs, lightly beaten
¼ pint/1½ dl. soured cream

6 tablespoons soured cream
1½ tablespoons chopped
  parsley
¼ teaspoon nutmeg
1 tablespoon lemon juice
Salt
1 lb./450 g. cooked rice
1 lb./450 g. mushrooms,
  sautéed in butter
5 hard-boiled eggs,
  chopped
½ oz./15 g. fresh dill,
  chopped
Egg for brushing

1. In a large saucepan combine the first 5 ingredients and boil for 15 minutes. Add the chicken, cover and simmer for 1½ hours. Chop meat and reserve stock.

2. Prepare the pastry as for shortcrust pastry (page 481).

3. Blend 12 fl. oz./3½ dl. of the stock with the soured cream and bring to a simmer. Remove from heat and add the parsley, nutmeg, lemon juice, chicken and salt.

4. Roll out half the pastry to ⅛-inch/3-mm. thickness and line a deep pie dish. Beginning and ending with a layer of rice, alternate a layer of the chicken mixture with a layer of the mushrooms and a layer of the eggs and dill. Press down filling, then cover with the remaining pastry, crimping the edges. Cut a steam hole, then brush lid with egg. Bake 15 minutes in a 400°F., 200°C., Gas Mark 6 oven, then reduce heat to 350°F., 180°C., Gas Mark 4 for 30 minutes.

Serves 8

SOUTHERN FRIED CHICKEN

USA

Preparation time: 10 minutes   **Cooking time:** 15 minutes

Ingredients

A 3-lb./1⅓-kg. frying
   chicken, cut into 12
   pieces
Salt
Freshly ground pepper

About 1⅓ pints/8 dl.
   groundnut oil
4 oz./100 g. flour

1. Rinse the chicken pieces, pat dry and season with salt and pepper. Over very high heat, pour enough oil into a deep-frier to deep-fry the chicken pieces.

2. Place the flour, salt and pepper in a bag. Beginning with the legs and thighs, add a few chicken pieces at a time and shake vigorously to coat thoroughly. Remove and press the flour into the skin of each piece.

3. Add the chicken pieces to the hot oil one by one, keeping the temperature of the oil constant. Continue frying until each piece is crisp and golden brown, about 15 minutes.

4. As each piece is cooked, remove with a slotted spoon and drain on absorbent paper. Keep warm in a slow oven or cool to room temperature before serving.

Serves 3 to 4

MEXICAN-STYLE TURKEY

Preparation time: 20 minutes

Cooking time: 2 hours

Mexico

Ingredients

2 oz./50 g. flour

Salt

A 12-lb./5½-kg. turkey (giblets reserved), cut into serving pieces

4 oz./100 g. lard

Mole Sauce:

1½ tablespoons oil

3 medium onions, chopped

2 cloves garlic, chopped

3 oz./75 g. seedless raisins

2 oz./50 g. plain chocolate, cut in pieces

1 teaspoon cinnamon

¼ teaspoon each of aniseed, cumin and cloves

1½ tablespoons chilli powder

1½ tablespoons white sesame seeds, toasted

4 oz./100 g. cornmeal

3 tomatoes, chopped

Freshly grated pepper

—

Lime slices and toasted sesame seeds for garnish

1. Season the flour with the salt. Dredge the turkey pieces in the flour. Heat lard in large pan. Brown the turkey, then transfer the turkey to a large flameproof casserole. Cover with water and season with salt. Bring to the boil, cover and simmer until turkey is tender, about 45 minutes.

2. Remove turkey pieces from casserole. Remove meat and reserve. Return turkey bones to casserole. Add the giblets and bring to the boil, then lower heat and simmer for ½ hour. Strain and reserve 2½ pints/1¼ litres stock.

3. Heat the oil in a frying pan. Sauté the onions, then add the remaining *mole* ingredients. Mix well. Using ¾ pint/ 4½ dl. of turkey stock, purée the onion mixture until the sauce is smooth. Mix in the remaining stock. Add the sauce and turkey to the casserole and simmer for 30 minutes. Garnish with lime slices and sesame seeds.

Serves 10 to 12

ROAST STUFFED DUCK

France

Preparation time: 20 minutes
Stuffing refrigerates—1 hour

Cooking time: 1½ hours

Ingredients

Stuffing:	Salt
Duck's liver, chopped	Freshly ground pepper
1½ oz./40 g. fresh bread- crumbs, moistened with milk	5 tablespoons brandy — A 4½-lb./2-kg. duck
1 onion, chopped	2 tomatoes, halved
½ clove garlic, crushed	⅓ pint/2 dl. chicken stock
½ teaspoon dried thyme	Salt
½ teaspoon dried savory	Freshly ground pepper
1 teaspoon dried rosemary	

1. Combine the duck's liver, breadcrumbs, onion, garlic and herbs. Season with salt and pepper, then sprinkle on the brandy, cover and refrigerate 1 hour.

2. Preheat oven to 400°F., 200°C., Gas Mark 6.

3. Stuff the duck, then truss and secure the vent. Place the duck in a roasting tin. Surround with the tomatoes. Roast until the juices running from the thigh, when pricked, are pale yellow, about 1½ hours.

4. Transfer duck to a heated serving platter and keep warm.

5. Spoon out all but 1 tablespoon of the fat in the roasting tin. Pour in the chicken stock and boil rapidly for a few minutes, deglazing the tin. Add the tomatoes. Strain and season with salt and pepper, then pour into a heated sauce boat.

6. Carve duck at the table, spooning the sauce over individual portions of the stuffing as they are served.

Serves 4

BRAISED DUCK WITH TURNIPS

Preparation time: 35 minutes   **Cooking time:** 1½–2 hours

France

Ingredients

Stuffing:

Duck's liver and giblets,
 diced

2 chicken livers, diced

3 oz./75 g. bacon, diced

2 oz./50 g. fresh bread-
 crumbs

1½ tablespoons milk

2 eggs, beaten

1 shallot, finely chopped

Salt and pepper

1 tablespoon chopped
 fresh parsley

½ teaspoon sage

1 teaspoon basil

1 teaspoon rosemary

—

3½ oz./90 g. butter

A 4½-lb./2-kg. duck

2 tablespoons tomato
 purée

5 tablespoons Madeira

10 small white onions

20 small turnips, sliced

1½ tablespoons cream

1 tablespoon cognac

1. Combine the stuffing ingredients listed above. Lightly brown the mixture in a frying pan in 1 oz./25 g. of the butter.

2. Rinse the duck well and rub with salt. Stuff the bird, then truss and secure the vent. Preheat oven to 350°F., 180°C., Gas Mark 4.

3. Brown the duck in 1½ oz./40 g. of butter in a flameproof casserole. Mix the tomato purée with the Madeira and stir into casserole. Season with salt and pepper. Cover and braise for 1 hour.

4. Brown the onions and turnips in a frying pan with the rest of the butter. Add the cream and cognac. Reserve.

5. After the duck has cooked about 1 hour, degrease the casserole and add the turnips and onions. Continue to braise until the vegetables are tender and the juices from the duck's thigh run pale yellow. Transfer the duck to a hot platter and surround with the vegetables.

Serves 4

BRAISED DUCK AND PERSIAN RICE

Iran

Preparation time: 30 minutes
Duck marinates—2 hours

Cooking time: 65 minutes

Ingredients

A 5- to 6-lb./2¼- to 2¾-kg. duck, cut into serving pieces
⅓ pint/2 dl. yoghurt
1 oz./25 g. butter
2 onions, chopped
1½ pints/9 dl. water
Salt
Freshly ground pepper
Persian Rice:
1½ oz./40 g. butter

½ duck's giblets, chopped
1½ oz./40 g. pistachio nuts, chopped
1½ oz./40 g. seedless raisins
1 lb./450 g. long-grain rice
Salt
Freshly ground pepper
½ teaspoon cinnamon
1½ pints/9 dl. chicken stock, hot

1. Coat the duck pieces with the yoghurt. Cover and let stand for 2 hours. Remove duck and reserve yoghurt.

2. Melt the butter in an enamelled cast-iron casserole. Sauté the onions for 5 minutes. Add the duck pieces and sauté until browned, about 10 minutes. Pour in the water and scrape up any particles in the casserole. Season with salt and pepper. Bring to the boil, then lower heat, cover and simmer until duck is tender, about 40 minutes.

3. Prepare the Persian rice: Melt the butter and sauté the duck's giblets until lightly browned. Add the nuts, raisins, rice, salt, pepper and cinnamon and fry, stirring, for 2 minutes. Pour in the chicken stock, then lower heat, cover and simmer gently until rice is nearly tender, about 15 minutes. Drain and reserve.

4. Preheat oven to 400°F., 200°C., Gas Mark 6. Drain the duck pieces and then alternate layers of the Persian rice and the duck in the casserole used to cook the duck. Cover and bake until heated through, about 10 minutes.

Serves 6

DUCKLING BRAISED IN RED WINE

Preparation time: 20 minutes

Cooking time 1½ hours

France

Ingredients

8 oz./225 g. bacon, diced

2 oz./50 g. butter

15 small white onions

4 shallots, chopped

A 4½-lb./2-kg. duckling,
   cut into serving pieces

2 tablespoons Calvados,
   warmed

1 oz./25 g. flour

1⅓ pints/8 dl. red wine

6 tablespoons stock

Salt

Freshly ground pepper

Bouquet garni (parsley,
   sage, rosemary, bay
   leaf, peppercorns)

8 oz./225 g. mushrooms,
   sliced

1 duck liver, minced

Beurre Manié:

2 tablespoons flour

1 oz./25 g. butter

1. In an enamelled cast-iron casserole, sauté the bacon until brown. Remove the bacon and reserve. Add the butter, onions and shallots to the casserole and sauté until onions are golden, but not brown. Remove and reserve.

2. Brown the pieces of duck in the casserole. Pour in the brandy and flambé. Mix in the flour and stir, then add the wine and stock and continue stirring until the sauce is smooth. Return the reserved bacon, onions and shallots to the casserole. Add salt, pepper and the bouquet garni. Cover and simmer for 1 hour over low heat.

3. Add the mushrooms and cook for an additional 30 minutes. Before serving, remove bouquet garni and transfer duck pieces, onions and mushrooms to a heated serving dish.

4. Add the liver and the *beurre manié* (page 471) to the sauce. Correct seasoning, then pour the sauce over the duck.

Serves 4

WILD DUCK IN MUSTARD SAUCE

France

Preparation time: 20 minutes **Cooking time:** 20–30 minutes

Ingredients

A 2-lb./1-kg. wild duck
Salt
Freshly ground pepper
2 to 3 rashers streaky
   bacon
Butter for basting
Mustard Sauce:
Duck's liver
1 oz./25 g. butter
2 shallots, finely chopped

⅓ pint/2 dl. rosé wine
Juice of ½ lemon
Grated peel of 1 lemon
1 teaspoon prepared
   Dijon mustard
Salt
Freshly ground pepper
1½ tablespoons chopped
   fresh parsley

1. Set the oven at 425°F., 220°C., Gas Mark 7.

2. Season the inside of the duck with salt and pepper. Bard the breast by covering it with rashers of streaky bacon and securing with string.

3. Place the duck, breast side up, on a trivet in a roasting tin. Baste frequently with butter. Roast 20 to 30 minutes for pink to well-done meat.

4. While the duck is roasting, prepare the mustard sauce: a) Sauté the duck liver in ½ oz./15 g. of the butter for 5 minutes; b) remove liver, mash to a paste and set aside; c) using the same pan, sauté the shallots with butter until translucent; d) pour in the wine and bring to the boil; e) lower heat and add the duck liver, lemon juice, grated lemon peel, mustard, salt, pepper and parsley.

5. Remove the duck from the oven, carve and arrange on a heated serving dish. Add the pan juices to the mustard sauce and serve in a separate sauce boat.

Serves 2

SAUTÉED DUCK LIVER WITH BRANDY SAUCE

France

Preparation time: 5 minutes

Cooking time: 10 minutes

Ingredients

8 oz./225 g. duck livers,
   cut in ½-inch/1-cm.
   slices

1½ tablespoons flour

Salt

Freshly ground pepper

2 tablespoons goose fat or
   olive oil

12 thin slices French
   bread, fried in olive oil

8 oz./225 g. small green
   seedless grapes

2 tablespoons Armagnac
   brandy

1. Dust livers with flour and season with salt and pepper.

2. Heat the goose fat (or olive oil) in a frying pan, add liver slices and sauté for 3 minutes on one side and 2 minutes on the other. They should be pink on the inside.

3. Arrange livers and bread slices in a circle on a hot serving dish. Keep warm.

4. Sauté the grapes in the pan juices for 3 minutes. Remove with a slotted spoon and arrange in the centre of the serving platter. Keep warm.

5. Dilute pan juices with the brandy, bring to the boil and pour over the livers. Serve immediately.

Serves 2

GOOSE WITH CHESTNUT STUFFING

France

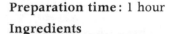

Preparation time: 1 hour

Roasting time: $2\frac{1}{4}$ hours

Ingredients

Chestnut Stuffing:

1 lb./450 g. chestnuts
$\frac{1}{3}$ pint/2 dl. Madeira
$\frac{1}{3}$ pint/2 dl. chicken stock
2 goose or chicken livers
1 onion, finely chopped
6 shallots, finely chopped
1 clove garlic, crushed
2 oz./50 g. butter
6 tablespoons chopped parsley

5 oz./150 g. breadcrumbs
2 tablespoons white wine
2 tablespoons cream
$\frac{1}{2}$ tablespoon sage
Salt
Freshly ground pepper
Pinch allspice
1 egg, beaten
—
An 8-lb./$3\frac{1}{2}$-kg. goose
Salt

1. Score the chestnuts, then blanch in a pot of boiling water for 3 minutes. Drain and peel. Combine the chestnuts, Madeira and stock and simmer until tender, about 30 minutes. Purée the chestnuts.

2. Sauté the livers, onion, shallots and garlic in butter for 3 minutes. Chop the livers, then add this mixture to the chestnuts. Add the remaining stuffing ingredients.

3. Preheat oven to 425°F., 220°C., Gas Mark 7. Stuff and truss the goose. Place the goose on a rack in a roasting tin. Salt lightly and prick the breast with a fork. Roast for 15 minutes, then baste with the pan juices. Reduce oven temperature to 350°F., 180°C., Gas Mark 4 and continue roasting until the juices from the thigh run pale yellow when pricked, about 2 hours.

4. When the goose is done, transfer to a heated serving platter. Skim the fat from the pan, then deglaze with the chestnut liquid. Reduce gravy to desired consistency. Carve the goose at the table, topping each portion with the hot gravy.

Serves 10

PARTRIDGES BRAISED IN RED WINE

Preparation time: 35 minutes   **Cooking time:** 1–1½ hours

France

Ingredients

Stuffing:

Partridges' livers, chopped
4 oz./100 g. ham, diced
*1½ tablespoons chopped
  fresh parsley*
1 egg, beaten
Salt
Freshly ground pepper

   —

2 partridges
Salt

Freshly ground pepper
3 tablespoons olive oil
1 tablespoon flour
⅓ pint/2 dl. red wine
⅓ pint/2 dl. chicken stock
1 tablespoon tomato purée
*Bouquet garni (thyme,
  bay leaf, parsley)*
*½ teaspoon grated orange
  peel*
6 cloves garlic, blanched

1. Combine the partridge livers, three-quarters of the ham and the parsley. Bind with the egg, then season with salt and pepper.

2. Stuff the partridges. Truss and season with salt and pepper.

3. In a flameproof casserole or saucepan, heat the olive oil. Add the partridges and brown evenly over moderately high heat, about 10 minutes. Remove birds and keep warm.

4. Add the remaining ham to the casserole. Sprinkle with the flour, then stir in the red wine, chicken stock and tomato purée.

5. Add the bouquet garni and orange peel. Bring rapidly to the boil, then lower heat, cover and simmer for 10 minutes.

6. Return the partridges to the casserole and add the blanched garlic cloves. Cover and simmer until birds are tender, about 1 to 1½ hours, depending on their age.

Serves 2

PARTRIDGES WITH GRAPES

France

Preparation time: 15 minutes **Cooking time:** 30 minutes

Ingredients

4 partridges, cleaned
3 oz./75 g. butter
4 thin slices pork fat or
   blanched barding bacon
7 dozen Muscat or other
   green seedless grapes

Salt
Freshly ground pepper
3 tablespoons brandy,
   warmed
4 slices French bread,
   fried in butter

1. Rub the partridges with a little butter, bard with the pork fat (or bacon) slices and truss.

2. Heat the remaining butter in a flameproof casserole or saucepan large enough to hold the partridges side by side. Add the birds and brown on all sides over moderately high heat. (This will take about 15 minutes.)

3. Add the grapes, salt and pepper, cover and continue cooking over moderate heat until birds are tender, about 15 minutes.

4. Remove the partridges, untruss and take off the barding strips.

5. Return birds to the casserole, sprinkle on the brandy and flambé.

6. Arrange the partridges on a heated serving platter. Garnish each bird with the grapes and the fried bread slices and cover with the remaining pan juices.

Serves 4

Partridges should be young and small to be cooked in this manner. Quail could very well be substituted.

PARTRIDGES WITH LENTILS

Preparation time: 30 minutes
Lentils soak—overnight

Cooking time: 1½ hours

France

Ingredients

8 oz./225 g. dry lentils
4 partridges
Salt
Freshly ground pepper
4 rashers bacon, blanched
2 oz./50 g. butter
2 carrots, quartered

6 shallots, chopped
2 bouquet garni (parsley,
    rosemary, thyme,
    peppercorns)
⅓ pint/2 dl. dry white wine
⅓ pint/2 dl. chicken stock
3 onions, chopped

1. Soak lentils overnight in a bowl of cold water.

2. Season the cavities of the partridges with salt and pepper. Wrap a rasher of blanched bacon around each breast and secure with string. Truss the legs and wings.

3. Heat the butter in a large flameproof casserole or saucepan. Add the partridges and brown evenly over fairly high heat. Add the carrots, shallots and 1 bouquet garni. Pour in the wine and stock. Cover and simmer over low heat until birds are tender, about 1 to 1½ hours.

4. While the partridges are cooking, prepare the lentils: a) Drain the soaked lentils; b) place them in a large saucepan; c) cover with cold water; d) add the remaining bouquet garni and the onions; e) bring to the boil, then lower heat, cover and simmer until tender, about 30 to 40 minutes; f) drain and keep hot.

5. Transfer the cooked partridges to a heated serving platter and surround them with the lentils. Strain the casserole juices and sprinkle over the birds.

Serves 4

YOUNG HARE IN WHITE WINE

France

Preparation time: 30 minutes

Cooking time: 1 hour

Ingredients

2 young hares (less than
 one year old), saddles
 and legs only
½ oz./15 g. butter
12 tiny white onions
1 tablespoon flour
⅓ pint/2 dl. dry white wine
6 tablespoons water
Salt

Freshly ground pepper
Bouquet garni (bay leaf,
 oregano, thyme)
2 egg yolks
6 tablespoons double
 cream
Juice of ½ lemon
1½ tablespoons chopped
 fresh parsley

1. Cut the meat into serving pieces.

2. Heat the butter in a large pan. Add the meat and brown evenly over moderately high heat. Remove meat and reserve.

3. Add the onions to the pan and brown lightly. Stirring continuously, sprinkle in the flour and cook for 30 seconds. Blend in the wine and water.

4. Return the meat to the pan and season to taste with salt and pepper. Add the bouquet garni, cover and simmer until the meat is tender, about 1 hour.

5. Discard the bouquet garni. Transfer the meat to a heated serving platter. Keep warm.

6. In a small bowl, beat the egg yolks well. Add the cream, lemon juice and parsley.

7. Blend a little of the liquid from the pan into the cream and egg mixture, then gently stir the mixture into the remaining liquid in the pan. Stirring constantly, heat through. Do not allow the sauce to boil. Cover the meat with the sauce and serve immediately.

Serves 4 to 6

HARE IN RED WINE SAUCE

Preparation time: 30 minutes   **Cooking time:** 2 hours   *France*

Ingredients

6 tablespoons olive oil

A 5-lb./2¼-kg. hare, cut
    into serving pieces

2 tablespoons cognac,
    warmed

1⅓ pints/8 dl. dry red wine

Salt

Freshly ground pepper

Bouquet garni (bay leaf,
    parsley, oregano, thyme)

10 small white onions

8 oz./225 g. small pork
    sausages

4 oz./100 g. stoned black
    olives

Chopped fresh parsley
    for garnish

1. Heat the oil in an enamelled cast-iron casserole or sauce-pan. Add the pieces of hare and brown evenly over moderately high heat.

2. Sprinkle on the warmed cognac and flambé.

3. Add the red wine, salt, pepper and bouquet garni. Cover and simmer over low heat for 1 hour.

4. While the hare is cooking, blanch the onions in boiling water for 5 minutes and brown the sausages in a frying pan.

5. Add the onions, sausages and olives to the casserole. Correct seasoning, if necessary, then continue to simmer hare for another hour.

6. Transfer the hare, sausages, olives and onions to a heated platter. Keep warm.

7. Reduce the sauce by about half over high heat. Pour sauce over the hare and garnish with chopped parsley.

Serves 6

FRICASSÉE OF RABBIT ÎLE DE FRANCE

France

Preparation time: 20 minutes　　**Cooking time:** $1\frac{1}{2}$ hours

Ingredients

1 oz./25 g. butter

4 oz./100 g. lean bacon, diced

A 3-lb./1$\frac{1}{3}$-kg. rabbit, cut into serving pieces

1$\frac{1}{2}$ tablespoons brandy, warmed

3 tablespoons flour

$\frac{1}{3}$ pint/2 dl. beef stock

$\frac{1}{3}$ pint/2 dl. white wine

1 clove garlic, finely chopped

Bouquet garni (bay leaf, parsley, oregano, thyme)

Salt

12 small white onions

8 oz./225 g. white mushrooms, halved

1. Heat the butter in an enamelled cast-iron casserole or saucepan. Add the bacon and brown. Using a slotted spoon, remove bacon and reserve.

2. Add the rabbit pieces to the casserole. Brown slightly over high heat, then sprinkle on the warmed brandy and flambé.

3. Stirring constantly, gradually add the flour and cook for 1 minute over low heat.

4. Blend in the stock and wine, then add the garlic, bouquet garni and salt. Cover and simmer over low heat for 1 hour.

5. While the rabbit is cooking, blanch the onions in boiling water for 5 minutes. Drain and reserve.

6. Add the reserved bacon and onions and the mushrooms to the casserole. Re-cover and cook until the rabbit is tender, about 30 minutes.

Serves 4

MEAT

ROAST BEEF AND YORKSHIRE PUDDING

Great Britain

Preparation time: 35 minutes
Batter stands—15 minutes

Cooking time: 15 minutes per lb./500 g. plus 15 minutes for rare meat

Ingredients

A 3-lb./1⅓-kg. sirloin, topside or rib

Salt

Freshly ground pepper

Yorkshire Pudding:

4 oz./100 g. flour

Salt

1 egg

½ pint/3 dl. milk

—

½ pint/3 dl. beef stock

1. Preheat the oven to 450°F., 230°C., Gas Mark 8. Season the meat with salt and pepper and place in a small roasting tin. Sear the roast for 15 minutes, then reduce the temperature to 350°F., 180°C., Gas Mark 4 and continue roasting until the meat reaches the desired degree of doneness.

2. About ¾ hour before the roast is done, prepare the Yorkshire pudding: Sift the flour and salt into a bowl. Make a well in the centre and break the egg into it. Add a little milk and beat until the batter is smooth. Stir in the remaining milk. Let the batter stand for 15 minutes.

3. Pour 3 tablespoons of dripping from the roast into a shallow ovenproof baking dish. Heat the fat to sizzling. Pour in the batter and bake near the top of the oven until crisp and brown, about 15 minutes for individual puddings or about 30 minutes for a large one. If large, cut the pudding into squares.

4. For the gravy, slowly pour off the fat from the roasting tin, saving the sediment and meat juices. Season with salt and pepper and stir over low heat until dark brown. Add the beef stock, bring to the boil and reduce slightly. Pour into a gravy boat and skim off any remaining fat.

Serves 6

POT ROAST WITH DUMPLINGS

Preparation time: 55 minutes   **Cooking time:** 3 hours

Meat marinates—2 days   **Dumplings cook**—10 minutes

Germany

Ingredients

Marinade:

2 onions, chopped

4 carrots, chopped

2 sticks celery, chopped

2 cloves

10 peppercorns

4 bay leaves

4 sprigs parsley

1 pint/6 dl. red wine
  vinegar

—

A 4-lb./1¾-kg. topside

Salt and pepper

Flour

2 oz./50 g. butter

¾ pint/4½ dl. beef stock

Dumplings:

6 potatoes

2 eggs, well beaten

4 oz./100 g. flour

Salt

Nutmeg

24 croûtons

1. Combine the marinade ingredients. Rub the joint with salt and pepper. Place the meat in the marinade and refrigerate for 2 days, turning occasionally. Remove meat, pat dry and dredge in flour. Strain the marinade.

2. Melt the butter in a large flameproof casserole and brown the meat evenly. Add the marinade vegetables and sauté for 10 minutes, then add the stock and half of the marinade. Cover and simmer for 3 hours, turning the meat once. About 30 minutes before serving, stir 2 tablespoons flour and water together and mix into the sauce. Continue to simmer.

3. Boil the potatoes until soft, then peel and grate. Mix in the eggs, flour and seasonings. Press a croûton into the centre of a spoonful of dumpling mixture. Repeat to make 24 balls. Boil the dumplings for 10 minutes.

4. Place the meat and vegetables on a serving dish with the dumplings. Reduce the gravy slightly and pour over.

Serves 8

BRISKET OF BEEF WITH FRUIT

Israel

Preparation time: 20 minutes

Ingredients

A 3-lb./1⅓-kg. brisket, boned
1 large onion, chopped
Salt
Freshly ground pepper
½ teaspoon ginger
¼ teaspoon cinnamon
6 cloves
3 oz./75 g. dried apricots
3 oz./75 g. dried prunes
1½ oz./40 g. currants

Cooking time: 1 hour 50
minutes

1 lb./450 g. potatoes,
  peeled
Sauce:
3 tablespoons beef
  dripping
2 tablespoons flour
Reserved liquid from
  cooking fruit
1 tablespoon sugar
⅓ pint/2 dl. red wine

1. Place the beef and chopped onion in an enamelled cast-iron casserole. Cover with boiling water. Return water to the boil. Skim surface until clear, then season with salt, pepper and the spices. Cover casserole and simmer for 1 hour.

2. While meat is cooking, place the fruits in a saucepan, cover with water and simmer for ½ hour. Drain and reserve liquid. Add the fruits and potatoes to casserole. Cover tightly and simmer until potatoes are nearly tender, about 20 minutes.

3. While the casserole is simmering, prepare the sauce: a) In a saucepan, heat the beef dripping; b) stirring constantly over moderate heat, blend in the flour and cook until lightly browned; c) add the reserved fruit liquid and continue stirring until sauce thickens, then add the sugar and wine; d) continue stirring until the sauce is smooth. Keep warm.

4. When the potatoes are nearly tender, blend in the sauce and cook until the meat is tender, about ½ hour.

Serves 4 to 6

TOURNEDOS WITH ARTICHOKE HEARTS

France

Preparation time: 2 hours

Cooking time: 6–8 minutes

Ingredients

4 beef marrow bones
4 artichokes
Salt
1 lemon, cut in half
1½ oz./40 g. butter
4 tournedos
Freshly ground pepper

1 tablespoon Calvados or
  other brandy, warmed
4 rounds of bread, fried
  in butter
6 fl. oz./1¾ dl. crème
  fraîche (page 473) or
  double cream
1 tablespoon chopped fresh
  tarragon or parsley

1. Poach the marrow bones in salted water for 2 hours. Remove the marrow from the bones and reserve.

2. Drop the artichokes into a large saucepan of lightly salted boiling water. Return water to the boil, then lower heat to moderate and cook artichokes until tender, about 35 minutes. Drain the artichokes. Discard leaves and remove the choke. Rub the artichokes hearts with the cut lemon and keep warm.

3. In a frying pan, melt the butter and sear the tournedos on both sides over high heat. Reduce heat and cook steaks for 3 to 4 minutes on each side. Remove from heat. Season with salt and pepper, then sprinkle on the brandy and flambé.

4. Arrange the bread rounds on a heated platter. Place one tournedos, topped with an artichoke heart, on each round.

5. Stir the *crème fraîche* into the meat juices. Heat sauce through to thicken, then season with salt and pepper and sprinkle in the tarragon (or parsley). Pour sauce over the artichoke hearts and top with strips of marrow.

Serves 4

STEAK WITH BORDELAISE SAUCE

France

Preparation time: 10 minutes

Cooking time: 12 minutes

Ingredients

2 1-lb./450-g. entrecôte
  steaks

Bordelaise Sauce:

4 shallots, minced

⅛ teaspoon dried thyme

6 tablespoons red Bordeaux
  wine

3 oz./75 g. butter, at
  room temperature

Salt

Freshly ground pepper

1 tablespoon tomato
  paste

2 oz./50 g. poached beef
  marrow (page 476),
  diced (optional)

1 tablespoon chopped
  fresh parsley

1. Preheat grill.

2. Grill steaks to preferred rareness. (For medium-rare steaks, allow about 6 minutes on each side.)

3. While the steaks are cooking, prepare the sauce: a) In a saucepan, combine the shallots, thyme and wine; b) reduce the liquid over high heat until syrupy; c) place the saucepan over hot water; d) using a wire whisk, beat in the butter, a little at a time (the butter should not melt but should retain a creamy consistency); e) season with salt and pepper, then add the tomato paste, marrow and parsley.

4. To serve, arrange the steaks on a hot platter and cover with the sauce.

Serves 4

STEAK WITH BERCY SAUCE

Preparation time: 10 minutes **Cooking time:** 12–15 minutes

France

Ingredients

2 1½- to 2-inch/4- to 5-cm.
  thick entrecôte steaks

Bercy Sauce:

3 shallots, minced

6 tablespoons white wine

Salt

Freshly ground pepper

3½ oz./90 g. butter, at
  room temperature

2 tablespoons chopped
  fresh parsley

Juice of ¼ lemon

—

Salt

Freshly ground pepper

Watercress for garnish

1. Grill steaks as desired. (For medium-rare meat, allow 6 to 8 minutes on one side and 6 minutes on the other.)

2. While the steaks are cooking, prepare the sauce: a) In an enamelled saucepan, combine the shallots, white wine, salt and pepper; b) reduce to a third over high heat; c) place the pan over hot water and beat in the butter a little at a time (the butter should not melt completely, but remain soft and creamy); d) add the chopped parsley and lemon juice.

3. When the steaks are done, season with salt and pepper and transfer to a heated platter. Pour the bercy sauce over the steaks, garnish with watercress and serve.

Serves 2

A sauce with red wine instead of white wine as its base turns this dish into steak marchand de vin.

STEAK WITH VEGETABLE GARNISH

France

Preparation time: 40 minutes   **Cooking time:** 8–10 minutes
Meat marinates—6 hours

Ingredients

Marinade:

6 tablespoons dry white
  wine

2 tablespoons Armagnac

1 teaspoon peppercorns

¼ teaspoon nutmeg

1 teaspoon thyme

1 bay leaf

——

2 lb./1 kg. porterhouse
  steak

3 tablespoons olive oil

2 small aubergines, peeled
  and diced

2 courgettes, sliced

2 tomatoes, sliced

2 green peppers, seeded
  and coarsely chopped

2 onions, chopped

1 clove garlic, crushed

Salt

Freshly ground pepper

1. Combine the marinade ingredients. Add the meat and
   let stand at room temperature for 6 hours, turning it
   occasionally. Drain and dry the meat. Reserve the
   marinade.

2. Preheat the grill. Heat the oil in a frying pan. Add the
   vegetables, garlic, salt and pepper. Add 1½ tablespoons
   of the marinade, cover and cook over low heat for 30
   minutes.

3. Grill steaks for 8 to 10 minutes. Baste occasionally with
   the marinade.

4. Transfer the meat to a hot platter. Dilute the cooking
   juices with the marinade, scrape up any brown particles
   and reduce the sauce. Pour the sauce over the meat and
   serve the vegetables separately.

Serves 4

SUKIYAKI

Preparation time: 15 minutes
Meat chills—to the freezing point

Cooking time: 8 minutes

Japan

Ingredients

2 lb./1 kg. beef fillet or
  sirloin
6 tablespoons soy sauce
3 tablespoons sake or dry
  sherry
3 tablespoons sugar
6 fl. oz./1¾ dl. chicken stock
Salt
Freshly ground pepper
3 tablespoons vegetable oil
½ head bok choy (Chinese
  cabbage) or green
  cabbage, cut in thin
  diagonal slices

2 onions, thinly sliced
4 oz./100 g. celery, sliced
4 oz./100 g. bamboo
  shoots, sliced lengthwise
8 mushrooms, sliced
8 oz./225 g. fresh spinach
  leaves, trimmed
12 spring onions, thinly
  sliced
1 cake tofu (bean curd),
  cubed
Raw egg for dipping

1. Chill meat to freezing point. Cut (across the grain) into very thin slices, then allow to warm to room temperature.

2. In a non-metallic bowl, combine the soy sauce, *sake* (or sherry), sugar, chicken stock, salt and pepper. Reserve.

3. Heat the oil in a large pan. Add the sliced meat and brown lightly over fairly high heat. Push meat to the side of the pan. Pour in half the soy mixture, then add the cabbage, onions, celery, bamboo and mushrooms. Stirring constantly, cook briskly for 3 minutes. Add the spinach, spring onions and bean curd. Stirring gently but briskly, cook another 3 minutes.

4. Serve immediately with hot rice and individual bowls of lightly beaten raw egg for dipping. (The hot *sukiyaki* placed in the egg has an unusual creamy texture. This can be omitted.) The remaining soy mixture is served as a dipping sauce.

Serves 4

BEEF ROLLS BRAISED IN RED WINE

France

Preparation time: 15 minutes   **Cooking time:** 1–1½ hours

Ingredients

Stuffing:

4 tablespoons chopped
  fresh parsley

1 shallot, minced

4 oz./100 g. sausage meat

Salt

Freshly ground pepper

———

4 very thin slices sirloin
  or topside, pounded to
  ⅛-inch/3-mm. thickness

1½ oz./40 g. butter

1 tablespoon tomato paste

6 tablespoons red wine

6 tablespoons beef stock

1. In a bowl, combine the parsley, shallot and sausage meat. Season to taste with salt and pepper. (To check seasoning, sauté a teaspoonful of the stuffing in butter until well cooked, then taste.)

2. Spread a layer of the stuffing on each slice of beef. Roll up and tie.

3. Heat the butter in a deep frying pan. Add the beef rolls and brown evenly on all sides.

4. Dilute the tomato paste with the wine and stock. Pour over the beef rolls.

5. Season with pepper, then cover and simmer over low heat for 1 to 1½ hours.

Serves 4

STUFFED BEEF ROLLS

Preparation time: 20 minutes   **Cooking time:** 1½ hours

Norway

Ingredients

1 lb./450 g. sirloin or
   topside, thinly sliced

1 teaspoon salt

½ teaspoon freshly ground
   pepper

¼ teaspoon ground ginger

¼ teaspoon ground cloves

4 oz./100 g. minced beef

1½ tablespoons chopped
   fresh parsley

*Flour for dredging beef
   rolls*

2 oz./50 g. butter

¾ pint/4½ dl. beef stock,
   heated

1. Place the meat slices between pieces of waxed paper and pound as thin as possible. (Each slice should be about 3 × 4 inches/7½ × 10 cm. when pounded.)

2. Sprinkle each slice with salt, pepper, ginger and cloves. Place some of the minced beef on each slice of seasoned steak, then sprinkle with the chopped parsley.

3. Roll up each slice, tucking in the edges as the slice is rolled and securing each end with string. Dredge the beef rolls in the flour. Reserve.

4. Melt the butter in a heavy pan. Add the beef rolls and brown evenly over fairly high heat. Pour in the heated stock, adding water if necessary, to cover rolls with liquid. Lower heat, cover pan and simmer for ¾ hour. Uncover the pan and simmer for another ¾ hour.

5. Remove the rolls with a slotted spoon and keep warm. Reduce the gravy to desired consistency over high heat.

6. To serve, discard strings from the beef rolls and transfer the meat to a heated platter. Pour the gravy over the meat or serve it in a warmed sauce boat.

Serves 2 to 3

SHREDDED BEEF WITH BAMBOO SHOOTS AND GREEN PEPPERS

China

Preparation time: 10 minutes

Cooking time: 6 minutes

Ingredients

12 oz./350 g. flank steak, sliced thinly and then shredded

Cornflour for dredging meat

2 tablespoons groundnut oil

2 oz./50 g. canned bamboo shoots, slivered into matchstick pieces

1 small green pepper, chopped

Salt

5 thick slices fresh root ginger, peeled and slivered

¼ teaspoon cayenne pepper

1 tablespoon soy sauce

½ teaspoon sugar

1 tablespoon Chinese rice wine or dry sherry

1. Dredge the beef in cornflour. Reserve.

2. Place a frying pan over high heat for ½ minute. Lower heat slightly and add 1 tablespoon of the oil. Swirl pan for ½ minute, then add the bamboo shoots, green pepper and a pinch of salt. Fry, stirring, for 2 minutes. Remove vegetables with a slotted spoon and reserve.

3. Add the remaining oil to the pan. Wait ½ minute, then add the ginger and fry, stirring, for ½ minute.

4. Add the cayenne pepper and the reserved beef. Stirring constantly, fry until the meat is nicely browned, about 1½ minutes. Remove from heat.

5. Stir in the soy sauce, sugar and rice wine (or sherry). Return pan to high heat. Stirring briskly, heat through. Add the vegetables and mix for ½ minute. Serve immediately.

Serves 2

BARBECUED STEAK

Preparation time: 15 minutes   **Cooking time:** 5–10 minutes

Steaks marinate—2–4 hours

Korea

Ingredients

4 rump steaks

Marinade:

1½ tablespoons fresh
  peeled and finely
  chopped root ginger

6 tablespoons soy sauce

3 tablespoons sugar or
  honey

2 cloves garlic, crushed

3 tablespoons ground
  sesame seeds

6 spring onions, chopped

1. Combine marinade ingredients in a non-metallic bowl.

2. Place steaks in shallow dish and pour marinade over them. Brush meat thoroughly with the marinade, then let stand 2 to 4 hours in the refrigerator, turning meat occasionally.

3. Preheat grill.

4. Transfer marinated steaks to grill pan. Reserve marinade.

5. Grill steaks for 5 to 10 minutes, turning once and brushing with the marinade.

Serves 4

BEEF BRAISED IN RED WINE

France

Preparation time: 20 minutes

Cooking time: 3 hours

Ingredients

3 lb./1⅓ kg. chuck steak, cut into 1½-inch/4-cm. cubes

Salt

Freshly ground pepper

¼ teaspoon ground allspice

8 oz./225 g. salt pork

8 oz./225 g. lean bacon, diced

3 tablespoons chopped fresh parsley

1 clove garlic, crushed

2 shallots, chopped

Bouquet garni (rosemary, thyme, mace, pepper-corns)

1 onion, stuck with 4 cloves

1¼ pints/7 dl. red wine

1. Season the steak with salt, pepper and allspice. Reserve.

2. Blanch the salt pork in boiling water for 10 minutes. Drain, slice and reserve.

3. In a bowl, combine the diced bacon, parsley, garlic and shallots. Mix well.

4. Place a layer of the salt pork slices in an enamelled cast-iron casserole. Add a layer of chuck steak, then one of the chopped mixture. Continue layering, ending with a layer of steak.

5. Add the bouquet garni and the onion stuck with cloves. Pour in the red wine.

6. Bring to the boil, then cover tightly and simmer over low heat for 3 hours.

7. Skim off the fat. Remove the onion and bouquet garni. Serve in the casserole.

Serves 8

BRAISED BEEF WITH RICE AND OLIVES

Tunisia

Preparation time: 15 minutes   **Cooking time:** 2½ hours

Ingredients

1½ tablespoons olive oil

1 lb./450 g. stewing beef,
  cut into 1-inch/2½-cm.
  cubes

2 onions, chopped

1 clove garlic, minced

4 oz./100 g. raw long-grain
  rice

⅓ pint/2 dl. beef stock

A 14-oz./397-g. can
  tomatoes

Salt

Freshly ground pepper

3 oz./75 g. stoned green
  olives, sliced

Chopped fresh parsley
  for garnish

1. Heat the olive oil in an enamelled casserole. Add the beef cubes and sauté evenly over moderately high heat until barely browned, about 10 minutes.

2. Stirring constantly, add the onions, garlic and rice and cook for a minute or two.

3. Reduce heat and stir in beef stock and tomatoes. Season with salt and pepper.

4. Bring to the boil, then lower heat and simmer for 2 hours.

5. Add the sliced olives and continue simmering until meat is tender, about 30 minutes.

6. Serve in the casserole, garnished with chopped parsley.

Serves 2

BRAISED BEEF AND ONIONS

France **Preparation time:** 10 minutes   **Cooking time:** 3 hours

Ingredients

2 lb./1 kg. braising steak,
  sliced

2½ lb./1¼ kg. onions, thinly
  sliced

1½ oz./40 g. butter

Salt

Freshly ground pepper

¾ pint/4½ dl. water

Dash red wine vinegar

*4 sour gherkins, finely
  sliced*

1. Layer the meat and onions in a buttered, enamelled cast-iron casserole. (Begin and end with a layer of onions and season each layer with salt and pepper.)

2. Add the water, cover and simmer over very low heat until the meat is tender, about 3 hours.

3. Just before serving, add a dash of vinegar and the finely sliced gherkins. Dot with butter and serve from the casserole.

Serves 4

STEWED BEEF WITH OKRA

Preparation time: 15 minutes   **Cooking time:** 2½ hours   *Egypt*

Ingredients

1½ tablespoons vegetable
   oil

1 oz./25 g. butter

1½ lb./700 g. stewing beef,
   cut into 1½-inch/4-cm.
   cubes

2 onions, chopped

2 cloves garlic, crushed

½ teaspoon ground
   coriander

1 lb./450 g. tomatoes,
   peeled and sliced

1 tablespoon tomato
   paste

2 lb./1 kg. fresh okra,
   trimmed, or 2
   10-oz./284-g. packages
   frozen okra

Salt

Freshly ground pepper

1. Heat the oil and butter in an enamelled cast-iron casserole. Add the meat cubes and sauté on all sides over moderate heat until nearly brown.

2. Add the onions, garlic and coriander and fry, stirring, for a minute or two.

3. Add the tomatoes and tomato paste and fresh okra. Correct seasoning. (If frozen okra is used, add in Step 5 where indicated.)

4. Cover stew mixture with water and bring to the boil, then reduce heat, cover casserole and simmer for 2 hours.

5. (Add the frozen okra.) Check level of liquid and add additional water, if necessary. Cover casserole again and continue simmering until the meat and vegetables are very tender, about ½ hour.

Serves 3 to 4

Very nice indeed!

SPICY SHREDDED BEEF

Venezuela

Preparation time: 25 minutes

Cooking time: 2½ hours

Ingredients

2-lb./1-kg. piece flank
   steak

¾ pint/4½ dl. beef stock or
   water

4 tablespoons olive oil

2 onions, finely chopped

3 cloves garlic, crushed

1 tin kidney beans

6 tomatoes, blanched,
   peeled and chopped

1½ teaspoon ground cumin

1 teaspoon salt

Freshly ground pepper

Cooked rice for garnish

1 teasp. oregano

1. Combine the steak and beef stock (or water) in an enamelled cast-iron casserole. Bring rapidly to the boil, then reduce heat, cover and simmer meat until extremely tender, about 2½ hours.

2. Remove casserole from heat and allow meat to cool in its broth.

3. Heat the olive oil in a large frying pan. Add the onions and garlic and sauté over moderately high heat until onions are translucent, about 5 minutes. Keep hot.

4. Add the tomatoes to the frying pan, then season with the cumin, salt and pepper. Blend sauce throughly, then simmer for 5 minutes. Keep hot.

5. Transfer the cooled meat to a carving board. Slice thinly, then shred.

6. Add the meat to the sauce and heat through.

7. To serve, spoon onto the centre of a heated platter. Surround with mounds of rice.

Serves 4 to 6

Added also 2 leeks + 1 red pepper

YANKEE MEAT LOAF

Preparation time: 15 minutes   **Cooking time:** 45 minutes   *USA*

Ingredients

1 lb./450 g. minced beef
⅓ pint/2 dl. milk
2 oz./50 g. seasoned
  breadcrumbs
1 egg
1 onion, parboiled and
  chopped
1 green pepper, chopped
Dash Worcestershire
  sauce

Dash Tabasco sauce
1 tablespoon oregano
1 teaspoon tarragon
1½ teaspoons parsley
1 teaspoon thyme
½ teaspoon sage
Freshly grated pepper
1 tomato, sliced
½ oz./15 g. butter

1. Preheat oven to 325°F., 160°C., Gas Mark 3.

2. Combine the first 14 ingredients and mix thoroughly. Shape into a loaf and place in a loaf tin. Arrange tomato slices on top and dot with the butter.

3. Bake for 45 minutes. Remove from oven and let rest for 15 minutes before serving.

Serves 4

Many cooks enjoy experimenting with different combinations and quantities of herbs. Try adding mustard, rosemary, dill, mushrooms, fresh parsley or pimento to spice up your meat loaf.

STEAK AND KIDNEY PIE

Australia

Preparation time: 15 minutes
Pastry chills—1 hour

Cooking time: 2½ hours

Ingredients

Flaky Pastry:
8 oz./225 g. flour
1 teaspoon salt
6 oz./175 g. butter
7 tablespoons iced water
—
1 tablespoon flour
Salt
Freshly ground pepper
1 lb./450 g. braising steak, cubed

2 lamb or ox kidneys, skinned, cored and sliced
2 tablespoons oil
1 onion, chopped
Dash Worcestershire sauce
12 fl. oz./3½ dl. beef stock
1 egg, beaten

1. Prepare the flaky pastry (page 474). Chill for 1 hour.

2. Season the flour with salt and pepper. Dredge the meats in the flour mixture. Heat the oil in an enamelled casserole and lightly brown the meat and onion. Add the Worcestershire sauce and stock and simmer over low heat for 2 hours.

3. Roll out the pastry to ¼-inch/5-mm. thickness. Preheat the oven to 425°F., 220°C., Gas Mark 7.

4. Transfer the meat to a deep pie dish and pour in the juice. Cover with the crust. Cut a hole in the centre of the crust and brush with the beaten egg. Bake until the crust is golden, about 30 minutes.

Serves 4

TOKÁNY OF VEAL

Preparation time: 40 minutes

Cooking time: 1 hour
20 minutes

Hungary

Ingredients

2 lb./1 kg. veal shoulder,
  cubed

Flour for dredging veal

2 tablespoons oil

1 oz./25 g. butter

3 onions, chopped

⅓ pint/2 dl. dry white wine

1 green pepper, seeded
  and sliced into rings

2 carrots, sliced

3 tomatoes, peeled and
  chopped

½ teaspoon marjoram

1 tablespoon paprika

Salt

Freshly ground pepper

⅓ pint/2 dl. veal or beef
  stock

6 oz./175 g. bacon, diced

8 oz./225 g. mushrooms,
  chopped

⅓ pint/2 dl. soured cream

1. Dredge the veal in flour. Heat the oil and butter in an enamelled cast-iron casserole. Brown the veal evenly over moderately high heat. Remove and reserve.

2. Add the onions to the casserole and sauté until tender, about 5 minutes. Pour in the wine, scraping up any browned particles in the casserole. Add the green pepper, carrots and tomatoes to the casserole. Simmer for 10 minutes.

3. Return the veal to the casserole. Add the seasonings and stock and bring to the boil, then lower heat, cover and simmer for 1 hour.

4. Blanch the bacon for 5 minutes. Drain, rinse under cold water and pat dry. Sauté bacon until lightly browned and add to the casserole. Replace cover and simmer for another 20 minutes.

5. Ten minutes before serving, add the mushrooms. Reduce the heat to low and stir in the soured cream. Heat to thicken but do not boil.

Serves 4

BREAST OF VEAL WITH CHESTNUT STUFFING

France

Preparation time: 1 hour　　　　**Cooking time:** 2½ hours

Ingredients

1½ lb./700 g. chestnuts
1 cabbage, quartered
6 rashers smoked bacon
3 oz./75 g. breadcrumbs
3 to 4 tablespoons milk
2 onions, chopped
1½ oz./40 g. butter

Salt
Freshly ground pepper
A 2½-lb./1¼-kg. veal breast, boned
1 oz./25 g. lard
1 pint/6 dl. dry white wine
1½ tablespoons chopped fresh parsley

1. Blanch the scored chestnuts in boiling water for 3 minutes. Drain and peel. Return chestnuts to the pot, cover with cold water and simmer for 15 minutes. Drain and chop half the chestnuts.

2. Blanch the cabbage for 3 minutes. Drain and refresh.

3. Blanch the bacon for 10 minutes. Drain, then arrange on the bottom of a large flameproof casserole.

4. Moisten the crumbs with the milk. Combine with the chopped chestnuts, onions and butter. Season with salt and pepper. Spread the stuffing over the meat, roll up and secure. Place the veal, cabbage, lard and whole chestnuts in the casserole. Pour in the wine and cover tightly. Simmer over low heat for 2½ hours.

5. Transfer the veal to a platter and garnish with the chestnuts and cabbage. Reduce the liquid in the casserole, skim off the fat and pour over the meat and vegetables. Sprinkle with parsley.

Serves 4

OSSO BUCO

Preparation time: 25 minutes   **Cooking time:** 2 hours

Italy

Ingredients

2 lb./1 kg. shin of veal,
   sawed into 2-inch/5-cm.
   sections

Flour for dredging veal

1½ tablespoons olive oil

1 oz./25 g. butter

2 carrots, finely chopped

2 onions, finely chopped

2 sticks celery, chopped

1 clove garlic, crushed

2 pieces lemon peel

1 bay leaf

½ teaspoon dried thyme

Salt

Freshly ground pepper

1½ tablespoons tomato
   purée

¾ pint/4½ dl. dry white
   wine

¾ pint/4½ dl. veal or beef
   stock

3 tablespoons chopped
   fresh parsley

1 tablespoon grated lemon
   rind

1. Roll the veal pieces in flour.

2. Heat the oil and butter in an enamelled cast-iron casserole. Add the floured veal and brown evenly over
   moderately high heat, Remove veal and reserve.

3. Add the carrots, onions, celery and garlic to the casserole.
   Stir over moderate heat until onions are tender, about 5
   minutes. (Do not let vegetables brown.)

4. Arrange the reserved veal on top of the vegetables. Add
   the lemon peel and bay leaf. Sprinkle on the thyme, then
   season with salt and pepper.

5. In a bowl, combine the tomato purée, wine and stock.
   Add to the casserole. Bring to the boil, then reduce heat,
   cover and simmer very gently for 2 hours. Discard bay
   leaf and lemon peel. Stir in the parsley and grated lemon
   rind. Cook for 5 more minutes. Taste and correct seasoning, if necessary, then serve with steamed or braised rice
   (page 339).

Serves 4

BREADED VEAL ESCALOPES WITH ANCHOVY BUTTER

Austria

Preparation time: 10 minutes   **Cooking time:** 6 minutes

Ingredients

Anchovy Butter:
2 anchovy fillets, chopped
3 oz./75 g. butter, at
* room temperature*
—
4 veal escalopes, pounded
* flat*
Seasoned flour

2 eggs, beaten
2 oz./50 g. dry bread-
* crumbs*
1½ oz./40 g. butter
Chopped fresh parsley
* for garnish*
Lemon wedges for garnish

1. Prepare the anchovy butter: In a mortar, pound the anchovies and mix in softened butter. Form into 4 pats, transfer to waxed paper and refrigerate until needed.

2. Dry the escalopes and dredge in seasoned flour. Dip in the beaten egg and then in the breadcrumbs.

3. Melt the butter in a large frying pan. Add the escalopes and sauté over high heat until nicely browned and crisp, about 3 minutes per side.

4. Arrange the escalopes on a serving platter. Top each one with a pat of anchovy butter, garnish with chopped fresh parsley and lemon wedges. Serve immediately.

Serves 4

Topping each escalope with a fried egg and an anchovy fillet instead of the anchovy butter turns this dish into Holstein veal.

VEAL ESCALOPES IN CREAM SAUCE

France

Preparation time: 25 minutes   **Cooking time:** 15 minutes

Ingredients

4 veal escalopes
Flour for dusting veal
2 oz./50 g. butter
Salt
Freshly ground pepper
2 onions, chopped
2 shallots, finely chopped
8 oz./225 g. mushrooms, chopped

3 oz./75 g. ham, cut in julienne strips
1½ tablespoons flour
⅓ pint/2 dl. milk
3 oz./75 g. Gruyère or other Swiss cheese, grated
1½ tablespoons cream

1. Dust the veal escalopes with flour.

2. Heat the butter in a frying pan and lightly brown the escalopes on both sides over moderately high heat. Transfer to an ovenproof baking dish, season to taste and set aside.

3. Set oven at 425°F., 220°C., Gas Mark 7.

4. Add the onions and shallots to the pan. Sauté briefly, then add the mushrooms. Cook until the onions are nearly tender.

5. Add the ham to the pan, stir in the flour and then slowly pour in the milk.

6. Stirring constantly, bring sauce to the boil, then lower heat and cook until thickened. Salt and pepper to taste.

7. Cover escalopes with half the grated cheese, pour sauce over and top with the remaining cheese.

8. Bake until nicely browned, about 15 minutes. Just before serving, sprinkle on the cream.

Serves 4

VEAL ESCALOPES WITH PIPÉRADE SAUCE

France

Preparation time: 35 minutes   **Cooking time:** 10 minutes

Ingredients

Pipérade:

1½ tablespoons olive oil

2 green peppers, seeded
  and thinly sliced

1 small chilli pepper,
  chopped

1 onion, chopped

2 cloves garlic, crushed

¼ teaspoon sugar

Salt

Freshly ground pepper

2 lb./1 kg. tomatoes, peeled,
  seeded and chopped

—

4 veal escalopes

Flour for dusting veal

1 egg, beaten

1 oz./25 g. dry bread-
  crumbs

1½ oz./40 g. butter

4 slices ham

3 oz./75 g. Gruyère or
  other Swiss cheese,
  grated

1. Prepare the *pipérade:* a) Heat the olive oil in a large frying pan; b) add the green peppers, chilli pepper, onion, garlic and sugar; c) season with salt and pepper and sauté until onion is translucent; d) add the tomatoes, then cover and simmer gently for 15 minutes; e) uncover and continue to cook until liquid has evaporated. Reserve.

2. Set oven at 425°F., 220°C., Gas Mark 7.

3. Dust the escalopes with a little flour. Dip them in the beaten egg and then in the breadcrumbs.

4. Melt the butter in a frying pan and sauté the escalopes over moderate heat until golden brown on both sides.

5. Arrange the veal in a buttered ovenproof baking dish. Place a slice of ham on each escalope and cover thoroughly with the *pipérade.* Sprinkle with the grated cheese and bake until nicely browned, about 10 minutes.

Serves 4

VEAL WITH MUSHROOMS LYONNAISE

France

Preparation time: 30 minutes   **Cooking time:** 1–1¼ hours

Ingredients

1½ lb./700 g. veal shoulder,
   cut into 1½-inch/4-cm.
   cubes
Flour for dusting veal
2 tablespoons olive oil
3 oz./75 g. butter
4 shallots, finely chopped
2 onions, chopped
4 oz./100 g. thickly sliced
   bacon, diced

Salt
Freshly ground pepper
12 oz./350 g. mushrooms,
   sliced
12 fl. oz./3½ dl. chicken
   stock
6 tablespoons double cream
Juice of 1 lemon
6 slices French bread,
   fried in butter

1. Pat the veal cubes dry and dust with flour.

2. Heat the olive oil and half of the butter in a large pan. Add the pieces of veal and brown evenly on all sides over high heat.

3. Lower heat to moderate and add the shallots, onions and bacon. Cook for 10 minutes, then add salt and pepper.

4. While the onions and bacon are cooking, heat the remaining butter in another pan and sauté the mushrooms. Add the sautéed mushrooms and the chicken stock to the veal. Simmer gently until the veal is tender, about 1 to 1¼ hours.

5. Add the cream and lemon juice to the pan. Bring sauce to the boil and thicken by cooking over moderate heat for about 3 minutes.

6. Serve in a deep heated platter garnished with the slices of fried bread.

Serves 3 to 4

VEAL AND HAM ROLLS

Italy

Preparation time: 45 minutes   **Cooking time:** 25 minutes

Ingredients

8 veal escalopes, pounded
  very thin
Salt
Freshly ground pepper
8 thin slices ham
Flour for dusting veal rolls
1 oz./25 g. butter
1½ tablespoons vegetable
  oil

5 shallots, finely chopped
6 tablespoons white wine
3 tablespoons Marsala
2 tomatoes, peeled, seeded
  and chopped
2 teaspoons dried basil

1. Season the veal escalopes with salt and pepper.

2. Place a slice of ham on each escalope. Roll up escalopes and secure with thread. Dust lightly with flour.

3. Heat the butter and oil in a large frying pan. Add the rolled escalopes and sauté evenly over moderately high heat until nicely browned, about 10 minutes. Remove veal rolls and reserve.

4. Add the shallots to the pan and sauté over moderate heat until tender, about 5 minutes.

5. Stir in the white wine and the Marsala. Bring rapidly to the boil, scraping up any brown particles in the pan.

6. Reduce heat to low and return the reserved veal rolls to the pan. Stir in the tomatoes and basil. Season generously with salt and pepper.

7. Cover pan and simmer gently until the rolls are tender, about 25 minutes.

8. Remove veal rolls from pan and discard trussing thread, then arrange on a heated platter and cover with the sauce.

Serves 4 or 8

STUFFED VEAL ROLLS

Preparation time: 45 minutes

Cooking time: 45 minutes

The Netherlands

Ingredients

Stuffing:

1 oz./25 g. butter
1 onion, chopped
4 oz./100 g. veal, minced
1½ tablespoons chopped parsley
2 eggs, hard-boiled
Salt
Freshly ground pepper

Freshly grated nutmeg

—

6 thin slices veal
Seasoned flour for dredging veal
2 oz./50 g. butter
6 tablespoons beef stock
2 slices lemon
Chopped fresh herbs for garnish

1. Prepare the stuffing: a) Heat the butter in a frying pan; add the onion and sauté over moderately low heat until translucent, about 5 minutes; remove from heat; b) in a bowl, combine the sautéed onion, minced veal and parsley; c) put eggs through a sieve, then add to mixture and blend thoroughly. Season to taste. Reserve.

2. Pound the veal slices to about ⅛-inch/3-mm. thickness. Trim and season lightly with salt and pepper. Place some of the stuffing on each veal slice. Roll up the slices, then secure the rolls with string. Dredge rolls lightly in seasoned flour.

3. Heat the butter in a large frying pan. Add the veal rolls and sauté evenly over moderately high heat until nicely browned on all sides, about 10 minutes. Add the stock and the lemon slices to the pan. Bring to the boil, then lower heat, cover and simmer for 45 minutes.

4. Remove the veal rolls from the frying pan, untie them and arrange on a heated serving platter. Keep hot. Reduce the pan juices slightly, then discard the lemon slices and pour sauce over the veal rolls. Garnish with chopped fresh herbs.

Serves 6

ROAST LEG OF LAMB WITH GARLIC SAUCE

France

Preparation time: 20 minutes

Cooking time: 20 minutes per lb./500 g. plus 20 minutes for pink lamb

Ingredients

8 oz./225 g. garlic cloves, peeled
A 5-lb./2¼-kg. leg of lamb
6 anchovy fillets, halved

Salt
Freshly ground pepper
⅓ pint/2 dl. beef stock

1. Preheat oven to 350°F., 180°C., Gas Mark 3.

2. Sliver 1 large clove garlic.

3. Make slits in the leg of lamb and insert the slivered garlic and the anchovy fillets. Lightly salt and pepper the meat.

4. Roast the lamb in the oven. (For pink lamb, cook 20 minutes per lb./500 g. plus 20 minutes.)

5. While the meat is cooking, prepare the remaining garlic cloves: Drop the garlic cloves into a pot of rapidly boiling water and cook until tender, about 8 minutes. Rinse under cold water, then drain and mash. Reserve.

6. When the lamb is done, remove the roasting tin from the oven and transfer lamb to a heated platter.

7. Stir the mashed garlic cloves into the roasting tin juices, add the stock and reduce sauce slightly over high heat.

8. Carve the lamb at the table and serve the sauce separately.

Serves 6

ROAST LEG OF LAMB WITH PÉRIGORD SAUCE

France

Preparation times 15 minutes

Cooking time: 20 minutes per lb./500 g. plus 20 minutes for pink lamb

Ingredients

A 5-lb./2¼-kg. leg of lamb
2 truffles, slivered
4 oz./100 g. bacon rashers
1½ tablespoons goose fat (page 475) or olive oil
Salt

Freshly ground pepper
2 tablespoons Armagnac or other brandy, warmed
6 tablespoons beef stock

1. Preheat oven to 450°F., 230°C., Gas Mark 8.

2. Make small slits in the lamb and insert the truffle slivers. Bard the lamb with the bacon, then brush on the goose fat (or olive oil). Place lamb on a rack in a roasting tin. Season with salt and pepper. Roast, uncovered, for 15 minutes.

3. Reduce heat to 325°F., 160°C., Gas Mark 3, baste lamb and then continue roasting until done. (For pink lamb, allow 20 minutes per lb./500 g. plus 20 minutes.)

4. About 15 minutes before the end of cooking time, sprinkle on the brandy and flambé.

5. Transfer the roasted lamb to a heated serving platter. Keep warm.

6. Place the roasting tin on top of the stove. Add the stock and scrape up any browned particles in the roasting tin. Reduce slightly over high heat. Pour into a heated sauce boat and serve with the lamb.

Serves 6

ROAST LEG OF LAMB WITH POTATOES

France

Preparation time: 20 minutes

Cooking time: 20 minutes per lb./500 g. plus 20 minutes for pink lamb

Ingredients

A 5- to 6-lb./2¼- to 2¾-kg. leg of lamb
3 cloves garlic
4 oz./100 g. bacon rashers
2 oz./50 g. butter
3 lb./1⅓ kg. potatoes, peeled and thinly sliced

Salt
Freshly ground pepper
Freshly grated nutmeg
3 tablespoons beef stock

1. Preheat oven to 425°F., 220°C., Gas Mark 7.

2. Make slits in the lamb and insert 1 clove garlic, slivered. Crush the remaining garlic and sliver 1 rasher bacon.

3. Coat a casserole with ½ oz./15 g. of the butter. Layer the potato slices in the casserole, seasoning each layer with the slivered bacon, garlic, salt, pepper and nutmeg.

4. Place the leg of lamb on top of the potatoes. Bard with the remaining bacon rashers and dot with the remaining butter. Place casserole in the oven and sear lamb for 15 minutes. Reduce oven temperature to 325°F., 160°C., Gas Mark 3 and baste lamb. Continue roasting until the meat is done. Baste frequently. (To determine total roasting time for pink lamb, allow 20 minutes per lb./500 g. plus 20 minutes.)

5. About 15 minutes before the end of the cooking time, pour the beef stock over the meat and potatoes.

6. When the lamb is done, remove from the casserole and carve. Cover the potatoes with the sliced lamb, pour on the carving juices and present dish in the casserole.

Serves 6 to 8

BRAISED LEG OF LAMB WITH ONIONS

France

Preparation time: 30 minutes   **Cooking time:** 2 hours

Ingredients

A 5-lb./2¼-kg. leg of lamb
2 oz./50 g. butter
3 tablespoons olive oil
3 tablespoons cold water
1½ tablespoons tomato paste
1 pint/6 dl. beef stock
Bouquet garni (bay leaf, thyme, garlic)

36 tiny white onions, unpeeled
1 teaspoon sugar
Salt
Freshly ground pepper
2 teaspoons potato flour or cornflour, dissolved in 1½ tablespoons cold water

1. Rub the leg of lamb with ½ oz./15 g. of the butter. Heat the olive oil in an enamelled cast-iron casserole and brown the lamb on all sides over high heat. Pour in the cold water and scrape up any brown particles.

2. Mix the tomato paste with ¾ pint/4½ dl. of the stock. Add the tomato paste mixture and the bouquet garni to the casserole. Bring to the boil, then lower heat, cover and simmer for 2 hours.

3. Drop the unpeeled onions into a large pot of rapidly boiling water. Cook for 3 minutes, then rinse under cold water. Drain and peel. About 30 minutes before the meat is done, heat the remaining butter in a large frying pan and sauté the onions until golden, about 5 minutes. Sprinkle the onions with the sugar, pour in the remaining stock and cook until nearly all the liquid has evaporated.

4. Season the cooked lamb with salt and pepper. Transfer to a heated serving platter and surround with the onions. Thicken the lamb pan juices by stirring in the potato flour (or cornflour) mixture. Heat through and pour over the dish.

Serves 6

LEG OF LAMB WITH HARICOT BEANS

France

Preparation time: 20 minutes
Beans soak—overnight

Cooking time: Lamb—20 minutes per lb./500 g. plus 20 minutes
Beans—2 hours

Ingredients

2 lb./1 kg. dried haricot beans

Bouquet garni (thyme, rosemary, parsley)

Salt

Freshly ground pepper

4 onions, chopped

3 cloves garlic, slivered

A 6-lb./2¾-kg. leg of lamb

2 oz./50 g. butter

2 tomatoes, peeled, seeded and quartered

2 shallots, chopped

1. Soak the beans in cold water overnight. Drain beans and transfer them to a saucepan. Add cold water to cover, the bouquet garni, salt, pepper and half the onions. Bring to the boil and simmer the beans until tender, at least 2 hours. When done, drain and discard the bouquet garni.

2. Preheat oven to 450°F., 230°C., Gas Mark 8.

3. While the beans are cooking, insert garlic slivers in the meat. Rub with 1 oz./25 g. butter and season to taste. Sear in the hot oven for 15 minutes. Reduce heat to 325°F., 160°C., Gas Mark 3 and roast for about a further 2 hours. Baste frequently. The outside of the meat should be golden brown and the inside slightly pink.

4. Prepare the garnish while the lamb and beans are cooking: Heat 1 oz./25 g. butter in a saucepan. Add the tomatoes, remaining onions and shallots. Cook slowly for 10 minutes, then add the beans. Simmer for about 5 minutes.

5. Transfer bean and tomato mixture to a serving platter. Remove lamb and place it on top of the beans.

Serves 8 to 10

STUFFED SHOULDER OF LAMB

Preparation time: 30 minutes

Roasting time: 15 minutes per lb./500 g. plus 15 minutes for pink meat

The Netherlands

Ingredients

A 4-lb./1¾-kg. shoulder of lamb, boned
1 garlic clove, crushed
Salt

Stuffing:

1 oz./25 g. butter
1 onion, chopped
1½ tablespoons flour
2 teaspoons curry powder
⅓ pint/2 dl. milk

1 apple, peeled, cored and diced
3 tablespoons chopped fresh parsley
4 oz./100 g. cooked rice
Salt
Freshly ground pepper
—
2 oz./50 g. butter, melted
⅓ pint/2 dl. beef stock
1½ tablespoons flour

1. Rub all surfaces of the shoulder of lamb with garlic and salt. Reserve. Preheat oven to 400°F., 200°C., Gas Mark 6.

2. To make the stuffing: Melt the butter in a saucepan and sauté the onion over moderate heat until translucent, about 5 minutes. Remove pan from heat and sprinkle on the flour and curry powder. Return pan to low heat and stir for 1 minute. Gradually add the milk and stir until smooth. Add in the apple, parsley, rice and salt and pepper.

3. Fill the pocket of the lamb shoulder with the stuffing. Secure the opening with skewers, then sew up. Place in a roasting tin and baste with the melted butter, then roast to desired tenderness. (For pink meat allow 15 minutes per lb./500 g. plus 15 minutes.) When lamb is done, remove from oven and cool slightly, then carve and serve. To prepare a gravy, deglaze the roasting tin with the beef stock and the flour. Serve in a sauce boat.

Serves 4 to 6

P. J. MORIARTY'S IRISH STEW

Ireland

Preparation time: 20 minutes

Cooking time: 2 hours

Ingredients

3 lb./1⅓ kg. potatoes,
  peeled and thinly sliced
Salt
Freshly ground pepper
1 lb./450 g. onions, thinly
  sliced

3 lb./1⅓ kg. stewing lamb,
  cut into cubes
1½ pints/9 dl. water or
  beef stock
Chopped fresh parsley
  for garnish

1. Line the bottom of an enamelled cast-iron casserole with a layer of sliced potatoes. Season with salt and pepper. Add a layer of onions and seasonings, then a layer of lamb. Continue layering, seasoning each layer with salt and pepper. End with a layer of potatoes.

2. Pour in the water (or stock) and bring rapidly to the boil.

3. Skim the surface of the stew, then lower heat, cover and simmer until meat is tender, about 2 hours.

4. Sprinkle stew with fresh chopped parsley and serve from the casserole.

Serves 6

LAMB PILAF WITH APRICOTS

Preparation time: 30 minutes   **Cooking time:** 2 hours   *Iran*

Ingredients

2 oz./50 g. butter

2 lb./1 kg. lean stewing
   lamb, cut into 1-inch/
   2½-cm. cubes

2 onions, finely chopped

Salt

Freshly ground pepper

¼ teaspoon ground
   cinnamon

¼ teaspoon ground allspice

¼ teaspoon freshly grated
   nutmeg

1 oz./25 g. seedless raisins

5 oz./150 g. dried apricots

1 lb./450 g. raw long-grain
   rice

1. Heat the butter in an enamelled cast-iron casserole. Add the meat and sauté evenly over moderate heat for 10 minutes.

2. Reduce heat, add the onion and fry, stirring, until the onion is golden and the meat nicely browned.

3. Add the seasonings, raisins and apricots. Sauté for a minute or two, then cover with cold water. Bring to the boil, then lower heat, cover and simmer until the meat is very tender, about 1½ hours.

4. Fifteen minutes before the meat is done, prepare the rice: a) Pour 1½ pints/9 dl. water into a saucepan and salt lightly; b) bring rapidly to the boil, then sprinkle in the rice; c) boil rapidly for 2 minutes, then lower heat, cover tightly and simmer for 10 minutes; d) drain.

5. Layer the rice and the cooked meat (with sauce) in another casserole, beginning and ending with a layer of rice.

6. Cover and cook over moderate heat until the rice is tender, about 20 minutes.

Serves 6

BAKED LAMB WITH CRACKED WHEAT

Lebanon

Preparation time: 30 minutes
Wheat soaks—15 minutes

Cooking time: 1 hour

Ingredients

1 lb./450 g. cracked wheat

2 lb./1 kg. lean lamb,
  minced twice

½ onion, grated

2 teaspoons salt

Freshly ground pepper

Filling:

1 onion, chopped

1½ tablespoons oil

8 oz./225 g. lean lamb,
  minced twice

1 oz./25 g. pine nuts,
  chopped

Salt

Freshly ground pepper

½ teaspoon cinnamon

Pinch grated nutmeg

Pinch ground allspice

—

4 oz./100 g. butter

1. Soak the cracked wheat in water for 15 minutes. Drain, pressing out excess water, until dry. Combine the wheat, lamb, onion, salt and pepper. Knead vigorously (or whirl in a blender) until mixture is smooth.

2. Set oven at 375°F., 190°C., Gas Mark 5.

3. Prepare the filling: Sauté the onion in the oil until soft, then mix in the remaining ingredients and sauté over high heat until the meat is lightly browned. Remove from heat.

4. Melt the butter in a saucepan. Reserve.

5. Spread half the reserved wheat-lamb mixture in the bottom of a buttered 9 × 12-inch/23 × 30-cm. baking tin. Press down firmly. Cover with the filling and then top with remaining wheat-lamb mixture. Smooth the top, pressing it down firmly. Cut diagonal lines across the surface to make diamond shapes. Pour the melted butter over the dish. Bake until crisp and brown, about 1 hour.

Serves 8

CAUCASIAN SKEWERED LAMB

Preparation time: 20 minutes   **Cooking time:** 10–15 minutes
Lamb marinates—24 hours

USSR

Ingredients

Marinade:

⅓ *pint/2 dl. olive oil*

⅓ *pint/2 dl. red wine*

3 *tablespoons lemon juice*

1½ *tablespoons fresh chopped dill*

1 *clove garlic, crushed*

1 *bay leaf*

Freshly ground pepper

2 *lb./1 kg. lamb, trimmed and cut into 1-inch/2½-cm. cubes*

16 *small onions*

4 *green peppers, seeded and quartered*

1. In a large non-metallic bowl, combine the marinade ingredients listed above.

2. Add the lamb chunks and stir to coat well. Cover and marinate in refrigerator for 24 hours (turn lamb frequently while it marinates).

3. Preheat grill.

4. Parboil the onions for 6 minutes. Drain and reserve.

5. Drain marinated lamb and reserve marinade.

6. Thread 4 skewers with the marinated lamb, onions and pepper quarters, alternating ingredients.

7. Baste with the reserved marinade, then grill. (For pink lamb, grill 10 minutes; for well-done, 15 minutes.) Once or twice during grilling turn skewers and baste again.

8. Serve immediately with rice.

Serves 4

CANBERRA LAMB FONDUE

Australia

Preparation time: 20 minutes

Ingredients

Mint Sauce:

12 sprigs fresh mint, chopped

4 tablespoons wine vinegar

½ onion, finely chopped

⅓ pint/2 dl. corn or groundnut oil

2 teaspoons salt

Freshly ground pepper

Cooking time: at table

Garlic Sauce:

6 large cloves garlic, crushed

2 egg yolks

⅓ pint/2 dl. fine olive oil

Juice of ½ lemon

Salt

Freshly ground pepper

—

1½ pints/9 dl. corn or groundnut oil

1½ lb./700 g. leg of lamb, cubed

1. Combine the above-listed ingredients for the mint sauce. Mix well and reserve.

2. Prepare the garlic sauce: Beat the garlic and yolks together, add the oil drop by drop, beating constantly, as for a mayonnaise (page 476). When thickened, add the lemon juice, salt and pepper. Reserve.

3. Heat oil to 400°F., 204°C. (or until a bread cube browns in 1 minute) in a fondue pot or chafing dish. To serve, place the fondue pot on the table, keeping the temperature constant. Spear a cube of lamb and cook to desired doneness—rare: 10 to 20 seconds; medium: 40 seconds; well done: 1 to 1½ minutes. Dip in either the mint or garlic sauce.

Serves 3 to 4

MEATBALLS WITH EGG-LEMON SAUCE

Greece

Preparation time: 30 minutes   **Cooking time:** 20 minutes

Ingredients

2 slices white bread
1½ lb./700 g. lamb, minced
*   twice*
1 onion, chopped
1 clove garlic, crushed
Salt
Freshly ground pepper

Egg-Lemon Sauce:
3 egg yolks
Juice of 1 lemon
6 fl. oz./1¾ dl. water
Salt
Freshly ground pepper

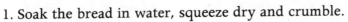

1. Soak the bread in water, squeeze dry and crumble.

2. In a blender or mixing bowl, combine the crumbled bread, lamb, onion, garlic, salt and pepper. Blend at high speed (or knead vigorously) until very smooth.

3. Form mixture into small teaspoon-size balls.

4. Drop the meatballs into a pot of lightly salted boiling water and poach over moderate heat until well cooked, about 20 minutes.

5. While the meatballs are poaching, prepare the sauce: a) In the top of a double saucepan, beat the egg yolks until light; b) add the lemon juice, water, salt and pepper and blend well; c) place over simmering water and heat gently until the sauce thickens slightly. (Do not allow the water under the sauce to boil.) Keep warm.

6. Drain the cooked meatballs thoroughly, then add them to the egg-lemon sauce and heat through. Serve immediately.

Serves 4

STUFFED VINE LEAVES

Turkey

Preparation time: 30 minutes   **Cooking time:** 1½ hours
Preserved vine leaves soak—20 minutes

Ingredients

20 large fresh vine leaves
  or a 1-lb./450-g. jar
  preserved vine leaves

Filling:

3½ oz./90 g. uncooked
  long-grain rice
1 lb./450 g. minced lamb
2 onions, finely chopped
1 clove garlic, crushed

1½ oz./40 g. seedless raisins
Salt
Freshly ground pepper
½ teaspoon cinnamon
—
Olive oil
1 egg yolk
1 tablespoon flour
¾ pint/4½ dl. beef stock

1. If fresh vine leaves are used, blanch in a pot of boiling water for 4 minutes, then refresh and drain. (Preserved leaves should be drained, then soaked in hot water for 20 minutes.)

2. Simmer the rice in a saucepan of boiling water for 5 minutes, then drain well and transfer to a mixing bowl. Add the other filling ingredients to the rice.

3. Spread out the vine leaves, vein side up. Place a spoonful of filling in each leaf centre, towards the stem end. Fold the leaf over the filling, tucking in the tip. Fold each side towards the middle, then roll up into a compact sausage-shape. Arrange in closely packed rows in a flameproof casserole coated with olive oil.

4. In a bowl, blend together the egg yolk, flour and a little of the beef stock. Mix until smooth, then blend in the remaining stock. Pour the stock mixture over the vine leaves, then weight with a heavy plate.

5. Cover casserole and cook until tender, about 1½ hours. Using a slotted spoon, transfer cooked vine leaves to a heated platter and top with an egg-lemon sauce (page 247).

Serves 4

CHRISTMAS BAKED HAM

Preparation time: 20 minutes   **Cooking time:** 3¾ hours

Sweden

Ingredients

*A 10- to 12-lb./4½- to 5½-
   kg. uncooked ham*

4 bay leaves

6 whole cloves

6 peppercorns

1½ pints/9 dl. Madeira

Coating:

1 egg white

1 tablespoon dry mustard

3 tablespoons brown sugar

*4 oz./100 g. dry bread-
   crumbs*

Sauce:

2 oz./50 g. butter

1 oz./25 g. flour

*¾ pint/4½ dl. stock from
   ham*

¾ pint/4½ dl. beef stock

*Cooked prunes and
   apple rings for garnish*

1. Place ham in a large pan and cover with boiling water. Add the seasonings and simmer until nearly tender, about 2½ hours. Drain, then pour in wine and simmer for 30 minutes more.

2. Preheat oven to 350°F., 180°C., Gas Mark 4. Combine the egg white, mustard and sugar. Mix thoroughly. Reserve.

3. Remove pan from heat and allow ham to cool slightly in liquid. Remove cooled ham from pan, reserving the wine. Strain the reserved wine and reserve ¾ pint/4½ dl. Skin ham but leave a collar of skin around the shank bone.

4. Place the ham in a roasting tin. Coat the surface of the meat with the egg white mixture, then pat on the bread-crumbs. Bake for 45 minutes.

5. For the sauce, melt the butter in a saucepan and blend in the flour; cook for 1 to 2 minutes. Gradually stir in the reserved wine stock and beef stock.

6. To serve, transfer the ham to a heated platter. Garnish with cooked prunes and apple rings. Serve the sauce in a heated gravy boat.

Serves 20

HAM AND CHICORY ROLLS AU GRATIN

Belgium

Preparation time: 15 minutes   **Cooking time:** 30 minutes

Ingredients

8 firm heads chicory

8 thin slices ham

Cheese Sauce:

1 oz./25 g. butter

1½ tablespoons flour

6 fl. oz./1¾ dl. milk

4 oz./100 g. Gruyère cheese, grated

Salt

Freshly ground pepper

1. Drop the heads of chicory into a saucepan of boiling water and cook for 2 minutes. Drain, then refresh under cold water and pat dry.

2. Roll up each head of chicory in a slice of the ham. Place rolls in a buttered baking dish. Reserve.

3. Set oven at 350°F., 180°C., Gas Mark 4.

4. Melt the butter in a saucepan, add the flour and milk, as for a béchamel sauce (page 471). Stirring constantly over low heat, gradually add half the grated cheese and cook until the cheese melts. Season to taste with salt and pepper. Keep warm.

5. Pour off any liquid that has accumulated in the baking dish, then cover the ham and chicory rolls with the sauce.

6. Top with the remaining grated cheese and bake for 30 minutes. Serve immediately.

Serves 4

ROAST PORK WITH APPLES

Preparation time: 15 minutes

Cooking time: 2¾ hours

The Netherlands

Ingredients

4 oz./100 g. butter

A 4-lb./1¾-kg. pork loin,
    boned and rolled

8 apples, peeled and sliced

Salt

Freshly ground pepper

1 teaspoon marjoram

1 teaspoon oregano

1 clove garlic, crushed

Juice of 2 oranges

1. Preheat oven to 350°F., 180°C., Gas Mark 4.

2. Melt the butter in a shallow roasting tin and brown the meat. Place in the oven and roast for ½ hour, then add the apples and seasonings. Continue roasting for a further 2¼ hours. Let the roast stand for 15 minutes, then carve and arrange on a serving platter with the apples.

3. Deglaze the pan with the orange juice and reduce the liquid slightly. Spoon over the meat and serve.

Serves 6

PORK WITH PLUM COMPOTE

France

Preparation time: 35 minutes   **Cooking time:** 2¼ hours

Ingredients

3 tablespoons olive oil
A 3-lb./1⅓-kg. pork loin
1½ oz./40 g. butter
Salt
Freshly ground pepper
2 teaspoons rosemary
1 teaspoon chopped sage
2 carrots, sliced
1 onion, sliced
3 cloves garlic, peeled

1 cabbage, cut into eighths
1 lb./450 g. potatoes,
 peeled
3 tablespoons chicken stock
Plum Compote:
1 lb./450 g. purple plums,
 halved and stoned
2 tablespoons sugar
1 tablespoon water
Peel of 1 lemon

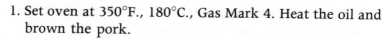

1. Set oven at 350°F., 180°C., Gas Mark 4. Heat the oil and brown the pork.

2. Melt the butter in a flameproof casserole and add the pork. Season with salt, pepper and herbs. Add the carrots, onions, and garlic. Cover and cook for 1¼ hours.

3. Blanch the cabbage in rapidly boiling salted water for 2 minutes. Remove and rinse under cold water. Drain.

4. After the pork has cooked for 1¼ hours add the potatoes and the cabbage. Baste with cooking juices. (Add 3 tablespoons chicken stock if there are not enough cooking juices for basting.) Season with salt and pepper. Re-cover and cook for another hour, basting a few times.

5. For the compote, put the plums in a saucepan with the sugar, water and lemon peel. Simmer until plums are soft, about 20 minutes; discard lemon peel.

6. Present the pork on a platter surrounded by the vegetables and sprinkled with 1 to 2 tablespoons of cooking juices. Serve the hot plum compote separately in a bowl.

Serves 4

ANDEAN-STYLE SWEET ROAST PORK

Peru

Preparation time: 35 minutes
Pork marinates—24 hours

Cooking time: 2¼ hours

Ingredients

A 3-lb./1⅓-kg. pork loin

1 tablespoon salt

Marinade:

⅓ pint/2 dl. dry white wine

4 whole cloves

2½ oz./65 g. brown sugar

—

2 oz./50 g. butter, melted

⅓ pint/2 dl. milk

½ teaspoon ground cinnamon

½ teaspoon nutmeg

4 oz./100 g. seedless raisins

1 oz./25 g. fresh bread-crumbs

1. Rub the pork loin with the salt. Let stand 20 minutes.

2. In a large non-metallic pan, combine marinade ingredients listed above. Add the pork loin, spooning marinade over meat to coat thoroughly. Cover and refrigerate 24 hours.

3. Preheat oven to 350°F., 180°C., Gas Mark 4.

4. Remove meat, pat dry and reserve.

5. Gradually add the melted butter, milk, cinnamon, nutmeg and raisins to the marinade. Mix thoroughly.

6. Sprinkle the pork with the breadcrumbs, then place in a roasting tin. Cover with the marinade mixture and cook until tender, about 2¼ hours. Baste meat frequently. Serve at once, spooning the gravy over the pork.

Serves 4

PORK STEWED IN CUMIN

Portugal

Preparation time: 20 minutes
Pork marinates—24 hours

Cooking time: 45 minutes

Ingredients

Marinade:

6 tablespoons white wine

Juice of 1 lemon

1½ teaspoons powdered cumin

3 cloves garlic, crushed

1 bay leaf

1 teaspoon salt

Freshly ground pepper

2 lb./1 kg. pork fillet, cubed

1½ tablespoons vegetable oil

2 tablespoons chopped parsley

Lemon wedges for garnish

Olives for garnish

—

1. In a shallow non-metallic bowl, combine the marinade ingredients.

2. Add the pork cubes and stir to coat thoroughly. Cover and refrigerate for 24 hours, turning meat occasionally.

3. Remove marinated pork from bowl with a slotted spoon. Pat dry. Reserve marinade.

4. Heat the oil in a heavy flameproof casserole, add the meat and sauté over moderately high heat until golden brown. Add the marinade. Reduce heat to low, cover and cook until the meat is tender, about 45 minutes. Lower heat, stir in parsley. Mix well and transfer to heated serving platter.

5. Garnish with lemon wedges and olives. Serve with fried potatoes.

Serves 4 to 6

SAVOY-STYLE FRICASSÉE OF PORK

France

Preparation time: 20 minutes **Cooking time:** 2 hours
Pork marinates—12 hours or overnight

Ingredients

Marinade:

¾ *pint/4½ dl. dry white wine*

2 tablespoons olive oil

Salt

6 peppercorns

2 onions, chopped

Bouquet garni (sage, rosemary, basil, chervil)

—

2 lb./1 kg. pork loin, cut into serving pieces

1½ oz./40 g. butter

2 tablespoons vegetable oil

1 tablespoon flour

1 tablespoon marinade (see above)

⅓ *pint/2 dl. red wine*

⅓ *pint/2 dl. water*

Salt

Freshly ground pepper

1 oz./25 g. butter

1 tablespoon flour

⅓ *pint/2 dl. cream*

8 slices French bread, fried in butter

1. Combine the above-listed marinade ingredients in a non-metallic bowl. Add the pieces of pork, cover and refrigerate for 12 hours or overnight. Remove the pieces of meat from the marinade and pat dry. Reserve 1 tablespoon of the marinade.

2. In a large frying pan, heat the butter and oil. Add the meat and sauté over moderate heat until nicely browned. Lower heat and sprinkle in the flour. Stir in the reserved marinade, then add the red wine and water. Season with salt and pepper. Bring to the boil, then lower heat, cover and simmer until the meat is tender, about 2 hours.

3. Prepare a *beurre manié* by combining the butter and flour. About 15 minutes before serving, thicken the sauce with the *beurre manié* and the cream. Serve garnished with fried bread.

Serves 4

PORK CHOPS BAKED WITH CABBAGE

France

Preparation time: 40 minutes

Cooking time: 40 minutes

Ingredients

1 cabbage, quartered
4 tablespoons cream
Salt
Freshly ground pepper
2 oz./50 g. butter
4 pork loin chops
6 tablespoons dry white wine

4 leaves fresh sage, chopped, or ¼ teaspoon dried sage
2 oz./50 g. Cantal or Cheddar cheese, grated

1. Blanch the cabbage quarters for 5 minutes in a large saucepan of boiling salted water. Refresh under cold running water, then drain and chop coarsely.

2. In a saucepan, combine the cabbage and cream. Season to taste with salt and pepper. Cover and cook over low heat for 15 minutes. Remove from heat.

3. Heat half the butter in a large frying pan and sauté the pork chops until nicely browned, about 10 minutes on each side. Season with salt and pepper. Remove chops from the pan and reserve.

4. Preheat oven to 325°F., 160°C., Gas Mark 3.

5. Add the wine and sage to the pan. Boil for a few minutes, then remove from heat and add the cabbage. Mix well.

6. Spread half the cabbage in a baking dish, add the chops and then cover with the remaining cabbage. Top with the grated cheese.

7. Dot with the remaining butter and bake, uncovered, for 40 minutes.

Serves 4

PORK CHOPS WITH SAUERKRAUT

Preparation time: 50 minutes   **Cooking time:** 45 minutes

Rumania

Ingredients

3 lb./1⅓ kg. sauerkraut

3 tablespoons vegetable oil

8 oz./225 g. bacon, diced

4 onions, chopped

2 cloves garlic, crushed

3 carrots, sliced

3 tablespoons tomato paste

Bouquet garni (juniper
   berries, peppercorns,
   parsley, bay leaf)

Salt

¾ pint/4½ dl. beer

¾ pint/4½ dl. beef or
   chicken stock

6 pork chops

Chopped fresh dill for
   garnish

⅓ pint/2 dl. soured cream

1. Briefly rinse the sauerkraut under cold running water. Squeeze out and reserve.

2. Heat half the oil in a flameproof casserole. Add the bacon and sauté until fat is rendered, about 10 minutes. Add the onions, garlic and carrots and sauté until golden, about 10 minutes.

3. Add the reserved sauerkraut and stir until coated with the fat. Blend in the tomato paste, then add the bouquet garni. Salt lightly. Pour in the beer and stock. Bring rapidly to the boil, then lower heat, cover and simmer for 20 minutes.

4. While the sauerkraut simmers, prepare the pork chops: Heat the remaining oil in a frying pan. Pat the chops dry, then sauté over moderately high heat until nicely browned on both sides.

5. Transfer the browned pork chops to the casserole, burying them in the sauerkraut. Cover and simmer until pork is tender, about 45 minutes.

6. Discard bouquet garni. Garnish with chopped fresh dill and serve accompanied by a dish of soured cream.

Serves 6

PORK FILLETS WITH PRUNES

France

Preparation time: 15 minutes
Prunes soak—overnight

Cooking time: 35 minutes

Ingredients

8 oz./225 g. dried stoned
  prunes

⅓ pint/2 dl. dry white wine

1½ lb./700 g. pork fillet
  (tenderloin) cut into
  1½-inch/4-cm. thick
  slices, flattened

1 oz./25 g. flour, seasoned
  with salt and pepper

1½ oz./40 g. butter

1 teaspoon redcurrant
  jelly

⅓ pint/2 dl. cream

1. Combine the prunes and wine in an enamelled cast-iron casserole. Soak prunes overnight.

2. Place the casserole over low heat and gently poach the prunes for 20 minutes. Remove from heat.

3. While the prunes are cooking, dust the pork fillets with the seasoned flour. Heat the butter in a frying pan and sauté the pork fillets for 10 minutes on each side. Lower heat, cover and cook for 10 minutes.

4. Using a slotted spoon, transfer the poached prunes to a heated serving dish. Surround with the fillets. Keep warm.

5. Pour the poaching liquid from the prunes into the juices in the meat pan. Over high heat, reduce liquid to about 6 tablespoons.

6. Lower heat to moderate. Stirring constantly, add the redcurrant jelly and the cream. Heat until sauce thickens slightly, then pour over the prunes and meat and serve immediately.

Serves 3 to 4

ROAST PORK STRIPS

Preparation time: 20 minutes
Pork marinates—3 hours

Cooking time: 50 minutes

China

Ingredients

1½ lb./700 g. pork tenderloin

Marinade:

3 tablespoons water

¼ teaspoon red food
  colouring

1½ tablespoons sugar

3 tablespoons soy sauce

1½ tablespoons hoisin
  sauce (optional)

1½ tablespoons Chinese
  rice wine or dry sherry

3 cloves garlic, crushed

½ teaspoon salt

1. Cut the pork into strips 5 inches/13 cm. long, 2 inches/5 cm. wide and 2 inches/5 cm. thick. Reserve.

2. In a shallow non-metallic dish, combine the marinade ingredients. Mix thoroughly. Add the pork strips to the marinade, coat well, then let stand at room temperature for 3 hours. (Baste strips with marinade from time to time.)

3. Preheat oven to 450°F., 230°C., Gas Mark 8.

4. Baste the pork one more time with the marinade, then transfer to a rack in a roasting tin. Discard marinade.

5. Place roasting tin on the top shelf of oven. Roast pork strips for 30 minutes, then turn meat over, baste with the pan juices and continue roasting until pork is tender, about 20 minutes. Transfer the roasted pork strips to a chopping board and slice at an angle into ¼-inch/5 mm.-thick pieces. Serve hot or cold.

Serves 3 to 4

SWEET AND SOUR PORK

China

Preparation time: 20 minutes
Batter stands—2 hours

Cooking time: 12 minutes

Ingredients

Batter:
4 oz./100 g. flour
½ teaspoon salt
1 egg, beaten
⅓ pint/2 dl. cold water

Marinade:
1½ tablespoons soy sauce
1½ tablespoons dry sherry
2 teaspoons sugar
—
1 lb./450 g. lean pork, cut
   in 1-inch/2½-cm. cubes
1¼ pints/7 dl. groundnut
   oil

Sweet and Sour Sauce:
2 cloves garlic, crushed

1½ tablespoons groundnut
   oil
3 green peppers, diced
2 oz./50 g. sweet pickled
   vegetables, chopped
6 fl. oz./1¾ dl. water
2 oz./50 g. sugar
1 tablespoon black treacle
6 tablespoons malt
   vinegar
1½ tablespoons tomato
   ketchup
1 tablespoon cornflour,
   dissolved in water

1. Combine the batter ingredients and beat until smooth.
   Let stand for 2 hours. Combine the marinade ingredients.
   Add the pork and let stand for 30 minutes.

2. Drain the pork and reserve the marinade. Heat the oil in
   a deep-frier until nearly smoking. Dip the pork in the
   batter and fry until brown, about 12 minutes. Drain.

3. Prepare the sauce: Add the garlic to the hot oil and fry,
   stirring, for ½ minute. Add the peppers and pickled
   vegetables and, still stirring, fry for 2 minutes. Blend in
   the water, reserved marinade, sugar, black treacle,
   vinegar and ketchup and stir for 3 minutes. Blend in the
   cornflour and simmer until sauce clears, about 2 minutes.
   Pour the sauce over the pork and serve.

Serves 2 to 3

BOK CHOY WITH PORK OR BEEF

Preparation time: 20 minutes   **Cooking time:** 8 minutes   *China*

Ingredients

*1 lb./450 g. bok choy
(Chinese cabbage) or
green cabbage*

*1 lb./450 g. pork tender-
loin or rump steak,
cubed*

Cornflour

1 egg white, beaten

*3 tablespoons groundnut
oil*

1 teaspoon salt

*1 teaspoon finely chopped
root ginger*

*1 tablespoon Chinese rice
wine or dry sherry*

1½ tablespoons soy sauce

¼ teaspoon sugar

1. Trim the leaves and stalks of the cabbage. Wash thoroughly and pat dry. Cut into 1- to 1½-inch/2½- to 4-cm. chunks. Reserve.

2. Dredge the pork (or beef) cubes in cornflour and dip in the egg white. (If using pork, omit egg white coating.)

3. Place a large frying pan over high heat for ½ minute. Swirl in 1½ tablespoons of the oil. Wait ½ minute, then reduce heat to moderate and add the stalks of cabbage. Fry, stirring, for 1 minute, then add the rest of the cabbage. Still stirring, fry until barely tender, about 1½ minutes. Remove pan from heat. Season with ½ teaspoon salt, then transfer to a heated serving platter. Keep warm.

4. Return pan to high heat. Wait ½ minute, then swirl in the remaining oil. Heat oil, then add the ginger and fry, stirring, for 1 minute. Add the meat and ½ teaspoon salt. Stirring continuously, fry meat until tender (pork—4 to 5 minutes; beef—2 to 3 minutes). Remove from heat.

5. One by one, add the rice wine (or sherry), soy sauce and sugar. Return pan to high heat and toss briefly. Pour over the bed of cabbage and serve immediately.

Serves 2 to 3

BEAN CURD AND PORK

China

Preparation time: 15 minutes
Dried shrimps soak—10 minutes

Cooking time: 7 minutes

Ingredients

1 tablespoon dried shrimps
8 oz./225 g. boneless lean pork, finely chopped
Cornflour
3 tablespoons groundnut oil
3 thick slices root ginger, peeled and finely chopped
1 chilli pepper, finely chopped
3 tablespoons soy sauce

1 tablespoon Chinese rice wine or dry sherry
½ teaspoon sugar
4 large spring onions, finely chopped
3 3-inch/7½-cm. square bean curd cakes
3 tablespoons chicken stock
1 tablespoon sesame seed oil

1. Soak the dried shrimps in cold water for 10 minutes. Drain.

2. Dredge the pork in cornflour. Place a large frying pan over high heat for ½ minute. Heat 1 tablespoon of the oil for ½ minute, then add the ginger, pork and chilli pepper. Fry, stirring, for 1½ minutes.

3. Stir in 2 tablespoons of the soy sauce, then add wine and sugar. Stir briskly for 1 minute, then mix in the white parts of the spring onions. Remove all ingredients from pan with a slotted spoon and reserve.

4. Add the remaining 2 tablespoons groundnut oil to the pan. Swirl over high heat for ½ minute, then add the bean curd cakes. Lower heat to moderate and fry, stirring, for 2 minutes, mashing down the cakes as they cook.

5. Stir in shrimps and remaining tablespoon soy sauce. Mix briefly. Return all ingredients to the pan and blend together. Add the chicken stock and the sesame oil. Stir briefly, then add the green portion of the spring onions. Toss lightly, transfer to a heated platter and serve.

Serves 2

STEAMED MINCED PORK

Preparation time: 10 minutes   **Cooking time:** 1½ hours
Chinese mushrooms soak—30 minutes

China

Ingredients

4 dried Chinese
  mushrooms

4 oz./100 g. canned water
  chestnuts, drained and
  chopped

1 lb./450 g. lean minced
  pork

3 tablespoons soy sauce

1½ tablespoons Chinese rice
  wine or dry sherry

Salt

1. Soak the Chinese mushrooms in a bowl of warm water
   for ½ hour. Remove with a slotted spoon, drain and pat
   dry. Discard stems. Chop caps finely.

2. In a bowl, combine the chopped mushroom caps with
   the water chestnuts and minced pork. Mix thoroughly,
   then gradually blend in the soy sauce, Chinese rice wine
   (or sherry) and salt.

3. Transfer mixture to an ovenproof serving bowl. Place
   bowl in a large pot of boiling water so that the water
   reaches two-thirds up the sides of the bowl. Cover pot
   and steam for 1½ hours.

4. Serve the pork cake in the bowl as an accompaniment to
   other Chinese dishes.

Serves 2 to 4

VARIATION: *Fifteen minutes before the end of cooking time, break
an egg over the pork cake. Re-cover and continue steaming until done.*

PORK SAUSAGES POACHED IN WHITE WINE

France

Preparation time: 20 minutes   **Cooking time:** 40 minutes

Ingredients

½ oz./15 g. butter

1 lb./450 g. best pork
   sausages

⅓ pint/2 dl. dry white wine

⅓ pint/2 dl. chicken stock

1 onion, chopped

2 cloves garlic, crushed

Bouquet garni (marjoram,
   mace, thyme, basil,
   peppercorns)

1 tablespoon tomato paste

1 lb./450 g. potatoes,
   peeled and halved

Salt

Freshly ground pepper

1 tablespoon chopped fresh
   parsley

1. In an enamelled cast-iron casserole, melt the butter and lightly brown the sausages. Cover with the wine and chicken stock. Add the onion, garlic, bouquet garni, tomato paste, potatoes, salt and pepper.

2. Bring to the boil. Cover and simmer gently for 40 minutes.

3. Transfer the sausages to a warmed platter and arrange the potatoes around them.

4. Skim fat from cooking liquid and reduce by half over moderately high heat. Correct seasoning and pour the strained liquid over the sausages. Sprinkle with the parsley.

Serves 2 to 4

Traditionally the people of Franche-Comté serve this dish with French bread and a selection of French mustards.

BRAISED PORK SAUSAGES WITH RED CABBAGE AND APPLES

Poland

Preparation time: 20 minutes   **Cooking time:** 45 minutes

Ingredients

1½ tablespoons vegetable
   oil

½ oz./15 g. butter

2 onions, chopped

1 small red cabbage,
   shredded

2 apples, peeled, cored
   and chopped

2 lb./1 kg. best pork
   sausages

Bay leaf

3 tablespoons red wine
   vinegar

6 tablespoons beef stock or
   water

Salt

Freshly ground pepper

1. Heat the oil and butter in a heavy pot or flameproof casserole. Add the chopped onions and sauté until tender, about 5 minutes.

2. Add the cabbage and apples. Mix well, then bury the sausages and bay leaf in the mixture.

3. Pour in the wine vinegar and stock (or water). Season with salt and pepper.

4. Cover pot and simmer over moderate heat for 45 minutes.

5. Discard bay leaf. Remove sausages from pot.

6. Transfer the cabbage mixture to a heated serving platter and arrange the sausages on top. Serve piping hot.

Serves 4 to 6

PHILADELPHIA SCRAPPLE

USA

Preparation time: 30 minutes **Cooking time:** 3½ hours

Ingredients

1 lb./450 g. pork shoulder
3 pigs' knuckles
½ teaspoon thyme
½ teaspoon marjoram
1 teaspoon sage
2 teaspoons salt

Freshly ground pepper
6 oz./175 g. buckwheat flour
6 oz./175 g. cornmeal
Flour for coating scrapple
Oil or butter for frying

1. Cover the meats with water and simmer until the meat separates easily from the bones, about 2½ hours.

2. Remove the meat from the bones and chop. Discard the bones. Strain the broth and return 1½ pints/9 dl. of broth to the pan. Add the chopped meats and the seasonings. Bring to the boil.

3. Combine the buckwheat and cornmeal with another 1½ pints/9 dl. broth, cooled. Pour into the pan and cook the mixture until thickened into a mush, about 1 hour.

4. Remove the scrapple from the heat and allow to cool. To serve, slice and coat lightly with flour. Fry in oil or butter until golden brown.

Serves 6 to 8

BAKED LIVER IN WINE SAUCE

Preparation time: 20 minutes   **Cooking time:** 40 minutes

Greece

Ingredients

2 tablespoons olive oil
3 onions, chopped
1 lb./450 g. pigs' liver,
  trimmed and cut in
  1-inch/2½-cm. squares
Flour for dredging liver
1½ tablespoons tomato
  paste

½ pint/3 dl. beef stock
⅓ pint/2 dl. red wine
Salt
Freshly ground pepper
Oregano
12 green olives, stoned

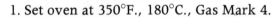

1. Set oven at 350°F., 180°C., Gas Mark 4.

2. Heat the olive oil in an enamelled cast-iron casserole. Add the onions and sauté over moderately high heat until golden, about 5 minutes. Remove with a slotted spoon and reserve.

3. Dredge the liver in flour.

4. Add the liver to the casserole and brown evenly, stirring over high heat for 2 minutes.

5. Add the tomato paste, stock, wine and the reserved onions. Season to taste with salt, pepper and oregano. Bring rapidly to the boil, then remove casserole from heat.

6. Cover and bake for 30 minutes, then add the olives. Re-cover and bake for 10 more minutes.

7. Serve with rice pilaf, if desired.

Serves 4

TONGUE WITH ALMOND SAUCE

Argentina

Preparation time: 20 minutes

Cooking time: 5½ hours

Ingredients

A 5- to 6-lb./2¼- to 2¾-kg.
 fresh ox tongue

1 onion studded with 2
 cloves

4 sprigs parsley

1 tablespoon salt

1 teaspoon oregano

4 peppercorns

2 bay leaves

Almond Sauce:

1 tablespoon olive oil

1 clove garlic, crushed

¾ pint/4½ dl. beef stock

2 oz./50 g. toasted
 almonds, slivered

2 teaspoons chopped
 fresh parsley

Dry breadcrumbs for
 thickening sauce
 (optional)

—

Capers for garnish

1. Rinse tongue and place in a large saucepan. Cover with cold water, then add the onion, parsley and seasonings.

2. Bring rapidly to the boil. Skim the surface, then lower heat, cover and simmer for 3 hours. Skim foam off surface of broth and turn tongue over. Re-cover and continue simmering until tender, about 2½ hours.

3. Remove pan from heat and allow tongue to cool slightly in its broth, then skin and trim gristle. Keep hot.

4. Prepare the almond sauce: a) Heat the olive oil in a small saucepan; b) add the garlic and sauté briefly, then add the stock, almonds and parsley; c) bring to the boil, then lower heat and simmer gently for 10 minutes. (If necessary, thicken with sifted dry breadcrumbs.)

5. To serve, slice tongue and arrange on a heated platter. Cover with the sauce and garnish with capers. Serve immediately.

Serves 6 to 10

TRIPE AND ONIONS

Preparation time: 40 minutes **Cooking time:** about 2½ hours

France

Ingredients

2 lb./1 kg. honeycomb tripe	Salt
1 onion stuck with 4 cloves	Freshly ground pepper
	1½ oz./40 g. butter
Bouquet garni (bay leaf, marjoram, peppercorns)	3 onions, sliced
	6 tablespoons olive oil
	3 tablespoons vinegar
2 carrots, quartered	Chopped fresh parsley

1. Wash tripe and blanch in boiling water for 2 minutes. Refresh under cold water and repeat process. Drain.

2. Put tripe in saucepan. Cover generously with cold water. Add the onion stuck with cloves, bouquet garni, carrots, salt and pepper. Cover and simmer until tender, about 2 hours.

3. Drain the tripe and pat dry. Cut into strips. Reserve.

4. Heat the butter in a frying pan, add the onions and cook over low heat for 20 minutes. Do not brown.

5. In another pan heat the oil and sauté the tripe until golden, about 10 minutes.

6. Add the sautéed onions to the tripe. Pour in the vinegar and heat through. Transfer to a heated platter and garnish with fresh chopped parsley.

Serves 6

Most tripe sold in the U.S., Britain and France has been cleaned, blanched and partly cooked. Additional cooking needed to make tripe tender may vary from 1 to 4 hours. Always check with the butcher how much longer it needs to be cooked. If the tripe has not been precooked, it will have to simmer 10 to 12 hours.

TRIPE IN WHITE WINE

France

Preparation time: 30 minutes

Cooking time: 4 hours

Ingredients

2 lb./1 kg. honeycomb
   tripe
2 leeks, thinly sliced
4 carrots, thinly sliced
10 small white onions
1 stick celery, thinly sliced
1 calf's foot or knuckle,
   quartered (optional)
2 cloves garlic, crushed

Bouquet garni (bay leaf,
   parsley, thyme,
   marjoram, peppercorns)
¼ teaspoon freshly grated
   nutmeg
Salt
Freshly ground pepper
1½ pints/9 dl. dry white
   wine
1½ pints/9 dl. water

1. Set oven at 300°F., 150°C., Gas Mark 2.

2. Prepare the tripe: Wash tripe under cold running water, then transfer to a large pot of rapidly boiling water and blanch for 2 minutes. Refresh tripe under cold water, then repeat blanching process. Drain tripe, dry throughly and cut into small serving pieces.

3. Line a buttered flameproof casserole with the leeks, carrots, onions and celery. Add the tripe pieces (calf's foot or knuckle), garlic, bouquet garni and nutmeg. Season with salt and pepper.

4. Pour in the wine and water and bring rapidly to the boil, then remove casserole from heat.

5. Cover casserole tightly and bake for at least 4 hours. (Since the flavour of the casserole improves with prolonged cooking, it may be cooked for much longer, if desired.)

Serves 4 to 6

LISBON-STYLE CALVES' LIVER

Preparation time: 10 minutes   **Cooking time:** 10 minutes

Liver marinates—24 hours

Portugal

Ingredients

Marinade:

⅓ *pint/2 dl. dry white wine*

1 bay leaf

2 cloves garlic, crushed

Salt

Freshly ground pepper

—

1 lb./450 g. calves' liver, thinly sliced

8 oz./225 g. bacon, diced

1. Combine the marinade ingredients in a shallow, non-metallic pan.

2. Add liver slices and stir to coat thoroughly. Cover and refrigerate for 24 hours, turning occasionally.

3. Remove liver slices, pat dry and reserve. Strain marinade and reserve.

4. In a frying pan, fry bacon until crisp. Add the liver and sauté over moderate heat until tender, about 3 minutes per side.

5. Transfer meat to a heated platter and keep warm.

6. Pour the reserved marinade into the pan and reduce by half over high heat.

7. Spoon reduced marinade over the liver and serve at once.

Serves 4

VEAL SWEETBREADS WITH SORREL

France

Preparation time: 40 minutes
Sweetbreads soak—4 hours

Cooking time: 40 minutes

Ingredients

1 lb./450 g. sweetbreads

3 tablespoons goose fat (page 475) or olive oil

8 small white onions

2 carrots, sliced

2 tomatoes, peeled, seeded and chopped

Salt

Freshly ground pepper

Bouquet garni (chervil, thyme, bay leaf, peppercorns)

6 tablespoons dry white wine

6 tablespoons stock

2 lb./1 kg. sorrel or spinach

1. Soak the sweetbreads in cold water until they turn white, about 4 hours. (Change the water every hour.) Drain sweetbreads, then blanch in a pot of simmering water for 10 minutes. Plunge them into ice water and soak for 5 minutes to firm. Remove and pat dry, then trim skin and membranes.

2. Heat 2 tablespoons of the goose fat (or oil) in a saucepan and brown the sweetbreads, onions and carrots. Add the tomatoes, salt, pepper, bouquet garni, wine and stock. Cover and simmer gently for 40 minutes.

3. Rinse the sorrel (or spinach) and trim the stalks. Blanch for 2 minutes in boiling salted water, then refresh. Drain well and chop. In another pan, heat the remaining fat. Add the sorrel, cover and cook gently for 20 minutes. Season to taste.

4. When the sweetbreads are done, discard bouquet garni and reserve juices. Arrange the sweetbreads and vegetables on a heated platter. Keep warm. Over high heat, reduce juice in saucepan by half. Strain and pour over the meat and vegetables.

Serves 4

CALVES' KIDNEYS IN MADEIRA SAUCE

France

Preparation time: 10 minutes   **Cooking time:** 15 minutes

Ingredients

2 whole calves' kidneys
2 oz./50 g. butter
8 oz./225 g. mushrooms, sliced
4 oz./100 g. ham, diced
Salt
Freshly ground pepper

2 tablespoons Calvados, warmed
6 tablespoons Madeira
6 tablespoons cream
1½ tablespoons chopped fresh parsley

1. Remove most of the fat and the very fine membrane from the kidneys. Slice and pat dry. Reserve.

2. Melt half the butter in a frying pan and sauté the mushrooms over high heat for 5 minutes. Add the ham and season with salt and pepper. Remove pan from heat.

3. In another pan, heat the remaining butter. Stirring constantly, sauté the kidneys over moderately high heat for about 6 minutes. Pour in the warmed Calvados and flambé. Remove pan from heat.

4. Add the Madeira to the pan with the mushrooms. Place over high heat. Stirring constantly, bring to the boil. Lower heat and stir in the cream. Heat slightly, then remove pan from cooker.

5. Add the kidneys to the mushrooms, sprinkle with the parsley and serve immediately. (The kidneys should not stand or they will get hard.)

Serves 2 to 3

This dish is often served with artichoke hearts braised in butter. Steamed rice would be another good accompaniment.

CALVES' KIDNEYS WITH NOODLES

France

Preparation time: 25 minutes   **Cooking time:** 25 minutes

Ingredients

2 whole calves' kidneys

12 oz./350 g. flat egg
  noodles

Salt

1½ oz./40 g. butter

2 tablespoons olive oil

1 clove garlic, crushed

3 shallots, finely chopped

Freshly ground pepper

2 tablespoons cognac,
  warmed

1. Preheat oven to 350°F., 180°C., Gas Mark 4.

2. Prepare the kidneys: a) Remove most of the fat as well as the very fine membrane; b) cut each kidney into four sections, following its natural divisions so that it will cook quickly and evenly; c) rinse very briefly under cold running water, pat dry and reserve.

3. Drop the noodles into salted boiling water and cook for 10 minutes.

4. While the noodles are cooking, sauté the kidneys in butter for about 10 minutes. Spoon butter over the kidneys as they cook. Drain the noodles and rinse with cold water.

5. In a separate pan, heat the olive oil and sauté the crushed garlic and the shallots. Add the noodles, coating them thoroughly with the oil. Season with salt and pepper and turn into a warm buttered baking dish.

6. Remove kidneys from heat, reserving pan juices. Slice the kidneys and season with salt and pepper. Place kidneys around noodles in the baking dish. Spoon half the pan juices onto the casserole. Bake for 15 minutes. Just before serving, add the warmed cognac to the remaining pan juices. Flambé and sprinkle over the top of the casserole.

Serves 4

LAMBS' KIDNEYS IN CHAMPAGNE SAUCE

France

Preparation time: 15 minutes   **Cooking time:** 25 minutes

Ingredients

10 lambs' kidneys, peeled
    and trimmed of fat
4 oz./100 g. butter
8 oz./225 g. mushrooms,
    sliced
Salt
Freshly ground pepper
Pinch grated nutmeg

2 tablespoons chopped
    fresh parsley
3 shallots, finely chopped
1 tablespoon flour
$\frac{1}{4}$ pint/$1\frac{1}{2}$ dl. champagne
    (or dry white wine)
$1\frac{1}{2}$ tablespoons beef stock
Juice of $\frac{1}{2}$ lemon

1. Prepare the kidneys by removing most of the fat and the fine membrane. Rinse under cold water. Pat dry and reserve.

2. Heat $1\frac{1}{2}$ oz./40 g. of the butter in a frying pan, add the mushrooms and sauté for 5 minutes. Remove from heat and sprinkle lightly with salt and pepper. Reserve.

3. In another pan, heat 2 oz./50 g. of the remaining butter. Add kidneys and cook over moderate heat for 5 minutes. Transfer the kidneys to a warm plate and season with salt, pepper, nutmeg and half the parsley. Keep warm.

4. In the same pan, cook the shallots over low heat until translucent. Stir in the flour and then add the wine and the stock. Blend well. Stir in the mushrooms. Cook sauce for 10 minutes, stirring to prevent boiling. Swirl in the rest of the butter and the lemon juice. Remove from heat.

5. Cut the kidneys crosswise into slices $\frac{1}{8}$ inch/3 mm. thick. Add the kidneys and the juices to the sauce. Return pan to low heat for a few minutes to allow kidneys to warm through. Garnish the dish with the remaining parsley.

Serves 4 to 5

CALVES' BRAINS IN BURGUNDY SAUCE

France

Preparation time: 45 minutes   **Cooking time:** 20–25 minutes
Brains soak—4 hours

Ingredients

1 lb./450 g. calves' brains	1¼ pints/7 dl. red wine
1 onion, sliced	1½ oz./40 g. butter
2 carrots, sliced	1 tablespoon flour
Bouquet garni (bay leaf, parsley, thyme)	1 egg yolk
1 clove garlic, crushed	8 slices French bread, fried in butter
Salt and pepper	Chopped fresh parsley
2 teaspoons sugar	

1. Soak brains in cold salted water until no traces of blood remain, about 4 hours. Remove the membrane enclosing the brains, rinse them under cold water and pat dry.

2. In a large saucepan combine the onion, carrots, bouquet garni, garlic, salt, pepper and sugar. Place the brains on top and pour in the wine. Bring to the boil, then lower heat, cover and simmer gently for 20 to 25 minutes.

3. Remove saucepan from heat and allow brains to cool in the sauce for 20 minutes. Remove brains and keep warm.

4. Strain the sauce through a sieve into a saucepan. Over high heat, reduce sauce to about ½ pint/3 dl.

5. Prepare a *beurre manié* by blending together the butter and flour. Beat the yolk well in a bowl. Beat in 3 tablespoons of the sauce, a tablespoon at a time. Slowly pour mixture into the remaining sauce, then beat in the *beurre manié*. Do not boil.

6. Slice the brains and arrange them in the centre of a warm serving dish. Surround with the fried bread, cover with the sauce and garnish with chopped parsley.

Serves 4

Composite Dishes and Casseroles

JANSSON'S TEMPTATION

Sweden

Preparation time: 15 minutes

Cooking time: 1 hour

Ingredients

8 medium potatoes,
  peeled and thinly sliced

Freshly ground pepper

2 onions, finely chopped

16 anchovy fillets,
  chopped

1 oz./25 g. dry bread-
  crumbs

12 fl. oz./3½ dl. double
  cream

1 oz./25 g. butter

1. Set oven at 375°F., 190°C., Gas Mark 5.

2. Place a layer of potatoes in a buttered ovenproof dish. Season lightly with pepper, then cover with a thin layer of onions and anchovies. Continue layering with the remaining potatoes, onions and anchovies, lightly seasoning the potato layers with pepper.

3. Sprinkle the top with the breadcrumbs, then pour in the cream and dot with the butter.

4. Bake until the potatoes are tender when tested with a knife, about 1 hour. Serve from the baking dish.

Serves 4

HERRING, POTATO AND ONION CASSEROLE

Sweden

Preparation time: 15 minutes   **Cooking time:** 50 minutes
Herring fillets soak—overnight

Ingredients

6 salt herring fillets	Freshly ground pepper
5 potatoes, peeled and sliced thinly	2 tablespoons dry bread-crumbs
4 onions, sliced thinly	1 oz./25 g. butter

1. Soak the salt herring fillets overnight in cold water.

2. Drain the herring fillets and pat dry, then cut into bite-size pieces.

3. Set oven at 400°F., 200°C., Gas Mark 6.

4. In a well-buttered rectangular baking dish, arrange the potatoes, herring and onions in alternating rows. Season lightly with pepper.

5. Sprinkle the top with breadcrumbs and dot with the butter.

6. Bake for 30 minutes, then turn oven heat down to 300°F., 150°C., Gas Mark 2 and continue baking until potatoes are tender, about 20 minutes. Serve immediately from the baking dish.

Serves 3 to 4

COBBLER'S PIE

Germany

Preparation time: 20 minutes
Herring fillets soak—4 hours

Cooking time: 1 hour

Ingredients

1 lb./450 g. herring fillets
¾ pint/4½ dl. soured cream
3 tablespoons milk
3 lb./1⅓ kg. cooked
  potatoes, thinly sliced
2 onions, minced

1 lb./450 g. cooked ham,
  cut in julienne strips
Dry breadcrumbs for
  topping pie
½ oz./15 g. butter

1. Soak the herring fillets for 4 hours in a bowl of cold water.

2. Drain herring fillets and pat dry, then mince. Reserve.

3. Set oven at 350°F., 180°C., Gas Mark 4.

4. In a bowl, blend together the soured cream and milk. Reserve.

5. Line the bottom of a well-buttered soufflé dish with a thin layer of sliced potatoes. Cover with a layer of minced herring and onions, then top with a layer of ham strips. Continue layering with the remaining potatoes, herring, onions and ham. (End with a layer of potatoes.)

6. Cover the mixture with the soured cream and milk mixture, then top with dry breadcrumbs and dot with the butter.

7. Bake cobbler's pie for 1 hour. Serve piping hot from the soufflé dish.

Serves 6

PAELLA VALENCIANA

Preparation time: 1 hour

Cooking time: 30–35 minutes

Spain

Ingredients

4 tablespoons olive oil

A 3-lb./1⅓-kg. frying chicken, cut into serving pieces

4 tablespoons water

1 large onion, chopped

1 clove garlic, crushed

2 oz./50 g. butter

1 lb./450 g. rice

¼ teaspoon saffron

1⅓ pints/8 dl. chicken stock

3 medium tomatoes, quartered

Salt

Freshly ground pepper

½ teaspoon cayenne pepper

A 2-lb./1-kg. lobster, cleaned and cut up (page 476)

1 lb./450 g. garlic sausage, sliced

6 oz./175 g. shelled peas

8 oz./225 g. cleaned and shelled prawns

18 mussels, cleaned

Fresh parsley for garnish

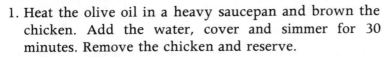

1. Heat the olive oil in a heavy saucepan and brown the chicken. Add the water, cover and simmer for 30 minutes. Remove the chicken and reserve.

2. In the same pan, cook the onion and garlic until soft, about 5 minutes. Add the butter, rice and saffron. Stir for 5 minutes to coat the rice thoroughly, then pour in the stock. Add the tomatoes and seasonings, cover and simmer for 15 minutes.

3. In a large baking dish, assemble the paella. Start with a layer of half the rice mixture and cover with layers of the chicken, lobster and sausage. Cover with the remaining rice. Bake, covered, for 20 minutes, then add the peas and prawns to the top layer of rice. Add the mussels, and more stock if the rice seems too dry. Cover the dish again and bake until the mussels open, about 12 minutes. Discard any mussels that do not open. Garnish with the parsley and serve.

Serves 8

LIBERIAN CHICKEN CASSEROLE

West Africa

Preparation time: 30 minutes

Cooking time: 30 minutes

Ingredients

3 tablespoons vegetable oil
*A 3-lb./1⅓-kg. chicken, cut
  into serving pieces*
8 oz./225 g. ham, chopped
2 onions, chopped
½ teaspoon ground allspice
Salt

Freshly ground pepper
8 oz./225 g. long-grain rice
6 tomatoes, peeled
6 oz./175 g. tomato paste
1¼ pints/7 dl. chicken stock
*8 oz./225 g. French beans,
  snapped*

1. Heat the oil in an enamelled cast-iron casserole. Add the chicken pieces and brown evenly over moderate heat.

2. Add the ham, onions and allspice to the casserole. Season with salt and pepper. Cook over moderate heat until the onions are tender, about 5 minutes.

3. Add the rice and mix well to coat grains. Stir in the tomatoes, tomato paste and chicken stock. Top with the French beans.

4. Cover casserole and simmer for 20 minutes.

5. Check amount of liquid in casserole. Add additional stock or water, if necessary, then cover casserole again and continue simmering until rice is done, about 10 minutes.

Serves 4

CHICKEN TETRAZZINI

Preparation time: 40 minutes   **Cooking time:** 20 minutes

Italy

Ingredients

Sauce:
4 oz./100 g. butter
2 tablespoons flour
1¼ pints/9 dl. milk
1 teaspoon salt
Freshly ground pepper
1 oz./25 g. Parmesan
　cheese, grated
1 egg yolk

—

6 oz./175 g. cooked
　chicken, cubed

4 oz./100 g. mushrooms,
　sliced
2 oz./50 g. butter
Salt
Freshly ground pepper
3 tablespoons white wine
1 lb./450 g. spaghettini
　(fine spaghetti)
4 oz./100 g. Parmesan
　cheese, grated
1½ tablespoons bread-
　crumbs

1. Prepare the sauce: Melt the butter in a saucepan and add
the flour. Stirring constantly, add the milk a little at a
time. Stir over low heat for 10 minutes. Add the salt and
pepper. Remove from the heat and stir in the cheese and
egg yolk. Reserve.

2. Sauté the chicken and mushrooms in the butter for about
3 minutes. Add salt, pepper and the wine and cook over
medium heat for about 5 minutes. Reserve.

3. Preheat the oven to 350°F., 180°C., Gas Mark 4.

4. Cook the spaghettini in boiling salted water until *al dente*,
about 6 to 8 minutes. Drain and return to pot. Add the
sauce, the chicken-mushroom mixture and the Parmesan
cheese. Mix well. Pour into a large buttered casserole and
sprinkle with the breadcrumbs. Bake for 20 minutes and
serve.

Serves 4 to 6

very tasty!

BEEF TAJINE

Morocco

Preparation time: 30 minutes   **Cooking time:** $1\frac{3}{4}$–$2\frac{1}{4}$ hours

Ingredients

2 lb./1 kg. topside, cubed
Salt
Freshly ground pepper
2 tablespoons olive oil
2 onions, chopped
1 teaspoon cumin
$\frac{1}{2}$ teaspoon ground ginger
$\frac{1}{2}$ teaspoon turmeric
Pinch cayenne pepper
1 cinnamon stick

6 tablespoons chopped
   parsley
4 tomatoes, peeled and
   chopped
2 tablespoons tomato
   paste
6 fl. oz./1$\frac{3}{4}$ dl. water
1 lb./450 g. green beans,
   sliced lengthwise
1 tablespoon sesame seeds,
   toasted

1. Pat the meat dry and season with salt and pepper. Heat the oil in a large flameproof casserole and brown the meat. Remove and reserve.

2. In the same pan, add the onions and sauté until lightly browned, about 10 minutes. Add the spices, parsley, tomatoes, tomato paste and water. Return the beef to the casserole, cover and simmer for $1\frac{1}{2}$ to 2 hours, stirring occasionally. Add more water if necessary.

3. In a separate saucepan, cook the green beans in boiling salted water until nearly tender. Reserve.

4. Preheat the oven to 400°F., 200°C., Gas Mark 6.

5. Place the green beans in the casserole, cover and bake in the oven for 15 minutes. Remove from the oven, sprinkle with the sesame seeds and serve with hot white rice.

Serves 4

DUTCH HOT POT

Preparation time: 30 minutes   **Cooking time:** 2 hours

The Netherlands

Ingredients

3 lb./1⅓ beef brisket
1 meat bone
5 onions, chopped
6 carrots, chopped
6 potatoes, cubed
3 knockwurst

3 tablespoons rendered
   beef suet or chicken fat
Salt
Freshly ground pepper
Cayenne pepper

1. Place the brisket and the meat bone in a large saucepan. Cover generously with cold water and bring to the boil over moderately high heat. Skim the surface of the water, then lower heat and simmer meat for 1½ hours.

2. Add the vegetables and knockwurst to the pan. Return to the boil, then lower heat and simmer until brisket is tender, about ½ hour. Remove saucepan from heat and discard the meat bone. Remove the brisket and knockwurst. Reserve.

3. Using a fine colander or sieve, drain the vegetables, then purée in a sieve or blender. Transfer vegetable purée to a mixing bowl. Blend in the suet (or fat), then season to taste with salt, pepper and cayenne. Reserve.

4. Remove the casing from the knockwurst. Slice the peeled knockwurst into ½-inch/1-cm.-thick rounds. Fold into the vegetable purée. Transfer mixture to a heated serving platter.

5. Slice the brisket. Arrange the slices on top of the vegetable purée and knockwurst. Serve immediately.

Serves 6

The strained cooking broth from this dish may be kept hot and used as an accompaniment to the dish, or it may be reserved for future use.

Very nice ✓

GOULASH WITH SAUERKRAUT

Austria

Preparation time: 30 minutes   **Cooking time:** 2½ hours

Ingredients

1½ lb./700 g. chuck steak, cubed

(Seasoned flour for *cornflour* dredging meat) *for thickening sauce*

2 tablespoons vegetable oil

2 large onions, chopped

1 clove garlic, chopped

4 tomatoes, peeled, seeded and chopped

1½ tablespoons tomato paste

2 carrots

Bouquet garni (parsley, bay leaf, thyme)

⅓ pint/2 dl. white wine (*used red*)

⅓ pint/2 dl. water

Salt

Freshly ground pepper

(12 oz./350 g. sauerkraut) *omitted*

3 potatoes, peeled

2 teaspoons paprika

(6 tablespoons soured cream) *1 small carton yoghurt*

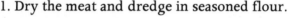

1. Dry the meat and dredge in seasoned flour.

2. Heat the oil in a large frying pan. Add the meat and brown evenly over moderately high heat. Using a slotted spoon, transfer meat to an enamelled cast-iron casserole. Reserve.

3. Add the onions to the pan and sauté until lightly browned, about 10 minutes. Transfer onions to the casserole. Add the garlic, tomatoes, tomato paste, bouquet garni, white wine and water. Season with salt and pepper. Bring to the boil, then lower heat. Cover and simmer for 1¾ hours.

4. While the casserole simmers, rinse the sauerkraut in cold water and squeeze dry. Add the sauerkraut, potatoes and paprika to the casserole. Re-cover and continue simmering until the potatoes are tender, about 45 minutes.

5. Correct seasoning. Stir in the soured cream and heat through. (Do not boil.)

Serves 3 to 4

CABBAGE ROLLS IN TOMATO SAUCE

USSR

Preparation time: 30 minutes   **Cooking time:** 35 minutes

Ingredients

12 large cabbage leaves

Stuffing:
1 large onion, chopped
3 oz./75 g. butter
1 lb./450 g. best minced beef
8 oz./225 g. minced pork
6 oz./175 g. cooked rice
1½ tablespoons chopped fresh parsley
1 egg, lightly beaten

Salt
Freshly ground pepper
Sour Cream Sauce:
1½ tablespoons flour
⅓ pint/2 dl. tomato juice
6 tablespoons water
⅓ pint/2 dl. soured cream
3 tablespoons chopped fresh dill
Salt
Freshly ground pepper

1. Blanch the trimmed cabbage leaves in a pot of boiling water for 5 minutes. Refresh and drain well.

2. Sauté the onion in 1 oz./25 g. of the butter. Combine the onion, meats, rice and parsley. Mix thoroughly, then bind with the egg and season with salt and pepper.

3. Flatten the cabbage leaves. Place a portion of the meat mixture on the end of each leaf. Roll up the leaves, tucking the edges around the mixture. Secure with string.

4. Sauté the rolls in the remaining butter until lightly browned, about 5 minutes. Reduce heat to low, cover pan and cook gently for 30 minutes. Remove from pan and discard string. Arrange on a heated platter and keep warm.

5. Stirring over moderate heat, add the flour to the pan and cook for 2 minutes. Blend in the tomato juice and water. Bring to the boil, blend in the soured cream, dill and salt and pepper. Pour sauce over the rolls and serve.

Serves 6

MINCED BEEF WITH RICE AND BEANS

Cuba

Preparation time: 20 minutes

Cooking time: 35 minutes

Ingredients

4 bacon rashers

1 large onion, chopped

2 cloves garlic, crushed

3 sticks celery, chopped

1 green pepper, seeded and chopped

1 pint/6 dl. water

Salt

8 oz./225 g. long-grain rice

1 lb./450 g. minced beef

3 tomatoes, peeled and quartered

A 16-oz./454-g. can kidney beans, partially drained

Freshly ground pepper

Dash of cumin

1. In a large frying pan, fry the bacon until crisp. Remove, drain and reserve. Sauté the onion, garlic, celery and green pepper in the bacon fat until soft, about 10 minutes.

2. Bring the water and ½ teaspoon salt to the boil in a saucepan. Add the rice, cover and simmer for 25 minutes.

3. Add the beef to the onion mixture, stirring constantly until the meat is browned. Add the tomatoes and kidney beans. Mix and season with salt, pepper and cumin. Cover and simmer over low heat for 20 minutes. Serve the bean mixture spooned over the rice and crumble the bacon on top.

Serves 4

HARICOT BEAN AND MEAT STEW

Preparation time: 30 minutes
Haricot beans soak—overnight

Cooking time: 4½ hours

Brazil

Ingredients

1¼ lb./600 g. dried haricot
  beans
A 4-lb./1¾-kg. pickled tongue
1 lb./450 g. pork sausages
A 1-lb./450-g. piece garlic
  sausage
An 8-oz./225-g. piece bacon
2½ lb./1¼ kg. chuck steak, cubed
1½ tablespoons oil

12 oz./350 g. onions,
  chopped
2 cloves garlic, crushed
3 tablespoons chopped
  parsley
1 lb./450 g. tomatoes,
  skinned
2 chilli peppers, chopped
Salt and pepper

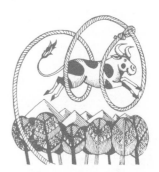

1. Soak the haricot beans and tongue overnight in separate
   bowls of cold water. Drain.

2. Place the tongue in a large saucepan and cover with fresh
   water. Simmer until tongue is tender, about 2½ hours.
   Remove from heat and cool tongue in its broth. Skin and
   trim the tongue.

3. Place the beans in a large saucepan and cover with cold
   water. Cover and simmer for 30 minutes.

4. Add all the meats to beans. Cover and simmer until the
   meats and beans are tender, about 2 hours.

5. Heat the oil in a frying pan. Sauté the onions, garlic,
   parsley, tomatoes and peppers until tender, about 5
   minutes. Add 4 oz./100 g. of the cooked beans to the
   vegetables and mash. Simmer for 5 minutes. Stir the
   vegetable mixture into the large pot of meat and beans.

6. Remove meats, slice and arrange on a heated platter.
   Traditionally, the tongue is placed in the middle, the
   smoked meats at one end and the fresh meats at the other.
   Serve the beans in a tureen with separate bowls of rice.

Serves 8 to 10

SOUTH AMERICAN MIXED-MEATS STEW

Uruguay

Preparation time: 25 minutes   **Cooking time:** 2 hours

Ingredients

2 lb./1 kg. stewing beef, cubed

A 3-lb./1⅓-kg. corner gammon

2 onions, quartered

3 carrots, sliced

½ small cabbage, cut in wedges

4 potatoes, peeled and quartered

1 stick celery, chopped

Small hot chilli peppers, to taste

8 oz./225 g. fresh corn kernels

1 green pepper, quartered

2 turnips, quartered

3 cloves garlic, crushed

3 sprigs fresh parsley, chopped

Bouquet garni (bay leaf, oregano, cumin)

Freshly ground pepper

7 oz./200 g. chick-peas, cooked

1. Place the beef and gammon in a large saucepan. Cover with cold water and bring to the boil. Reduce heat, skim the surface and simmer until tender, about 1½ hours.

2. Add the remaining ingredients. Bring rapidly to the boil, then lower heat, cover and simmer until vegetables are tender, about 30 minutes. Skim the fat from the broth and correct seasoning. Discard the bouquet garni.

3. Transfer the gammon to a carving board. Slice into bite-sized pieces. Return to the casserole and heat through. To serve, arrange the meats and vegetables on a heated serving platter. Serve the broth in a tureen.

Serves 6 to 8

CORSICAN MEAT AND MACARONI CASSEROLE

France

Preparation time: 25 minutes   **Cooking time:** 3 hours

Ingredients

6 tablespoons olive oil

6 bacon rashers

8 oz./225 g. braising steak, cubed

8 oz./225 g. veal shoulder, cubed

8 oz./225 g. pork shoulder, cubed

1 onion, sliced

1 clove garlic, crushed

1 tomato, chopped

1½ pints/9 dl. red wine

⅓ pint/2 dl. water

Salt

Freshly ground pepper

Bouquet garni (rosemary, bay leaf, parsley)

8 oz./225 g. macaroni

6 oz./175 g. Gruyère or other Swiss cheese, grated

1. Heat the olive oil in a large frying pan. Sauté the bacon rashers and the meats over moderately high heat until nicely browned, about 10 minutes. Remove and drain.

2. Transfer the meats to an enamelled cast-iron casserole. Add the onion, garlic and tomato. Pour in the wine and water. Salt and pepper to taste, then add the bouquet garni. Bring to the boil, then lower heat, cover and simmer gently until meats are tender, about 2½ hours.

3. Set oven at 350°F., 180°C., Gas Mark 4.

4. Drop the macaroni into a pot of boiling, salted water. Cook until *al dente*, about 15 minutes, then drain.

5. When the meats are tender, remove with a slotted spoon and reserve. Reduce casserole liquid to ¾ pint/4½ dl. over high heat. Arrange a layer of meat in a large ovenproof dish. Cover with a layer of macaroni and then a layer of cheese. Pour in the reduced casserole liquid and bake for 20 minutes.

Serves 4

COTTAGE PIE

Great Britain

Preparation time: 35 minutes   **Cooking time:** 15 minutes

Ingredients

3 oz./75 g. butter
2 onions, chopped
2 cloves garlic, minced
1 lb./450 g. minced beef
4 carrots, sliced
1½ tablespoons tomato
   paste
1½ tablespoons chopped
   fresh parsley
1 tablespoon dried thyme

1 bay leaf
½ pint/3 dl. beef stock
Salt
Freshly ground pepper
6 medium potatoes,
   peeled
1 sprig mint
1 oz./25 g. Swiss or
   Cheddar cheese, grated

1. Heat 1 oz./25 g. of the butter in a frying pan. Sauté the onions, garlic and beef over moderate heat for 10 minutes. Add carrots, tomato paste, herbs and stock. Mix thoroughly, then season heavily with salt and pepper. Bring mixture to the boil, then lower heat and simmer until most of the stock has evaporated and the carrots are tender, about 20 minutes. Discard bay leaf. Keep warm.

2. While the meat mixture simmers, drop the potatoes and mint into a pot of rapidly boiling salted water and cook until tender, about 20 minutes. Drain, and discard the mint. Return the potatoes to the pot and toss briefly over low heat to remove excess moisture. Transfer potatoes to a bowl and mash well. Beat in the remaining butter and season to taste with salt and pepper.

3. Set oven at 375°F., 190°C., Gas Mark 5 or preheat grill.

4. Spoon the meat mixture into an ovenproof dish. Cover with the mashed potatoes, smoothing the surface. Sprinkle with the grated cheese, then bake for 15 minutes or place briefly under grill.

Serves 4

MEAT TIMBALES

Preparation time: 20 minutes   **Cooking time:** 45 minutes

South Africa

Ingredients

1 oz./25 g. butter
1 onion, chopped
1 clove garlic, crushed
1 slice white bread
⅓ pint/2 dl. milk
2 eggs, beaten
1 lb./450 g. minced beef or
  lamb
1 tablespoon curry
  powder

Juice of 1 lemon
1 oz./25 g. almonds,
  chopped
8 dried apricots, soaked
  and chopped
1½ oz./40 g. raisins
3 tablespoons chutney
Salt
Freshly ground pepper

1. Preheat oven to 350°F., 180°C., Gas Mark 4.

2. Melt the butter and sauté the onion and garlic for 10 minutes.

3. Soak the bread in the milk, then squeeze dry. Beat the eggs into the milk.

4. Combine the meat, bread and onions with the remaining ingredients. Stir in half the egg-milk mixture.

5. Place the mixture in a greased baking dish or 4 to 6 individual ovenproof dishes. Top with the remaining egg mixture and bake until the custard sets, about 45 minutes. Serve with plain rice.

Serves 4 to 6

BEEF, LAMB AND PORK HOT POT

Finland

Preparation time: 5 minutes   **Cooking time:** 5 hours

Ingredients

1 lb./450 g. chuck steak, cut into 1½-inch/4-cm. cubes

1 lb./450 g. boneless stewing lamb or mutton, cut into 1½-inch/4-cm. cubes

1 lb./450 g. boneless pork shoulder, cut into 1½-inch/4-cm. cubes

5 onions, thinly sliced

Allspice

Salt

1½ pints/9 dl. hot water or beef stock

1. Set oven at 275°F., 140°C., Gas Mark 1.

2. Layer the meats and sliced onion in an enamelled cast-iron casserole, alternating the ingredients. Season each layer with allspice and salt.

3. Pour in the water or stock, cover and bake until the meats are tender, about 5 hours.

Serves 8

GASCON LAMB AND CHICKEN BOILED DINNER

France

Preparation time: 20 minutes   **Cooking time:** 3 hours

Ingredients

A 4-lb./1¾-kg. shoulder of
   lamb

1 veal knuckle

Bouquet garni (juniper
   berries, bay leaf,
   parsley, thyme)

1 celery stick with leaves

1 onion stuck with 3 cloves

2 cloves garlic

Salt

Freshly ground pepper

A 3-lb./1⅓-kg. chicken,
   trussed

8 carrots, quartered

3 small white turnips,
   scraped

4 leeks

⅓ pint/2 dl. dry white wine

1. Put the lamb and veal knuckle in a large saucepan. Cover with cold water.

2. Bring to the boil. Skimming the surface occasionally, continue to boil until the broth is clear.

3. Add the bouquet garni, celery, onion, garlic, salt and pepper. Lower heat, cover and simmer for 1½ hours.

4. Add the chicken, carrots, turnips, leeks and wine. Continue cooking until chicken is tender, about 1½ hours. Taste and correct seasoning, if necessary.

5. To serve, arrange the meats, chicken and vegetables on a hot platter and strain the broth into a warmed soup tureen.

Serves 8

LAMB AND CHICKEN STEW WITH COUSCOUS

Morocco

Preparation time: 1½ hours
Couscous stands—15 minutes

Cooking time: 2 hours

Ingredients

6 tablespoons olive oil

3 lb./1⅓ kg. lamb, cubed

A 3-lb./1⅓-kg. chicken, cut into serving pieces

3 onions, chopped

3 leeks, cleaned and split

3 green peppers, seeded and cut in strips

4 carrots, cut in 2-inch/ 5-cm. lengths

4 turnips, cut in 2-inch/ 5-cm. lengths

2 cloves garlic, crushed

1 tablespoon coriander

Salt

Freshly ground pepper

Couscous:

1 lb./450 g. couscous (wheat-grain semolina)

1 teaspoon saffron

⅓ pint/2 dl. hot water

1½ oz./40 g. butter, at room temperature

3 tablespoons olive oil
—
4 oz./100 g. raisins

3 courgettes, sliced

3 tomatoes, peeled and quartered

1 teaspoon paprika

A 20-oz./567-g. can chick-peas

Hot Sauce:

¾ pint/4½ dl. meat-vegetable broth

⅛ teaspoon turmeric

1 teaspoon grated fresh root ginger

½ to ¾ teaspoon harissa (red pimento concentrate) or cayenne pepper

½ teaspoon grated nutmeg

1. Heat the olive oil in the bottom section of a *couscoussière* or in a large saucepan. Add the lamb, chicken, onions, leeks, peppers, carrots and turnips. Sauté evenly over moderately high heat until lightly browned, about 10 minutes. Cover the meats and vegetables with cold water. Add the garlic, coriander and season to taste with salt and pepper. Bring rapidly to the boil, then lower heat and simmer for about 2 hours in total.

2. Meanwhile prepare the *couscous*: a) Spread out the

couscous on a large platter; sprinkle on the saffron and hot water, then dot with $\frac{1}{2}$ oz./15 g. of the butter; b) rub the moistened grains between your palms until the water has been completely absorbed, then cover platter tightly with aluminium foil and let stand 15 minutes; c) stir the *couscous* thoroughly, then transfer it to the upper section of the *couscoussière* (or a muslin-lined sieve that fits snugly above the simmering stew in the saucepan); d) place on top of the meats and vegetables and steam until the grains are puffy, about 30 to 45 minutes. Spread the *couscous* on a platter and sprinkle with a little cold water, the olive oil and $\frac{1}{2}$ oz./15 g. butter.

Morocco

3. Add the raisins, courgettes, tomatoes and paprika to the simmering stew. Mix thoroughly. Continue simmering.

4. Place the top section of the *couscoussière* over the simmering stew again. A handful at a time, add the *couscous* to the *couscoussière*, making sure each addition has warmed thoroughly before adding the next. Steam until grains are swollen and separate, about 30 minutes.

5. While the *couscous* steams, drain the chick-peas, then transfer to a sieve and steam over lightly salted boiling water until tender, about 20 minutes. Drain and keep hot.

6. When the *couscous* is done, transfer to a platter and work in the remaining butter. Keep hot. When meats and vegetables are done, remove and keep warm. Strain the cooking liquid into a saucepan and keep hot.

7. Prepare the hot sauce: Transfer $\frac{3}{4}$ pint/$4\frac{1}{2}$ dl. of the strained broth to another saucepan. Bring to the boil, then stir in the turmeric, ginger, harissa (or cayenne pepper) and nutmeg. Keep hot.

8. To serve, pile the *couscous* in the centre of a large wooden or earthenware serving platter. Make a well in the centre and fill with the meats and vegetables. Surround with the chick-peas. Serve the hot sauce and meat-vegetable broth separately. Or serve as picture facing page 320.

Serves 8

AEGEAN PASTA WITH LAMB

Greece

Preparation time: 1½ hours

Cooking time: 45 minutes

Ingredients

1 lb./450 g. minced lamb

2 onions, chopped

5 garlic cloves, crushed

2½ oz./65 g. butter

A 28-oz./681-g. can Italian
  plum tomatoes, chopped

Pinch oregano

Salt and pepper

¼ teaspoon each nutmeg,
  allspice and cinnamon

3 eggs, lightly beaten

3 oz./75 g. Parmesan, grated

1 large aubergine, peeled
  and thinly sliced

Olive oil

12 oz./350 g. macaroni,
  cooked

Custard Sauce:

1 oz./25 g. butter

1½ tablespoons flour

1¼ pints/7 dl. milk, heated

Salt and pepper

4 eggs, lightly beaten

8 oz./225 g. Ricotta cheese

1. Sauté the lamb, onions and garlic in 1½ oz./40 g. butter for 10 minutes. Blend in the tomatoes and seasonings. Cook uncovered until the liquid is nearly evaporated, about 45 minutes. Remove from heat and allow to cool slightly, then stir in the eggs and 2 oz./50 g. cheese.

2. Preheat grill. Arrange the aubergine on a baking sheet, sprinkle lightly with olive oil and grill until both sides are golden. Turn oven to 325°F., 160°C., Gas Mark 3.

3. Add the macaroni to the meat mixture. Pour into a greased baking dish. Sprinkle with half the remaining Parmesan cheese, then layer in the aubergine slices.

4. Melt the butter for the custard sauce. Sprinkle in the flour and stir over low heat for 2 minutes. Add the milk, salt and pepper, stir over low heat until mixture thickens, 2 minutes. Blend a little of the heated mixture into the eggs, then stir the eggs into the saucepan. Blend in the Ricotta. Pour the custard over the aubergine. Dot with remaining butter and cheese. Bake until set.

Serves 6

MOUSSAKA

Preparation time: 30 minutes
Aubergine stands—1 hour

Cooking time: 1¼ hours

Bulgaria

Ingredients

*4 medium aubergines,
  peeled and sliced*
1 onion, chopped
1 oz./25 g. butter
2 lb./1 kg. minced lamb
2 teaspoons salt
1 teaspoon paprika

Freshly ground pepper
Pinch oregano
Olive oil
4 tomatoes, sliced
⅓ pint/2 dl. yoghurt
4 egg yolks
2 oz./50 g. flour

1. Salt both sides of the aubergine slices and let stand 1 hour.

2. Sauté the onion in the butter for 10 minutes. Add the lamb, salt, paprika, pepper and oregano. Brown the mixture and reserve.

3. Preheat the oven to 350°F., 180°C., Gas Mark 4.

4. Rinse the aubergine slices and pat dry. Sprinkle with olive oil and grill until lightly browned on one side, then turn and grill on other side.

5. In a greased baking dish, arrange alternate layers of the meat mixture with the aubergine slices. Top with the tomato slices. Bake for 1 hour.

6. Combine the yoghurt, egg yolks and flour, mixing well. Pour over the casserole and bake until custard is golden, about 15 minutes.

Serves 6

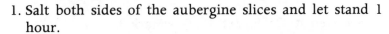

ALSATIAN MEAT AND POTATO CASSEROLE

France

Preparation time: 20 minutes   **Cooking time:** 2 hours

Ingredients

*2½ lb./1¼ kg. potatoes,
  peeled and thinly sliced*

*12 oz./350 g. lean pork
  (boned), thinly sliced*

*12 oz./350 g. lamb (boned
  shoulder), thinly sliced*

*1 lb./450 g. onions, thinly
  sliced*

Salt

Freshly ground pepper

Freshly grated nutmeg

*Bouquet garni (bay leaf,
  parsley, thyme)*

1 oz./25 g. butter

1 pint/6 dl. dry white wine

1. Set oven at 325°F., 160°C., Gas Mark 3.

2. Place a layer of potatoes in a buttered casserole, add a layer of pork and lamb and then a layer of onions. Season with salt, pepper and a dash of nutmeg. Continue alternating layers, seasoning each layer with salt, pepper and nutmeg and finishing with a layer of potatoes.

3. Bury the bouquet garni in the middle of the casserole, then dot casserole with the butter and pour in the white wine.

4. Cover tightly and bake until meat is tender, about 2 hours. Serve from the casserole.

Serves 4 to 6

ANDALUSIAN STEW

Preparation time: 30 minutes
Chick-peas soak—overnight

Cooking time: 2 hours

Spain

Ingredients

3 tablespoons olive oil

4 oz./100 g. salt pork, diced

4 oz./100 g. bacon, cubed

12 oz./350 g. pork loin, cubed

12 oz./350 g. chicken, chopped

Salt

Freshly ground pepper

3 pints/1½ litres cold water

8 oz./225 g. soaked chick-peas

6 turnips, peeled and diced

4 carrots, chopped

4 onions, quartered

8 oz./225 g. green beans

1 small cabbage, quartered

3 medium potatoes, quartered

3 cloves garlic, crushed

Pinch saffron

½ teaspoon cumin

Pinch coriander

1. In a large flameproof casserole, heat the olive oil. Add the salt pork and sauté over fairly high heat for 5 minutes. Remove with a slotted spoon and reserve.

2. Add the pieces of bacon, pork and chicken to the casserole. Brown over high heat then season with salt and pepper.

3. Return the reserved salt pork to the casserole. Pour in the cold water and bring rapidly to the boil. Skim the surface. Add the chick-peas and return to the boil, then lower heat, cover and simmer gently for 1½ hours. Add the vegetables, re-cover and continue simmering for ½ hour.

4. Season the stew with the garlic, saffron, cumin and coriander, then remove vegetables and meats with a slotted spoon and arrange on a heated serving platter. Bring broth to the boil and reduce slightly over high heat. Pour broth over meat and vegetables. Serve immediately.

Serves 4 to 6

CASSOULET

France

Preparation time: 1¼ hours
Beans soak—overnight

Cooking time: 3 hours

Ingredients

1½ lb./700 g. dried haricot beans
1¾ pints/1 litre beef stock
4 oz./100 g. pork rind or bacon, blanched
2 carrots, quartered
3 whole cloves garlic
1 onion
2 tablespoons flour
6 tablespoons tomato purée
8 tablespoons pork fat
8 oz./225 g. pork, cubed

1 lb./450 g. lamb, cubed
4 oz./100 g. salt pork, cubed
2 onions, chopped
3 cloves garlic, minced
Bouquet garni (thyme, bay leaf, rosemary)
Salt and pepper
12 oz./350 g. garlic sausage
8 oz./225 g. pork sausages
2 oz./50 g. breadcrumbs
3 tablespoons fresh parsley

1. Soak the beans overnight in cold water. Drain and place in a large saucepan. Add the stock, pork rind, carrots, garlic and onion. Cover and simmer for 1 hour. Remove the pork rind and the beans. Reserve. Strain the liquid, stir in the flour mixed with the tomato purée. Discard the vegetables.

2. Heat 5 tablespoons of the fat and brown the cubed meats. Pour in the bean liquid, then add the onions and seasonings. Cover and simmer for 1¾ hours, then add the garlic sausage in one piece. Simmer for 20 minutes.

3. Set oven at 350°F., 180°C., Gas Mark 4. Heat the remaining fat and brown the pork sausages. Slice the pork rind and layer in a large casserole. Add half the beans.

4. Discard bouquet garni. Transfer cubed meats to the beans. Cover with remaining beans, then add the sausages and sliced garlic sausage. Pour in the liquid from the casserole, sprinkle with breadcrumbs and parsley and bake for 1 hour.

Serves 8

PORK AND SEAFOOD MAGELLAN

Preparation time: 30 minutes
Pork marinates—overnight

Cooking time: 1 hour

Portugal

Ingredients

Marinade:

¼ pint/1½ dl. dry white
   wine

1 tablespoon paprika

1 bay leaf

2 cloves

3 cloves garlic, crushed

—

2 lb./1 kg. lean boneless
   pork, cubed

1 oz./25 g. lard

2 onions, sliced

2 cloves garlic, crushed

4 tomatoes, chopped

2 lb./1 kg. clams or
   mussels, scrubbed

Chopped fresh parsley

Chopped fresh thyme

Lemon wedges

1. Combine the marinade ingredients and coat the pork cubes thoroughly. Cover bowl and refrigerate overnight, turning occasionally. Remove pork from marinade and pat dry. Reserve the marinade.

2. Heat half of the lard in a large frying pan and brown the pork. Add the marinade to the pan, cover and simmer for 40 minutes. Remove cover before end of cooking time to reduce liquid by half. Reserve.

3. Melt the remaining lard and sauté the onions and garlic for 5 minutes. Add the tomatoes, the reserved pork and its liquid. Simmer for 10 minutes.

4. Add the clams, cover and simmer over moderate heat until the clams open, about 5 minutes. Discard bay leaf and any clams that do not open. Arrange the pork and clams (in their shells) on a heated serving platter. Top with the sauce from the casserole, then garnish with parsley, thyme and lemon wedges.

Serves 6

PORK AND SAUERKRAUT

France

Preparation time: 20 minutes   **Cooking time:** 4 hours

Ingredients

2 onions, sliced

2 tablespoons goose fat
(page 475) or olive oil

1 lb./450 g. sauerkraut,
rinsed and drained

2 apples, peeled and sliced

20 juniper berries

6 to 8 peppercorns

¾ pint/4½ dl. dry white
wine

¾ pint/4½ dl. beef stock

A 1-lb./450-g. piece of
lean bacon or salt pork

4 pork loin chops

2 tablespoons kirsch

8 potatoes, in jackets

4 frankfurters

1. In a large enamelled cast-iron casserole, sauté the onions
in the goose fat (or oil). Add the sauerkraut and apples.
Tie the juniper berries and peppercorns in muslin and
add to the pot. Pour in enough wine and stock to cover
the sauerkraut. Cover and cook over low heat for 2½
hours.

2. While the sauerkraut is stewing, blanch the bacon (or
salt pork) in plenty of simmering water for 15 minutes.
Drain.

3. Add the bacon and the pork chops to the sauerkraut.
Cover and simmer for 1 hour, then stir in the kirsch, re-
cover and continue simmering for an additional 30
minutes.

4. Boil the potatoes in salted water until tender and then
peel. Keep warm.

5. In a separate saucepan, simmer the frankfurters in water
for 15 minutes.

6. Place the sauerkraut in a serving dish. Cut the bacon into
slices and arrange on top with the chops. Surround the
sauerkraut with the potatoes and frankfurters.

Serves 4

PORK AND VEAL PIE

Preparation time: 25 minutes
Meats marinate—24 hours

Cooking time: 50 minutes
Pastry chills—1 hour

France

Ingredients

8 oz./225 g. pork fillet
8 oz./225 g. veal

Marinade:
6 tablespoons dry white wine
2 shallots, finely chopped
2 teaspoons salt
Freshly ground pepper
$\frac{1}{8}$ teaspoon allspice

Flaky Pastry:
8 oz./225 g. flour
1 teaspoon salt
6 oz./175 g. butter
7 tablespoons iced water
—
3 eggs
6 tablespoons cream

1. Cut the pork fillet and the veal into julienne strips.

2. In a glass bowl, combine the marinade ingredients listed above. Add the pork and veal. Cover and marinate in the refrigerator for 24 hours.

3. Prepare flaky pastry (page 474) with the ingredients listed above. Chill for 1 hour.

4. Set oven at 425°F., 220°C., Gas Mark 7. Roll out two-thirds of the pastry into a rectangle $\frac{1}{4}$ inch/5 mm. thick. Place on a buttered baking sheet.

5. Drain the marinated meats and pat dry. Arrange on the pastry, leaving a $\frac{3}{4}$-inch/2-cm. margin around the edge of the pastry. Roll out the rest of the pastry to form the top crust. (This should be thinner than the bottom portion.) Place pastry top over the meat, moisten the edges and seal. Cut a $\frac{1}{2}$-inch/1-cm. opening in the top crust.

6. Beat 1 egg well in a small bowl, then brush on the top crust for a glaze. Bake pie for 40 minutes. Remove from oven. Beat together the remaining eggs and the cream. Pour the mixture into the pie opening. Return pie to oven for 10 more minutes. Serve immediately.

Serves 4 to 6

EASTER PIE

France

Preparation time: 30 minutes **Cooking time:** 40–45 minutes
Pastry chills—2 hours

Ingredients

Flaky Pastry:
8 oz./225 g. flour
1 teaspoon salt
6 oz./175 g. butter
7 tablespoons ice water

Filling:
1 lb./450 g. sausage meat
2 tablespoons chopped
   fresh parsley

1 tablespoon salt
1 tablespoon pepper
⅛ teaspoon ground allspice
4 hard-boiled eggs,
   peeled and halved

—

1 beaten egg for glazing

1. Using the ingredients listed above, prepare the flaky pastry (page 474). Chill for 2 hours.

2. In a bowl, combine the sausage meat, parsley, salt, pepper and allspice.

3. Set oven at 425°F., 220°C., Gas Mark 7. Roll out two-thirds of the pastry into a rectangle about ¼ inch/5 mm. thick. Cut off the corners to form a 6-sided piece of pastry. Place on a buttered baking sheet.

4. Spread half the sausage mixture in the middle of the pastry, leaving a fairly wide border. Place the hard-boiled eggs on top, cut side down, then add the rest of the filling.

5. Cover filling with a 6-sided pastry lid made from remaining dough. Moisten, pinch and seal the edges. Make 2 or 3 slits in the lid. Brush pie with the beaten egg and bake for 40 to 45 minutes. Serve at room temperature.

Serves 4

HAM AND PORK CUSTARD

Preparation time: 10 minutes   **Cooking time:** 30 minutes

France

Ingredients

8 oz./225 g. ham, sliced
8 oz./225 g. cooked pork, sliced
1¼ pints/7 dl. milk

Salt
6 eggs
4 tablespoons flour
½ oz./15 g. butter

1. Set oven at 325°F., 160°C., Gas Mark 3.

2. Arrange the meats in a buttered 3½-pint/2-litre flame-proof dish. Reserve.

3. Pour the milk into a saucepan, salt lightly, bring to the boil, then lower heat.

4. In a mixing bowl, beat together the eggs and the flour. Beating constantly, add the hot milk.

5. Pour custard mixture over the meat, then dot with the butter.

6. Bake until set, about 30 minutes. Serve warm or cold as a breakfast or light luncheon dish.

Serves 4 to 6

This savoury custard somewhat resembles a quiche. In Burgundy it has many variations. Without meat and made with sweetened milk, it is often topped with fruit purée to serve as dessert.

FRIED NOODLES WITH PORK

China

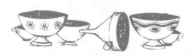

Preparation time: 20 minutes
Cooked noodles chill—24 hours

Cooking time: 10 minutes

Ingredients

8 oz./225 g. Chinese or other egg noodles	8 oz./225 g. boneless pork or chicken, cut into julienne strips
7 tablespoons groundnut oil	$1\frac{1}{2}$ tablespoons soy sauce
8 oz./225 g. mushrooms	1 tablespoon Chinese rice wine or dry sherry
1 lb./450 g. fresh mung bean sprouts or 1 large can bean sprouts	$\frac{1}{4}$ teaspoon salt
1 slice ginger, minced	1 clove garlic, minced
	3 spring onions, minced

1. Cook the noodles in a large pot of rapidly boiling unsalted water until tender, about 12 minutes. Drain and spread out on a platter to cool. Toss with 1 tablespoon of the oil, then cover and refrigerate for at least 24 hours.

2. Discard mushroom stems and slice caps into julienne strips. Reserve. Rinse bean sprouts. Discard husks, drain.

4. Place a frying pan over high heat for 1 minute. Add 2 tablespoons of the oil and heat for $\frac{1}{2}$ minute. Add the ginger and, stirring, fry for 1 minute. Add the pork (or chicken) and fry for 3 minutes. Remove from heat. Mix in 1 tablespoon of the soy sauce, the Chinese rice wine and salt. Remove ingredients from pan and reserve.

5. Return pan to high heat. Add 2 more tablespoons of the oil to the pan. Wait $\frac{1}{2}$ minute, then add the garlic, bean sprouts, spring onions and mushrooms. Fry, stirring, for 2 minutes. Season with salt. Remove ingredients from pan and reserve.

6. Heat the remaining oil in the pan and fry the noodles for 1 minute. Return all the reserved ingredients. Mix well and season with the remaining soy sauce.

Serves 4

LASAGNE AL FORNO

Preparation time: 2¼ hours   **Cooking time:** 45 minutes

Italy

Ingredients

1 lb./450 g. minced beef

1 large onion, chopped

1 clove garlic, crushed

A 16-oz./454-g. can Italian
    plum tomatoes

2 8-oz./227-g. cans
    tomato juice

2 teaspoons oregano

1 teaspoon basil

1½ tablespoons chopped
    fresh parsley

2 teaspoons salt

1 tablespoon sugar

8 oz./225 g. cooked sweet
    or hot Italian sausage,
    sliced

8 oz./225 g. lasagne

12 oz./350 g. Ricotta cheese

4 oz./100 g. Parmesan
    cheese, freshly grated

8 oz./225 g. Mozzarella
    cheese, shredded

1. Sauté the beef, onion and garlic in a large saucepan until
   the meat is brown and the onion is tender, about 5
   minutes. Drain off any fat. Add the plum tomatoes,
   tomato juice, 1 teaspoon of the oregano, basil, parsley,
   1 teaspoon salt and the sugar. Stir well and heat to
   boiling. Add the sausage and simmer, uncovered, for
   about 1½ hours.

2. While the sauce is cooking, prepare the lasagne accord-
   ing to package directions. This should take about 25
   minutes. Drain and separate the lasagne.

3. Preheat the oven to 350°F., 180°C., Gas Mark 4. Mix together the Ricotta, 2 oz./50 g. of the Parmesan cheese, 1
   teaspoon salt and the remaining teaspoon of oregano.

4. In an ungreased 13 × 9 × 2½-inch/33 × 23 × 6-cm. baking dish, assemble the lasagne. Start with a layer of a
   quarter of the sauce, then a third of the lasagne, a third
   of the Ricotta mixture and a third of the Mozzarella.
   Repeat twice. End with the remaining sauce and sprinkle
   with the remaining Parmesan cheese. Bake for 45
   minutes. Remove from oven and let stand for 10 minutes.

Serves 6

CHINESE FRIED RICE

China   **Preparation time:** 10 minutes   **Cooking time:** 15 minutes

Ingredients

*5 tablespoons groundnut
oil or vegetable oil*

2 eggs, lightly beaten

*8 spring onions, finely
chopped*

*1 thick slice fresh root
ginger, finely chopped*

*8 oz./225 g. raw prawns,
shelled and de-veined*

8 oz./225 g. ham, chopped

3 oz./75 g. cooked peas

1 lb./450 g. cooked rice

2 tablespoons soy sauce

1. Place a large frying pan over high heat for 1 minute. Add 2 tablespoons of the oil and swirl pan for ½ minute. Lower heat and pour in the beaten eggs with a few spring onions. Cook until eggs set, then transfer to a bowl and break up into small pieces. Reserve.

2. Swirl 1 more tablespoon oil into the pan. Heat through, then add the ginger and, stirring continuously, fry over moderate heat for 1 minute.

3. Add the prawns and fry over high heat until firm and pink, about 2 minutes. Add the ham and fry for 1 minute. Add the peas and fry for 1 more minute. Remove all ingredients from pan and reserve.

4. Heat the remaining 2 tablespoons oil in the pan for ½ minute. Add the cooked rice and fry for 2 to 3 minutes. Stir in the soy sauce. Return all the ingredients to the pan, mix briefly over high heat, then transfer to a platter and serve immediately.

Serves 4

Meatless Dishes and Vegetables

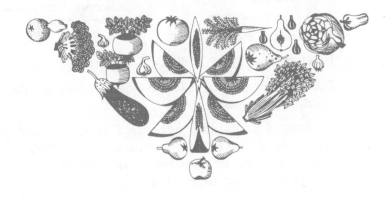

BAKED EGGS WITH BÉCHAMEL SAUCE

France

Preparation time: 10 minutes   **Cooking time:** 20 minutes

Ingredients

4 eggs

3 tablespoons cream

Salt

Freshly ground pepper

Béchamel Sauce:

1 oz./25 g. butter

1½ tablespoons flour

⅓ pint/2 dl. milk

1½ tablespoons cream

Salt

Freshly ground pepper

—

*4 slices white bread,
    toasted and buttered*

*Chopped fresh parsley
    for garnish*

1. Set oven at 350°F., 180°C., Gas Mark 4.

2. Beat the eggs well, as for an omelette, and add the cream, salt and pepper.

3. Butter 4 individual ovenproof ramekins and pour a quarter of the egg mixture into each one. Place ramekins in a roasting tin half filled with hot water and bake until set, about 20 minutes.

4. While the eggs are baking, prepare the béchamel sauce (page 471), using the above-listed ingredients. Keep warm.

5. When eggs are done, turn out the ramekins onto slices of buttered toast. Cover with béchamel sauce and sprinkle with chopped parsley.

Serves 2 to 4

BAKED EGGS EINDHOVEN

Preparation time: 10 minutes   **Cooking time:** 15 minutes

The Netherlands

Ingredients

2 oz./50 g. butter
1 onion, grated
Salt
2 oz./50 g. Cheddar
  cheese, grated

6 eggs
6 tablespoons double
  cream
Cayenne pepper

1. Preheat oven to 350°F., 180°C., Gas Mark 4.

2. In a small frying pan, heat the butter. Add the grated onion and sauté over moderate heat until onion is translucent, about 5 minutes. Remove from heat.

3. Pour the sautéed onions into a shallow baking dish. Salt lightly, then sprinkle with half the grated cheese.

4. One by one, gently break the eggs onto the bed of cheese. (Do not break the yolks.) Cover with the double cream, then top with the remaining grated cheese.

5. Sprinkle dish with cayenne, then bake for 15 minutes. Serve piping hot from the baking dish.

Serves 3 to 6

CORSICAN CHEESE OMELETTE

France

Preparation time: 5 minutes   **Cooking time:** 6 minutes

Ingredients

6 eggs

2 tablespoons cold water

⅛ teaspoon crushed mint

Salt

Freshly ground pepper

1½ oz./40 g. butter

4 oz./100 g. Broccio or
   other fresh goat cheese

Parsley sprigs for garnish

1. In a bowl, combine eggs and water. Beat eggs until light and fluffy, then add the mint and season with salt and pepper.

2. Place a large omelette pan over moderate heat. Heat until a drop of water sprinkled in pan disappears immediately, then swirl in the butter.

3. When the foam of the butter begins to subside, quickly pour in the eggs. Using the flat side of a fork, briskly swirl the eggs in the pan until they begin to set. (Shake pan back and forth while stirring to prevent omelette from sticking.)

4. Crumble in the cheese, fold omelette over and remove from heat. Garnish with parsley sprigs and serve.

Serves 2

EGGS WITH PIPÉRADE SAUCE

Preparation time: 15 minutes   **Cooking time:** 30 minutes

France

Ingredients

Pipérade:

1½ tablespoons olive oil

2 green peppers, seeded and thinly sliced

1 chilli pepper, chopped

1 onion, chopped

2 cloves garlic, crushed

Salt

Freshly ground pepper

2 lb./1 kg. tomatoes, peeled, seeded and chopped

¼ teaspoon sugar

—

8 slices of ham, cut in strips

1½ tablespoons olive oil

8 eggs, lightly beaten

Fresh parsley for garnish

1. Prepare the *pipérade*: a) Heat the olive oil in a large frying pan; b) add the green peppers, chilli pepper, onion and garlic; c) season with salt and pepper and sauté until onion is translucent; d) add the tomatoes and sugar, cover and simmer gently for 15 minutes; e) uncover and continue to cook until liquid has evaporated; f) correct seasoning. Keep warm.

2. In another pan, brown the ham in the olive oil. Remove ham and keep warm.

3. Stirring constantly over high heat, pour eggs into the pan in which the ham was cooked. Continue stirring until lightly scrambled. With a spatula, transfer the eggs to a hot platter and spoon the *pipérade* over them. Surround with the reserved ham and garnish with fresh parsley. Serve immediately.

Serves 4

EGGS POACHED IN WINE SAUCE

France

Preparation time: 10 minutes

Cooking time: 20 minutes

Ingredients

Meurette Sauce:

1 onion, sliced

2 shallots, sliced

2 cloves garlic, crushed

2 leeks (white part only), sliced

2 carrots, sliced

1 pint/6 dl. red Burgundy wine

1 bouquet garni (rosemary, basil, dill)

Salt

Freshly ground pepper

1 teaspoon sugar

2 tablespoons cognac

——

1 tablespoon flour

1½ oz./40 g. butter

8 eggs

8 slices French bread, fried in butter

1. Prepare the *meurette* sauce: a) In a saucepan combine the vegetables, wine, bouquet garni, salt, pepper and sugar; b) bring to the boil, then lower heat and simmer gently for 15 minutes; c) using a fine sieve, strain the sauce into a frying pan; d) add the cognac and flambé. Keep sauce over moderate heat.

2. Prepare a *beurre manié* (page 471) by kneading the flour and butter together. Reserve.

3. Poach the eggs in the simmering sauce. Transfer the poached eggs to a warm platter and keep hot.

4. Thicken the *meurette* with the *beurre manié*. Correct seasoning. Place the eggs on the fried bread and cover with the sauce. Serve immediately.

Serves 4

VARIATION: *In lower Burgundy the* meurette *is made with dry white wine, and sautéed mushrooms are added to the sauce.*

FRIED EGGS WITH HAM AND AUBERGINE

France

Preparation time: 25 minutes
Aubergine stands—1 hour

Cooking time: 12 minutes

Ingredients

1 aubergine, peeled and
　sliced
Salt
5 tablespoons olive oil
8 slices ham

8 eggs
½ pint/3 dl. tomato juice
　flavoured with garlic
Chopped fresh parsley
　for garnish

1. Sprinkle the aubergine slices with salt and allow to stand for 1 hour. Pat dry.

2. Heat half the oil in a frying pan and sauté the aubergine slices until tender, about 5 minutes on each side. Arrange on a heated platter. Keep warm.

3. In another pan, heat the remaining oil. Brown the ham and fry the eggs.

4. In a small saucepan, heat the tomato juice. Keep warm.

5. Arrange the ham and eggs on top of the aubergine, cover with the tomato juice and sprinkle with chopped fresh parsley.

Serves 4

CHEESE FONDUE

Switzerland

Preparation time: 10 minutes   **Cooking time:** 15 minutes

Ingredients

¾ pint/4½ dl. dry white wine

1 clove garlic, split

8 oz./225 g. Gruyère cheese, grated

8 oz./225 g. Emmenthal cheese, grated

1 tablespoon cornflour

2 tablespoons kirsch

Salt

Freshly ground pepper

Freshly grated nutmeg

1 loaf French bread, cubed

1. Pour the wine into a fondue pot or chafing dish rubbed with garlic. Heat almost to the boiling point.

2. Little by little, slowly add the grated cheese to the hot wine. (Make sure each addition is thoroughly melted and blended in before adding the next.) Keep hot.

3. In a small cup, combine the cornflour and the kirsch. Reserve.

4. Stirring constantly, bring the cheese and wine mixture to the boil, then reduce heat and blend in the cornflour and kirsch mixture. Continue stirring over moderately low heat until mixture thickens, about 3 minutes, then season to taste with salt, freshly ground pepper and nutmeg.

5. To serve, place the fondue pot over low heat at the table, regulating the heat so that the fondue barely simmers. Spear small pieces of the French bread with long-handled forks and swirl in the fondue until nicely coated.

Serves 4

WELSH RAREBIT

Preparation time: 5 minutes   **Cooking time:** 1–2 minutes   *Wales*

Ingredients

12 oz./350 g. Cheddar
  cheese, grated

2 oz./50 g. butter, at
  room temperature

1 to 2 teaspoons mustard

Dash cayenne pepper

1 tablespoon milk or beer

6 slices bread, toasted
  and buttered

1. Preheat the grill.

2. Combine the cheese, butter, mustard and pepper. Add the milk (or beer) and stir until smooth.

3. Spread the mixture onto the hot toast and place under the grill until the cheese has melted. Serve immediately.

Serves 3 or 6

CHEESE RAMEKIN LORRAINE

France

Preparation time: 15 minutes   **Cooking time:** 30–35 minutes

Ingredients

¾ pint/4½ dl. milk

4 tablespoons flour

5 oz./150 g. Gruyère or
other Swiss cheese,
grated

Salt

Freshly ground pepper

4 eggs, separated

2 oz./50 g. cottage cheese,
sieved

2 tablespoons double
cream

1. Set oven at 325°F., 160°C., Gas Mark 3.

2. In a saucepan, bring the milk to the boiling point. Remove pan from heat. Beating well, add to the flour in a bowl. Return to the saucepan and cook over moderate heat for 5 minutes.

3. Remove mixture from heat, blend in the grated cheese and season with salt and pepper.

4. Beat the egg yolks and mix into the custard.

5. Beat the egg whites until stiff and fold into the mixture.

6. Whip the sieved cottage cheese with the cream.

7. Transfer the custard to a buttered 3-pint/1½-litre ovenproof soufflé dish and cover with the cottage cheese mixture.

8. Bake custard until set, about 30 to 35 minutes. Serve immediately as a luncheon or supper dish.

Serves 4

QUICHE LORRAINE

Preparation time: 20 minutes   **Cooking time:** 30 minutes

Pastry chills—1 hour

France

Ingredients

Flaky Pastry:

6 oz./175 g. flour

½ teaspoon salt

4 oz./100 g. butter

3 to 5 tablespoons iced
   water

Filling:

6 rashers lean bacon

1 oz./25 g. butter, cut
   in small pieces

3 eggs

6 tablespoons single cream

¼ teaspoon nutmeg

Salt

Freshly ground pepper

1. Using the above-listed ingredients, prepare the flaky pastry (page 474) and chill for 1 hour.

2. Set oven at 400°F., 200°C., Gas Mark 6.

3. Roll out pastry to ⅛-inch/3-mm. thickness and line a buttered 9-inch/23-cm. flan ring. Bake blind until golden, about 10 minutes. Remove from oven and reduce temperature to 350°F., 180°C., Gas Mark 4.

4. Cut bacon into quarters and brown the pieces in a frying pan. Remove and drain.

5. Place the bacon and ½ oz./15 g. butter in the partially cooked pastry case. Reserve.

6. Beat the eggs and cream together. Season with nutmeg, salt and pepper. Pour mixture over the bacon and dot with the rest of the butter.

7. Bake quiche until a knife inserted in the middle of the filling comes out clean, about 30 minutes. Cool slightly before cutting. The quiche may be served hot or cold.

Serves 4 to 6

THREE-CHEESE QUICHE

France

Preparation time: 15 minutes
Pastry chills—1 hour

Cooking time: 30 minutes

Ingredients

Flaky Pastry:
6 oz./175 g. flour
½ teaspoon salt
4 oz./100 g. butter
3 to 5 tablespoons iced
   water

Filling:
4 oz./100 g. cottage
   cheese

1½ tablespoons milk
1 teaspoon salt
2 oz./50 g. Gruyère or
   other Swiss cheese,
   grated
3 oz./75 g. diced Maroilles
   or Pont l'Evêque cheese
2 eggs, beaten
Freshly ground pepper

1. Using the above-listed ingredients, prepare the flaky pastry (page 474) and chill for 1 hour.

2. Preheat oven to 400°F., 200°C., Gas Mark 6.

3. Roll out the pastry to ⅛-inch/3-mm. thickness and line a 9-inch/23-cm. flan ring. Bake blind for 10 minutes. Remove from oven and reserve.

4. Reduce oven temperature to 350°F., 180°C., Gas Mark 4.

5. In a bowl, combine the cottage cheese, milk and salt. Blend in the other cheeses and the eggs. Season well with pepper.

6. Pour the cheese mixture into the partially cooked pastry case and bake until the filling is golden and the pastry lightly browned, about 30 minutes. Serve immediately.

Serves 4 to 6

VARIATION: *Make bite-size quiches and serve as an appetiser.*

CHEESE AND ONION TART

Preparation time: 50 minutes
Pastry chills—1 hour

Cooking time: 30 minutes

France

Ingredients

Flaky Pastry:
6 oz./175 g. flour
½ teaspoon salt
4 oz./100 g. butter
3 to 5 tablespoons iced
  water

Filling:
1 oz./25 g. butter
4 large onions, sliced

2 eggs
1½ tablespoons cream
6 tablespoons milk
1 teaspoon flour
1 oz./25 g. Gruyère or
  other Swiss cheese,
  grated
Salt
Freshly ground pepper

1. Using the above-listed ingredients, prepare the flaky pastry (page 474). Chill for 1 hour.

2. Heat the butter in a frying pan. Add the onions, cover and cook over low heat for 30 minutes. Stir the onions occasionally. Do not brown. Remove pan from heat.

3. In a bowl, beat the eggs, cream and milk. Blend in the flour and cheese. Season with salt and pepper. Reserve.

4. Set oven at 400°F., 200°C., Gas Mark 6.

5. Roll out pastry and line a 9-inch/23-cm. flan ring. Bake blind for 10 minutes.

6. Beat the egg mixture into the onions. Pour mixture into the pastry case and bake until the filling has set and the pastry is lightly browned, about 30 minutes. Serve hot or cold.

Serves 4 to 6

ALSATIAN ONION TART

France

Preparation time: 35 minutes
Pastry chills—1 hour

Cooking time: 30 minutes

Ingredients

    Flaky Pastry:
    6 oz./175 g. flour
    ½ teaspoon salt
    4 oz./100 g. butter
    3 to 5 tablespoons iced
      water

    Filling:
    1½ lb./700 g. onions, sliced
    6 tablespoons water

Salt
Freshly ground pepper
Freshly grated nutmeg
5 rashers lean bacon, cut
  into small strips
2 eggs
6 tablespoons double cream
2½ oz./65 g. butter

1. Using the above-listed ingredients, prepare the flaky pastry (page 474) and chill for 1 hour.

2. Simmer the onions in 6 tablespoons water until all the liquid has evaporated, about 15 minutes. Season with salt, pepper and nutmeg. Reserve.

3. While the onions are cooking, briefly sauté bacon to eliminate some of the fat. Remove the bacon and reserve.

4. Set oven at 400°F., 200°C., Gas Mark 6.

5. In a bowl, beat the eggs and add the cream. Reserve.

6. Roll out the pastry and line a 9-inch/23-cm. flan ring. Bake blind for 10 minutes, then remove and reduce oven temperature to 350°F., 180°C., Gas Mark 4.

7. Melt the butter in a saucepan and stir in the onions. Remove pan from heat and pour in the egg and cream mixture. Correct seasoning. Pour mixture into the pastry case. Dot with the bacon and bake for 30 minutes. Serve immediately.

Serves 6

ONION FLAN

Preparation time: 45 minutes

Pastry chills—1 hour

Cooking time: 30 minutes

France

Ingredients

Flaky Pastry:

6 oz./175 g. flour

½ teaspoon salt

4 oz./100 g. butter

3 to 5 tablespoons iced
  water

Filling:

4 tablespoons olive oil

1½ lb./700 g. onions,
  thinly sliced

1 clove garlic, crushed

Salt

Freshly ground pepper

12 anchovy fillets

15 black olives, sliced

1. Prepare the flaky pastry (page 474) using the above-listed ingredients. Chill for 1 hour.

2. Heat 3 tablespoons of the oil in a frying pan. Add the onions and garlic and season with salt and pepper. Cover pan and braise over low heat for 30 minutes. Do not allow onions to brown.

3. Preheat the oven to 400°F., 200°C., Gas Mark 6.

4. While onions are cooking, roll out dough into a circle ⅛ inch/3 mm. thick. Line a buttered 9-inch/23-cm. flan ring with the pastry and bake blind for 10 minutes. Remove from oven and lower oven heat to 350°F., 180°C., Gas Mark 4.

5. Place the onions in the pastry case. Lay the anchovy fillets in a lattice arrangement over the onions. Top with the olive slices and sprinkle with remaining oil.

6. Return flan to oven and bake for 30 minutes.

Serves 4 to 6

LEEK PIE

France

Preparation time: 45 minutes
Pastry chills—1 hour

Cooking time: 45 minutes

Ingredients

Flaky Pastry:
8 oz./225 g. flour
1 teaspoon salt
6 oz./175 g. butter
7 tablespoons iced water
Filling:
12 leeks (white parts only),
   split

2½ oz./65 g. butter
1 tablespoon flour
6 tablespoons single cream
Salt
Freshly ground pepper
—
1 egg, beaten

1. Using the above-listed ingredients, prepare the flaky pastry (page 474) and chill for 1 hour.

2. Wash the leeks thoroughly, then blanch for 2 minutes in boiling water. Drain and refresh in cold water. Pat dry.

3. Heat 1½ oz./40 g. of the butter in a frying pan. Add the blanched leeks, cover pan and braise leeks over low heat until barely tender, about 30 minutes.

4. While the leeks are cooking, prepare a béchamel sauce (page 471) with the remaining butter, flour and cream. Season to taste with salt and pepper. Remove from heat. Add the braised leeks to the sauce. Mix well. Reserve.

5. Set oven at 400°F., 200°C., Gas Mark 6.

6. Roll out half the chilled pastry to line a buttered 9-inch/23-cm. pie or flan dish. Pour in the reserved leek mixture. Roll out the remaining pastry. Cover the leeks with the lid and seal the edges of the pie. Brush the crust with the beaten egg and bake for 45 minutes. Serve at once.

Serves 6

PASTA ST. AMBROSE

Preparation time: 10 minutes   **Cooking time:** 20 minutes

Italy

Ingredients

Sauce:

4 oz./100 g. unsalted
   butter

1 onion, finely chopped

1 large stick celery,
   finely chopped

1 clove garlic, crushed

6 tablespoons dry white
   wine or 3 tablespoons
   dry vermouth

⅓ pint/2 dl. double cream

1 tablespoon tomato
   paste

—

4 oz./100 g. Parmesan
   cheese, grated

1 lb./450 g. thin Italian
   spaghetti (spaghettini)

1. In a saucepan, melt 1 oz./25 g. of the butter. Add the chopped onion and celery and sauté over low heat until translucent, about 5 minutes. Add the remaining butter and the garlic. Stir over low heat until the butter has melted. Add the wine (or vermouth) and cook over high heat until nearly all the liquid has evaporated. Reduce heat to low. Add the cream and tomato paste and stir for 1 minute. Stir in the Parmesan cheese. Continue stirring over low heat until sauce is smooth. Keep warm.

2. In a large pot of rapidly boiling salted water, cook spaghettini until barely tender (*al dente*), about 6 to 8 minutes. Drain in a colander.

3. Return spaghettini to pot. Cover with the sauce and toss lightly. Transfer to a heated serving bowl and serve immediately, accompanied by a dish of freshly grated Parmesan cheese.

Serves 4 to 6

ALSATIAN DUMPLINGS

France

Preparation time: 20 minutes
Dough stands—2 hours

Cooking time: 10 minutes
per batch

Ingredients

14 oz./400 g. flour
3 eggs, beaten
⅓ pint/2 dl. milk
1 teaspoon salt

1½ oz./40 g. butter, melted
3 oz./75 g. Gruyère or other Swiss cheese, grated

1. Prepare the dough by mixing together the flour, eggs, milk and salt and allow it to stand for 2 hours.

2. Using a teaspoon dipped in boiling water, form the dough into little balls.

3. Into a large saucepan of boiling water, drop as many dumplings as can be accommodated without crowding. Cook over moderate heat for 10 minutes. Remove dumplings with a slotted spoon and drain. Add another batch to the boiling water.

4. Transfer cooked dumplings to a buttered baking dish and keep warm. Continue as above until all dumplings are cooked.

5. Just before serving, preheat grill. Pour the melted butter over the dumplings, sprinkle with the grated cheese and heat under the grill until the cheese turns golden. Serve hot as a side dish with a meat stew or casserole.

Serves 8 to 10

POTATO AND SAUERKRAUT SALAD

France

Preparation time: 20 minutes   **Cooking time:** 20 minutes

Ingredients

1 lb./450 g. medium
* potatoes*

Salt

Vinaigrette Sauce:

3 tablespoons wine
* vinegar*

9 tablespoons olive oil

½ teaspoon salt

Freshly ground pepper
—
3 tablespoons mayonnaise

12 oz./350 g. garlic
* sausage*

6 rashers bacon

1 lb./450 g. sauerkraut,
* rinsed and drained*

1. Cook the potatoes in salted boiling water until just tender, about 15 to 20 minutes. (It is important not to overcook potatoes for a salad.) Drain, peel and cut into thin slices.

2. Prepare the vinaigrette sauce by combining the above-listed ingredients.

3. Marinate the warm potato slices in a mixture of 3 tablespoons of the vinaigrette sauce and 1 tablespoon mayonnaise.

4. Poach the sausage in boiling water for 10 minutes. Drain, slice and toss with 3 tablespoons of vinaigrette.

5. Sauté the bacon until crisp, drain on absorbent paper and crumble.

6. Drop the sauerkraut into boiling water. Bring back to the boil, then remove from the heat. Leave sauerkraut in hot water for 2 minutes, drain, refresh and squeeze dry. Transfer to a platter and toss with the remaining vinaigrette and mayonnaise. To serve, sprinkle the bacon over the sauerkraut and arrange the sausage and potatoes around it.

Serves 4 to 6

POTATO AND ONION CASSEROLE

France

Preparation time: 15 minutes
Potatoes boil—20 minutes

Cooking time: 20 minutes

Ingredients

2 lb./1 kg. medium potatoes	Salt
3 medium onions, chopped	Freshly ground pepper
4 oz./100 g. butter	Freshly grated nutmeg

1. Boil the potatoes in their jackets until barely tender, about 20 minutes.

2. While the potatoes are cooking, prepare the onions.

3. Heat half the butter in a frying pan. Add the onions and sauté gently until translucent, about 5 minutes. Do not brown. Remove from heat and reserve.

4. Set oven at 375°F., 190°C., Gas Mark 5.

5. Peel the potatoes, then transfer to a mixing bowl and mash.

6. Mix the sautéed onions into the mashed potatoes. Season to taste with salt, pepper and nutmeg. Blend in 1 oz./25 g. of the remaining butter.

7. Transfer mixture to a buttered 3-pint/1½-litre baking dish, dot with the remaining butter and bake in the oven until top is nicely browned, about 20 minutes. Serve in the baking dish.

Serves 4 to 6

GAND-STYLE POTATO CASSEROLE

Belgium

Preparation time: 30 minutes   **Cooking time:** 20 minutes

Ingredients

6 large potatoes, peeled
  and quartered

2 leeks, chopped

12 sticks celery, coarsely
  chopped

1½ oz./40 g. butter, melted

2 egg yolks, beaten

6 oz./175 g. Swiss cheese,
  grated

Salt

Freshly ground pepper

1. Set oven at 350°F., 180°C., Gas Mark 4.

2. Drop potatoes into a large pan of boiling salted water and cook for 10 minutes.

3. Add the leeks and celery to the pan and simmer until the vegetables are tender, about 15 minutes.

4. Drain the vegetables. Purée through a sieve or in a blender.

5. Transfer the vegetable mixture to a large bowl and beat in the butter, the egg yolks and half the grated cheese. Season to taste with salt and pepper.

6. Pour the vegetable mixture into a buttered baking dish. Bake for 20 minutes.

7. Sprinkle the casserole with the remaining grated cheese and put under the grill until the cheese is golden, about 2 minutes. Serve immediately.

Serves 4

SAVOY POTATOES

France

Preparation time: 20 minutes   **Cooking time:** 1½ hours

Ingredients

2 lb./1 kg. potatoes, peeled and thinly sliced	*5 oz./150 g. Beaufort or Swiss cheese, grated*
Salt	*¾ pint/4½ dl. beef stock*
Freshly ground pepper	*2 oz./50 g. butter*

1. Set oven at 325°F., 160°C., Gas Mark 3.

2. Butter an ovenproof casserole.

3. Dry the potato slices. Place one thin layer of potatoes in the casserole. Season with salt and pepper, then cover with a layer of grated cheese. Continue layering and seasoning, ending with a layer of grated cheese.

4. Pour the stock over the cheese and dot with the butter.

5. Bake until all the liquid has evaporated, about 1½ hours.

Serves 4 to 6

DAUPHINÉ POTATOES

Preparation time: 15 minutes   **Cooking time:** 1½ hours   *France*

Ingredients

2 lb./1 kg. potatoes,
   peeled and thinly sliced
1 clove garlic, crushed
1½ oz./40 g. butter
Salt
Freshly ground pepper

½ teaspoon freshly grated
   nutmeg
2 eggs, beaten
¾ pint/4½ dl. milk
1 tablespoon cream

1. Set oven at 325°F., 160°C., Gas Mark 3.

2. Pat the potato slices dry.

3. Rub a baking dish with the crushed garlic, then coat with ½ oz./15 g. of the butter.

4. Layer the potato slices in the dish, seasoning each layer with salt, pepper and nutmeg.

5. In a bowl, beat together the eggs, milk and cream.

6. Pour the mixture over the potatoes, dot with the remaining butter and bake for 1½ hours.

Serves 4 to 6

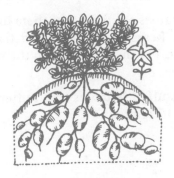

BAKED STUFFED POTATOES

France

Preparation time: 30 minutes

Cooking time: 1¼ hours

Ingredients

8 medium potatoes
8 anchovy fillets
2 eggs, hard-boiled
4 shallots, chopped
1½ tablespoons chopped
    fresh parsley
1½ tablespoons chopped
    fresh chives
½ oz./15 g. butter

Béchamel Sauce:
1½ oz./40 g. butter
1½ tablespoons flour
⅓ pint/2 dl. milk
2 tablespoons cream
Salt
Freshly ground pepper
½ teaspoon freshly grated
    nutmeg

1. Preheat oven to 350°F., 180°C., Gas Mark 4.

2. Prick potatoes with a fork and bake until tender, about 1 hour.

3. In a bowl, mash together the anchovies, eggs, shallots, parsley and chives. Reserve.

4. Fifteen minutes before the potatoes are done, prepare the béchamel sauce (page 471). Blend in the reserved anchovy-herb mixture. Keep warm over hot water.

5. When the potatoes are done, cut them in half and scoop out the pulp. Reserve jackets. Mash the pulp and the sauce together. Fill the jackets with the mixture and dot with the butter.

6. Arrange the stuffed potatoes in a buttered baking dish and bake for 15 minutes.

Serves 8

HASH-BROWN POTATOES ANGOUMOIS

France

Preparation time: 5 minutes   **Cooking time:** 35 minutes

Ingredients

*1½ lb./700 g. potatoes,
    peeled and grated*

6 rashers bacon, diced

1 clove garlic, crushed

Salt

Freshly ground pepper

*3 tablespoons lard or
    vegetable oil*

1. In a bowl, combine the potatoes, bacon and garlic. Mix well, then season with salt and pepper.

2. Heat the lard (or oil) in a frying pan. Add the potato mixture and cook over moderate heat until underside is golden.

3. Turn potatoes and continue cooking until the second side is crisp and golden, about 15 minutes.

Serves 4

YAM FRITTERS

Ghana

Preparation time: 30 minutes
Yams boil—20 minutes

Cooking time: 15 minutes
per batch

Ingredients

1 lb./450 g. yams or sweet
  potatoes
Salt
2 eggs, lightly beaten
3 tablespoons single cream
1 onion, grated
Flour

Ground cloves
Freshly grated nutmeg
Freshly ground pepper
Flour for dredging fritters
Vegetable oil or lard for
  frying

1. Drop the yams (or sweet potatoes) into a pot of rapidly boiling salted water and boil until tender, about 20 minutes.

2. Drain yams, then peel and trim any discoloured areas.

3. Mash the yams in a large mixing bowl until smooth.

4. Incorporate the eggs, beat in the cream and then add the grated onion and enough flour to bind. Mix thoroughly, then season to taste with ground cloves, grated nutmeg, salt and pepper.

5. Shape the mixture into flat cakes, then dredge lightly in flour.

6. Pour enough oil (or lard) into a large heavy frying pan to reach a depth of $\frac{1}{4}$ inch/5 mm. Heat until oil is almost at smoking point.

7. Add a few fritters to the hot oil and fry until crisp and brown, about 8 minutes per side. Remove fritters with a slotted spoon, drain and keep hot.

8. Repeat until all fritters are fried, then transfer to a heated platter and serve immediately.

Serves 4 to 6

BARLEY AND MUSHROOM CASSEROLE

Scotland

Preparation time: 25 minutes   **Cooking time:** 45 minutes

Ingredients

3 oz./75 g. butter
2 cloves garlic, crushed
2 onions, finely chopped
1 lb./450 g. mushrooms, thinly sliced
7 oz./200 g. pearl barley

½ tablespoon dried basil
½ pint/3 dl. chicken stock
Salt
Freshly ground pepper
3 tablespoons chopped fresh parsley

1. Set oven at 325°F., 160°C., Gas Mark 3.

2. Melt the butter in a small enamelled cast-iron casserole. Add the garlic and onion and sauté over moderately low heat until onion is translucent, about 5 minutes.

3. Add the mushrooms and sauté over moderate heat until mushrooms are golden, about 5 minutes.

4. Add the barley and the basil to the mushroom mixture and toss lightly, then pour in the chicken stock and season to taste with salt and pepper.

5. Slowly bring casserole to the boil, then remove from heat. Cover casserole and bake until barley is tender, about 45 minutes.

6. Before serving, add the chopped parsley and toss gently. Serve piping hot.

Serves 2 to 4

LENTILS WITH TOMATOES

Syria

Preparation time: 15 minutes
Lentils soak—3 hours

Cooking time: 1 hour

Ingredients

8 oz./225 g. lentils

3 tablespoons vegetable oil

1 large onion, finely chopped

2 cloves garlic, crushed

1 teaspoon ground cumin

6 tablespoons beef stock

4 tomatoes, peeled and chopped

Salt

Freshly ground pepper

1. Soak the lentils in a bowl of cold water for 3 hours.

2. Discard any lentils that have floated to the surface, then drain the remaining lentils thoroughly.

3. Transfer lentils to a pot of rapidly boiling salted water and cook over moderate heat for ½ hour. Drain and reserve.

4. Heat the oil in a large saucepan. Add the onion and garlic and sauté until translucent, about 5 minutes.

5. Stirring constantly, add the cumin and cook over high heat for 2 minutes.

6. Add the stock and the reserved lentils. Mix thoroughly, then simmer, uncovered, over moderately low heat until lentils are nearly tender, about 15 minutes.

7. Stir in the tomatoes and season to taste with salt and pepper. Continue simmering until tomatoes are tender, about 15 minutes.

8. Transfer to a heated serving dish and serve immediately.

Serves 4

BRAISED RICE, MILAN STYLE

Preparation time: 15 minutes   **Cooking time:** 25 minutes   *Italy*

Ingredients

¾ pint/4½ dl. beef or
   chicken stock, heated

Pinch saffron

1½ tablespoons oil

1½ oz./40 g. butter

½ onion, chopped

1½ tablespoons beef
   marrow, diced

7 oz./200 g. short-grain
   rice

2 tablespoons freshly
   grated Parmesan cheese

Salt

Freshly ground pepper

1. In a cup, combine 3 tablespoons of the hot stock and the saffron. Reserve.

2. Heat the oil and 1 oz./25 g. of the butter in a large frying pan. Add the onion and sauté over moderate heat until onion is translucent, about 5 minutes. Add the marrow and the rice. Stir briefly until rice is thoroughly coated, then sauté for 1 minute over moderate heat.

3. Add 6 tablespoons of the remaining stock to the rice. Stir gently over moderate heat until the stock is absorbed, then add another 6 tablespoons stock and stir until that is absorbed. Add half the remaining stock to the rice and stir as above, then add the remaining stock. Continue stirring gently until the rice is tender and creamy and all the stock has been absorbed. (This entire process will take 20 to 25 minutes.)

4. Stir the saffron and stock mixture into the rice, then blend in the remaining butter and the Parmesan cheese. Season with salt and pepper and serve accompanied by a bowl of freshly grated Parmesan cheese.

Serves 2 to 3

GINGERED STRING BEANS

China

Preparation time: 10 minutes   **Cooking time:** 8 minutes

Ingredients

*1 lb./450 g. fresh string
(runner) beans, sliced*

Salt

*1½ tablespoons groundnut
oil or flavourless
vegetable oil*

*3 thick slices fresh
root ginger, crushed*

1 tablespoon soy sauce

3 tablespoons chicken stock

3 spring onions, chopped

*Chopped walnuts for
garnish*

1. Plunge the beans into a saucepan of lightly salted boiling water and blanch over moderately high heat for 3 minutes. Drain and refresh under cold water, then pat dry and reserve.

2. Place a large frying pan over high heat for ½ minute, then swirl in the oil. Wait ½ minute, then add the crushed ginger and, stirring, fry over moderately high heat for 1 minute.

3. Add the beans and fry until barely tender, about 2 minutes.

4. Add the soy sauce and chicken stock. Bring rapidly to the boil, then cover and simmer over moderate heat until beans are tender, about 4 minutes.

5. Stir in the spring onions and toss briefly over high heat, then transfer to a heated serving platter, garnish with chopped walnuts and serve immediately.

Serves 4

GASCONY GREEN BEANS

Preparation time: 15 minutes   **Cooking time:** 30 minutes

France

Ingredients

1½ lb./700 g. green beans

3 leeks (white parts only),
    split

1 clove garlic, crushed

Salt

1½ tablespoons goose fat
    (page 475) or olive oil

2 onions, chopped

3 thin slices ham, diced

1½ tablespoons flour

1 egg yolk

1 teaspoon wine vinegar

Chopped fresh parsley
    for garnish

1. Parboil the beans, leeks and garlic in a pan of boiling salted water for 10 minutes. Drain vegetables, reserving ⅓ pint/2 dl. of the broth. Reserve vegetables.

2. In a frying pan, heat the goose fat (or olive oil) and sauté the onions and the ham over moderate heat for 10 minutes. Stirring constantly, sprinkle in the flour and pour in the reserved vegetable broth. Continue stirring over moderate heat until the sauce is smooth. Add the reserved vegetables to the sauce and simmer gently for 10 minutes. Keep hot.

3. Beat the egg yolk and vinegar in a bowl. Gradually beat a little of the hot sauce into egg mixture, then pour into the frying pan.

4. Heat until sauce thickens. (Do not boil.) Garnish with chopped parsley and serve.

Serves 6

SAVOURY GRATED BEETS

USSR

Preparation time: 10 minutes   **Cooking time:** 35 minutes

Ingredients

1½ oz./40 g. butter

1 onion, finely chopped

1 lb./450 g. raw beetroots, grated

1 teaspoon grated lemon rind

1½ tablespoons lemon juice

1 tablespoon flour

6 tablespoons beef stock, heated

Salt

Freshly ground pepper

1½ tablespoons chopped chives

1½ tablespoons chopped fresh parsley

1. Heat the butter in a frying pan. Add the chopped onion and sauté over moderately low heat until translucent, about 5 minutes.

2. Add the grated beetroots, lemon rind and lemon juice. Mix gently until beets are evenly coated, then cover pan and simmer over low heat until barely tender, about 20 minutes.

3. Mix the flour with a little of the hot stock. Return to the remaining stock and mix vigorously until well blended, then pour over the beets. Stir beet mixture over moderate heat until well blended, then simmer, uncovered, until beets are tender, about 10 minutes.

4. Reduce heat to low. Season beets to taste with salt and pepper, then add the chopped chives and parsley. Toss gently. Serve hot or cold.

Serves 4

BROCCOLI, BERLIN STYLE

Preparation time: 15 minutes   **Cooking time:** 15 minutes

France

Ingredients

1½ lb./700 g. broccoli	2 egg yolks, beaten
Salt	1 tablespoon lemon juice
1½ oz./40 g. butter	Pinch nutmeg
½ oz./15 g. flour	Pinch freshly ground
⅓ pint/2 dl. milk	pepper
3 tablespoons chicken stock	

1. Place the broccoli in a small amount of boiling salted water. Cover tightly and cook until just tender, about 10 to 15 minutes.

2. Prepare the sauce: Melt the butter and blend in the flour. Gradually add the milk and chicken stock and stir until thickened, about 2 minutes. Add the yolks and cook for another minute, then stir in the lemon juice, nutmeg and pepper.

3. Arrange the broccoli on a heated serving dish and cover with the sauce.

Serves 4

BRUSSELS SPROUTS WITH CELERY

Great Britain

Preparation time: 20 minutes

Cooking time: 10 minutes

Ingredients

1½ oz./40 g. butter
2 sticks celery, chopped
1 onion, chopped
1½ lb./700 g. small
   Brussels sprouts,
   trimmed
½ oz./15 g. flour

⅓ pint/2 dl. milk, heated
Salt
Freshly ground pepper
Freshly grated nutmeg
1 oz./25 g. breadcrumbs

1. Set oven at 350°F., 180°C., Gas Mark 4.

2. In a frying pan heat 1 oz./25 g. of the butter. Add the celery and onion and sauté over low heat until tender, about 10 minutes.

3. While the onions and celery are cooking, steam the Brussels sprouts for 7 minutes over boiling water. Drain and reserve.

4. Sprinkle the flour into the onion and celery mixture. Stir over low heat until well blended, then gradually add the milk and cook gently until sauce thickens.

5. Season to taste with salt, pepper and nutmeg, then add the reserved Brussels sprouts.

6. Pour mixture into a buttered baking dish. Top with the breadcrumbs, dot with the remaining butter and bake for 10 minutes. Serve hot.

Serves 4 to 6

PURÉED BRUSSELS SPROUTS

Preparation time: 10 minutes **Cooking time:** 15–20 minutes

The Netherlands

Ingredients

Salt

⅓ pint/2 dl. water

1 lb./450 g. Brussels
  sprouts, trimmed and
  scored

Pinch nutmeg

1 teaspoon lemon juice

⅓ pint/2 dl. double cream

1. Bring salted water to the boil in a saucepan. Add the Brussels sprouts. Return to the boil, lower the heat, cover and simmer until tender, about 10 to 15 minutes. Drain and refresh under cold water.

2. Using a sieve or blender, purée the Brussels sprouts, then return to the saucepan. Add salt to taste and the nutmeg, then stir in the lemon juice and cream. Blend well.

3. Stir over low heat for 5 minutes. Serve piping hot.

Serves 3 to 4

This purée makes an ideal accompaniment to duck or pork.

BEDFORD COLESLAW

USA

Preparation time: 20 minutes

Marination time: 2 hours

Ingredients

1 small head cabbage
2 carrots, peeled
½ green pepper, chopped
1 small onion, chopped
1 clove garlic, crushed
(optional)

1½ tablespoons vinaigrette
dressing (page 482)
6 tablespoons mayonnaise
Salt
Freshly ground pepper

1. In a non-metallic bowl, shred the cabbage and the carrots. Add the pepper and onion and toss well.

2. Stir in the garlic, vinaigrette and mayonnaise. Season to taste with salt and pepper. Cover and refrigerate for at least 2 hours (or overnight) before serving.

Serves 4

STUFFED CABBAGE

Preparation time: 30 minutes   **Cooking time:** 2 hours   *France*

Ingredients

*A 2-lb./1-kg. green
    cabbage*

Stuffing:

1 lb./450 g. sorrel, chopped

*6 tablespoons chopped
    fresh parsley*

8 oz./225 g. lettuce, chopped

8 oz./225 g. spinach, chopped

8 oz./225 g. bacon, diced

8 oz./225 g. pork, minced

2 onions, chopped

2 shallots, finely chopped

4 eggs

1 oz./25 g. flour

2½ oz./65 g. breadcrumbs

2 tablespoons cream

Salt and pepper

—

*2½ pints/1¼ litres chicken
    stock*

1. Blanch the cabbage in boiling water for 10 minutes. Drain.

2. For the stuffing combine the greens with the bacon, pork, onions and shallots. Add the eggs, flour, breadcrumbs and cream. Blend until smooth and season with salt and pepper.

3. Remove a few outer leaves of the cabbage and carefully open out the remaining leaves. Cut out the central stalk, leaving the base of the core intact. Fill the cabbage with the stuffing and gently reshape the cabbage to its original form. Cover the top of the cabbage with the detached outer leaves.

4. Wrap the cabbage tightly in muslin. Place in a pan just large enough to hold the cabbage. Cover with the chicken stock and simmer, covered, for 2 hours. Serve the cabbage immediately, accompanied by a sauce boat of the hot cooking liquid.

Serves 4

BAVARIAN RED CABBAGE

Germany

Preparation time: 15 minutes   **Cooking time:** 30 minutes

Ingredients

5 rashers bacon

3 onions, chopped

1 tablespoon flour

3 tablespoons red wine
  vinegar

6 tablespoons red wine

2 lb./1 kg. red cabbage,
  shredded

¼ teaspoon caraway seeds
  (optional)

1 apple, peeled, cored
  and diced

Salt

Freshly ground pepper

1. In a heavy enamelled casserole, sauté the bacon over moderate heat to render the fat. Do not allow the fat to brown. Remove the bacon and reserve for other uses.

2. Add the onions to the casserole and sauté until translucent. Sprinkle in the flour while stirring. Cook for about 30 seconds, then slowly pour in the vinegar and the wine. Stir briskly to avoid lumps.

3. Add the red cabbage, caraway seeds and apple. Season with salt and pepper. Mix all the ingredients together and cover.

4. Cook for about 30 minutes, or until the cabbage is tender but not soggy.

Serves 4 to 6

HONEYED CARROTS AND SWEET POTATOES

Israel

Preparation time: 15 minutes   **Cooking time:** 1 hour

Ingredients

1 lb./450 g. carrots, thickly
  sliced

3 large sweet potatoes,
  peeled and quartered

⅓ pint/2 dl. water, boiling

8 oz./225 g. prunes,
  stoned

4 tablespoons honey

Salt

1. Place the carrots and sweet potatoes in a saucepan. Pour in the water, then add the prunes.

2. Cover the pan tightly and cook the mixture over low heat for 15 minutes.

3. Add the honey and season to taste with salt. Simmer over very low heat until the vegetables are tender, about 45 minutes.

Serves 4 to 6

BALKAN BRAISED CARROTS

Yugoslavia

Preparation time: 5 minutes   **Cooking time:** 15–30 minutes

Ingredients

2 oz./50 g. butter
1 teaspoon sugar
8 carrots, thinly sliced
3 spring onions, cut into
  1-inch/2½-cm. pieces
Cayenne pepper

Salt
Freshly ground pepper
⅓ pint/2 dl. plain yoghurt
1½ tablespoons chopped
  fresh dill

1. Melt the butter in a saucepan. Add the sugar, carrot slices and spring onions. Cover and braise gently until carrots are tender, about 15 to 30 minutes.

2. Season to taste with the cayenne pepper, salt and pepper.

3. Add the yoghurt and dill. Stirring constantly, heat through. (Do not allow to boil.) Serve immediately.

Serves 2 to 4

CAULIFLOWER WITH BREADCRUMB GARNISH

France

Preparation time: 10 minutes   **Cooking time:** 25 minutes

Ingredients

1 cauliflower, trimmed
Salt
4 oz./100 g. butter
4 oz./100 g. dry bread-
  crumbs

Juice of ½ lemon
Freshly ground pepper
4 eggs, hard-boiled
6 tablespoons chopped
  fresh parsley

1. Drop the cauliflower into a heavy pan of boiling salted water. Quickly return to the boil, then lower heat, cover tightly and cook until tender, about 25 minutes.

2. While the cauliflower is cooking, prepare the breadcrumb garnish: a) Melt the butter in a frying pan; b) add the breadcrumbs and stir until the mixture is golden; c) sprinkle in the lemon juice and add salt and pepper to taste. Keep warm.

3. Remove the cauliflower and drain well. Reserve.

4. Finely chop the hard-boiled eggs and mix with the chopped parsley. Season to taste with salt and pepper.

5. To serve, arrange the cauliflower on a heated platter. Sprinkle on the reserved breadcrumbs and surround with the egg and parsley mixture.

Serves 2 to 4

CAULIFLOWER SOUFFLÉ

France

Preparation time: 25 minutes   **Cooking time:** 35–40 minutes

Ingredients

1 small cauliflower,
    broken into florets
½ teaspoon salt
Freshly ground pepper
Freshly grated nutmeg
Cayenne pepper
1 teaspoon rosemary
1½ oz./40 g. butter

2 tablespoons flour
12 fl. oz./3½ dl. milk,
    boiling
5 eggs, separated
6 oz./175 g. Swiss cheese,
    grated
½ oz./15 g. dry bread-
    crumbs

1. Preheat oven to 400°F., 200°C., Gas Mark 6.

2. Cook the cauliflower in boiling salted water until tender, about 10 minutes. Purée and season with salt, pepper, nutmeg, cayenne pepper and rosemary.

3. Melt the butter in a saucepan, stir in the flour and cook for 2 minutes. Add the milk and stir until thickened. Remove the pan from the heat and blend in 4 of the egg yolks, one at a time. Add the cauliflower purée and all but 2 tablespoons of the grated cheese.

4. Beat the 5 egg whites with a pinch of salt until stiff. Fold carefully into the cheese mixture. Pour into a buttered soufflé dish and sprinkle with the remaining grated cheese and the breadcrumbs. Bake for 35 to 40 minutes.

Serves 4

CORN PUDDING

Preparation time: 15 minutes   **Cooking time:** 45 minutes   *USA*

Ingredients

2 oz./50 g. butter
1 small onion, finely
*   chopped*
6 oz./175 g. fresh corn
*   kernels*

⅓ pint/2 dl. single cream
Salt
Freshly ground pepper
4 eggs, separated

1. Set oven at 325°F., 160°C., Gas Mark 3.

2. In a frying pan, melt the butter and sauté the onion over low heat for 3 minutes. Do not allow the butter to brown. Scrape into a bowl.

3. Add the corn, cream, salt and pepper. Lightly beat the egg yolks and stir into the corn. Mix well.

4. In a separate bowl, beat the egg whites until frothy. Add a pinch of salt and continue beating until stiff. Fold the egg whites into the corn mixture.

5. Pour into a buttered baking dish. Bake for 40 minutes. Increase heat to 400°F., 200°C., Gas Mark 6 and bake for an additional 5 minutes.

Serves 4

FRIED SWEET CORN

Indonesia

Preparation time: 5 minutes

Cooking time: 5 minutes

Ingredients

6 oz./175 g. cooked sweet corn or an 8-oz./225-g. can corn kernels

1 small onion, chopped

1 stick celery, chopped

1½ tablespoons chopped parsley

½ teaspoon salt

1 egg, lightly beaten

1 to 2 tablespoons flour

2 tablespoons groundnut oil

1. Combine the first seven ingredients in a large bowl. Mix thoroughly.

2. Heat the oil in a large frying pan. Add the vegetable mixture and fry, stirring, until golden, about 5 minutes.

Serves 2

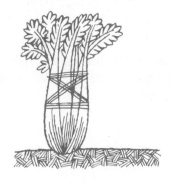

BRAISED CUCUMBERS WITH DILL AND SOURED CREAM

USSR

Preparation time: 20 minutes   **Cooking time:** 15 minutes

Ingredients

6 small cucumbers, peeled
Salt
3 oz./75 g. butter
1 onion, finely chopped
3 tablespoons soured
  cream

1½ tablespoons chopped
  fresh dill
Freshly ground pepper
Pinch nutmeg

1. Halve the cucumbers lengthwise and scrape out the seeds. Cut into 2-inch/5-cm. strips. Sprinkle the cucumbers with salt and let stand for 20 minutes. Drain and pat dry.

2. Melt 2 oz./50 g. of butter in a saucepan. Add the cucumbers, cover and cook over low heat until tender, about 10 minutes.

3. Melt the remaining butter and sauté the onion for 5 minutes. Remove from the heat and stir in the soured cream and dill. Season with salt, pepper and nutmeg. Stir in the cucumbers, heat through and serve.

Serves 4 to 6

STUFFED AUBERGINE AMMAN

Jordan

Preparation time: 40 minutes
Aubergine drains—30 minutes

Cooking time: 5 minutes

Ingredients

3 medium aubergines

Salt

6 tablespoons olive oil

2 onions, chopped

1 lb./450 g. mushrooms, thinly sliced

2 cloves garlic, crushed

A 15-oz./425-g. can Italian tomatoes, drained and chopped

2 oz./50 g. fresh bread-crumbs

Freshly ground pepper

1½ tablespoons chopped fresh parsley

1 teaspoon crushed dried mint leaves

½ teaspoon oregano

¼ teaspoon marjoram

Pinch cayenne pepper

¼ teaspoon ground allspice

2 oz./50 g. Parmesan cheese, freshly grated

1. Preheat oven to 350°F., 180°C., Gas Mark 4.

2. Boil the aubergines in a large saucepan of water for 15 minutes. Drain and cut in half lengthwise. Scoop out most of the pulp, leaving ½-inch/1-cm. thickness of pulp in the skins. Sprinkle hollowed-out shells with salt and drain for ½ hour. Rinse, pat dry and reserve. Chop the scooped-out pulp.

3. Heat the olive oil in a large frying pan. Add the chopped aubergine pulp, onions, mushrooms and garlic. Sauté over moderately high heat until lightly browned.

4. Add the tomatoes, breadcrumbs, 1½ teaspoons salt, pepper, herbs and spices. Mix well, then remove from heat and spoon the sautéed mixture into the reserved shells.

5. Arrange the stuffed aubergines in a greased baking dish, sprinkle with the grated Parmesan and bake until cheese has melted or nearly browned.

Serves 6

SAUTÉED MUSHROOMS

Preparation time: 20 minutes **Cooking time:** 20 minutes
Chinese mushrooms soak—30 minutes

France

Ingredients

*8 to 12 cèpes (boletus
    mushrooms) or Chinese
    mushrooms or 1 lb./
    450 g. firm white
    mushrooms*

6 tablespoons olive oil

2 cloves garlic, crushed

6 shallots, chopped

4 slices ham, diced

*1 tablespoon chopped
    fresh parsley*

1 bay leaf

Salt

Freshly ground pepper

Juice of ½ lemon

1. Clean the mushrooms and remove stalks. Chop stalks. Reserve caps and stalks. (If Chinese mushrooms are used; soak them in lukewarm water for 30 minutes, remove with a slotted spoon and discard stalks. Pat caps dry.)

2. In a frying pan, heat half the oil with the garlic. Stir in the shallots and sauté until translucent, about 3 minutes. Add the ham, parsley, bay leaf and the chopped mushroom stalks. Lower heat and cook gently for 15 minutes.

3. Heat the remaining oil in a frying pan and sauté the mushroom caps over high heat. Season with salt and pepper. Keep warm.

4. Arrange the mushroom caps on a heated platter and surround with the ham garnish. Sprinkle with the lemon juice and serve immediately.

Serves 4

CREAMED WILD MUSHROOMS

France

Preparation time: 25 minutes **Cooking time:** 20 minutes

Ingredients

*1 lb./450 g. chanterelles or
  white mushrooms*
Vinegar for rinsing
1½ oz./40 g. butter
1½ tablespoons oil
Salt
Freshly ground pepper

4 tablespoons double cream
*Pinch freshly grated
  nutmeg*
*8 slices French bread,
  fried in butter*
*Chopped fresh parsley
  for garnish*

1. Carefully clean the mushrooms, rinsing them several times in water with a dash of vinegar until no dirt remains. Pat dry. (If the *chanterelles* are large, cut them lengthwise into strips.)

2. Heat the butter and oil in a frying pan. Add the mushrooms and stir over moderately high heat until moisture starts coming out of the mushrooms, about 10 minutes.

3. Season with salt and pepper. Cook, uncovered, over moderate heat for 10 minutes to reduce liquid.

4. Reduce heat to low and stir in the cream and a pinch of nutmeg. Continue stirring over low heat until the cream begins to thicken, then remove pan from heat.

5. Arrange the fried bread on a heated platter. Pour the creamed mushrooms on top and garnish with chopped fresh parsley. Serve immediately.

Serves 4

OKRA OLYMPIA

Preparation time: 10 minutes   **Cooking time:** 35 minutes   *Greece*

Ingredients

1½ lb./700 g. okra,
  trimmed and sliced
⅓ pint/2 dl. olive oil
3 onions, finely chopped
5 tomatoes, peeled and
  chopped
½ lemon, sliced

Salt
Freshly ground pepper
¼ teaspoon oregano
¼ teaspoon sugar
6 tablespoons water

1. Blanch the okra briefly in a pan of boiling salted water. Drain.

2. Heat the olive oil and sauté the onions until translucent, about 10 minutes. Add the okra slices and cook for 5 minutes.

3. Add the remaining ingredients, cover and simmer over low heat for 20 minutes. Correct seasoning and serve hot.

Serves 6

ONIONS STUFFED WITH RICE AND MEAT

Sweden

Preparation time: 50 minutes　　**Cooking time:** 1 hour

Ingredients

10 medium onions, peeled
Salt
8 oz./225 g. minced beef
6 oz./175 g. cooked rice
1 egg
⅓ pint/2 dl. cream
Freshly ground pepper

1½ oz./40 g. butter
1 tablespoon brown sugar
¾ pint/4½ dl. beef stock
1½ tablespoons flour
2 tablespoons each chopped
　fresh dill and parsley

1. Parboil the onions in salted water for 5 minutes. Remove with a slotted spoon and drain. Carefully scoop out the centres with a spoon, keeping the shape. Reserve centres.

2. Combine the meat, rice, egg and half the cream. Season well with salt and pepper. Fill the onions with the mixture. Cover with reserved onion centres and secure with string.

3. Set oven at 350°F., 180°C., Gas Mark 4.

4. Melt the butter in a flameproof casserole, then brown the filled onions a few at a time. Sprinkle with the brown sugar. Pour in the stock, half covering the onions. Cover the casserole, place in the oven and simmer for 1 hour, basting occasionally. Discard the string and arrange the onions on a serving platter. Keep warm.

5. Heat the cooking liquid. Mix the flour and remaining cream together, then whisk into the liquid. Stir until thickened. Correct seasoning. Pour the sauce over the onions. Sprinkle with dill and parsley.

Serves 4 to 6

BASSE-TERRE CREAMED PEAS

Preparation time: 10 minutes   **Cooking time:** 10–15 minutes

Guadeloupe

Ingredients

2 thick rashers bacon, diced

2 lb./1 kg. young green peas, shelled

½ pint/3 dl. beef stock

Bouquet garni (parsley, peppercorns, small onion, bay leaf)

6 tablespoons double cream

Salt

Freshly ground pepper

½ oz./15 g. butter, softened

1 teaspoon flour

1 tablespoon rum

Pinch brown sugar

1. In a small saucepan, sauté the bacon cubes until crisp. Drain and reserve.

2. Put the peas in a medium saucepan and add the stock and the bouquet garni. Simmer over medium heat for 10 to 15 minutes, until peas are tender. Remove the bouquet garni. Add the double cream and season with salt and pepper.

3. Make a *roux* by combining the butter and flour and add it into the peas. Stir sauce until smooth and thick. Add the rum and sugar and serve piping hot.

Serves 4 to 6

FRIED SPINACH

China

Preparation time: 10 minutes   **Cooking time:** 11 minutes

Ingredients

2 lb./1 kg. spinach,
   trimmed
1½ tablespoons groundnut
   or flavourless vegetable
   oil

1 clove garlic, crushed
A 1-inch/2½-cm. piece
   fresh root ginger, peeled
   and minced

1. Wash the spinach thoroughly and dry lightly. The leaves should be slightly moist.

2. Place a saucepan over high heat for 1 minute. Add the oil, garlic and ginger. Swirl oil in pan for ½ minute.

3. Reduce heat to moderate, add the spinach and cover immediately. Cook spinach for 1 minute, then toss lightly.

4. Replace cover and cook until just tender, about 10 more minutes. Serve immediately.

Serves 4

Any leafy vegetable, such as bok choy, *watercress or romaine lettuce, can be cooked this same way.*

MARROW AND TOMATO CASEROLE

West Indies

Preparation time: 45 minutes **Cooking time:** 40 minutes

Ingredients

1 medium marrow
Salt
2 small onions, diced
½ teaspoon salt

Béchamel Sauce:
1 oz./25 g. butter
½ oz./15 g. flour
⅓ pint/2 dl. milk

Freshly ground pepper
—
2 garlic cloves, crushed
2 oz./50 g. butter
2 tomatoes, peeled and
   sliced
Chopped parsley for
   garnish

1. Cut the marrow into ½-inch/1-cm. slices, sprinkle with salt and allow to stand for 15 minutes, then drain and pat dry.

2. Place the marrow, onion and salt in a saucepan with cold water to cover. Bring to the boil, cover and lower heat. Simmer 10 minutes, drain well and transfer to a buttered baking dish.

3. Set oven at 325°F., 160°C., Gas Mark 3.

4. Prepare the béchamel sauce (page 471) using the above-listed ingredients. Pour the béchamel sauce over the vegetables, sprinkle with the garlic and dot with the butter. Cover with overlapping slices of tomato and bake for 40 minutes. Garnish with parsley and serve.

Serves 4 to 6

ROMAN-STYLE STUFFED TOMATOES

Italy

Preparation time: 20 minutes   **Cooking time:** 20 minutes

Ingredients

6 large firm tomatoes
4 oz./100 g. cooked rice
4 oz./100 g. butter, melted
4 oz./100 g. Mozzarella
  cheese, shredded
1 oz./25 g. Romano or
  other hard cheese, grated

1 teaspoon dried oregano
1 tablespoon finely
  chopped parsley
Salt
Freshly ground pepper
1½ tablespoons bread-
  crumbs

1. Cut off the top of each tomato and scoop out the centre.
   Be careful not to make the walls too thin.

2. Preheat oven to 325°F., 160°C., Gas Mark 3.

3. In a mixing bowl, toss the rice with 3 oz./75 g. of the
   butter. Add the cheeses, oregano, parsley, salt and
   pepper and mix well.

4. Stuff each tomato with one-sixth of the rice mixture and
   then place in buttered baking dish. Sprinkle the top of
   each tomato with 1 teaspoon breadcrumbs and 1 teaspoon of the remaining melted butter. Bake for 20
   minutes.

Serves 6

BAKED TURNIPS IN CREAM

Preparation time: 25 minutes   **Cooking time:** 15 minutes

France

Ingredients

*2 lb./1 kg. small white
  early turnips, peeled
  and quartered*

Sauce Normande:

2 oz./50 g. butter

*1 medium onion, finely
  sliced*

½ oz./15 g. flour

*⅓ pint/2 dl. dry cider or
  dry white wine*

Salt

Freshly ground pepper

*½ pint/3 dl. crème fraîche
  or double cream*

*Pinch freshly grated
  nutmeg*

Lemon juice

1. Blanch the turnips in boiling salted water for 10 minutes. Drain and arrange in a buttered baking dish.

2. Set oven at 400°F., 200°C., Gas Mark 6.

3. Prepare the *sauce normande*: a) Melt the butter in a saucepan and lightly sauté the onion until translucent; b) stir in the flour and continue cooking for a few minutes; c) add the cider, stirring constantly until the sauce thickens; d) season with salt and pepper, then add the *crème fraîche* (page 473) or double cream, nutmeg and a squeeze of lemon juice.

4. Pour the sauce over the turnips and bake for 15 minutes.

Serves 6 to 8

YELLOW TURNIP SOUFFLÉ

Norway

Preparation time: 15 minutes   **Cooking time:** 50 minutes

Ingredients

1 lb./450 g. yellow main-
crop turnips, scraped
and coarsely grated

2 oz./50 g. fresh bread-
crumbs

⅓ pint/2 dl. milk

3 eggs, separated
1½ oz./40 g. butter, melted
Salt
Freshly ground pepper

1. Preheat oven to 350°F., 180°C., Gas Mark 4.

2. Add the grated turnips to a pot of boiling water and cook over moderately high heat until barely tender, about 3 minutes.

3. While the turnips parboil, combine the breadcrumbs, milk, lightly beaten egg yolks and butter in a mixing bowl. Blend thoroughly, then season to taste with salt and pepper. Reserve.

4. Drain the parboiled turnips, mash, then stir into the breadcrumb mixture. Reserve.

5. In another bowl, beat the egg whites with a wire whisk or electric beater until frothy. Add a pinch of salt, then continue beating until egg whites are stiff.

6. Gently fold the egg whites into the turnip mixture, then transfer mixture to a buttered baking dish.

7. Set the baking dish in a shallow pan of hot water and bake until the soufflé is puffed and lightly browned, about 50 minutes. (Do not open the oven door during baking.)

8. Serve piping hot from the baking dish.

Serves 6

COURGETTES IN TOMATO SAUCE

Preparation time: 10 minutes   **Cooking time:** 30 minutes   *France*

Ingredients

Tomato Sauce:

2 tablespoons olive oil

2 lb./1 kg. ripe tomatoes,
  peeled, seeded and
  quartered

2 onions, chopped

Several leaves fresh
  basil or 1 teaspoon
  dried basil

1 tablespoon chopped
  fresh parsley

Salt

Freshly ground pepper
——

5 small courgettes, sliced

3 sprigs fresh tarragon,
  chopped, or 1 teaspoon
  dried tarragon

1. Heat the olive oil in a pan. Add the tomatoes, onions,
   basil and parsley and mix well.

2. Cover pan and simmer over low heat until the tomatoes
   soften, about 15 minutes. Season with salt and pepper.

3. Add the courgettes, cover and cook over moderately low
   heat until the courgettes are tender, about 15 minutes.

4. Just before serving, sprinkle with the tarragon. Serve
   hot or cold.

Serves 4 to 6

COURGETTES IN SOURED CREAM

Bulgaria

Preparation time: 20 minutes   **Cooking time:** 25 minutes

Ingredients

1 lb./450 g. courgettes,
  coarsely grated or cut
  into thin strips
Salt
½ oz./15 g. flour
⅓ pint/2 dl. soured cream
1½ oz./40 g. butter

1 medium onion, chopped
1 clove garlic, crushed
Freshly ground pepper
2 tablespoons chopped
  fresh dill
1½ tablespoons vinegar

1. Sprinkle the courgettes with salt and let stand for 15 minutes.

2. In a small bowl, combine flour and soured cream. Reserve.

3. Melt the butter in a frying pan. Add the onion and garlic and sauté gently until translucent, about 10 minutes.

4. Drain the courgettes, then transfer to the frying pan. Season with salt and pepper. Cook until tender, about 10 minutes.

5. Spoon the reserved soured cream mixture over courgettes. Cook over low heat for 5 minutes.

6. Blend in the dill and vinegar. Heat through and serve at once.

Serves 4

COURGETTES STUFFED WITH LAMB AND RICE

Greece

Preparation time: 45 minutes   **Cooking time:** 20 minutes

Ingredients

6 courgettes	Salt
2 tablespoons olive oil	Freshly ground pepper
2 onions, finely chopped	⅓ pint/2 dl. water
8 oz./225 g. lamb, minced	8 oz./225 g. cooked rice
1½ tablespoons chopped fresh parsley	1½ tablespoons lemon juice
1 teaspoon dried thyme	2 eggs, beaten
½ teaspoon fennel seeds	1½ oz./40 g. butter
2 bay leaves	Dry breadcrumbs for garnish
½ teaspoon dried mint	

1. Slice the courgettes in half lengthwise. Scoop out the pulp and chop. Reserve the shells.

2. Heat the oil and sauté the onion until limp, then add the lamb and sauté until browned, about 10 minutes. Add the courgette pulp and flavourings. Pour in the water and simmer meat mixture gently until the water has evaporated, about 15 minutes.

3. Set oven at 350°F., 180°C., Gas Mark 4.

4. Discard the bay leaves from the meat mixture, then transfer mixture to a large bowl. Add the rice and the lemon juice and mix thoroughly, then bind with the eggs. Correct seasonings. Stuff the reserved courgette shells with the rice and meat mixture, dot with butter, sprinkle with dry breadcrumbs. Arrange on a buttered baking sheet and bake until shells are tender, about 20 minutes.

Serves 6

VEGETABLES AU GRATIN

Sweden

Preparation time: 25 minutes   **Cooking time:** 10 minutes

Ingredients

Cream Sauce:
1 oz./25 g. butter
½ oz./15 g. flour
⅓ pint/2 dl. double cream
⅓ pint/2 dl. vegetable stock
  or milk
2 egg yolks
Salt
Freshly ground pepper

8 oz./225 g. cauliflower,
  cooked
8 oz./225 g. carrots,
  cooked
10 oz./275 g. peas, cooked
½ oz./15 g. butter
4 tomatoes, sliced
1 oz./25 g. Emmenthal
  cheese, grated

—

1. Preheat oven to 400°F., 200°C., Gas Mark 6.

2. In a saucepan melt the butter. Stirring constantly over moderate heat, sprinkle in the flour and cook for 1 minute.

3. Gradually beat in the cream and vegetable stock (or milk). Stir over low heat for 10 minutes. Keep hot.

4. In a bowl, beat the egg yolks well. Gradually beat in a few tablespoons of the hot sauce, then stir mixture into the saucepan. Heat through but do not boil. Remove saucepan from heat and season to taste with salt and pepper. Reserve.

5. Layer the cauliflower, carrots and peas in a well-buttered baking dish. Pour in the sauce. Layer on the tomato slices, season well with salt and pepper, then top with the grated cheese. Bake until the cheese is melted, about 10 minutes, then brown quickly under the grill.

Serves 4 to 6

BATTER-FRIED VEGETABLES

Preparation time: 20 minutes
Batter and sauce chill—15 minutes

Cooking time: 1 minute
per batch

Japan

Ingredients

Batter:

2 eggs
¾ pint/4½ dl. water
8 oz./225 g. flour
Salt
1 teaspoon baking
powder

Dipping Sauce:

⅓ pint/2 dl. chicken stock
2 oz./50 g. sugar
6 tablespoons soy sauce
1½ tablespoons mirin
(sweet rice wine) or
dry sherry
1 slice fresh root ginger,
peeled and minced
1 teaspoon grated radish

1 spring onion, minced

—

1¼ pints/7 dl. vegetable oil
⅓ pint/2 dl. sesame seed oil
4 carrots, sliced
2 sweet potatoes, sliced
2 green peppers, sliced
8 oz./225 g. small
mushrooms, halved
1 small aubergine, sliced
2 onions, sliced in rings
24 French beans, snapped
in half
2 courgettes, sliced
Rice

1. Prepare the batter by combining the eggs with the water
   and mixing well. Gradually stir in the flour, salt and
   baking powder. Mixture should have consistency of
   whipping cream. Refrigerate for 15 minutes.

2. Combine dipping sauce ingredients and refrigerate.

3. Heat the oil in a large pot to 350°F., 177°C. Dip each
   vegetable into the batter and drop it gently into the hot
   oil. Fry until golden brown, about 30 seconds to 1
   minute. Drain each piece briefly and serve at once.
   Serve with individual bowls of dipping sauce and hot rice.

Serves 4 to 6

VEGETABLE CURRY

India

Preparation time: 15 minutes

Cooking time: 40 minutes

Ingredients

Curry Powder:

*1 tablespoon each
coriander, cumin,
turmeric*

*2 whole cardamom pods,
ground*

*1 teaspoon each ginger,
fenugreek, chilli
powder, garam masala
(optional)*

—

2 tablespoons groundnut oil

*2 large onions, finely
chopped*

2 cloves garlic, crushed

2 chilli peppers, chopped

*6 tablespoons tomato
purée*

¼ teaspoon sugar

4 medium potatoes

4 carrots, sliced

*10 oz./275 g. Brussels
sprouts*

2 oz./50 g. raisins

6 courgettes, sliced

4 apples, chopped

Salt

Lemon juice

1. In a small bowl, combine the curry powder ingredients.

2. Heat the oil in a large pan. Add the onion, garlic and chilli peppers and sauté over moderate heat for 10 minutes. Blend in the curry powder mixture and stir until the spices darken in colour, about 3 minutes. Blend in the tomato purée and the sugar, then pour in enough water to make a thick sauce. Cover and simmer gently for 10 minutes.

3. While the sauce simmers, parboil the potatoes for 5 minutes then drain, peel and cut into small pieces. Add the potatoes, carrots, Brussels sprouts and raisins to the sauce. Pour over enough water to barely cover the vegetables. Mix thoroughly, then simmer for 5 minutes. Add the courgettes and the apples. Season to taste with salt and lemon juice, then continue to simmer until vegetables are tender, about 10 minutes. Serve the curry with a meat dish or as a main course with rice.

Serves 6 to 8

Goods

ARAB BREAD

Lebanon

Preparation time: 20 minutes
Dough rises—1¾ hours

Baking time: 8–10 minutes

Ingredients

2 teaspoons dried yeast
Pinch sugar
About ½ pint/3 dl. warm
 water
1 teaspoon salt

1½ tablespoons oil
14 oz./400 g. strong
 plain flour, sifted
Cornmeal

1. In a large mixing bowl, dissolve the yeast and sugar in 3 tablespoons of the water. Let stand for 10 minutes, then add the remaining water, the salt and the oil. Stir 4 oz./100 g. of the flour at a time into the yeast mixture, forming a sticky dough. (Add a little more flour if dough is too sticky.)

2. Transfer the dough to a lightly floured board and knead vigorously until smooth, about 10 minutes. Shape the dough into a ball and coat lightly with oil. Cover and let rise until doubled in bulk, about 1½ hours.

3. Punch down the dough and form 6 or 7 balls. On a lightly floured board, roll or press out the dough with the hands into 6-inch/15-cm. circles that are ¼ inch/5 mm. thick. Dust lightly with flour, cover and let rise again for 15 minutes.

4. Preheat oven to 450°F., 230°C., Gas Mark 8.

5. Place the bread on lightly oiled baking sheets dusted with cornmeal. Bake until puffy, about 8 to 10 minutes. Wrap the bread in foil immediately after removing from the oven to preserve moistness.

Makes 6 or 7 round loaves

IRISH SODA BREAD

Preparation time: 15 minutes   **Baking time:** 1 hour   *Ireland*

Ingredients

1 lb./450 g. plain flour
1 teaspoon bicarbonate of
   soda
1 teaspoon cream of tartar
1 teaspoon salt

6 oz./175 g. sugar
4 oz./100 g. butter, melted
3 oz./75 g. seedless raisins
¾ pint/4½ dl. buttermilk

1. Preheat oven to 375°F., 190°C., Gas Mark 5.

2. Sift the dry ingredients into a large mixing bowl.

3. Add the butter, raisins and buttermilk. Mix well, making
   a soft, moist dough. Dust with additional flour if dough
   is too sticky to handle.

4. Transfer the dough to a lightly floured surface. Knead
   vigorously for 3 or 4 minutes until dough is firm, then
   shape into 2 round loaves.

5. Moisten each loaf with buttermilk and dust with flour.

6. Score the top of each loaf with an *X*.

7. Place the bread on a buttered and floured baking sheet
   and bake until nicely browned, about 1 hour. Cool on a
   wire rack.

Makes 2 loaves

SWEDISH SAFFRON BREAD

Sweden

Preparation time: 20 minutes
Dough rises—1½–3½ hours

Baking time: 15–30 minutes

Ingredients

2 oz./50 g. butter
⅓ pint/2 dl. milk
2 teaspoons dried yeast
4 oz./100 g. sugar
½ teaspoon ground saffron
½ teaspoon salt

1 egg
1¼ lb./600 g. strong plain
   flour
Beaten egg for glaze
Raisins for decoration

1. Melt the butter over low heat and gradually add the milk. Heat until mixture is warm, but not hot.

2. Place the yeast in a large mixing bowl. Add a little of the warm milk mixture and half the sugar. Blend thoroughly. Leave to stand for 10 to 15 minutes, then stir in the remaining milk, saffron, sugar, salt and egg. Mix well. Gradually stir in 1 lb./450 g. of the flour. Work the dough with fingers until smooth and firm.

3. Sprinkle a little of the remaining flour over the dough, then cover bowl and let stand in a warm place until the dough doubles in bulk (1 to 3 hours).

4. Transfer the dough to a lightly floured surface and knead until smooth. If dough is too moist, add some of the remaining flour. Divide into portions and shape dough into small cakes, braided loaves or buns. Arrange the breads on a buttered baking sheet, cover and let stand for ½ hour.

5. Preheat oven to 450°F., 230°C., Gas Mark 8. Brush the breads with the egg, decorate with the raisins and bake until golden, about 15 minutes for small cakes and braided buns, about 30 minutes for larger loaves.

Serves 6

BRIOCHE

Preparation time: 30 minutes   **Baking time:** 20 minutes   *France*
Dough rises—2½ hours

Ingredients

2 teaspoons dried yeast

2 teaspoons sugar

3 tablespoons warm water

6 fl. oz./1¾ dl. milk, warmed

1 lb./450 g. strong plain flour, sifted

½ teaspoon salt

8 oz./225 g. butter, softened

6 eggs

1 egg mixed with 1½ tablespoons water for glazing

1. In a large mixing bowl dissolve the yeast and sugar in the warm water. Leave to stand for 10 to 15 minutes. Add the milk, half of the flour, and the salt, then beat well with a wooden spoon. Cover with a damp towel and let rise until double in bulk, about 1 hour.

2. Add the butter, eggs, and the remaining 8 oz./225 g. of flour and mix well until the dough is smooth and satiny. Cover again with a damp towel and let rise until doubled in bulk, about 1½ hours.

3. With very well-floured hands, form 18 (2-inch/5-cm.) balls of dough. Place each one in a buttered brioche tin. Now roll 18 (½-inch/1-cm.) balls. Firmly press one small ball in the centre of each large ball.

4. Preheat oven to 425°F., 220°C., Gas Mark 7.

5. Brush each brioche with glaze and let them rise for another 15 minutes. Bake for 20 minutes, until golden brown.

Makes 18 brioches

GLAZED PRETZEL BREAD

USSR

Preparation time: 30 minutes
Dough rises—2 hours

Baking time: 50 minutes

Ingredients

2 teaspoons dried yeast

3 tablespoons warm water

1 teaspoon sugar

14 oz./400 g. strong plain
   flour, sifted

1½ oz./40 g. castor sugar

½ teaspoon salt

2 oz./50 g. butter, chilled

2 eggs

6 tablespoons single
   cream

Butter, melted

1 egg lightly beaten with
   1 tablespoon cream

2 teaspoons honey

2 teaspoons peach brandy

1. In a cup, soak the yeast in the warm water with the sugar for about 10 minutes.

2. Sift together flour, castor sugar and salt. Cut butter into the flour until it reaches the consistency of breadcrumbs.

3. In a large mixing bowl, lightly beat together the eggs and the cream, then stir in the yeast mixture. Gradually blend in the flour mixture. Knead the dough on a lightly floured surface until it is smooth and shiny, about 10 minutes. Shape it into a ball and coat it lightly with butter. Cover and let dough rise until doubled in bulk, about 1½ hours.

4. Preheat the oven to 425°F., 220°C., Gas Mark 7.

5. Punch down the dough. Roll into a long 2-inch/5-cm. thick rope. Twist the rope into a pretzel shape and transfer to a buttered baking sheet. Let dough rise until doubled again, about 30 minutes.

6. Brush the dough with the lightly beaten egg and cream. Bake for 15 minutes, then cover with foil and bake for 25 more minutes. Remove from oven and transfer to a wire rack to cool. Combine the honey and brandy and glaze the loaf.

Serves 6

GINGERBREAD

Preparation time: 15 minutes   **Baking time:** 1¼ hours   *USA*

Ingredients

8 oz./225 g. butter, in
   small pieces
4 oz./100 g. castor sugar
8 oz./225 g. black treacle
⅓ pint/2 dl. milk, scalded
9 oz./250 g. plain flour
1 teaspoon ginger
1 teaspoon cinnamon
1 teaspoon allspice

1 teaspoon salt
1½ teaspoons bicarbonate
   of soda
2 eggs
Rind of 1 orange, grated
Whipped cream for
   topping
Orange slices for
   decoration

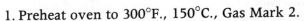

1. Preheat oven to 300°F., 150°C., Gas Mark 2.

2. In a large mixing bowl, combine the butter, sugar and black treacle. Pour in the hot scalded milk and stir until the butter is melted, then let stand until cool.

3. Sift together into a bowl the flour, ginger, cinnamon, allspice, salt and bicarbonate of soda. Reserve.

4. One by one, beat the eggs into the cooled milk mixture, then gradually beat in the spiced flour. Add the orange rind and mix thoroughly.

5. Scrape the mixture into a 10-inch/25-cm. square buttered cake tin and bake until a warmed skewer inserted in the centre comes out clean, about 1¼ hours.

6. Cut into squares and serve piping hot, topped with whipped cream and decorated with orange slices.

Serves 8 to 12

FREE-FORM ALMOND CAKES

France

Preparation time: 15 minutes   **Baking time:** 45–60 minutes
Batter chills—2 hours

Ingredients

14 oz./400 g. plain flour, sifted

8 oz./225 g. butter, at room temperature

2 eggs

8 oz./225 g. castor sugar

4 oz./100 g. ground almonds

Few drops almond essence

1½ tablespoons water

1½ tablespoons lemon juice

5 oz./150 g. mixed glacé fruits, finely chopped

Blackcurrant jam for topping

1. Sift the flour into a large bowl. Make a well in the middle of the flour and add the butter and eggs. Work mixture lightly with fingertips until well blended, then briskly work in the sugar, almonds, almond essence, water, lemon juice and glacé fruits.

2. Shape dough into a ball, wrap in greaseproof paper and refrigerate for 2 hours.

3. Preheat oven to 325°F., 160°C., Gas Mark 3.

4. Transfer the chilled dough to a sheet of greaseproof paper and cut in half. Using the bottom of a plate, press each half into a flat round cake about ¾ inch/2 cm. thick.

5. Place the cakes on a buttered baking sheet. Streak the surfaces with a fork and bake until golden, about 45 to 60 minutes. (The cakes will be quite flat.)

6. When the cakes are done, transfer to a wire rack to cool. Serve at room temperature, topped with blackcurrant jam.

Serves 8

NUTTED TEA CAKE

Preparation time: 15 minutes **Baking time:** 50–60 minutes

France

Ingredients

4 oz./100 g. unsalted
  butter, at room
  temperature

3 eggs

4 oz./100 g. castor sugar

4 oz./100 g. walnuts,
  finely ground

Juice of 1 lemon

Grated peel of ¼ lemon

5 oz./150 g. plain flour

½ teaspoon bicarbonate of
  soda

1. Set oven at 350°F., 180°C., Gas Mark 4.

2. Cream the butter in a bowl. Beat in the eggs one at a time.

3. Beat vigorously, then add the sugar, nuts, lemon juice, grated lemon peel, flour and bicarbonate of soda. Mix carefully until ingredients are thoroughly blended.

4. Pour into a buttered 2½-pint/1¼-litre loaf tin and bake until the cake shrinks slightly from the sides of the tin and a skewer inserted into the centre of the cake comes out clean, about 50 to 60 minutes.

Serves 6

NUT CAKE

France

Preparation time: 10 minutes   **Baking time:** 1 hour

Ingredients

5 eggs, separated
5 oz./150 g. castor sugar

18 oz./500 g. hazelnuts,
  ground

1. Preheat oven to 350°F., 180°C., Gas Mark 4.

2. Using a wire whisk, beat the egg yolks well in a bowl. Gradually beat in the sugar. Continue beating until the mixture is light yellow. Stir the nuts into the egg yolk mixture.

3. In another bowl, beat the egg whites until stiff. Carefully fold the egg whites into the mixture.

4. Pour the mixture into a buttered and floured charlotte mould or 8-inch/20-cm. round cake tin.

5. Bake until a skewer inserted into the centre of the cake comes out clean, about 1 hour. (Do not open the oven door during baking time.)

6. When the cake is done, transfer to a cake rack and allow to cool thoroughly before removing from tin.

Serves 8

SAND CAKE

Preparation time: 45 minutes

Baking time: 1 hour

Austria

Ingredients

8 oz./225 butter, at room
  temperature

8 oz./225 g. castor sugar

5 eggs, separated

4 oz./100 g. plain flour

4 oz./100 g. cornflour

½ teaspoon baking powder

1 tablespoon rum

Rind of 3 lemons, grated

Pinch salt

1. Preheat oven to 350°F., 180°C., Gas Mark 4.

2. In a mixing bowl, cream the butter well with a wooden spoon, then beat until light and fluffy with a whisk or an electric beater. Add 2 oz./50 g. of the sugar to the butter. Beat until all the sugar is thoroughly incorporated, then add one egg yolk at a time, blending thoroughly. (This will take at least 20 minutes by hand or 10 minutes using an electric beater.)

3. A tablespoon at a time, beat the plain flour and cornflour into the mixture. Blend thoroughly before adding each remaining tablespoon. Beat the baking powder into the mixture, then add the rum and grated lemon rind. Reserve.

4. In another mixing bowl, beat the egg whites with a pinch of salt until stiff. Gently fold the egg whites into the mixture.

5. Pour the mixture into a buttered 2½-lb./1¼-kg. loaf tin and bake until golden and a skewer inserted into the centre of the cake comes out clean, about 1 hour.

6. Transfer cake (in tin) to a wire rack and cool for ½ hour, then remove from tin and cool to room temperature.

Serves 8

GUGELHUPF

Germany

Preparation time: 15 minutes
Dough rises—2 hours

Baking time: 1 hour

Ingredients

½ oz./15 g. dried yeast

4 oz./100 g. castor sugar

6 tablespoons warm water

1 lb./450 g. strong plain
    flour, sifted

½ teaspoon salt

4 oz./100 g. butter,
    softened

4 eggs, lightly beaten

6 fl. oz./1¾ dl. milk,
    warmed

6 oz./175 g. raisins

1½ oz./40 g. candied citron
    peel, chopped

1½ oz./40 g. candied
    orange peel, chopped

2 teaspoons vanilla
    essence

2 oz./50 g. coarsely
    chopped almonds

Melted butter

Icing sugar for dusting
    cake

1. Dissolve the yeast and 1 teaspoon of the sugar in the warm water. Add 2 oz./50 g. of the flour and mix lightly. Let the dough rise for 30 minutes in a warm draught-free corner.

2. Resift the remaining flour and the salt into the dough. With a wooden spoon, beat in the butter and eggs alternately with the milk. Beat the mixture well.

3. Add the raisins, citron, orange peel, vanilla, nuts and the remaining sugar. Beat until the batter is smooth and elastic. Cover the dough and let rise until doubled in bulk, about 1 hour.

4. Place the dough in a buttered 3½- to 4-pint/2- to 2½-litre Gugelhupf mould. Let it rise for another 30 minutes.

5. Preheat oven to 350°F., 180°C., Gas Mark 4. Brush the top of Gugelhupf with melted butter and bake until deep golden brown, about 1 hour. Dust with icing sugar.

Serves 6 to 8

KING'S CAKE

Preparation time: 30 minutes   **Baking time:** 1¼ hours   *Germany*

Ingredients

12 oz./350 g. unsalted
  butter
10 oz./275 g. castor sugar
5 eggs, separated
12 oz./350 g. self-raising
  flour, sifted
Pinch salt
1½ oz./40 g. currants
1½ oz./40 g. raisins

1 oz./25 g. slivered
  almonds
1½ tablespoons chopped
  citron peel
Grated rind of 1 lemon
¼ teaspoon vanilla essence
1½ tablespoons cognac or
  rum

1. Preheat oven to 350°F., 180°C., Gas Mark 4.

2. Cream the butter, then add the sugar and beat until fluffy. Add the egg yolks, one at a time. Slowly stir in the flour, mixing well. Add the salt, currants, raisins, almonds, citron peel, lemon rind, vanilla essence and cognac.

3. Beat the egg whites with a little salt until stiff. Gently fold the egg whites into the mixture, then pour into a 10-inch/25-cm. round buttered cake tin.

4. Bake until a skewer inserted in the cake comes out clean, about 1¼ hours. Cool the cake in the tin.

Serves 10

CHOCOLATE DREAM CAKE

Sweden

Preparation time: 30 minutes

Baking time: 15 minutes

Ingredients

1 oz./25 g. plain flour
1 oz./25 g. cornflour
1½ tablespoons cocoa
1 teaspoon baking powder
3 eggs
1 egg white
5 oz./150 g. castor sugar

Mocha Butter Cream:
4 oz./100 g. butter, softened

4½ oz./125 g. icing sugar
1 tablespoon cocoa
1 tablespoon instant coffee, dissolved in 1 teaspoon water
1 teaspoon vanilla essence
1 egg yolk

1. Preheat oven to 400°F., 200°C., Gas Mark 6. Line a 9 × 12-inch/23 × 30-cm. Swiss roll tin with greaseproof paper. Reserve.

2. Sift the plain flour, cornflour, cocoa and baking powder into a bowl. Reserve.

3. In a large mixing bowl, beat the eggs and extra egg white very well. Beating constantly, gradually add the sugar. Continue beating until mixture is fluffy. A tablespoon at a time, beat the sifted ingredients into the egg and sugar mixture. Beat thoroughly after each addition.

4. Using a spatula, spread the mixture into the Swiss roll tin and bake until cake springs back to the touch, about 15 minutes. Invert the cake onto a floured towel, cover with greaseproof paper, roll up loosely and cool.

5. Prepare the mocha butter cream. Cream the butter well in a mixing bowl and blend in the sugar and cocoa. Beat mixture until fluffy. Add the coffee, vanilla and egg yolk. Unroll the cake and spread the mocha cream evenly on top. Holding the shorter end of the towel, re-roll the cake into a cylinder. Place on a platter and serve.

Serves 6

CHOCOLATE TORTE

Preparation time: 30 minutes   **Baking time:** 50 minutes

Germany

Ingredients

8 oz./225 g. plain chocolate

1½ tablespoons instant
   coffee powder

8 oz./225 g. butter, softened

8 oz./225 g. castor sugar

8 eggs, separated

1 oz./25 g. dry breadcrumbs

Pinch salt

Glaze:

6 oz./175 g. plain
   chocolate

1½ tablespoons instant
   coffee powder

Knob butter

Whipped cream

1. Set oven at 350°F., 180°C., Gas Mark 4. Combine the chocolate and coffee in a double saucepan. Melt over simmering water. Reserve.

2. In a large bowl, cream the butter. Gradually add the sugar and beat until light and fluffy. Beat the egg yolks until pale yellow, then gradually incorporate into the butter and sugar mixture. Add the breadcrumbs. Blend thoroughly, then stir in the melted chocolate.

3. In another large bowl, beat the egg whites with the salt until stiff. Gently fold into the mixture. Pour three-quarters of the mixture into 2 (8-inch/20-cm.) sandwich tins. Refrigerate the rest of mixture until needed.

4. Bake torte until a skewer inserted in the centre comes out clean, about 50 minutes. Cool torte slightly in the tins, then transfer to a cake rack and cool.

5. Remove chilled mixture from refrigerator about 10 minutes before using. Spread it on the bottom layer of the torte, then cover with the other layer. Refrigerate.

6. Prepare the glaze: Melt the chocolate with the coffee, then beat in the butter. Remove from heat and cool slightly. Spread over torte. Serve with whipped cream.

Serves 6 to 8

CHEESECAKE

Israel

Preparation time: 25 minutes

Baking time: 45 minutes

Ingredients

4 oz./100 g. butter, melted

8 oz./225 g. digestive
   biscuit crumbs

1 oz./25 g. castor sugar

Filling:

3 8-oz./225-g. packets
   cream cheese, at room
   temperature

4 eggs

10 oz./275 g. castor sugar

Few drops vanilla essence

1 tablespoon lemon juice

—

10 oz./275 g. strawberries,
   hulled

1. Preheat oven to 350°F., 180°C., Gas Mark 4.

2. Pour the melted butter over the digestive biscuit crumbs and the sugar, then toss lightly. Press the crumbs firmly to all sides of an 8-inch/20-cm. spring-form pan or ovenproof flan dish and refrigerate.

3. Combine the filling ingredients in a large mixing bowl. Beat until smooth, then pour into the chilled crust. Bake for 45 minutes, then turn off the heat and allow the cake to cool in the oven.

4. Place the cheesecake on a serving platter (if baked in a spring-form pan) and arrange the strawberries in an attractive pattern on the top. Serve chilled.

Serves 6 to 8

PRUNE CAKE

Preparation time: 20 minutes   **Baking time:** 1½ hours   *USA*

Ingredients

8 oz./225 g. castor sugar

1 teaspoon salt

1 teaspoon nutmeg

1 teaspoon cinnamon

1 teaspoon bicarbonate of
   soda

8 oz./225 g. plain flour

3 eggs

⅓ pint/2 dl. vegetable oil

⅓ pint/2 dl. buttermilk

6 oz./175 g. prunes,
   soaked and chopped

6 oz./175 g. shelled filberts
   or walnuts, chopped

Few drops vanilla essence

Glaze:

8 oz./225 g. sugar

½ teaspoon bicarbonate of
   soda

4 oz./100 g. butter

6 tablespoons buttermilk

1 tablespoon golden syrup

½ teaspoon vanilla essence

1. Preheat oven to 300°F., 150°C., Gas Mark 2.

2. Sift the dry ingredients into a mixing bowl. Reserve.

3. In another mixing bowl beat the eggs until pale yellow.
   Gradually beat in the oil and the buttermilk, then stir in
   the prunes, nuts and vanilla. Gradually blend the dry
   ingredients into the egg mixture. Continue beating until
   mixture is thoroughly blended.

4. Pour the mixture into a buttered and floured 9-inch/
   23-cm. square cake tin and bake until a skewer inserted
   comes out clean, about 1½ hours. Transfer cake (in tin)
   to a wire rack. Reserve.

5. As soon as the cake is removed from the oven, prepare
   the glaze. Combine all the ingredients in a saucepan. Boil
   and stir over high heat until mixture is frothy and slightly
   thickened, about 2 minutes. Pour the glaze over the hot
   cake. Let stand for at least 3 hours. Serve at room
   temperature.

Serves 8 to 10

CARROT CAKE

Canada

Preparation time: 15 minutes

Baking time: 1½ hours

Ingredients

8 oz./225 g. castor sugar
½ pint/3 dl. vegetable oil
4 eggs
8 oz./225 g. plain flour
2 teaspoons bicarbonate of
    soda

1 teaspoon salt
3 teaspoons cinnamon
½ teaspoon nutmeg
Few drops vanilla essence
12 oz./350 g. grated
    carrots

1. Preheat oven to 325°F., 160°C., Gas Mark 3.

2. Combine the sugar, oil and eggs.

3. Sift together the dry ingredients. Add to the sugar mixture, beating well. Add the vanilla and carrots.

4. Pour into an 8-inch/20-cm. square cake tin and bake until a skewer comes out clean, about 1½ hours.

Serves 6 to 8

DUNDEE CAKE

Preparation time: 20 minutes   **Baking time:** 2 hours

Scotland

Ingredients

6 oz./175 g. butter

6 oz./175 g. castor sugar

3 eggs

8 oz./225 g. plain flour

2 teaspoons baking powder

1 teaspoon mixed spice

2 tablespoons milk

2 oz./50 g. almonds, chopped

2 oz./50 g. glacé cherries

14 oz./400 g. mixed dried fruit

3 oz./75 g. candied peel, chopped

2 oz./50 g. flaked almonds

Egg white for glaze

1. Preheat oven to 325°F., 160°C., Gas Mark 3.

2. Cream the butter in a large mixing bowl. Gradually blend in the sugar and beat until fluffy. Gradually incorporate the eggs into the mixture.

3. Sift together the dry ingredients. Blend into the butter mixture, adding enough milk to make a thick batter. Stir in the chopped almonds and fruits.

4. Put the mixture into a buttered and floured 8-inch/ 20-cm. round cake tin. Cover with the almond flakes and brush with the egg white. Bake until a skewer inserted in the cake comes out clean, about 2 hours. Cool cake slightly in the tin before transferring to a wire rack.

Serves 8

ALMOND TORTE

Portugal

Preparation time: 30 minutes　　**Baking time:** 30 minutes

Ingredients

8 oz./225 g. castor sugar
4 tablespoons water
6 oz./175 g. ground
　almonds
1 oz./25 g. plain flour
8 egg yolks
1½ teaspoons ground
　cinnamon

1 teaspoon almond essence
2 oz./50 g. flaked almonds
*Whipped cream flavoured
　with almond essence and
　sugar*

1. Set oven at 400°F., 200°C., Gas Mark 6.

2. In a heavy saucepan, combine the sugar and water. Bring to a gentle boil until liquid clears. Stirring over moderate heat, add the ground almonds and flour and cook for 5 minutes. Remove pan from heat and reserve.

3. In a bowl, beat the egg yolks with a wire whisk until pale yellow. Stir the almond mixture into the egg yolks a spoonful at a time, beating well. Return mixture to saucepan. Stir in cinnamon and almond essence.

4. Stirring constantly, gently cook almond mixture over low heat until it thickens slightly, about 10 minutes. Do not boil. Remove from heat.

5. Pour mixture into a buttered fluted flan tin and top with the almond flakes. Bake pie until set, about 30 minutes. (Cover with foil after 10 minutes.) Serve cold accompanied by whipped cream flavoured with almond essence and sugar.

Serves 6 to 8

RASPBERRY JAM TORTE

Preparation time: 30 minutes   **Baking time:** 25 minutes

Pastry chills—30 minutes

Germany

Ingredients

4 oz./100 g. plain flour

1 teaspoon cinnamon

8 oz./225 g. hazelnuts, ground

4 oz./100 g. castor sugar

8 oz./225 unsalted butter, chilled

2 egg yolks

8 oz./225 g. raspberry jam

Icing sugar for dusting top of tart

1. Sift the flour and cinnamon into a large mixing bowl, then add the hazelnuts and sugar. Using 2 knives, cut the butter into the dry ingredients until pastry has the consistency of fine breadcrumbs. Add the egg yolks and briskly work mixture with fingertips until smooth. Do not overhandle the pastry. Wrap in greaseproof paper and refrigerate for 30 minutes.

2. Preheat oven to 375°F., 190°C., Gas Mark 5.

3. On a lightly floured surface, roll out two-thirds of the chilled pastry to ¼-inch/5-mm. thickness and line a 9-inch/23-cm. loose-bottomed flan tin.

4. Smooth the raspberry jam into the prepared pastry case.

5. Roll out the remaining pastry on a lightly floured surface. Cut into long ½-inch/1-cm. wide strips with a fluted pastry wheel or knife. Lay the strips in a lattice pattern on top of the filled tart. Pinch the strips together with the edges of tart case, then refrigerate for 15 minutes.

6. Bake tart until pastry is lightly browned, about 25 minutes. Cool in the dish for 15 minutes, then remove tart from dish and cool to room temperature on a cake rack. Dust with icing sugar.

Serves 6 to 8

MERINGUE SPONGE CAKE

France

Preparation time: 30 minutes   **Baking time:** 30 minutes
Meringue syrup simmers—15 minutes

Ingredients

A 1-lb./450-g. Genoese or
  other sponge cake
6 oz./175 g. apricot jam
1½ tablespoons cognac
1½ oz./40 g. sugar
Meringue:
4 oz./100 g. sugar

6 tablespoons water
4 egg whites
Pinch salt
Pinch cream of tartar
—
Glacé cherries

1. Cut the cake into 2 layers. Reserve.

2. Combine the apricot jam, cognac and sugar in a small heavy saucepan. Stir over moderate heat until sugar dissolves and mixture is runny, then remove from heat and cool slightly. Using a knife or spatula, spread the filling over one layer of the cake. Top with the remaining layer. Transfer to an ovenproof platter and reserve.

3. Set oven at 225°F., 110°C., Gas Mark ¼.

4. In another saucepan, combine the sugar and water. Stir over moderate heat until sugar dissolves and liquid clears, about 2 to 3 minutes. Then boil until syrup reaches the soft ball stage (238°F., 114°C. on a sugar thermometer), about 10 minutes.

5. While the syrup cooks, beat the egg whites in a large bowl with the salt and the cream of tartar until stiff. Gradually fold the hot syrup into the egg whites. Beat meringue until cooled to 100°F., 38°C., about 10 minutes.

6. Spread the meringue with a spatula over the cake. Top with glacé cherries. Bake cake for 30 minutes. (Do not brown meringue.) Serve hot or cool to room temperature.

Serves 4

STRAWBERRY CREAM CAKE

Preparation time: 1½ hours

Baking time: 10 minutes

France

Ingredients

5 egg yolks

4 oz./100 g. castor sugar

½ oz./15 g. self-raising flour

1½ oz./40 g. hazelnuts, toasted and ground

1½ oz./40 g. pecans, toasted and ground

Few drops vanilla essence

6 egg whites

Pinch salt

Strawberry Cream:

10 oz./275 g. fresh strawberries

2½ oz./65 g. castor sugar

2 tablespoons kirsch

¼ oz./7 g. gelatine

12 fl. oz./3½ dl. double cream

—

Redcurrant jelly, melted

1. Preheat oven to 400°F., 200°C., Gas Mark 6. Beat the yolks until pale yellow. Gradually add the sugar, beating until fluffy. Fold in the flour, nuts and vanilla.

2. In another bowl, beat the egg whites with salt until stiff. Fold the whites into the yolk mixture. Pour into 2 well-buttered and floured 8-inch/20-cm round sandwich tins and bake until done, about 8 to 12 minutes. Cool the cake in the tins for 10 minutes, then turn onto a wire rack.

3. Slice half of the strawberries, then sprinkle with 1 tablespoon of the sugar and 1½ tablespoons of the liqueur. Combine the remaining liqueur and 2 tablespoons of water in a small saucepan. Add the gelatine and stir over low heat until dissolved. Stir in remaining sugar; cool. Whip the cream until stiff. Stir the gelatine mixture into the cream, blend in the drained strawberries; chill.

4. Spread the redcurrant glaze over the cooled cake layers. Place one layer on a serving plate and spread a third of the strawberry cream over the top. Cover with the other layer of cake and coat the entire *gâteau* with the remaining strawberry cream. Arrange whole strawberries on top and glaze. Refrigerate for 2 hours.

Serves 6

ALMOND MACAROONS

France

Preparation time: 5 minutes   **Baking time:** 30–35 minutes

Ingredients

4 egg whites
10 oz./275 g. castor sugar
10 oz./275 g. blanched
  almonds, finely chopped

1½ tablespoons lemon juice
¼ teaspoon almond essence
Castor sugar for sprinkling

1. Using a wire whisk lightly beat the egg whites.

2. Fold in the sugar, almonds, lemon juice and almond essence.

3. Preheat oven to 275°F., 140°C., Gas Mark 1. Line a baking sheet with oiled greaseproof paper. Using 2 teaspoons, shape the mixture into small mounds and drop onto the paper. Sprinkle with castor sugar and bake until golden, about 30 to 35 minutes. (Do not open oven door during baking.)

4. When the macaroons are done, transfer (on paper) to a cake rack and allow to cool to room temperature. Remove cooled macaroons from paper by placing the paper on a damp cloth and lifting off the macaroons with a spatula.

Makes about 36 macaroons

ALMOND MERINGUES

Preparation time: 15 minutes   **Baking time:** 2–3 hours   *France*

Ingredients

2 egg whites

Pinch salt

Pinch cream of tartar

4 oz./100 g. castor sugar

1½ oz./40 g. ground
    almonds

1. Set oven at 225°F., 110°C., Gas Mark ¼.

2. Line a baking sheet with greaseproof paper and butter generously.

3. In a bowl beat the egg whites until frothy. Add a pinch of salt and a pinch of cream of tartar, then continue beating until very stiff.

4. Gently fold in the sugar and almonds.

5. Using a tablespoon, drop little mounds of the mixture onto the buttered paper.

6. Bake meringues until they can be removed from the paper without sticking, about 2 to 3 hours.

Makes about 15 meringues

ALSATIAN CHRISTMAS BISCUITS

France

Preparation time: 20 minutes
Dough chills—overnight

Baking time: 10–15 minutes
per batch

Ingredients

8 oz./225 g. unsalted
butter, at room
temperature

8 oz./225 g. castor sugar

7 oz./200 g. plain flour

8 oz./225 g. ground
almonds

4½ oz./125 g. candied
orange peel, finely
chopped

4 teaspoons ground
cinnamon

1 egg

½ teaspoon rose water
(optional) or ½ teaspoon
lemon juice

½ teaspoon salt

1 egg yolk, beaten, for
glazing

Sugar and ground almonds
for decoration

1. In a bowl, cream the butter with the sugar. Blend until fully integrated. Gradually beat in the flour, then add the rest of the ingredients. Mix thoroughly.

2. Knead the dough well, then cover with a damp cloth and refrigerate overnight.

3. Set oven at 400°F., 200°C., Gas Mark 6.

4. Place the chilled dough on waxed paper and roll out to ¼-inch/5-mm. thickness. Using biscuit cutters or a knife, cut the dough into various Christmas-shaped biscuits. Brush the tops with the beaten egg and sprinkle with sugar and ground almonds.

5. Arrange the biscuits on buttered and floured baking sheets and bake for 10 to 15 minutes.

Makes about 60 biscuits

BRANDY RING TWISTS

Preparation time: 25 minutes   **Baking time:** 15 minutes

Sweden

Ingredients

8 oz./225 g. butter, at
  room temperature
5 oz./150 g. castor sugar

3 tablespoons brandy
10 oz./275 g. plain flour,
  sifted

1. Preheat oven to 350°F., 180°C., Gas Mark 4.

2. In a mixing bowl cream the butter well. Gradually blend in the sugar and beat until light and fluffy. Beat in the brandy, a tablespoon at a time, then gradually blend in the flour. Mix thoroughly.

3. Transfer the dough to a lightly floured board. Roll out dough to $\frac{1}{4}$-inch/5-mm. thickness, then cut into thin 5-inch/13-cm. strips.

4. Assemble the brandy rings: Twist 2 of the dough strips together to form a rope, then join the ends of the rope to form a ring. Repeat process with the remaining strips of dough.

5. Transfer the brandy rings to a buttered baking sheet and bake until golden, about 15 minutes.

Makes about 72 brandy ring twists

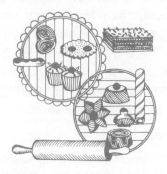

DUTCH SPICE COOKIES

*The
Netherlands*

Preparation time: 30 minutes   **Baking time:** 15–20 minutes

Ingredients

1 lb./450 g. plain flour
4 teaspoons baking powder
½ teaspoon salt
1 teaspoon ground
  cinnamon
1 teaspoon ground cloves
1 teaspoon ground nutmeg
½ teaspoon white pepper

8 oz./225 g. unsalted
  butter, at room
  temperature
8 oz./225 g. brown sugar
1 tablespoon grated lemon
  peel
4 to 6 tablespoons milk
6 oz./175 g. almonds,
  slivered

1. Preheat oven to 350°F., 180°C., Gas Mark 4.

2. Sift the flour, baking powder, salt, cinnamon, cloves, nutmeg and white pepper into a mixing bowl. Reserve.

3. In a large mixing bowl, cream the butter well with a wooden spoon. Gradually work in the sugar, then beat mixture until light and fluffy. Blend the spiced flour, a little at a time, into the butter and sugar mixture, and then add the lemon zest. Gradually add 4 tablespoons of the milk to the mixture. Blend thoroughly, adding a little more milk, if necessary, to make a soft dough.

4. On a lightly floured surface, roll out dough to ¼-inch/ 5-mm. thickness, then cut dough into 3-inch/7½-cm. squares. Using a spatula, transfer the squares to buttered baking sheets, then sprinkle with the slivered almonds.

5. Bake cookies until light brown, about 15 to 20 minutes. Cool slightly on baking sheets, then transfer to a wire rack and cool to room temperature.

Makes 40 cookies

In the Netherlands, windmill-patterned moulds are pressed onto the rolled-out dough. At Christmas time, tree, star, or Santa Claus biscuit cutters can be used.

SCANDINAVIAN GINGERSNAPS

Preparation time: 40 minutes
Dough refrigerates—2 hours

Baking time: 10–15 minutes
per batch

Sweden

Ingredients

5 oz./150 g. light brown
  sugar
4 oz./100 g. granulated
  sugar
4 oz./100 g. black treacle
4 tablespoons water
5 oz./150 g. butter
1½ teaspoons ground
  cinnamon

2 teaspoons ground ginger
1 teaspoon ground nutmeg
1½ teaspoons baking
  powder
11 oz./300 g. wholemeal
  flour, sifted

1. In a saucepan combine the brown sugar, granulated sugar, black treacle and water. Bring to the boil.

2. Stirring constantly over moderate heat, add the butter ½ oz./15 g. at a time. Continue stirring until butter is melted, then remove pan from heat and cool for 20 minutes.

3. Add the cinnamon, ginger, nutmeg and baking powder to the sugar mixture, then gradually blend in the flour.

4. Cover the dough and refrigerate until firm, about 2 hours.

5. Preheat oven to 350°F., 180°C., Gas Mark 4.

6. Transfer the chilled dough to a lightly floured surface. Knead dough until smooth and even, then roll out to ⅛-inch/3-mm. thickness.

7. Using the rim of a small glass or a 2-inch/5-cm. cutter, cut the dough into rounds. Place on a buttered baking sheet and bake until golden, about 10 to 15 minutes.

Makes about 100 gingersnaps

SHORTBREAD COOKIES

Canada

Preparation time: 15 minutes
Dough chills—1 hour

Baking time: 20 minutes

Ingredients

6 oz./175 g. butter,
  softened
12 oz./350 g. plain flour
9 oz./250 g. icing sugar
2 oz./50 g. desiccated
  coconut

6 oz./175 g. walnuts,
  finely chopped
Sugar for sprinkling
  cookies

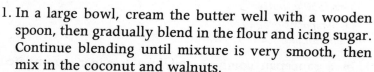

1. In a large bowl, cream the butter well with a wooden spoon, then gradually blend in the flour and icing sugar. Continue blending until mixture is very smooth, then mix in the coconut and walnuts.

2. Roll dough into a ball, wrap in greaseproof paper and refrigerate for 1 hour.

3. Set oven at 350°F., 180°C., Gas Mark 4.

4. On lightly floured greaseproof paper, roll out the dough to ½-inch/1-cm. thickness. Using a sharp knife or biscuit cutter, cut dough into various shapes.

5. Arrange cookies on an unbuttered baking sheet and bake for 20 minutes. When the cookies are done, transfer to a cake rack and sprinkle with sugar.

Makes about 48 cookies

CAEN COOKIES

Preparation time: 15 minutes   **Baking time:** 10–12 minutes
Dough chills—1 hour

France

Ingredients

7 oz./200 g. plain flour	4 oz./100 g. castor sugar
¼ teaspoon salt	Peel of 1 orange, grated
3 hard-boiled egg yolks	8 oz./225 g. butter, chilled

1. Sift the flour and salt into a mixing bowl. Make a well in the centre of the flour and sieve the egg yolks into the well.

2. Add the sugar and grated orange peel. Mix lightly.

3. Using 2 knives, cut the butter into the flour mixture, cutting the butter down to pea-sized pieces.

4. Using fingertips, lightly work the dough until smooth, then shape into a ball, wrap in greaseproof paper and refrigerate for 1 hour.

5. Set oven to 400°F., 200°C., Gas Mark 6.

6. On lightly floured greaseproof paper, roll out the dough to about ¼-inch/5-mm. thickness. Using biscuit cutters, cut dough into desired shapes.

7. Arrange the cookies on a buttered baking sheet, score the tops with a fork and bake for 10 to 12 minutes.

Makes about 36 cookies

WALNUT DELIGHTS

Denmark

Preparation time: 10 minutes

Baking time: 25 minutes

Ingredients

*4 oz./100 g. digestive
   biscuit crumbs*

6 oz./175 g. castor sugar

1 teaspoon baking powder

2 eggs, separated

*3 oz./75 g. walnuts,
   chopped*

Few drops vanilla essence

Salt

*Ice cream or whipped
   cream for decoration*

1. Preheat oven to 350°F., 180°C., Gas Mark 4.

2. Combine the digestive biscuit crumbs, sugar and baking powder in a large mixing bowl.

3. Lightly beat the egg yolks and stir into the dry ingredients. Add the walnuts and vanilla. Mix well.

4. In a separate bowl beat the egg whites with a pinch of salt until stiff. Fold carefully into the biscuit crumb mixture, then pour the mixture into an 8 × 8-inch/20 × 20-cm. buttered and floured tin.

5. Bake until golden, about 25 minutes. Cool in the tin, then cut into bars. Top with ice cream or whipped cream.

Serves 6

HONEY AND NUT PASTRY

Preparation time: 30 minutes   **Baking time:** 45 minutes   *Turkey*

Ingredients

Syrup:
8 oz./225 g. castor sugar
6 tablespoons water
1 tablespoon lemon juice
1 tablespoon rose water
—

20 sheets phyllo pastry
8 oz./225 g. butter, melted
8 oz./225 g. shelled
   walnuts or almonds,
   chopped
$1\frac{1}{2}$ oz./40 g. castor sugar

1. Preheat oven to 350°F., 180°C., Gas Mark 4.

2. Combine the sugar and water in a saucepan. Stir over low heat until sugar dissolves, then add the lemon juice. Bring to a gentle boil and simmer until thickened. Stir in rose water, simmer 1 to 2 minutes; cool and chill.

3. Lay a sheet of phyllo pastry in a well-buttered rectangular baking dish. Brush some of the melted butter over the pastry. Add another sheet of pastry, then brush with butter. Continue until half the pastry and half the butter have been used.

4. Top the stacked pastry sheets with the chopped walnuts (or almonds), then sprinkle with the sugar. Cover the nuts and sugar with a layer of phyllo, then brush with butter. Repeat until all the phyllo and all the butter have been used.

5. Using a very sharp knife, cut through the finished dish to make large diamond shapes.

6. Bake for 30 minutes, then raise oven temperature to 450°F., 230°C., Gas Mark 8 and continue baking until the pastry has puffed and coloured slightly, about 15 minutes more. Remove from oven and cover with the chilled syrup. Cool to room temperature. To serve, slice along original incisions.

Makes about 24 pastries

PEACH COBBLER

USA

Preparation time: 30 minutes   **Baking time:** 45 minutes

Ingredients

8 large fresh peaches,
peeled and sliced

3 oz./75 g. shelled walnuts,
chopped

4 oz./100 g. soft brown
sugar

1 tablespoon lemon juice

½ teaspoon cinnamon

4 oz./100 g. flour

1 teaspoon baking powder

¼ teaspoon salt

4 oz./100 g. unsalted
butter, at room
temperature

4 oz./100 g. castor sugar

2 eggs, beaten

Rind of 1 lemon, grated

1. Preheat oven to 375°F., 190°C., Gas Mark 5.

2. Toss the peaches and walnuts in a deep ovenproof dish
with 3 oz./75 g. of the brown sugar, the lemon juice and
the cinnamon. Reserve.

3. Sift the flour, baking powder and salt into a bowl.
Reserve.

4. In a mixing bowl, cream the butter well with a wooden
spoon, then gradually blend in the castor sugar. Beat
until light and fluffy.

5. Beat the eggs into the butter and sugar mixture, then
blend in the lemon rind.

6. Gradually beat the flour mixture into the butter and
sugar mixture. Stir until thoroughly blended.

7. Spread the mixture over the reserved fruit. Top with the
remaining brown sugar. Bake until crust is golden, about
45 minutes. Serve piping hot from the baking dish.

Serves 4

*Top each portion of cobbler with a generous helping of whipped
cream, vanilla ice cream or brandy butter.*

APPLE TART

Preparation time: 45 minutes
Pastry chills—1 hour

Baking time: 25 minutes

France

Ingredients

Sweet Shortcrust Pastry:
10 oz./275 g. plain flour,
   sifted
¼ teaspoon salt
1½ oz./40 g. castor sugar
3 oz./75 g. unsalted butter
3 oz./75 g. shortening
1 egg yolk
2½ tablespoons iced water

Filling:
5 lb./2¼ kg. cooking apples,
   peeled and sliced
4 oz./100 g. apricot jam
5 oz./150 g. sugar
6 tablespoons Calvados
1½ oz./40 g. butter
1 tablespoon lemon juice

Glaze:
6 oz./175 g. apricot jam,
   melted

1. Using the above-listed ingredients, prepare the sweet shortcrust pastry (page 481). Chill for 1 hour.

2. Set oven at 400°F., 200°C., Gas Mark 6.

3. Roll out the pastry to ⅛-inch/3-mm. thickness and line a buttered 11-inch/28-cm. flan tin. Prick and bake blind for 10 minutes.

4. Place 3 lb./1⅓ kg. of the apples in a saucepan, cover pan and cook apples over low heat until very soft, about 15 minutes. Beat in the apricot jam, 4 oz./100 g. sugar, Calvados and butter. Stirring constantly, bring to the boil and cook until apple purée is very thick, about 5 minutes. Remove from heat.

5. In a bowl, toss the remaining sliced apples with the lemon juice and the remaining sugar.

6. Pour the slightly cooled apple purée into the pastry case. Top with the sliced apples. Bake tart until apple slices are tender, about 25 minutes. Glaze with apricot jam.

Serves 6 to 8

FRENCH APPLE-CUSTARD PIE

France

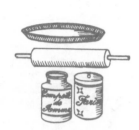

Preparation time: 45 minutes
Pastry chills—1 hour

Baking time: 1 hour

Ingredients

Sweet Shortcrust Pastry:
12 oz./350 g. plain flour, sifted
¼ teaspoon salt
1½ oz./40 g. castor sugar
4 oz./100 g. unsalted butter
3 oz./75 g. shortening
1 egg yolk
3 tablespoons iced water

Filling:
1½ lb./700 g. cooking apples,
    peeled and sliced

½ teaspoon ground
    cinnamon
6 tablespoons sugar
2 tablespoons flour
12 fl. oz./3½ dl. milk,
    scalded
1½ teaspoons orange-
    flower water (optional)
4 egg yolks

—

1 egg, beaten, for glazing

1. Using the above-listed ingredients, prepare the sweet shortcrust pastry (page 481). Chill for 1 hour.

2. Toss the apples, cinnamon and half the sugar in a bowl.

3. Place the flour in a saucepan. Whisking constantly, gradually add the scalded milk, then stir in the remaining sugar (and the orange-flower water). Beat over moderate heat for 5 minutes. Remove from heat.

4. In a bowl, beat the yolks with a whisk until pale yellow. Gradually beat in the milk mixture. Cool until needed. Set oven at 400°F., 200°C., Gas Mark 6.

5. Roll out two-thirds of the pastry and line an 11-inch/28-cm. buttered flan tin. Bake blind for 15 minutes, then reduce oven temperature to 350°F., 180°C., Gas Mark 4. Pour the custard mixture into the pastry case. Layer the sliced apples on top. Roll out the remaining pastry and cover the pie. Seal the edges and make 2 or 3 slits on the top. Brush with the beaten egg. Bake for about 1 hour.

Serves 6 to 8

APPLE ENVELOPES

Preparation time: 30 minutes
Pastry chills—1 hour

Baking time: 30 minutes

France

Ingredients

Sweet Shortcrust Pastry:
1 lb./450 g. plain flour, sifted
½ teaspoon salt
2½ oz./65 g. castor sugar
5 oz./150 g. unsalted butter
5 oz./150 g. shortening
2 egg yolks
4 tablespoons iced water
—

6 cooking apples
Juice of 2 lemons
6 teaspoons cinnamon
6 teaspoons brandy
6 knobs butter
8 oz./225 g. castor sugar
1 tablespoon cinnamon
Double cream for topping

1. Using the above-listed ingredients, prepare the sweet shortcrust pastry (page 481). Refrigerate for 1 hour.

2. Peel and core the apples, leaving a ¼-inch/5-mm. plug of core at the base of each apple. Trim bottoms evenly so that apples will stand. Sprinkle all surfaces of the apples with the lemon juice. Place a teaspoon each of cinnamon and brandy and a knob of butter in each core. Refrigerate.

3. Combine sugar and cinnamon in a small bowl. Reserve.

4. Divide pastry into 6 equal pieces. Roll out 1 section of pastry to ⅛-inch/3-mm. thickness between 2 sheets of greaseproof paper.

5. Using a plate as a guide, cut out a 10-inch/25-cm. circle. Cover a prepared apple with dough round. Fold edges around apple and pinch pastry to seal. Sprinkle outsides with cinnamon-sugar. Repeat entire step for remaining apples. Chill for 30 minutes.

6. Preheat oven to 400°F., 200°C., Gas Mark 6. Bake on a buttered baking sheet for 30 minutes. Serve piping hot, topped with chilled double cream.

Serves 6

APPLE STRUDEL

Germany

Preparation time: 1 hour

Ingredients

2 lb./1 kg. tart apples,
  peeled, cored and sliced

Juice of 1 lemon

4 oz./100 g. sugar

6 oz./175 g. raisins

Rind of 1 lemon, grated

½ teaspoon cinnamon

Dough 1:

½ oz./15 g. dried yeast

1 teaspoon sugar

Baking time: 40 minutes

6 tablespoons warm water

4 oz./100 g. plain flour

2 egg yolks

Dough 2:

4 oz./100 g. unsalted
  butter, chilled

4 oz./100 g. plain flour
——

3 oz./75 g. raspberry jam,
  melted

1 egg yolk, lightly beaten

1. Preheat oven to 400°F., 200°C., Gas Mark 6. Toss the first six ingredients and cover. Prepare Dough 1: Combine the yeast, sugar and warm water. Leave to stand for 10 to 15 minutes. Add 1 oz./25 g. of the flour, stirring well. Rest for 5 minutes. Add remaining flour, kneading well. Add the egg yolks, shape into a ball, cover and reserve.

2. Prepare Dough 2: Quickly cut the butter into the flour until mixture is the consistency of breadcrumbs. Roll into a ball, cover and refrigerate for 20 minutes.

3. Roll out each of the doughs separately between pieces of very well-floured wax paper to ⅛-inch/3-mm. thickness. Place Dough 1 on top of Dough 2. Fold in half, roll out to ¼-inch/5-mm. thickness. Repeat the process of folding and rolling the dough 2 more times. Transfer the dough to a well-floured cloth; roll thinly to a rectangle.

4. Trim the edges, then brush with the raspberry jam and spread with the apple mixture. Carefully roll the dough into a compact cylinder. Tuck in the edges and seal. Glaze with the egg yolk and bake until golden, about 40 minutes. Cover with foil after 25 minutes in the oven.

Serves 6

PEAR FLAN

Preparation time: 1 hour
Pastry chills—1 hour

Baking time: 25 minutes

France

Ingredients

Sweet Shortcrust Pastry:
10 oz./275 g. plain flour, sifted
¼ teaspoon salt
1½ oz./40 g. castor sugar
3 oz./75 g. unsalted butter
3 oz./75 g. shortening
1 egg yolk
2½ tablespoons iced water
—
1¼ lb./600 g. castor sugar

½ oz./15 g. cornflour
2 egg yolks
⅓ pint/2 dl. milk
Pinch salt
2 oz./50 g. ground almonds
A vanilla pod
2 oz./50 g. unsalted butter
¾ pint/4½ dl. water
6 pears, peeled
12 oz./350 g. apricot jam

1. Using the above-listed ingredients, prepare the pastry (page 481). Chill for 1 hour.

2. Preheat oven to 400°F., 200°C., Gas Mark 6.

3. Roll out the pastry and line a 10-inch/25-cm. flan tin. Bake blind until golden, about 25 minutes.

4. Combine 4 oz./100 g. of the sugar and all the cornflour in a mixing bowl. Add the yolks and 3 tablespoons of the milk, mixing well. Blend in the salt and the almonds. Heat the remaining milk and add the vanilla pod. Bring almost to the boil, then pour a small amount of the hot milk into the yolk mixture. Pour the eggs back into the saucepan, remove the vanilla pod and stir until thickened. Cool to room temperature, then incorporate the butter. Pour into the pastry case and chill.

5. Combine the remaining sugar and the water and stir until the mixture clears. Poach the pears in the liquid until tender, about 10 minutes. Remove, drain and slice. Arrange the pears in an attractive pattern on top of the custard and glaze with the melted apricot jam.

Serves 6

SWISS PLUM TART

Switzerland

Preparation time: 40 minutes
Pastry chills—1 hour

Baking time: 30 minutes

Ingredients

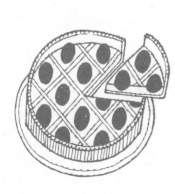

Sweet Shortcrust Pastry:
8 oz./225 g. plain flour, sifted
¼ teaspoon salt
1½ oz./40 g. castor sugar
2½ oz./65 g. unsalted butter
2½ oz./65 g. shortening
1 egg yolk
2 tablespoons iced water

Filling:
3 oz./75 g. sponge cake crumbs

1 oz./25 g. ground almonds
12 to 16 fresh purple plums, stoned and quartered
1 oz./25 g. castor sugar
1 tablespoon lemon juice
1½ oz./40 g. unsalted butter, softened
—
6 oz./175 g. apricot jam, melted
Icing sugar

1. Using the above-listed ingredients, prepare the sweet shortcrust pastry (page 481). Chill for 1 hour.

2. Preheat oven to 400°F., 200°C., Gas Mark 6.

3. Roll out the pastry and line a 9-inch/23-cm. flan tin. Spread the cake crumbs and almonds over the dough. Arrange the plums in concentric circles over the crumbs. Sprinkle the sugar and the lemon juice over the plums and dot with the butter. Bake the tart until the plums are soft and the crust is golden brown, about 30 minutes. Brush with the apricot glaze. Cool. Sprinkle with icing sugar just before serving.

Serves 6

PRUNE AND CUSTARD TART

Preparation time: 30 minutes
Pastry chills—1 hour

Baking time: 40 minutes

France

Ingredients

Sweet Shortcrust Pastry:

8 oz./225 g. plain flour,
   sifted

¼ teaspoon salt

1½ oz./40 g. castor sugar

2½ oz./65 g. unsalted butter

2½ oz./65 g. shortening

1 egg yolk

2 tablespoons iced water

1 lb./450 g. prunes, stoned
   and soaked

Custard:

12 fl. oz./3½ dl. milk

½ vanilla pod or ¼ teaspoon
   vanilla essence

3 egg yolks

1 egg

2½ oz./65 g. castor sugar

1. Using the above-listed ingredients, prepare the sweet shortcrust pastry (page 481). Chill for 1 hour.

2. Set oven at 400°F., 200°C., Gas Mark 6.

3. Drain and reserve the soaked prunes.

4. Roll out pastry and line a 9-inch/23-cm. flan tin. Prick the surface with a fork and bake blind for 15 minutes. Reserve. Reduce oven to 350°F., 180°C., Gas Mark 4.

5. In a small saucepan, combine the milk and the vanilla. Bring to the boil, then immediately remove pan from heat. Discard vanilla pod (if used) and let milk cool.

6. In a bowl beat the egg yolks and whole egg. Beating constantly, slowly add the sugar. Continue beating until mixture is light and fluffy, then gradually beat in the scalded milk.

7. Arrange prunes in the pastry case and cover with the custard. Bake until the custard sets, about 40 minutes. Serve cold.

Serves 6

VERMONT PUMPKIN PIE

USA

Preparation time: 1½ hours
Pastry chills—1 hour

Baking time: 45 minutes

Ingredients

Flaky Pastry:
8 oz./225 g. plain flour
1 teaspoon salt
6 oz./175 g. butter
7 tablespoons iced water
—

*A 3-lb./1⅓-kg. pumpkin or
a 16-oz./454-g. can
pumpkin purée*
5 oz./150 g. brown sugar
1 teaspoon ground cinnamon

½ teaspoon ground ginger
⅛ teaspoon ground nutmeg
⅛ teaspoon ground cloves
½ teaspoon salt
*12 fl. oz./3½ dl. double
cream*
2 eggs, slightly beaten
3 tablespoons rum
Whipped cream

1. Using the above-listed ingredients prepare the pastry (page 474). Chill for 1 hour.

2. Preheat oven to 325°F., 160°C., Gas Mark 3. Halve the pumpkin and remove the seeds and strings. Place cut sides down on a baking sheet and bake until soft, about 1 hour.

3. Roll out the dough to ¼-inch/5-mm. thickness on a lightly floured surface. Line a 9-inch/23-cm. flan tin.

4. Remove the cooked pumpkin from the oven. Increase oven temperature to 400°F., 200°C., Gas Mark 6. Purée the pulp in a sieve or blender. Combine ¾ pint/4½ dl. of the purée (or canned pumpkin) with the brown sugar, cinnamon, ginger, nutmeg, cloves and salt. Mix thoroughly. Beat the cream into the mixture, then thoroughly beat in the eggs. Add the rum.

5. Pour the mixture into the shell and bake until a knife inserted in the centre of pie comes out clean, about 45 minutes. Serve at room temperature or chilled, either plain or topped with whipped cream.

Serves 6 to 8

Sweet Dishes

GLAZED APPLES

China

Preparation time: 15 minutes **Cooking time:** 10 minutes

Ingredients

3 tablespoons groundnut oil
4 apples, peeled, cored and cut in pieces

Syrup:
8 oz./225 g. sugar
6 tablespoons water

1½ tablespoons groundnut oil
1 tablespoon sesame seeds

—

Bowl of iced water

1. Heat the oil in a large frying pan over moderately high heat.

2. Add the apple pieces and fry, stirring over moderately high heat for 3 minutes. Using a slotted spoon, transfer apples to absorbent paper and drain thoroughly.

3. Prepare the syrup: Combine the sugar and water in a saucepan and bring to the boil over moderate heat. Stir in the groundnut oil, then lower heat slightly and simmer until syrup turns golden brown, about 10 minutes. Stir in the sesame seeds, then remove pan from heat.

4. Add the fried apples to the syrup mixture, stirring gently so that each piece is thoroughly coated.

5. Plunge the coated apples into the iced water until the syrup hardens, a few seconds, then transfer to a platter and serve immediately.

Serves 4

Some cooks arrange the glazed fruit on an oiled platter, and guests dip individual portions into the iced water at the table.

BAKED APPLES MARZIPAN

Preparation time: 15 minutes **Cooking time:** 45–60 minutes

Sweden

Ingredients

Almond Paste Filling:
*3 oz./75 g. blanched
    almonds, ground*
2 oz./50 g. castor sugar
1½ tablespoons water
—
*2½ tablespoons fine dry
    breadcrumbs*
2½ tablespoons sugar
6 firm apples

Lemon juice
1 oz./25 g. butter, melted
**Sugar-Almond Whipped
    Cream:**
*½ pint/3 dl. double cream,
    whipped*
Pinch castor sugar
*½ teaspoon almond
    essence*

1. Set oven at 375°F., 190°C., Gas Mark 5.

2. Work the almonds, sugar and water to a paste in a mortar or blender. Reserve.

3. In a bowl, combine the breadcrumbs and sugar. Reserve.

4. Peel and core the apples, sprinkling each apple with lemon juice to prevent browning.

5. Coat the apples with the butter, then roll in the breadcrumb and sugar mixture.

6. Arrange the apples on a buttered baking dish, then fill the cores with the reserved almond mixture.

7. Bake until apples are tender but still hold their shape, about 45 to 60 minutes. Serve piping hot, accompanied by chilled whipped cream flavoured with sugar and almond essence.

Serves 6

WITCHES' FROTH

Hungary

Preparation time: 30 minutes   **Refrigeration time:** 1 hour

Ingredients

*6 firm cooking apples,
    peeled and quartered*
Juice of 2 lemons
14 oz./400 g. castor sugar
Rind of 2 lemons, grated
1½ tablespoons brandy

*Pinch freshly grated
    nutmeg*
3 egg whites
Pinch salt
Pinch cream of tartar

1. Combine the apples and the juice of 1 lemon in a saucepan. Place over low heat, cover and cook until apples are tender, about 30 minutes.

2. Press apples through a sieve into a large bowl. Beating vigorously with a wire whisk, gradually add the sugar, remaining lemon juice, lemon rind, brandy and nutmeg. Continue beating until mixture is very frothy. Adjust flavouring. Cover bowl and refrigerate for 1 hour.

3. In another bowl, beat the egg whites until frothy. Add the salt and cream of tartar. Continue beating until stiff.

4. Carefully fold the egg whites into the chilled apple mixture. Pour the froth into a glass serving bowl or individual dessert dishes. Serve chilled.

Serves 4

APPLE OMELETTE

Preparation time: 15 minutes
Apples simmer—5 minutes

Cooking time: 5 minutes

France

Ingredients

1½ lb./700 g. firm cooking
    apples
3 oz./75 g. butter
2 tablespoons Calvados,
    warmed

6 eggs
Pinch salt
Castor sugar
2 tablespoons water

1. Peel and core the apples, then slice thinly.

2. Heat half the butter in a frying pan. Add the apple slices and 1 tablespoon of the Calvados. Stir briefly to coat with the butter, then cover pan and cook over low heat until barely tender, about 5 minutes.

3. In a mixing bowl, combine the eggs, salt, a pinch of sugar and water. Beat lightly.

4. Place a large omelette pan or frying pan over high heat for 1 to 2 minutes, then swirl in the remaining butter. When the butter foam subsides, quickly pour in the eggs and stir briskly until eggs begin to set.

5. Using a slotted spoon, transfer the apples to the eggs and cook until omelette is set. (Lift the edge of the omelette and tilt the pan as the omelette cooks to allow all egg liquid to cook.) Fold the omelette in half. Sprinkle with a little sugar and the remaining Calvados. Flambé and serve immediately.

Serves 3 to 4

BEVERLOO APPLE SOUFFLÉ

The Netherlands

Preparation time: 35 minutes   **Cooking time:** 45 minutes

Ingredients

8 tart apples	⅓ pint/2 dl. hot milk
Juice of 1 lemon	Rind of 1 lemon, grated
6 oz./175 g. butter	Pinch salt
5 oz./150 g. sugar	4 eggs, separated
2 oz./50 g. plain flour	8 rusks, crumbled

1. Peel, core and slice the apples. Toss with the lemon juice. Set oven at 325°F., 160°C., Gas Mark 3.

2. In a saucepan, melt 1½ oz./40 g. of the butter. Add the apples and 4 oz./100 g. of the sugar. Stir briefly over low heat, then cover and cook for 15 minutes.

3. Meanwhile, melt remaining butter, add flour, then stir over moderate heat for 2 minutes. Slowly add the milk, stirring constantly. When thoroughly blended, stir in the lemon rind, the remaining sugar and a little salt. Continue stirring until smooth and thick. Remove from heat.

4. Beat the egg yolks, one by one, into the milk mixture. Stir in the apples.

5. Beat the egg whites with a pinch of salt until stiff, then carefully fold into the apple mixture.

6. Fill a buttered and floured 2½-pint/1¼-litre soufflé dish with alternating layers of the apple mixture and the crumbled rusks. Bake for 45 minutes. Serve hot.

Serves 6

CHILLED APRICOT PURÉE

Preparation time: 15 minutes
Apricots soak—15 minutes

Cooking time: 40 minutes
Prepared dish chills—1 hour

Lebanon

Ingredients

1½ lb./700 g. dried apricots
10 oz./275 g. sugar
3 pints/1½ litres water
1½ teaspoons cornflour
  dissolved in 6 table-
  spoons water

2 teaspoons lemon juice
Whipped cream flavoured
  with sugar for garnish
Chopped almonds for
  decoration

1. Soak the apricots in a bowl of hot water for 15 minutes. Drain and reserve.

2. Combine the sugar and water in a large saucepan, and bring to the boil. Stirring constantly, cook over moderate heat until liquid is clear. Add the drained apricots and cook over moderate heat until fruit is very tender, about 20 minutes. (Stir occasionally while apricots cook.)

3. Purée the apricot mixture through a sieve or in a blender.

4. Return mixture to saucepan. Stirring briskly over moderate heat, add the cornflour mixture and cook until purée thickens, about 3 minutes. Remove from heat. Stir in the lemon juice.

5. Spoon the purée into a large serving bowl or into individual dessert dishes. Refrigerate for 1 hour. Serve chilled, topped with sweetened whipped cream and chopped almonds.

Serves 6

DATE AND BANANA COMPOTE

Jordan

Preparation time: 20 minutes

Cooking time: 3–4 minutes
Compote chills—3 hours

Ingredients

*6 bananas, peeled, thinly
sliced and sprinkled with
lemon juice*

*1 lb./450 g. stoned dates,
halved*

*6 oz./175 g. almonds,
halved*

⅓ pint/2 dl. single cream
Brown sugar for glazing

1. Layer the sliced bananas in deep ovenproof dish, covering each layer of bananas with date halves and almonds.

2. Pour in the cream. The cream should barely cover the last layer of fruit. Refrigerate for at least 3 hours.

3. Just before serving, sprinkle a very thin layer of brown sugar on the fruit. Glaze for 3 or 4 minutes under grill and serve immediately.

Serves 4

BANANA WHIP WITH ORANGE CREAM

Jamaica

Preparation time: 15 minutes
Banana chills—2 hours

Cooking time: 5 minutes
Orange chills—2 hours

Ingredients

6 bananas

Lemon juice

1 oz./25 g. castor sugar

2 oz./50 g. almonds, coarsely chopped

2 tablespoons orange juice

Pinch ground cinnamon

2 tablespoons light rum

1 oz./25 g. desiccated coconut

3 egg whites

Salt

Orange Cream:

3 egg yolks

1½ oz./40 g. castor sugar

⅓ pint/2 dl. orange juice

1. Mash the bananas in a non-metallic bowl and sprinkle them with lemon juice to stop them turning black. Add the sugar, almonds, orange juice, cinnamon, rum and coconut, mixing well.

2. In a separate bowl, beat the egg whites with a pinch of salt until stiff.

3. Carefully fold banana mixture and egg whites together. Do not overmix. Pour into a serving bowl and chill for at least 2 hours.

4. Prepare the orange cream topping: Beat the egg yolks with the sugar until lemon-coloured. Pour the eggs into a double saucepan, then add the orange juice, whisking constantly until foamy. (Do not boil.)

5. Chill the topping for 2 hours, then serve with the banana whip.

Serves 6 to 8

AVIGNON FIG ROLL

France

Preparation time: 10 minutes   **Refrigeration time:** 3 hours

Ingredients

1 lb./450 g. dried figs,
chopped

4 oz./100 g. blanched
almonds, coarsely
chopped

1 oz./25 g. icing sugar

1. In a mortar or blender, crush together the figs and almonds.

2. Form the mixture into a sausage shape and roll in the icing sugar. Wrap in aluminium foil and refrigerate for at least 3 hours.

3. To serve, unwrap, place on a serving plate and slice thinly.

Serves 6

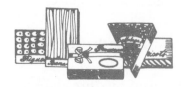

FRESH FIGS IN HONEY AND WINE

Preparation time: 10 minutes

Cooking time: 20 minutes
Compote chills—1 hour

Tunisia

Ingredients

1½ lb./450 g. under-ripe
  green figs
¾ pint/4½ dl. dry white
  wine

9 oz./250 g. honey
Vanilla-flavoured whipped
  cream for topping

1. Wash figs and trim stems. Place in a saucepan and cover with the white wine. Bring to the boil over low heat, then stir in the honey. Cover pan and simmer until figs are tender, about 15 minutes.

2. Using a slotted spoon, transfer the figs to a serving bowl. Reserve.

3. Reduce fig syrup slightly over high heat, then pour over the fruit. Cover bowl and refrigerate for at least 1 hour. Serve chilled, topped with vanilla-flavoured whipped cream.

Serves 6

ORANGE FLOWERS

Spain

Preparation time: 10 minutes   **Cooking time:** 20 minutes

Ingredients

6 navel oranges
1 lb./450 g. sugar
¾ pint/4½ dl. water

1½ tablespoons
  orange-blossom water
Vanilla ice cream

1. Using a vegetable peeler, peel the oranges, then cut the peel into julienne strips. Carefully remove the pith from the oranges, leaving the oranges whole.

2. Blanch the oranges and peel in a large saucepan of boiling water for 5 minutes, then drain and reserve.

3. Also in a large saucepan, combine the sugar, water and orange-blossom water. Stir over moderately high heat until mixture reaches a slow boil. Add the blanched oranges and peel, then lower heat and poach fruit gently for 10 minutes. Transfer the oranges with a slotted spoon to a wire rack and cool.

4. Reduce the orange-peel syrup over moderately high heat until it reaches the soft ball stage (238°F., 114°C. on a sugar thermometer).

5. Assemble the orange flowers while the syrup reduces: Partially separate the segments of the oranges, then transfer to individual dessert dishes and place a scoop of vanilla ice cream in the centre of each orange.

6. Pour the reduced syrup over the orange flowers and serve immediately.

Serves 6

ORANGE PUFFS

Preparation time: 30 minutes   **Cooking time:** 20 minutes   *France*

Ingredients

4 large oranges
1½ oz./40 g. sugar
1 tablespoon kirsch
Custard:
⅓ pint/2 dl. milk

2 egg yolks
1½ oz./40 g. castor sugar
1 oz./25 g. flour
———
2 egg whites

1. Set oven at 250°F., 120°C., Gas Mark ½. Cut the top third off the oranges. Carefully carve out the flesh from the oranges. Reserve both the top sections (caps) and the bottom sections (cups) of the shells.

2. Remove the membrane and the seeds from the orange segments, then arrange pulp on a greased baking sheet. Sprinkle lightly with sugar and place in the oven for 10 minutes. Reset oven to 325°F., 160°C., Gas Mark 3.

3. While the orange segments are drying, remove the peel from the caps with a vegetable peeler; cut into julienne strips, then place in a small saucepan. Add the kirsch and place over low heat until the kirsch has evaporated.

4. Prepare the custard: Pour the milk into a saucepan; bring to the boil, then remove from heat. In a bowl, beat the egg yolks until pale yellow, then gradually add the sugar and the flour. Pour in the scalded milk and transfer mixture to a double saucepan, then beat over moderate heat until custard thickens. Combine two-thirds of the custard in a bowl with the orange segments and mix well.

5. Beat the egg whites until stiff, then fold in remaining custard. Spoon the custard-orange mixture into the orange cups. Add the orange peels, then top with the egg white mixture. Arrange in a shallow dish containing 6 tablespoons water. Bake for 20 minutes.

Serves 4

SICILIAN STUFFED PEACHES

Italy

Preparation time: 25 minutes

Cooking time: 20 minutes

Ingredients

6 large peaches

1 egg yolk

2 oz./50 g. castor sugar

4 oz./100 g. stale macaroons, finely crushed

¼ teaspoon almond essence

2 pinches freshly grated nutmeg

1 oz./25 g. unsalted butter, at room temperature

Double cream, whipped and flavoured with sugar and almond essence

Fresh mint sprigs for decoration

1. Set oven at 325°F., 160°C., Gas Mark 3.

2. Blanch the peaches in a pan of boiling water and drain. Peel, halve and stone the peaches. Reserve.

3. In a small bowl beat the egg yolk well. Gradually beat in the sugar. Continue beating until mixture is light and fluffy.

4. Add the crushed macaroons, almond essence and nutmeg to the egg-sugar mixture. Blend thoroughly, then work in the butter until well incorporated.

5. Fill 6 of the reserved peach halves with the macaroon mixture. Top with the remaining peach halves.

6. Arrange the stuffed peaches in a buttered ovenproof dish and bake until tender, about 20 minutes. (The peaches should not lose their shape.)

7. Serve hot or cold with double cream, whipped and flavoured to taste with sugar and almond essence. Decorate baked peaches with mint sprigs.

Serves 6

PEACHES WITH STRAWBERRY CREAM

France

Preparation time: 20 minutes   **Refrigeration time:** 2 hours

Ingredients

8 peaches, peeled and
  sliced
Juice of ½ lemon
4 oz./100 g. brown sugar
2 tablespoons water
1¼ lb./600 g. strawberries

1 oz./25 g. icing sugar
1 tablespoon cassis
¼ pint/1½ dl. double cream,
  whipped

1. Toss the peaches with the lemon juice in a serving bowl.

2. In a small saucepan, combine the brown sugar and water. Bring to the boil over moderate heat and swirl until the liquid starts to thicken, about 2 minutes. Stir the syrup into the peaches. Cover and refrigerate.

3. In a blender, purée the strawberries with the sugar and cassis. Fold the whipped cream into the purée and refrigerate 2 hours. Just before serving, spoon strawberry cream over the peaches.

Serves 6

CARAMELISED BAKED PEARS

France

Preparation time: 10 minutes   **Cooking time:** 30 minutes

Ingredients

2 lb./1 kg. pears, peeled
   and quartered
2½ oz./65 g. sugar
3 oz./75 g. butter

1½ tablespoons water
6 tablespoons double
   cream

1. Set oven at 400°F., 200°C., Gas Mark 6.

2. Arrange the pears in a buttered ovenproof dish. Sprinkle on the sugar, then dot with the butter. Moisten slightly with the water.

3. Bake, uncovered, until the pears are tender and the sugar becomes caramel coloured, about 30 minutes.

4. Remove dish from the oven, pour in the cream and serve immediately.

Serves 4

PINEAPPLE PAVLOVA

Preparation time: 10 minutes   **Cooking time:** 1 hour   *New Zealand*

Ingredients

3 egg whites
1 teaspoon cream of tartar
¼ teaspoon salt
6 oz./175 g. castor sugar
½ teaspoon vanilla
  essence

½ pint/3 dl. double cream,
  whipped
A 16-oz./454-g. can sliced
  pineapple, drained

1. Preheat the oven to 275°F., 140°C., Gas Mark 1.

2. Beat the egg whites, cream of tartar and salt until frothy. Add the sugar and vanilla and continue beating until stiff and glossy.

3. Line an 8-inch/20-cm. round tin with siliconised paper, then pour in the egg-white mixture. Make a slight indentation in the centre. Bake until cream coloured and firm, about 1 hour. Cool the meringue in the tin.

4. Transfer the meringue to a serving platter. Cover with the whipped cream and arrange the pineapple slices on the top.

Serves 6

RHUBARB FOOL

Great Britain

Preparation time: 15 minutes   **Cooking time:** 5 minutes
Rhubarb purée chills—1 hour

Ingredients

1 lb./450 g. rhubarb

*2 oz./50 g. soft brown or
  granulated sugar*

Rind of 1 lemon, grated

Rind of ½ orange, grated

2 pinches ground cloves

*⅓ pint/2 dl. double cream,
  chilled*

*Toasted almonds for
  topping*

1. Wash the rhubarb and trim stalks. Discard the leaves (they are poisonous). Cut the stalks into 2-inch/5-cm. sections.

2. Place the rhubarb in a saucepan and cover with cold water. Add the sugar, grated lemon and orange rinds and the cloves. Mix briefly. Bring to the boil, then lower heat and simmer until the rhubarb is just tender, about 5 minutes.

3. Using a slotted spoon, transfer the rhubarb to a blender. Add a little of the cooking liquid and purée. Transfer purée to a bowl and refrigerate for 1 hour.

4. Whip the cream lightly, then stir in the purée. Serve cold, topped with toasted almonds and accompanied by shortbread cookies (page 402).

Serves 4

SUMMER PUDDING

Preparation time: 30 minutes   **Cooking time:** 10 minutes   *Great Britain*
Pudding chills—12–24 hours

Ingredients

8 oz./225 g. fresh
  raspberries

8 oz./225 g. fresh cherries,
  stoned

8 oz./225 g. redcurrants

4 oz./100 g. demerara
  or granulated sugar

10 slices white bread,
  crusts trimmed

Whipped cream

1. In a heavy saucepan, combine the fruit and sugar. Cover and cook gently over low heat until fruit is soft, about 10 minutes. (Stir fruit once or twice during cooking to prevent sticking.)

2. Drain the hot fruit in a sieve, reserving the cooking juices.

3. Line all sides of a glass bowl or dish with trimmed bread slices. Patch any gaps between the slices with smaller pieces of bread.

4. Pour the fruit into the bread case. Sprinkle with the reserved fruit juice, then top with a lid of bread slices.

5. Cover with a double thickness of waxed paper and weight with a heavy plate. Chill for 12 to 24 hours.

6. Before serving, discard the waxed paper and unmould the pudding onto a serving dish. Serve with whipped cream.

Serves 6

CHOCOLATE MOUSSE

France

Preparation time: 10 minutes

Cooking time: 10 minutes
Mousse chills—2 hours

Ingredients

8 oz./225 g. plain
 chocolate

5 eggs, separated

½ teaspoon vanilla essence

2 teaspoons strong black
 coffee

⅓ pint/2 dl. double cream

2 tablespoons rum or
 brandy

4 oz./100 g. castor sugar

1. Melt the chocolate in a double saucepan.

2. Beat egg yolks until pale and gradually stir into the chocolate. Add the vanilla and coffee.

3. In a mixing bowl, beat the cream until thick. Stir in the rum (or brandy) and fold into the chocolate mixture.

4. In another mixing bowl, beat the egg whites and the sugar until stiff and carefully fold into the chocolate mixture a little at a time.

5. Pour mousse into a large bowl or individual serving dishes. Chill for 2 hours.

Serves 6 to 8

LEMON MOUSSE

Preparation time: 25 minutes

Cooking time: 10 minutes
Mousse chills—1 hour

France

Ingredients

5 egg yolks
4 oz./100 g. castor sugar
Juice of 2 lemons
Rind of 2 lemons, grated

3 egg whites
Pinch salt
6 tablespoons double
cream

1. In a mixing bowl, beat the egg yolks with a wire whisk until pale yellow. Beating constantly, gradually add the sugar. Continue beating until mixture is light and fluffy, then blend in the lemon juice and rind.

2. Transfer mixture to the top section of a double saucepan. Using a wire whisk, beat over simmering water until mixture is the consistency of soft custard, about 10 minutes. Remove from heat and reserve.

3. In a bowl, beat the egg whites with a pinch of salt until stiff.

4. Beat 2 tablespoons of the egg whites into the custard to lighten mixture, then fold in the remaining egg whites. Pour into a bowl and refrigerate for 1 hour.

5. Whip the cream in a bowl and gently fold into the chilled mousse. Pour into a serving bowl or individual dessert dishes. Serve chilled.

Serves 3 to 4

For a tarter lemon mousse, omit the cream in Step 5.

LEMON SNOW

Canada

Preparation time: 15 minutes

Dessert chills—2 hours

Ingredients

1 lemon jelly

4 oz./100 g. honey

⅛ teaspoon salt

½ pint/3 dl. boiling water

2 tablespoons lemon juice

⅓ pint/2 dl. double cream

7 oz./200 g. wafer crumbs

1. Dissolve the jelly, honey and salt in the boiling water. Stir in the lemon juice, then refrigerate until the mixture is syrupy, about 20 minutes. Whip until frothy.

2. Whip the cream until stiff, then lightly fold it into the lemon mixture.

3. Line an 8 × 10-inch/20 × 25-cm. dish with half the wafer crumbs. Pour in the mixture and top with the remaining crumbs. Chill until firm, about 2 hours.

Serves 6 to 8

CRANBERRY PURÉE

Preparation time: 5 minutes   **Cooking time:** 15 minutes   *USSR*

Ingredients

8 oz./225 g. cranberries,
  uncooked
½ pint/3 dl. water
2 oz./50 g. sugar

1½ oz./40 g. cornflour
Single or double cream
  flavoured with sugar
  and vanilla essence

1. Place the cranberries in a saucepan and cover with the water. Bring to the boil, then lower the heat and simmer for 10 minutes.

2. Purée the fruit in a blender or through a sieve, then return the mixture to the saucepan. Add the sugar and bring to the boil.

3. Dissolve the cornflour in a little water. Blend into the fruit mixture, stirring constantly, and cook until thickened. Pour into a large serving dish and chill for 3 hours. Serve with cream.

Serves 4

ESPRESSO ICE CREAM

Italy

Preparation time: 30 minutes

Cooking time: 3 minutes
Ice cream freezes—6 hours

Ingredients

*12 fl. oz./3½ dl. milk,
scalded*

2 oz./50 g. ground coffee

4 egg yolks

4 oz./100 g. castor sugar

⅓ pint/2 dl. double cream

¼ teaspoon cinnamon

1. Combine the scalded milk and the ground coffee in a saucepan. Place over very low heat and steep for 15 minutes.

2. Using a fine sieve lined with muslin, strain the coffeed milk into a bowl and reserve. (Discard grounds.)

3. In a mixing bowl, beat the egg yolks with a wire whisk until pale yellow, then gradually beat in the sugar. Continue beating until mixture is light and fluffy. Gradually beat the coffeed milk into the egg and sugar mixture, then slowly beat in the cream.

4. Transfer the ice cream mixture to a large saucepan. Stir in the cinnamon. Using a wooden spoon, stir mixture over low heat until nearly doubled in volume, about 2 to 3 minutes, then immediately remove from heat.

5. Pour mixture into a metallic container. Cool to room temperature. Freeze for 6 hours, beating thoroughly with a wooden spoon every ½ hour to break down ice crystals.

Serves 4

MOULDED VANILLA CREAM

Preparation time: 20 minutes   **Refrigeration time:** 24 hours

France

Ingredients

6 oz./175 g. cottage cheese

5 tablespoons double
  cream

2 oz./50 g. castor sugar

2 egg whites

Pinch salt

Crème fraîche for topping
  (page 473)

Vanilla sugar for topping
  (page 481)

1. Put the cottage cheese in a sieve. Drain off the excess liquid, then sieve the curds into a large mixing bowl.

2. Add the cream and beat vigorously until thickened, then beat in the sugar.

3. In another bowl, beat the egg whites with a pinch of salt until stiff. Gently fold the egg whites into the cottage cheese mixture.

4. Spoon the mixture into small heart-shaped pierced moulds lined with muslin. Place moulds on a plate and refrigerate for 24 hours. (If moulds are unavailable, spoon the mixture onto muslin. Tie up the muslin and hang in the refrigerator for 24 hours. Place a bowl under the muslin bag to catch any liquid that drips out.)

5. To serve, unmould the vanilla cream (or remove from the muslin), transfer to a serving dish and top with *crème fraîche* and vanilla sugar.

Serves 4

MARSALA CREAM

France

Preparation time: 10 minutes

Cooking time: 20 minutes
Prepared dish chills—1 hour

Ingredients

6 tablespoons Marsala
　wine

1 piece lemon peel

A 3-inch/7½-cm. stick
　cinnamon

1 clove

4 egg yolks

2 oz./50 g. castor sugar

3 tablespoons kirsch or
　rum

Sponge fingers for decoration

1. In a small saucepan, combine the Marsala, lemon peel, cinnamon stick and clove. Bring to the boil and simmer for 3 minutes, then remove from heat, strain and reserve.

2. In a mixing bowl, beat the egg yolks with a wire whisk until pale yellow. Beating constantly, gradually add the sugar. Continue beating until mixture is very light and fluffy.

3. Beat in the strained Marsala, then transfer mixture to the top section of a double saucepan.

4. Beat over hot water until mixture clings to a wooden spoon, about 10 minutes. (Do not let the water in the bottom section of the pan come to the boil as the mixture cooks.)

5. Beating constantly, very slowly add the kirsch (or rum) and cook for 5 more minutes. Remove from heat.

6. When the Marsala cream has cooled to room temperature, pour into a serving bowl and refrigerate for at least 1 hour. Serve chilled, decorated with sponge fingers.

Serves 4

For a delicious hot variation, gently fold 4 stiffly beaten egg whites into the Marsala cream at the end of Step 5 and serve immediately.

CHAMPAGNE CREAM

Preparation time: 10 minutes   **Cooking time:** 10 minutes   *France*
Prepared dish chills—1 hour

Ingredients

10 small sugar cubes
2 lemons, washed

⅓ pint/2 dl. champagne or
   dry white wine, heated
4 eggs, separated

1. Rub each sugar cube over the rind of the lemon to absorb the oil, then place cubes in a bowl.

2. Pour the hot champagne (or wine) over the sugar cubes. Stir until the sugar dissolves.

3. In another bowl, beat the egg yolks until pale yellow. Beating constantly, gradually add the sugar mixture.

4. Transfer mixture to the top section of a double saucepan and place over low heat. (The water in the bottom section of the double saucepan should not boil.) Beat with a wire whisk until mixture thickens. Remove from heat.

5. Cool mixture slightly, then refrigerate for 1 hour.

6. Just before serving, beat the egg whites until very stiff and fold into the chilled champagne cream.

Serves 2 to 3

PISTACHIO DELIGHT

France

Preparation time: 10 minutes   **Cooking time:** 10 minutes
Prepared dish chills—1 hour

Ingredients

3 egg yolks
4 oz./100 g. castor sugar
1½ tablespoons kirsch
¾ pint/4½ dl. double cream

5½ oz./160 g. pistachio
 nuts, coarsely ground
Halved pistachios for
 decoration

1. In a mixing bowl, beat the egg yolks until pale yellow. Beating constantly, gradually add the sugar. Continue beating until mixture is light and fluffy, then gradually beat in the kirsch and double cream.

2. Transfer egg yolk mixture to the top section of a double saucepan. Blend in the ground pistachios.

3. Place pan over barely simmering water and beat mixture with a wire whisk until very thick and fluffy, about 10 minutes. Remove from heat.

4. Pour into a serving bowl and decorate with halved pistachios. Refrigerate for at least 1 hour. Serve chilled.

Serves 4 to 6

CARAMEL CUSTARD

Preparation time: 15 minutes   **Cooking time:** 40–45 minutes

France

Ingredients

Caramel:

4 oz./100 g. sugar
1½ tablespoons water
—
4 whole eggs

4 egg yolks
5 oz./150 g. castor sugar
1¼ pints/7 dl. milk, scalded
2 tablespoons cognac

1. Set oven at 350°F., 180°C., Gas Mark 4.

2. Using the ingredients listed above, caramelise (page 472) a 2½-pint/1¼-litre fluted metal mould. Reserve.

3. In a mixing bowl, beat the whole eggs and extra egg yolks with a wire whisk or an electric beater until pale yellow. Beating constantly, gradually add the sugar. Continue beating until mixture is very light and fluffy.

4. Beating constantly, gradually add the scalded milk and cognac to the egg and sugar mixture. Continue beating until very smooth and light.

5. Strain the custard mixture into the caramelised mould. Place in a shallow pan of hot water and bake until a knife inserted into the centre of the custard comes out clean, about 40 to 45 minutes.

6. When the custard is done, remove mould from the oven. Cool to room temperature in the mould, then unmould by running a knife around the edge of the mould and quickly inverting onto a platter.

Serves 6

COFFEE CUSTARD

Brazil

Preparation time: 20 minutes

Cooking time: 45 minutes to 1 hour

Ingredients

12 fl. oz./3½ dl. milk
A 1-inch/2½-cm. piece
 vanilla pod
4 whole coffee beans
6 tablespoons very strong
 coffee

5 egg yolks
4 oz./100 g. castor sugar
1 teaspoon cornflour

1. Set oven to 325°F., 160°C., Gas Mark 3.

2. Combine the milk, vanilla pod and coffee beans in a saucepan. Bring rapidly to the boil, then remove pan from heat.

3. Stir in the strong coffee. Reserve.

4. In a bowl, beat the egg yolks, then gradually blend in the sugar and cornflour. Mix well.

5. Strain the cooled milk, a little at a time, through a fine sieve lined with muslin into the egg and sugar mixture.

6. Pour the mixture into a buttered baking dish or into individual ovenproof dishes.

7. Cover the baking dish, set in a pan of hot water and bake until a knife inserted into the centre of the custard comes out clean, about 45 minutes to 1 hour.

8. Cool custard to room temperature, then chill until needed. Before serving, run a knife around the inside edge of the baking dish and invert custard onto a serving dish.

Serves 4

RAISIN CUSTARD

Preparation time: 15 minutes   **Cooking time:** 45 minutes   *France*
Raisins soak—1 hour

Ingredients

3 oz./75 g. seedless raisins

3 tablespoons rum

4 eggs

6 oz./175 g. castor sugar

7 oz./200 g. plain flour

1½ pints/9 dl. milk,
  warmed

1 oz./25 g. vanilla sugar
  (page 481)

1. Soak the raisins in the rum for 1 hour, then drain and reserve.

2. Set oven at 325°F., 160°C., Gas Mark 3.

3. In a mixing bowl, beat the eggs until pale yellow. Beating constantly, gradually add the sugar. Continue beating until mixture is light and fluffy, then gradually beat in the flour and the warm milk.

4. Pour a quarter of the milk mixture into a buttered and floured 3-pint/1½-litre ovenproof dish. Bake for 10 minutes, then remove from oven.

5. Reset oven at 425°F., 220°C., Gas Mark 7.

6. Sprinkle the raisins into the baking dish, then cover with the remaining milk mixture and bake until set, about 35 minutes.

7. Sprinkle the baked raisin custard with the vanilla sugar and serve piping hot.

Serves 6

BASQUE BROWN SUGAR CUSTARD

Spain

Preparation time: 20 minutes   **Cooking time:** 1 hour

Ingredients

1¾ pints/1 litre milk
6 oz./175 g. cornflour
5 oz./150 g. butter, at
  room temperature
8 eggs

8 oz./225 g. dark soft
  brown sugar
1 tablespoon orange-
  flower water (optional)

1. Set oven at 325°F., 160°C., Gas Mark 3.

2. Pour the milk into a large saucepan. Bring rapidly to the boil, then immediately remove pan from heat.

3. Beating constantly, gradually add the cornflour to the milk. Continue beating until the mixture is smooth.

4. Allow mixture to cool slightly, then beat in the butter, ½ oz./15 g. at a time. Beat in the eggs, incorporating each one well before adding the next, then gradually beat in the sugar. (When the mixture is thoroughly blended, stir in the orange-flower water.)

5. Pour custard into a buttered 3-pint/1½-litre ovenproof dish and bake until set, about 1 hour. Serve hot.

Serves 8

PENANG COCONUT CUSTARD

Preparation time: 40 minutes   **Refrigeration time:** 2 hours

Malaysia

Ingredients

Coconut Milk:

1½ lb./700 g. coconut flesh, grated

¾ pint/4½ dl. scalded milk

—

4 oz./100 g. sugar

⅛ teaspoon salt

½ teaspoon vanilla essence

1½ tablespoons cornflour

3 tablespoons cold water

4 tablespoons crushed pineapple

4 teaspoons desiccated coconut

1. Steep the coconut flesh in the hot milk for 20 minutes. Strain through a double thickness of muslin, squeezing all the liquid out of the coconut.

2. In a saucepan, heat the coconut milk over a low flame to the boiling point. Add the sugar, salt, vanilla and the cornflour dissolved in the water. Stir constantly until thickened, about 5 minutes. Pour into individual dishes and refrigerate for about 2 hours.

3. To serve, top each custard with 1 tablespoon crushed pineapple and 1 teaspoon desiccated coconut.

Serves 4

NOTE: *Canned coconut milk or coconut cream can be substituted for the fresh, if necessary.*

SWEET MILK CLOUDS

Portugal

Preparation time: 15 minutes   **Cooking time:** 8 minutes

Ingredients

Custard:	**Sweet Milk 'Clouds':**
¾ pint/4½ dl. milk	4 egg whites
4 oz./100 g. sugar	1 oz./25 g. castor sugar
4 egg yolks	⅓ pint/2 dl. milk

1. Boil the milk in a saucepan and stir in the sugar until dissolved. Cool slightly.

2. Beat the egg yolks until pale. Add a small amount of the milk syrup to the yolks, beating constantly, then stir mixture into remaining syrup. Cook over low heat until mixture thickens. Do not boil.

3. Pour the custard into a serving dish or individual bowls and chill.

4. In a mixing bowl, whip the egg whites, add the sugar and whisk until stiff.

5. Boil the milk in a large saucepan. Drop a large tablespoonful of the egg whites into the hot milk. Poach each 'cloud' for 4 minutes. Remove and drain. Float the 'clouds' on the custard and serve.

Serves 4

GLAZED FRUIT PUDDING

Preparation time: 30 minutes   **Cooking time:** 10 minutes

France

Ingredients

2½ oz./65 g. sugar

⅓ pint/2 dl. water

4 pears, peeled and
   quartered

1 banana, sliced

2 oz./50 g. seedless raisins

2 oz./50 g. currants

Custard:

½ pint/3 dl. milk

3½ oz./90 g. sugar

6 eggs, separated

1 oz./25 g. plain flour

1 oz./25 g. butter

2 oz./50 g. almond
   macaroons, crushed

—

Icing sugar

1. Combine the sugar and water in a saucepan and boil until clear, about 5 minutes. Add the pears to the syrup and poach gently until tender, about 10 minutes. Remove with a slotted spoon and reserve.

2. Keeping the syrup over low heat, add the banana, raisins and currants. Remove from heat and let stand for 2 minutes, then drain and arrange all fruit in a deep oven-proof dish. Strain the syrup back into the saucepan and reduce over moderate heat to about 3 tablespoons. Pour over fruit and refrigerate.

3. Prepare the custard: a) Boil the milk and sugar; b) beat the egg yolks in a bowl and blend in the flour; c) gradually beat in the heated milk; d) return mixture to pan and cook over low heat, beating until mixture is thickened; e) remove from heat and stir in butter a little at a time; f) beat the egg whites until stiff and fold into the custard; g) add the macaroons.

4. Pour custard over cooled fruit. Sprinkle with icing sugar and glaze under grill until light brown. Cool and serve.

Serves 4 to 6

SURREY SUMMER TRIFLE

Great Britain

Preparation time: 15 minutes

Ingredients

1 lb./450 g. raspberries
  (fresh or frozen)
4 oz./100 g. redcurrants
4 oz./100 g. sugar
4 trifle sponge cakes

Custard:

6 egg yolks

2 oz./50 g. sugar
2 teaspoons cornflour
¾ pint/4½ dl. single cream
Few drops vanilla essence
—
1 oz./25 g. flaked almonds,
  toasted

1. Combine the raspberries, redcurrants and sugar in a saucepan. Place over low heat to dissolve the sugar, then simmer for 5 minutes. Remove from the heat and allow to cool.

2. Break the sponge cakes into a glass serving bowl and cover with the fruit and the juices.

3. Prepare the custard: Beat the egg yolks well; then add the sugar and cornflour and whisk thoroughly to blend. Heat the cream to the simmering point. Pour the cream into the egg mixture, a little at a time, blending well. Strain the custard back into the saucepan and stir over low heat until thickened. (Do not boil.) Add the vanilla and cool slightly.

4. Pour the custard over the fruit. Cool and chill until firm. Sprinkle with the almond flakes just before serving.

Serves 4

BLUEBERRY PUDDING

Preparation time: 15 minutes
Blueberries stand—30 minutes

Cooking time: 45 minutes

Canada

Ingredients

1 lb./450 g. blueberries
1 oz./25 g. plain flour
4 oz./100 g. brown sugar
1½ tablespoons white wine
  vinegar
Juice of 1 lemon
Pinch salt

8 oz./225 g. dry bread-
  crumbs
¾ pint/4½ dl. milk, heated
1 egg, lightly beaten
1 oz./25 g. butter
Single cream for topping

1. Preheat oven to 350°F., 180°C., Gas Mark 4.

2. Place the blueberries in a buttered baking dish. Sprinkle on the flour, brown sugar, vinegar, lemon juice and salt. Toss lightly, then let stand for ½ hour.

3. Put 6 oz./175 g. of the breadcrumbs in a mixing bowl. Cover with the milk. Stir until well blended, then incorporate the beaten egg.

4. Spoon the breadcrumb mixture into the baking dish with the blueberries. Stir gently, then sprinkle on the remaining breadcrumbs and dot with the butter.

5. Bake pudding for 45 minutes. Serve warm with cream.

Serves 6

YOGHURT PUDDING

India

Preparation time: 10 minutes
Yoghurt drains—overnight

Refrigeration time: 2 hours

Ingredients

1½ pints/9 dl. natural
  yoghurt

2 oz./50 g. castor sugar

¾ teaspoon ground
  cardamom

¼ teaspoon saffron, soaked
  in 1 tablespoon warm
  milk

¼ teaspoon freshly grated
  nutmeg

¼ teaspoon ground
  cinnamon

Salt

2 oz./50 g. pistachio nuts,
  shelled and sliced, for
  decoration

1. Place yoghurt in muslin bag and suspend over a bowl in
   the refrigerator overnight so the liquid drips out.

2. The next day add the sugar, cardamom, saffron, nutmeg,
   cinnamon and salt to the yoghurt curds remaining in
   the muslin. Mix well and chill for 2 hours in a serving
   bowl.

3. Serve the pudding cold, decorated with the pistachio
   slices.

Serves 4 to 6

SWEET MILK TREAT

Preparation time: 10 minutes   **Cooking time:** 45 minutes

Argentina

Ingredients

1 pint/6 dl. milk
6 oz./175 g. sugar
*A 1-inch/2½-cm. piece
  vanilla pod*

1 stick cinnamon
*1 oz./25 g. ground
  almonds*
Grated peel of 1 lemon

1. Combine all ingredients in a heavy saucepan and cook over low heat until pudding thickens, about 45 minutes.

2. Remove vanilla pod and cinnamon and pour into a large serving dish or individual soufflé dishes. Chill thoroughly before serving.

Serves 4

Sweet milk is used in Honduras and Argentina as a topping for many desserts.

BUTTERMILK LEMON MOULD

The
Netherlands

Preparation time: 15 minutes   **Refrigeration time:** 1 hour

Ingredients

6 tablespoons cold water
¾ oz./20 g. powdered
* gelatine*
⅓ pint/2 dl. fresh lemon
* juice, heated*

8 oz./225 g. castor sugar
1 pint/6 dl. buttermilk
Sweetened whipped cream
* for topping*

1. Pour the water into a saucepan. Sprinkle the gelatine on top, then let stand for 5 minutes.

2. Place the saucepan over low heat and stir gently until gelatine is completely dissolved. Reserve.

3. In a bowl, combine the lemon juice and sugar. Stir until sugar is completely dissolved, then pour in the buttermilk. Mix thoroughly.

4. Pour the buttermilk mixture into the gelatine mixture. Stir until well blended.

5. Pour the mixture into a lightly oiled 1¾-pint/1-litre mould. Refrigerate until firm, about 1 hour.

6. Unmould the chilled dessert onto a serving plate. Serve chilled, topped with sweetened whipped cream.

Serves 6

CHERRY PUDDING

Preparation time: 10 minutes   **Cooking time:** 45 minutes

France

Ingredients

1 lb./450 g. fresh black
  cherries or canned
  black cherries
6 oz./175 g. plain flour
Pinch salt

3 eggs
1½ oz./40 g. castor sugar
1¼ pints/7 dl. milk
1 oz./25 g. icing sugar

1. Preheat oven to 375°F., 190°C., Gas Mark 5.

2. Prepare the cherries: If fresh cherries used, wash and dry, then remove stones and stems. Reserve. (If canned cherries used, drain thoroughly and reserve.)

3. In a mixing bowl, combine the flour and salt. Beat in the eggs, one at a time, thoroughly incorporating each egg before adding the next. Beat in the sugar. Gradually pour in the milk, stirring until mixture is smooth.

4. Pour a ¼-inch/5-mm. layer of mixture into a buttered ovenproof dish. Spread the cherries over the mixture and then cover with the remaining mixture.

5. Bake until the pudding begins to set, about 25 minutes, then dust with the icing sugar and continue baking until golden, about 20 minutes. Serve hot.

Serves 4 to 6

PARSONAGE PUDDING

Finland

Preparation time: 10 minutes   **Cooking time:** 1½ hours

Ingredients

4 oz./100 g. dry bread
  cubes

⅓ pint/2 dl. buttermilk

1 teaspoon bicarbonate of
  soda

4 oz./100 g. castor sugar

½ teaspoon ground
  cinnamon

¼ teaspoon freshly grated
  nutmeg

1 egg, beaten

Raspberry jam for
  decoration

Single cream for topping

1. In a mixing bowl, combine the bread cubes and buttermilk. Let stand until the buttermilk is completely
   absorbed, about 15 minutes.

2. Add the bicarbonate of soda, sugar, cinnamon and nutmeg to the soaked bread cubes. Mix thoroughly, then
   incorporate the beaten egg.

3. Transfer the pudding mixture to a well-buttered pudding
   mould. (The mould should be two-thirds full.) Cover
   tightly with a buttered lid or foil.

4. Rest the mould on a rack in a saucepan of boiling water
   so that the water reaches two-thirds of the way up the
   sides of the mould. Cover and steam the pudding over
   moderately low heat for 1½ hours. (If necessary, add
   more water to the saucepan during steaming.)

5. Serve pudding piping hot, topped with raspberry jam
   and cream.

Serves 4

NOODLE PUDDING

Preparation time: 30 minutes   **Cooking time:** 1 hour

Germany

Ingredients

8 oz./225 g. egg noodles

4 oz./100 g. unsalted
  butter, at room
  temperature

6 oz./175 g. castor sugar

6 eggs, separated

Rind of 1 lemon, grated

Juice of 1 lemon

5 oz./150 g. raisins

4 oz./100 g. blanched
  almonds, slivered

Pinch salt

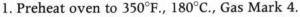

1. Preheat oven to 350°F., 180°C., Gas Mark 4.

2. Plunge the noodles into a large pan of boiling water and cook until noodles are *al dente* (page 470), about 12 minutes. Drain, rinse under cold water, then drain thoroughly. Reserve.

3. While the noodles cook, cream the butter in a large mixing bowl, then gradually blend in the sugar and beat until light and fluffy. Beat the egg yolks into sugar mixture, incorporating each yolk before adding the next. Stir in lemon rind, lemon juice, raisins and almonds. Combine the noodles with the sugar mixture. Blend thoroughly, then reserve.

4. In another large bowl, beat the egg whites with a pinch of salt until stiff. Carefully fold the egg whites into the noodle mixture. Pour into a large buttered soufflé dish and bake until browned, about 1 hour. Serve hot from the dish.

Serves 6

For variety, top each portion with raspberry sauce.

SEMOLINA PUDDING WITH BLACKCURRANT SAUCE

France

Preparation time: 20 minutes   **Cooking time:** 25 minutes

Ingredients

12 fl. oz./3½ dl. white wine
12 fl. oz./3½ dl. water
4½ oz./125 g. semolina
1 egg
4½ oz./125 g. castor sugar

2 egg whites
12 oz./350 g. fresh black-
    currants
Castor sugar

1. Pour the wine and water into a saucepan. Bring rapidly to the boil, then remove from heat and gradually beat in the semolina. Cover pan and simmer over low heat for 20 minutes, stirring occasionally. Remove pan from heat.

2. In a bowl, beat the egg well, then gradually stir in the sugar. Reserve.

3. In another bowl, beat the egg whites until stiff. Gently fold the egg whites into the sugar mixture, then fold this mixture into the semolina.

4. Pour into a 2-pint/generous-litre buttered savarin mould. Place in a pan filled with enough hot water to reach halfway up the sides of the mould. Do not cover the pan. Cook the pudding over low heat until set, about 25 minutes. (The water should barely simmer while the pudding cooks.)

5. When the pudding has set, remove from pan and cool to room temperature. Chill until needed.

6. While the pudding chills, prepare the blackcurrant purée by pressing the currants through a sieve, then adding sugar to taste. To serve, turn the pudding onto a plate and cover with the purée.

Serves 4 to 6

RICE PUDDING

Pakistan

Preparation time: 10 minutes   **Cooking time:** 1¼ hours

Ingredients

1½ pints/9 dl. milk

3 oz./75 g. round-grain rice

2 tablespoons seedless raisins

2 oz./50 g. sugar

¼ teaspoon ground cardamom

¼ teaspoon ground cinnamon

10 unsalted pistachio nuts, shelled and slivered

1. Bring the milk to the boil in a saucepan, then lower the heat and add the rice. Cook, stirring frequently, until the rice is done, about 1 hour.

2. Add the raisins and sugar. Cook for 10 minutes over very low heat.

3. Stir in the cardamom and cinnamon. Pour mixture into a serving bowl.

4. Serve hot or cold, sprinkled with pistachio slivers.

Serves 6

RICE MOULD WITH CUSTARD SAUCE

France

Preparation time: 1½ hours

Cooking time: 40 minutes

Ingredients

10 oz./275 g. sugar
3 tablespoons water
2 oz./50 g. glacé fruits
1 oz./25 g. raisins
1½ tablespoons cognac
1 pint/6 dl. milk
1 oz./25 g. butter
1 vanilla pod
7 oz./200 g. round-grain
   rice
3 egg whites

Pinch salt and cream of
   tartar
Glacé cherries and
   angelica for decoration

Custard Sauce:

3 egg yolks
2½ oz./65 g. castor
   sugar
12 fl. oz./3½ dl. milk,
   scalded
Few drops vanilla essence

1. Caramelise (page 472) a 3¼-pint/1¾-litre ring mould with 8 oz./225 g. sugar and the water. Soak the fruits and raisins in the cognac.

2. Combine the milk, 2 oz./50 g. sugar, butter and vanilla pod in a saucepan. Bring to the boil, then stir in the rice and simmer until milk is absorbed, about 45 minutes. Discard the vanilla pod, then stir in the cognac and fruit.

3. Preheat oven to 375°F., 190°C., Gas Mark 5. Beat the egg whites with the salt and cream of tartar until stiff. Gently fold into the rice, then pour into the mould. Cover with buttered waxed paper and bake until set, about 40 minutes. Remove from oven and invert onto a platter. Decorate with cherries and angelica. Serve hot or cold.

4. In a small saucepan, beat the yolks until pale yellow, then beat in the sugar until mixture is fluffy. Slowly stir in the milk and cook over low heat until thickened. Beat in the vanilla and serve in a heated sauce boat or poured around the mould.

Serves 6

CHILLED CHOCOLATE-ALMOND PUDDING

Poland

Preparation time: 30 minutes   **Refrigeration time:** 2 hours

Ingredients

8 oz./225 g. unsalted butter

8 oz./225 g. castor sugar

Few drops vanilla essence

8 oz./225 g. plain chocolate, melted

4 oz./100 g. ground almonds

Juice of 1 lemon

Topping:

2 oz./50 g. plain chocolate, melted

¾ pint/4½ dl. cream

1. Cream the butter in a mixing bowl. Gradually beat in 4 oz./100 g. of the sugar. Continue beating until smooth, then blend in the vanilla.

2. Beating constantly, slowly pour in the melted chocolate. Blend until creamy.

3. Pour mixture into small soufflé dishes or *pots de crème* and refrigerate.

4. In another bowl, combine the almonds, the remaining sugar and the lemon juice.

5. Cover the chocolate mixture with the almond mixture, then refrigerate again.

6. Combine the chocolate and cream for the topping. Mix well, then spread over the chocolate-almond layers. Return to refrigerator and chill for at least 2 hours before serving.

Serves 6 to 8

COTTBUS STEAMED CHOCOLATE PUDDING

Germany

Preparation time: 25 minutes   **Cooking time:** 1½ hours

Ingredients

6 oz./175 g. unsalted
   butter, softened

5 oz./150 g. castor sugar

6 eggs, separated

2 egg yolks

4 oz./100 g. plain
   chocolate, melted

1½ tablespoons Grand
   Marnier (optional)

6 oz./175 g. almonds,
   grated

3 oz./75 g. dry bread-
   crumbs

Pinch salt

1. Cream the butter in a large mixing bowl. Beating constantly, gradually add the sugar.

2. Lightly beat the 8 egg yolks in a separate bowl, then gradually add to the butter and sugar mixture. Beat until fluffy, about 10 minutes. Stir in the chocolate, (Grand Marnier), almonds and breadcrumbs. Mix well.

3. In another bowl, beat the egg whites with a pinch of salt until stiff. Gently fold the egg whites into the chocolate mixture.

4. Pour pudding into a buttered 2½-pint/1¼-litre pudding mould. Cover tightly. Set the mould in a pan of boiling water and steam over moderate heat for 1½ hours. (During steaming the level of water in the pan should remain near the top of the mould. Add more boiling water when necessary.)

5. When the steamed pudding is done, unmould by running a knife around the inside edge of the mould. Quickly invert the mould over a serving platter. Serve hot.

Serves 6

CHOCOLATE TRUFFLES

Preparation time: 15 minutes   **Cooking time:** 15 minutes

Chocolate mixture chills—3 hours

France

Ingredients

8 oz./225 g. plain
    chocolate, slivered

6 tablespoons milk

1½ oz./40 g. unsalted
    butter, at room
    temperature

1½ tablespoons rum or
    cognac

2 egg yolks, well beaten

Cocoa powder for coating
    truffles

1. Combine the slivered chocolate and milk in the top half of a double saucepan. Place over gently simmering water until the chocolate melts. (Do not boil.)

2. When the chocolate has melted, beat in the butter, ½ oz./ 15 g. at a time. Continue beating over the simmering water until mixture is very smooth, then remove from heat and stir in the rum (or cognac).

3. Cool the mixture slightly, then beat in the egg yolks.

4. Transfer the mixture to a small bowl. Cover with grease-proof paper and refrigerate until chocolate is firm enough to be moulded, about 3 hours.

5. Form the chocolate into small balls, then roll in cocoa powder until well coated.

Makes about 30 truffles

FLANDERS RAISIN CRÊPES

Belgium

Preparation time: 20 minutes
Batter chills—2 hours

Cooking time: 2 minutes
per crêpe

Ingredients

4 oz./100 g. plain flour,
  sifted
½ pint/3 dl. milk
1 tablespoon melted
  butter
1 egg
1 egg yolk
¼ teaspoon salt

Rind of 1 orange, grated
4½ oz./125 g. raisins
6 fl. oz./1¾ dl. kirsch or
  brandy
Oil for coating pan
Sugar for sprinkling
  crêpes

1. Combine the first 7 ingredients in a large mixing bowl and beat thoroughly until smooth. (This can also be done in a blender.) The batter should be the consistency of cream. Refrigerate for 2 hours.

2. Soak the raisins in 6 tablespoons of the kirsch (or brandy) for ½ hour. Stir the raisins into the batter.

3. Brush a crêpe pan or frying pan with oil. Heat to the smoking point, then pour in approximately 3 tablespoons of batter. Swirl quickly to lightly coat the pan and cook until golden. Turn the crêpe over and cook lightly on the other side. Reserve. Re-grease the pan and repeat until all the batter is used.

4. Fold the crêpes in thirds and arrange on a heated serving dish. Lightly sprinkle with sugar and the remaining kirsch. Flambé and serve.

Serves 4

APRICOT CRÊPE CAKE

Preparation time: 20 minutes
Batter chills—2 hours

Cooking time: 2 minutes
per crêpe

France

Ingredients

4 oz./100 g. plain flour,
  sifted
½ pint/3 dl. milk
1 tablespoon melted butter
1 egg
1 egg yolk

¼ teaspoon salt
Oil for coating pan
1 lb./450 g. apricot jam,
  melted
3 oz./75 g. almonds or
  walnuts, ground

1. Combine the first 6 ingredients in a large mixing bowl and beat thoroughly until smooth. (This can also be done in a blender.) The batter should be the consistency of cream. Refrigerate for 2 hours.

2. Brush a 6-inch/15-cm. crêpe pan or frying pan with oil. Heat to the smoking point, then pour in approximately 3 tablespoons of batter. Swirl quickly to lightly coat the pan and cook until golden. Turn the crêpe over and cook lightly on the other side. Reserve. Re-grease the pan and repeat until all the batter is used, preparing 12 crêpes.

3. To prepare the *gâteau*, glaze each crêpe with the apricot jam. Sprinkle lightly with the nuts and stack the crêpes one upon the other. Cover with a cloth to keep warm. Slice the *gâteau* like a cake when serving.

Serves 4

LEMON FRITTERS

France

Preparation time: 15 minutes
Batter stands—40 minutes

Cooking time: 3–4 minutes
per fritter

Ingredients

8 oz./225 g. plain flour
1 egg
½ pint/3 dl. milk
1 tablespoon castor sugar
¼ teaspoon salt

Grated rind of ½ lemon
Groundnut or vegetable oil
for deep-frying
Icing sugar for dusting

1. In a large mixing bowl, combine the flour, egg, milk, sugar and salt. Mix thoroughly, then add the lemon rind. Cover and let stand for 40 minutes.

2. Pour enough groundnut (or vegetable) oil into a large saucepan to reach a depth of 4 inches/10 cm. Place pan over high heat.

3. When the oil begins to sizzle, dip a long-handled rosette mould (or a long-handled deep-well gravy ladle) into the oil. Coat mould thoroughly in oil.

4. Pour the excess oil off the coated mould, then dip into the batter, filling the ladle about three-quarters full.

5. Plunge filled ladle into the hot oil (the fritter will detach itself). Fry until golden brown, about 3 to 4 minutes, then remove with a slotted spoon and drain on absorbent paper. Repeat Steps 4 and 5 until all the batter has been used.

6. Dust the fritters with icing sugar. Serve hot or cold.

Makes about 20 fritters

PILAR PUFFS

Preparation time: 15 minutes

Cooking time: 3–5 minutes per batch

Spain

Ingredients

4 oz./100 g. unsalted butter

1 oz./25 g. sugar

⅛ teaspoon salt

⅓ pint/2 dl. water

4 oz./100 g. flour

4 eggs

1 tablespoon brandy

Rind of 1 lemon, grated

Vegetable oil for deep frying

1 lb./450 g. apricot jam

Icing sugar

1. In a large saucepan, melt the butter. Over moderate heat blend in the sugar, salt and water. Bring to the boil.

2. Remove saucepan from heat and beat in the flour, a tablespoon at a time. Add the eggs (one at a time), beating well after each addition.

3. Stir mixture over moderate heat until batter pulls away from sides of saucepan.

4. Remove saucepan from heat. Blend in the brandy and lemon rind. Reserve.

5. Pour enough vegetable oil into a large saucepan to reach a depth of 4 inches/10 cm. Heat almost to smoking point (385°F., 196°C. to 390°F., 199°C.).

6. Using 2 teaspoons dipped in water, shape batter into small balls. Drop balls into the hot oil and deep fry until golden, about 3 to 5 minutes, then remove with a slotted spoon and drain thoroughly on a wire rack or absorbent paper.

7. Split the fried puffs. Fill each with apricot jam and dust with icing sugar.

Makes about 36 puffs

PLUM SURPRISES

Czechoslovakia

Preparation time: 30 minutes   **Cooking time:** 12 minutes

Ingredients

12 oz./350 g. plain flour
1 teaspoon salt
3½ oz./90 g. butter
2 eggs, lightly beaten
6 to 9 tablespoons milk

3 tablespoons castor sugar
1 teaspoon cinnamon
Pinch freshly grated
*   nutmeg*
16 plums, stoned

1. Sift the flour and salt into a bowl. Reserve.

2. In a large mixing bowl, cream well 2 oz./50 g. of the butter, softened, with a wooden spoon or beater, then gradually beat in the eggs. Blend thoroughly.

3. Stir the salted flour into the butter-egg mixture, then blend in enough of the milk to make a stiff dough.

4. Transfer the dough to a lightly floured board and roll out to ¼-inch/5-mm. thickness. Using a lightly floured 3½-inch/9-cm. biscuit cutter or glass, cut dough into 32 rounds.

5. Combine the sugar, cinnamon and nutmeg in a small bowl. Mix thoroughly. Reserve.

6. Top half the dough rounds with plums and sprinkle with some of the spiced sugar, then cover plums with the remaining dough rounds. Firmly seal edges.

7. Drop the dumplings into a saucepan of salted boiling water, cover and simmer until tender, about 12 minutes.

8. Using a slotted spoon, transfer the cooked dumplings to a serving dish. Dot with the remaining butter and sprinkle with the remaining sugar mixture. Serve hot or cold.

Makes 16 dumplings

Apricots, cherries or peaches can be substituted for the plums.

Fundamentals

al dente:

An Italian cookery term most often used to describe the cooking of pasta. It means that the spaghetti, noodle, macaroni, etc. should be cooked until barely tender (it should retain a 'bite')— anywhere from 5 to 6 minute for thin pasta to 12 to 15 minutes for broad noodles. Check packet instructions if in doubt. Other foods that are also cooked *al dente* are rice and certain vegetables.

bard:

To tie strips of pork fat or bacon around a piece of meat, fowl or fish before cooking to improve the flavour and to protect the delicate portions of the flesh during cooking.

baste:

To moisten foods with a marinade, butter or pan juices during cooking. Basting prevents drying and adds to the flavour.

bean curd (tofu):

A white, square cake made from ground, softened soya beans and water. It is available canned or fresh in Chinese or Japanese shops. *Tofu* may be refrigerated for up to 2 weeks if kept in a bowl of water. Change the water daily.

béarnaise sauce:

3 tablespoons vinegar
3 tablespoons white wine
2 teaspoons dried tarragon
1 tablespoon finely chopped shallots
Salt
Freshly ground pepper
8 oz./225 g. butter
4 egg yolks
1 to 2 tablespoons boiling water

A rich, creamy sauce served with grilled red meats and fish. A béarnaise sauce is prepared in the same way as a hollandaise, but the vinegar or lemon of the hollandaise is replaced by a reduced mixture of vinegar, wine, tarragon, shallots and seasonings.

1. Combine the vinegar, wine, tarragon, shallots, salt and pepper in a saucepan and reduce to 2 tablespoons over moderately high heat. Cool and strain.

2. Melt the butter and add the reduced liquid. Bring nearly to the boiling point.

3. Beat the egg yolks with salt and pepper in a small saucepan. Beat the hot butter mixture into the yolks until thickened. If the sauce curdles, beat in a little boiling water until smooth.

béchamel sauce:

1 oz./25 g. butter
1 oz./25 g. flour
½ pint/3 dl. milk, scalded
Salt
Freshly ground pepper

A basic thick white sauce prepared by adding hot milk, salt and pepper to a *roux*. Used in cream dishes or in the preparation of more complex white sauces.

1. In a small saucepan, prepare a *roux* with the butter and flour. Remove pan from the heat, pour in the scalded milk and beat with a whisk until blended.

2. Beating with the whisk, return to moderate heat, bring to the boil and cook for 3 minutes. Season to taste with salt and pepper.

Variation: Add an onion, ½ bay leaf and pinch nutmeg to the milk before scalding. Remove from heat and leave to infuse for 15 minutes. Strain the milk before adding it to the *roux*.

beurre manié:

French cookery term (literally 'kneaded butter') for a mixture of softened butter and flour that is used to thicken sauces, soups and stews. To prepare a *beurre manié*, combine 1 oz./25 g. butter and 1 oz./25 g. flour in a bowl. Knead the mixture thoroughly, then shape into tiny balls. Stir the prepared *beurre manié* into the sauce, soup or stew a few minutes before serving and beat briskly over low heat for 1 to 2 minutes. Do not boil.

bind:

To use beaten eggs or a sauce to hold other ingredients together—i.e., if a stuffing calls for breadcrumbs, onion, celery, sausage, etc., beaten eggs are used to 'bind' these ingredients together.

blanch:

To briefly heat foods in a large quantity of boiling water. Blanching is done for several reasons: to remove the excess salt or bitter taste of a food; to firm white meats such as brains, sweetbreads, chicken or veal; to make some fruits or vegetables easier to peel, or as a preliminary step in freezing, preserving and canning.

boil:

To heat a liquid until bubbles form rapidly on the surface.

bok choy: The Chinese cabbage that looks like common celery but has large, dark green leaves and white stalks. If this is not available, a firm green cabbage may be used.

bouquet garni: A 'bunch' of herbs tied together with string or secured in a muslin bag. It is used to flavour soups, stews and foods during cooking and then discarded before the dish is served. The traditional bouquet garni contains a bay leaf, parsley and thyme, but numerous other herbs are also used. Both the quantity and type of herbs chosen will depend on the particular recipe.

braise: To sear meat over high heat in oil or fat and then cook slowly in the oven in a covered dish with a small quantity of liquid.

caramelise: To heat sugar until it forms a golden brown syrup or to coat a mould or food with caramelised sugar. To caramelise a $2\frac{1}{2}$-pint/$1\frac{1}{4}$-litre metal mould, combine 4 oz./100 g. sugar and $1\frac{1}{2}$ tablespoons water in the mould. Place the mould over moderate heat and boil the mixture until the syrup turns golden brown, about 3 to 4 minutes. Swirl the mould gently during cooking. When the sugar caramelises, set mould briefly into a shallow pan of cold water to stop the cooking, then remove and swirl the caramel until all surfaces of the mould are coated and the syrup has cooled.

Chinese parsley: Very similar to coriander or cilantro but having a more pronounced flavour and pungent aroma. The best substitute is Italian flat-leaved parsley.

chop: Using a sharp knife, cut off a slice of the meat or vegetable. Hold the slice firmly on the chopping board and cut straight $\frac{1}{8}$-inch/3-mm. strips. Turn and cut the strips at $\frac{1}{8}$-inch/3-mm. intervals.

court bouillon: A liquid used for poaching fish, chicken or vegetables to give extra flavour. A basic court bouillon is prepared by boiling 2 carrots, 2 onions, a celery stick and bouquet garni in salted water for at least 30 minutes. When preparing a court bouillon for fish, white wine and a lemon are frequently added.

crème fraîche: A French term for double cream that has been allowed to mature and ferment slightly. It is served cold as a topping on sweet dishes, fruits or puddings. *Crème fraîche* is difficult to find but a good substitute can be prepared by combining 2 parts double cream to 1 part soured cream or buttermilk. Blend mixture thoroughly, then cover bowl and let stand at room temperature until the mixture thickens, about 4 hours. Refrigerate.

croûtons: Small cubes of bread that have been toasted in a 300°F., 150°C., Gas Mark 2 oven for 5 minutes, then tossed with melted butter or oil. Another way to make croûtons is to fry bread cubes in oil until golden brown. A good way to use up stale bread. A garlic clove can be added to the oil for variety.

cube: To cut food into pieces 1 inch/2½ cm. on all sides.

deglaze: To scrape the juices and brown particles from a meat cooking utensil by adding water, stock or wine. When a small quantity of flour mixed with water is briskly stirred into the liquid and heated, a simple gravy is formed.

dice: To cut meat or vegetables into regular ½-inch/1-cm. squares—about half the size of cubes.

dredge: To sprinkle foods lightly with flour or sugar to coat.

flaky pastry:

8 oz./225 g. plain flour
½ teaspoon salt
6 oz./175 g. butter, chilled and cut into pieces
7 tablespoons iced water

The basic dough used in the preparation of savoury pies such as quiches, flans, flamîches and pissaladières.

1. Sieve the flour and salt into a bowl. Divide the fat into quarters and rub one-quarter into the flour and salt until the mixture resembles breadcrumbs. Add the water and mix to a soft dough.

2. Turn onto a lightly floured board and knead gently. Place the dough in a polythene bag and leave to rest in the refrigerator for 20 minutes.

3. Roll out the dough into a rectangle about ¼ inch/ 5 mm. thick and three times as long as it is wide. Take one portion of the remaining fat and dot it in small knobs over the top two-thirds of the dough and to within ½ inch/1 cm. of the edges. Bring the bottom third of the dough up and the top third down to cover the centre third. Seal the edges by pressing down with a rolling pin. Cover the dough and leave it to rest until firm to the touch.

4. Half turn the dough so that the folds are on the sides. Repeat the rolling and continue as before until all the fat is used up. Rest the pastry until it is firm to the touch.

5. Roll out the dough to the desired thickness (usually ¼ inch/5 mm.) and carefully place in the flan tin. Trim the edges and prick the surface of the pastry. Line the prepared case with aluminium foil or waxed paper and fill with dried beans to prevent the crust from puffing. Bake in a preheated 400°F., 200°C., Gas Mark 6 oven until golden, about 10 to 15 minutes. Remove the foil and beans. Allow to cool slightly before adding a filling.

garam masala:

A prepared mixture of ground spices used to flavour the meat and vegetable dishes of India and Pakistan. It consists of black pepper, coriander, black and white cumin, cardamom, cloves, ginger, mace, nutmeg, cassia and fenugreek. It can be bought in the delicatessen sections of department stores or in speciality shops.

garnish: To decorate a dish just before serving with colourful extras (parsley, watercress, croûtons, tomatoes or lemon) or to accompany a main dish with complementary foods such as rice, noodles or beans.

glaze: 1) To put a dish under the grill to form a golden-brown crust just before serving. 2) To coat with an icing or syrup when preparing breads, pastries, cakes and pies.

goose fat: Rendered goose fat from a roast bird can be stored in an earthenware dish for months. Rendered chicken fat may be substituted for goose fat where necessary.

hoisin sauce: A thick, sweet brownish sauce made from soya beans, flour, sugar and spices, obtainable from Chinese stores. Possible substitutes are bottled duck sauce (Chinese plum sauce) or combine equal amounts of tomato ketchup and soy sauce and add a little sugar.

hollandaise sauce:

4 egg yolks
1 tablespoon water
2 tablespoons vinegar or lemon juice
Salt
Freshly ground pepper
6 oz./175 g. butter, at room temperature

A rich, thick sauce with a base of egg yolks, butter and vinegar or lemon juice. Served hot or cold with fish, eggs, chicken and vegetables or used as the basis for other sauces.

1. Place the egg yolks in the top section of a double saucepan. Using a wire whisk, beat yolks for 1 minute, then add the water, vinegar or lemon juice, salt and pepper. Beat for 1 minute. Place over barely simmering water.

2. Beating constantly with a whisk, gradually incorporate the butter, $\frac{1}{2}$ oz./15 g. at a time. Stir until thickened.

lard: 1) Solid pork fat that has been rendered and clarified. Commonly used as a cooking fat and in the preparation of pastries and biscuits. 2) To thread thin pieces of pork fat or unsmoked bacon through the flesh of uncooked lean meat or fowl to give it extra juiciness and flavour.

lobster:

To prepare a live lobster, place it shell side up on a chopping board. To kill it humanely, cut its spinal cord (where the tail and body meet) with a sharp heavy knife. Split the undershell lengthwise. Remove and discard the dark vein, the tough sac behind the eyes and the dead men's fingers. Retain the soft green liver and the red roe (known as 'coral')—these are great delicacies. Separate the tail from the chest—if the recipe calls for cut-up lobster. Cut off the claws and crack them. Lobsters should be prepared just before using them.

marinate:

To soak food in a liquid (the marinade) to season and tenderise it before cooking. A marinade is usually made of oil and vinegar (or lemon juice or wine) and appropriate seasonings for the dish.

marrow, bone:

This delicacy is found in the thigh and shoulder bones of an ox. Ask your butcher to saw the bones into reasonable lengths. Wash them and seal the ends with flour and water paste. Wrap in a cloth. Simmer in water or a court bouillon for 2 hours. Drain and dig out the marrow with a small spoon.

mayonnaise:

2 egg yolks, at room
   temperature
¼ teaspoon salt
Pinch sugar
½ teaspoon dry mustard
½ pint/3 dl. olive oil
2 tablespoons white wine
   vinegar (or lemon juice)

A creamy, cold sauce made from egg yolks, oil and vinegar or lemon juice. Served with fish, eggs, chicken and vegetables. Make sure all the ingredients are at room temperature.

1. Place the egg yolks in a bowl and beat with a wire whisk for 1 minute. Add the salt, sugar and dry mustard. Beat for 1 minute.

2. Beating constantly, add 3 tablespoons of the olive oil *a drop at a time*, then blend in the vinegar (if lemon juice is used, add when indicated below). Still beating, very slowly add enough of the remaining olive oil to make a thick and fluffy sauce. Correct the seasonings (and stir in the lemon juice). If it curdles, place another egg yolk in a clean bowl and blend in mayonnaise.

mince:

To cut an ingredient into very small pieces. Meat or vegetables can be put through a mincer.

---

pastry:

See entries under *flaky pastry* and *sweet shortcrust pastry*.

---

portions:

The number of servings given in the main-course recipes in this book are based on the assumption that the dish will be served with accompaniments and/or an appetiser, a soup, perhaps a dessert. If served alone, the portions could be increased—e.g., a recipe that 'Serves 6' might be served to 4.

---

preserved goose (confit d'oie):

Pieces of a goose (wing, leg and breast sections) preserved in their own fat for storage. Available canned in delicatessen sections of department stores or supermarkets. To prepare *confit d'oie:*

1. Clean a 10- to 14-lb./4½- to 5½-kg. goose, reserving all the fat. Cover the goose with approximately 2 lb./1 kg. of coarse salt and let stand in a cool place overnight.

2. Render the goose fat with four crushed cloves of garlic in a large frying pan.

3. Rinse the salt from the goose, joint and pat dry. Place the pieces in the fat, cover and cook for 30 minutes. Remove the goose with a slotted spoon and place in a large earthenware dish.

4. Allow the fat to cool, then strain through a double thickness of muslin. Pour over the goose pieces.

5. Melt 8 oz./225 g. of lard and let cool slightly. Pour over the goose, forming a 1-inch/2½-cm. topping. Whenever a piece of goose is removed, melt the lard and pour over the remaining pieces of goose to seal. Can be refrigerated for several months.

reduce:

To decrease the amount of a liquid by boiling, uncovered, over high heat. Reducing is done to intensify the flavour and improve the consistency of the liquid.

refresh:

To stop the cooking process by immediately plunging cooked foods into cold water. Refreshing helps retain flavour and sets the colour.

rouille:

1 slice white bread or 1 medium potato, cooked
1 hot red chilli pepper
1 clove garlic
6 tablespoons olive oil
Salt
Freshly ground pepper
1½ tablespoons hot fish stock

A thick creamy, cold sauce prepared like a mayonnaise but also incorporating a highly seasoned paste of garlic, hot red peppers and potatoes (or breadcrumbs). Served with soups, stews and fish.

1. Soak the bread in water and squeeze dry. In a mortar, pound the bread (or potato), pepper and garlic into a smooth paste.

2. Add the oil by drops. Season with salt and pepper, then slowly add the hot stock. Serve cold in a sauce boat.

roux:

A mixture of butter and flour, cooked gently over low heat. Used to thicken sauces or soups or as the base of a variety of white and brown sauces. To prepare a *roux*: Melt 1 oz./25 g. of butter over low heat, remove pan from heat and briskly beat in 1 oz./25 g. of flour with a wire whisk. Return the pan to low heat and beat briskly until the mixture is well blended and the flour is cooked through, about 3 minutes.

sauté:

To fry quickly in a small amount of fat.

score:

To partially gash the surface of foods, e.g. whole hams, steaks and chestnuts.

sesame seed oil: A topaz-coloured oil made from roasted sesame seeds. It has a special nutty flavour that heightens the taste of any dish. It is available in bottles in Chinese or Japanese shops and many supermarkets with a delicatessen or foreign food section.

shred: To cut or pull apart a meat or vegetable into thin strips, especially for Chinese dishes. Raw vegetables are best done by straight slicing, then cutting into narrow strips about 1 inch/$2\frac{1}{2}$ cm. long and $\frac{1}{8}$ to $\frac{1}{4}$ inch/3 to 5 mm. wide. Cooked meats or poultry can be shredded with your fingers.

shrimp, dried: Amber-coloured small brine shrimps with a strong salty taste. Tiny canned shrimps marinated in a good soy sauce may be substituted, but dried shrimps are obtainable from specialist Chinese shops.

simmer: To cook foods in a liquid heated to just below the boiling point.

sliver: To chop food, especially nuts, into thin strips.

sorrel: A green, leafy vegetable that is sometimes called 'sourgrass'. In recipes calling for sorrel, spinach may be substituted but add a little fresh lemon juice to achieve the best taste. As with spinach, use only enamel or stainless steel cooking utensils.

star anise: A liquorice-flavoured spice that resembles a tiny 8-pointed star. It is sold only in Chinese shops. Anise powder can be substituted if the whole spice is not available.

steam:

To cook meat, fish, vegetables or puddings in a covered pan placed over boiling water. The food is cooked by the intense steam given off by the water.

Puddings can be cooked in a basin in a pan of boiling water which should not come more than two-thirds of the way up the basin.

stock:

A liquid base for soups, sauces, stews or gravies made from the slow cooking of the bones and the trimmings of meat, fish or chicken. A stock can simmer between 30 minutes and 5 hours, with the flavours intensifying during the cooking. Stocks can be refrigerated in covered containers for up to 1 week or frozen for several months.

meat stock:

2 lb./1 kg. shin of beef
3 lb./1⅓ kg. veal or beef bones
5 pints/3 litres water
Salt
3 carrots, chopped
3 onions, chopped
2 leeks
2 celery sticks
Bouquet garni (thyme, bay leaf, peppercorns, parsley)
1 clove garlic

1. Cover the meat and bones with cold water. Bring to the boil and skim the surface. Add the remaining ingredients.

2. Partially cover the pan and simmer over moderate heat for 4 hours. Skim the surface occasionally. Strain the liquid, allow to cool and skim the fat again. Correct the seasonings and refrigerate.

chicken stock:

Substitute a 4-lb./1¾-kg. whole chicken and any extra giblets available for the beef and bones listed in the meat stock. Remove the chicken when tender, about 1¾ hours, and use for other purposes. Continue to simmer the broth for another hour. Strain, cool and refrigerate.

fish stock:

2 lb./1 kg. fish flesh and trimmings

2 onions

1 carrot

1 celery stick

Bouquet garni (bay leaf, fennel seed, parsley, peppercorns, thyme)

⅓ pint/2 dl. dry white wine

1 clove garlic

Salt

1. Place all the ingredients in a saucepan, cover with cold water and simmer for 45 minutes.

2. Pour the broth through a strainer lined with muslin and cool.

sweet shortcrust pastry:

8 oz./225 g. plain flour, sifted

¼ teaspoon salt

1½ oz./40 g. sugar

2½ oz./65 g. unsalted butter

2½ oz./65 g. shortening

1 egg yolk

2 tablespoons iced water

The basic dough used for dessert pastries and pies.

1. Mix the flour, salt and sugar together in a mixing bowl.

2. Cut the fat into pieces and, using your fingertips, rub it into the flour, salt and sugar until the mixture resembles fine bread-crumbs.

3. Add the egg yolk and a little water. Mix with a round-bladed knife until the mixture begins to hold together. Do not make the dough too wet or it will produce tough pastry.

4. Gather the mixture into a ball, wrap in a polythene bag and chill for 1 hour.

5. Roll out the dough to ¼-inch/5-mm. thickness and place in the flan tin. Trim the edges and use the blunt end of a knife to make a decorative edge. Prick the surface of the pastry and line the pastry case with aluminium foil or waxed paper. Fill with dried beans to prevent puffing and bake in a preheated 400°F., 200°C., Gas Mark 6 oven until golden, about 10 to 15 minutes. Remove foil and beans. Cool slightly before adding the filling.

truffles:

Many fanciful tales have been told about these exotic and expensive fungi, but the facts about them are equally intriguing. Black truffles come from France, where they are hunted for and dug up by trained pigs. White truffles, which are actually beige, come from Italy and are hunted by 'truffle hounds'. Truffles are available fresh (during certain months of the year at delicatessens) and canned. To prepare fresh truffles, wash them at least twice before slicing thinly. Save all the peelings and any small bits for garnishes, sauces and soups. Canned truffles need no advance preparation. Leftover truffles can be refrigerated, soaked in oil or wine to cover, for up to a month. If truffles are not available, mushrooms (perhaps marinated in Madeira for $\frac{1}{2}$ hour) can be substituted in most recipes.

vanilla sugar:

Granulated sugar with a slight vanilla flavour. To prepare, add a vanilla pod to a jar of sugar, cover tightly and store for at least 1 day. Vanilla sugar may be stored indefinitely.

vinaigrette sauce:

3 tablespoons red wine vinegar
9 tablespoons olive oil
$\frac{3}{4}$ teaspoon salt
Freshly ground pepper
1 to 2 cloves garlic, crushed (optional)
2 shallots, finely chopped (optional)

A basic dressing usually consisting of about 3 parts oil to 1 part vinegar. Served on salads, vegetables, cold meats and fish.
Combine all the ingredients listed and beat until thoroughly blended.

Variation: Add 1 tablespoon mixed herbs or $\frac{1}{2}$ tablespoon dry mustard.

Useful Facts and Figures

NOTES ON METRICATION

In this book quantities are given in both imperial and metric measures. Exact conversion from imperial to metric measures does not usually give very convenient working quantities and so the metric measures have been rounded off into units of 25 grams.

Ounces/fluid ounces	Approx. g. and ml. to nearest whole figure	Recommended conversion to nearest unit of 25
1	28	25
2	57	50
3	85	75
4	113	100
5 ($\frac{1}{4}$ pint)	142	150
6	170	175
7	198	200
8	227	225
9	255	250
10 ($\frac{1}{2}$ pint)	283	275
11	312	300
12	340	350
13	368	375
14	397	400
15 ($\frac{3}{4}$ pint)	425	425
16 (1 lb.)	454	450
17	482	475
18	510	500
19	538	550
20 (1 pint)	567	575

NOTE: When converting quantities over 20 oz., first add the appropriate figures in the centre column, *then* adjust to the nearest unit of 25. As a general guide, 1 kg. (1000 g.) equals 2·2 lb. or about 2 lb. 3 oz.; 1 litre (1000 ml.) equals 1·76 pints or almost exactly 1¾ pints. This method of conversion gives good results in nearly all cases but in certain cake recipes a more accurate conversion is necessary (or the liquid in the metric recipe must be reduced slightly) to produce a balanced recipe.

Liquid measures. The millilitre is a very small unit of measurement and we felt that to use decilitres (units of 100 ml.) would be better. The following table gives a few examples.

Imperial	Approx. ml. to nearest whole figure	Recommended dl.
¼ pint	142	1½
½ pint	283	3
¾ pint	425	4½
1 pint	567	6
1¼ pints	709	7
1½ pints	851	9
1¾ pints	992	10 (1 litre)

NOTE: For quantities of 1¾ pints and over we have used litres and fractions of a litre.

Spoon measures. All spoon measures given in this book are *level* unless otherwise specified.

Can sizes. At present, cans are marked with the exact (usually to the nearest whole number) metric equivalent of the imperial weight of the contents, so we have followed this practice when giving can sizes.

OVEN TEMPERATURES

The table below gives recommended equivalents.

	°F.	°C.	Gas Mark
Very cool	225	110	$\frac{1}{4}$
	250	120	$\frac{1}{2}$
Cool	275	140	1
	300	150	2
Moderate	325	160	3
	350	180	4
Moderately hot	375	190	5
	400	200	6
Hot	425	220	7
	450	230	8
Very hot	475	240	9

INGREDIENTS

We have tried, as far as possible, to use ingredients which are readily available in this country but if you do have difficulty purchasing any of the slightly more unusual products, try specialist shops such as health food stores for the cereals like cracked wheat, cornmeal (or maizemeal) and buckwheat; Chinese supermarkets for the special items which give the Chinese recipes their distinctive appeal; and good delicatessens for Continental sausages or other specialities.

Please note that unless otherwise specified all herbs are dried and all spices are ground.

Recipes by Country of Origin

ARGENTINA:

sweet milk treat (*dulce de leche*), 453

tongue with almond sauce (*lengua con salsa alemendras*), 268

AUSTRALIA:

Canberra lamb fondue, 246

steak and kidney pie, 226

AUSTRIA:

goulash with sauerkraut (*Szeged Goulasch*), 286

sand cake (*Sandkuchen*), 383

soup with liver meatballs (*Leberklössesuppe*), 83

Tyrolean beef soup (*Rindsuppe*), 84

veal escalopes with anchovy butter, breaded (*Schnitzel mit Sardelenbutter*), 230

BELGIUM:

Flanders raisin crêpes (*bouquettes aux raisins*), 464

Flemish fish soup (*waterzooi de poissons*), 97

Gand-style potato casserole (*potée de Gand*), 331

ham and chicory rolls au gratin (*lof, ham en kaassaus*), 250

BRAZIL:

Bahia fish soup (*bouquet de mar*), 99

coffee custard (*crème de café*), 444

haricot bean and meat stew (*feijoada à Brasileira*), 289

BULGARIA:

courgettes in soured cream (*tökfäzelék*), 368

moussaka, 299

CANADA:

blueberry pudding, 451

carrot cake, 390

chicken liver pâté, 58

lemon snow, 436

salmon in aspic, cold, 137

shortbread cookies, 402

split pea soup, 82

CHINA (All the Chinese recipe titles have been rendered in the Mandarin transliteration, the national language of China):

bean curd and pork (*dou fu ru*), 262

beef with bamboo shoots and green peppers, shredded (*tung sun chao new ru*), 218

bok choy with pork or beef (*bai tsai ru*), 261

chicken

with asparagus (*lu sun chao jee pien*), 189

with bamboo shoots and mushrooms (*jum bao-chee ting*), 187

wings with ginger (*chiang jee yeh*), 190

five spiced cold beef (*uni shiang new ru*), 53

fried noodles with pork (*tzu ru chao mien*), 308

fried prawns (*chao sha*), 161

fried rice, Chinese (*chow fan*), 310

fried spinach (*po tsai*), 362

gingered string beans (*chiang pien tou*), 340

glazed apples (*la szeping kuo*), 416

hot and sour soup (*shran la tong*), 70

pineapple chicken (*po la jee*), 188

roast pork strips (*tsa sow ru*), 259

roast spare ribs (*tas sow py kua*), 54

sea bass with ginger (*tsing lu yu*), 108

sesame seed chicken (*jee ma jee*), 174

spring rolls (*chun chuan*), 36–7

steamed minced pork (*tsing tzu ru*), 263

sweet and sour pork (*koo loo ru*), 260

wonton soup (*won ton*), 71

CUBA:

beef with rice and beans, minced (*carne con arroz y frijoles*), 288

kidney bean salad (*ensalada de habichuelas*), 23

CZECHOSLOVAKIA:

plum surprises (*svestkove knedl ky*), 468

DENMARK:

Christmas pickled herring (*sild*), 40

walnut delights (*koeka*), 404

EGYPT:

beef with okra, stewed (*bamia*), 223

ETHIOPIA:

chicken with hot sauce (*doro-weutt*), 183

FINLAND:

beef, lamb and pork hot pot (*karjalanpaisti*), 294

marinated herring with 3 dressings (*suolasilli*), 41

parsonage pudding (*pappilau pudding*), 456

vegetable soup (*kesäkeitto*), 72

FRANCE:

Albigeois main-course soup (*potée albigeoise*), 92

almond

cakes, free-form (*galettes charolaises*), 380

macaroons (*macarons de Saint-Emilion*), 396

meringues (*gâteaux soufflés aux amandes*), 397

Alpine brook trout (*truites de torrent à la jurassienne*), 141

Index

COLOUR PLATES

Between pages 32 and 33
1. A French kitchen.
   Photo by J.-C. Nicolas
2. The cocktail hour.
   Photo by Ledoyen
3. A selection of cheeses.
   Photo by G. d'Hotman
4. Stuffed mussels. See recipe
   on page 46.
   Photo by R. Montigny

Between pages 64 and 65
1. Still life with wine.
   Photo by Printemps Nation
2. Artichokes with green
   vinaigrette. See recipe on
   page 17.
   Photo by G. d'Hotman
3. Savoury sautéed scallops. See
   recipe on page 157.
   Photo by R. Montigny
4. Crispy vegetables. See recipe
   on page 30.
   Photo by R. Montigny

Between pages 128 and 129
1. Spices and herbs.
   Photo by Larousse
2. Tuna fish croquettes. See
   recipe on page 148.
   Photo by R. Montigny
3. Shellfish in white wine sauce.
   See recipe on page 151.
   Photo by R. Montigny
4. Baked sea bream provençal.
   See recipe on page 109.
   Photo by R. Montigny

Between pages 192 and 193
1. Roast chicken in Madeira
   sauce. See recipe on page
   164.
   Photo by R. Montigny
2. Chicken with red wine
   auvergnaise. See recipe
   on page 177.
   Photo by J.-C. Nicolas

Between pages 224 and 225
1. Still life.
   Photo by Printemps Nation
2. Still life.
   Photo by R. Montigny

Between pages 256 and 257
1. Wine cellar of the Tour
   d'Argent.
   Photo by Printemps Nation
2. Pork fillets with prunes. See
   recipe on page 258.
   Photo by R. Montigny
3. Braised leg of lamb with
   onions. See recipe on page
   239.
   Photo by R. Montigny
4. A mixed grill.
   Photo by J.-C. Nicolas

Between pages 320 and 321
1. Lamb and chicken stew with
   couscous. See recipe on
   pages 296 and 297.
   Photo by R. Montigny
2. Cassoulet. See recipe on page
   302.
   Photo by R. Montigny

Between pages 352 and 353
1. Cauliflower with breadcrumb
   garnish. See recipe on page
   351.
   Photo by R. Montigny
2. Still life with baking utensils.
   Photo by J.-C. Nicolas

Between pages 384 and 385
1. Orange puffs. See recipe on
   page 427.
   Photo by R. Montigny
2. Gugelhupf. See recipe on
   page 384.
   Photo by G. d'Hotman
3. Swiss plum tart. See recipe on
   page 412.
   Photo by G. d'Hotman
4. Apple tart. See recipe on page
   407.
   Photo by G. d'Hotman

Between pages 448 and 449
1. Rice mould with custard sauce.
   See recipe on page 460.
   Photo by R. Montigny
2. Caramel custard. See recipe
   on page 443.
   Photo by R. Montigny
3. Flanders raisin crêpes. See
   recipe on page 464.
   Photo by R. Montigny
4. A country kitchen.
   Photo by J.-C. Nicolas

*Drawings by Christiane Neuville,
Claude Rougeot, Jacques Dehornois.*